# Conversation: An Interdisciplinary Perspective

## INTERCOMMUNICATION SERIES

### Series Editors

Howard Giles, *Department of Psychology, University of Bristol, Bristol BS8 1HH, U.K.*

Cheris Kramarae, *Department of Speech Communication, University of Illinois, Urbana, IL 61801, U.S.A.*

### Editorial Advisory Board

William M. O'Barr, *Department of Anthropology, Duke University, Durham, NC 27706, U.S.A.*

Suzanne Romaine, *Merton College, Oxford University, Oxford, U.K.*

Rod Watson, *Department of Sociology, University of Manchester, Manchester, U.K.*

### Other Books in the Series

Talk and Social Organisation
GRAHAM BUTTON and JOHN R. E. LEE (eds)

Communication and Crosscultural Adaptation
YOUNG Y. KIM

Communication and Simulation
DAVID CROOKALL and DANNY SAUNDERS (eds)

### Other books of Interest

Perspectives on Marital Interaction
PATRICIA NOLLER and MARY-ANNE FITZPATRICK (eds)

Please contact us for the latest information on all our book and journal publications:

**Multilingual Matters Ltd,**
**Bank House, 8a Hill Road,**
**Clevedon, Avon BS21 7HH,**
**England**

INTERCOMMUNICATION 3
Series Editors: Howard Giles & Cheris Kramarae

# Conversation: An Interdisciplinary Perspective

Edited by
Derek Roger and Peter Bull



MULTILINGUAL MATTERS LTD
Clevedon · Philadelphia

**Library of Congress Cataloguing-in-Publication Data**

Conversation: an interdisciplinary perspective
edited by Derek Roger and Peter Bull
p. cm. — (Intercommunication: 3)
1. Conversation. 2. Interpersonal communication.
I. Roger, Derek. II. Bull, Peter. III. Series:
Intercommunication (Clevedon, Avon); 3.
P95.45C664 1988 88-2977
001.54′2--dc19 CIP

**British Library Cataloguing in Publication Data**

Conversation: an interdisciplinary approach.
—(Intercommunication; 3)
1. Interpersonal relationships. Conversation.
Psychosocial aspects.
I. Bull, Peter, *1949–* II. Roger, Derek
III. Series
302.2′242

ISBN 0-905028-87-2
ISBN 0-905028-86-4 Pbk

**Multilingual Matters Ltd,**

Bank House, 8a Hill Road, Clevedon, Avon BS21 7HH England & 242 Cherry Street, Philadelphia, PA 19106–1906 USA



Index compiled by Meg Davies
Typeset by Editorial Enterprises, Devon
Printed and bound in Great Britain by Short Run Press, Exeter

# Contents

# Preface

In April 1984, the editors of this book organised a conference at the University of York on Interdisciplinary Approaches to Interpersonal Communication. The conference was intended to bring together academics from diverse disciplines sharing a common interest in the study of conversation, and led to the formation of the interdisciplinary Communication Studies Group at the University of York.

Several of the chapters in this book are based on papers presented at the conference; there are also some invited contributions. The chapters are organised around five principal themes, namely, Concepts of Interpersonal Communication, Methods of Observation, Transcription Procedures, Data Analysis, and Research Applications. These themes represent particular issues which must be addressed by any researcher working on conversation and are prefaced by linking sections written by the editors, which highlight the topic of each section and evaluate the different approaches represented by the individual chapters.

In this way, the book is intended to provide an integrated and structured approach to the study of conversation. It should fill an obvious gap in the available literature, since it focuses explicitly on the ways in which interpersonal communication is investigated by researchers from different academic disciplines.

# Acknowledgements

The Conference on Interdisciplinary Approaches to Interpersonal Communication, from which several of the chapters in this book were derived, was supported in part by financial contributions from the Institute for Research in the Social Sciences at the University of York and the Social Psychology Section of the British Psychological Society.

# SECTION 1: Concepts of interpersonal communication

## Introduction

Researchers from different academic disciplines approach the study of interpersonal communication from widely differing theoretical perspectives. In this context, a major distinction can be drawn between the approach traditionally used by psychologists, which relies heavily on experimentation and quantitative techniques, and research which is based on naturally occurring situations, such as conversation analysis. This section contains two chapters which represent these contrasting theoretical positions: Bull & Roger present a psychological approach to the study of communication; and John Heritage reviews current trends in work on conversation analysis.

The final chapter of this section is written by Robert Hopper. Hopper describes his own field of research as 'speech communication', which in the United States is dedicated broadly to improving communication skills and the study of communicative competence. In this chapter Hopper, who is one of the few scholars to have used the techniques of both experimental and conversation-analytic research, attempts to make a direct comparison between the two approaches; his chapter has consequently been written with reference to the remaining sections of the book.

## The experimental approach

In Chapter 1, Bull & Roger outline the use of traditional psychological techniques in the study of interpersonal communication. The most important feature of this approach is a belief in the value of the experimental method, which in itself represents the distinctive theoretical perspective of psychology. The experimental method has a number of characteristic features, which are discussed below.

The first of these is that psychological research on communication is typically conducted in a laboratory setting, where the control and manipulation of variables can be systematically implemented. Associated with this is a belief in the importance of quantification and the value of inferential statistics for the analysis of the data. Hence, a second important feature of the psychological approach is that the significance of a particular behaviour rests on a statistical criterion, i.e. whether it occurs at a level which is significantly above what would be expected by chance.

A major implication of a quantitative approach to the study of communication is the need for categorisation. If the experimenter wishes to compare communication under different experimental conditions, he needs to establish independent categories into which different communicative events can be classified. Hence, another feature of the psychological approach to communication research has been a preoccupation with the development of scoring systems.

The belief in the experimental method has important consequences not only for the way in which psychologists carry out research but also for the particular aspects of communication which they choose to study. For example, there is an extensive research literature in experimental social psychology concerned with the effects of medium of communication on social interaction; an example of this is given in Section 5 in Derek Rutter's chapter on 'cuelessness and social interaction: an examination of teaching by telephone' (Chapter 13). This is the kind of topic which readily lends itself to psychological techniques of investigation, since it is relatively easy to compare communication under a number of different experimental conditions (face to face, over the telephone, or over a closed-circuit television link). Indeed, it might be argued that the popularity of this topic in recent years with social psychologists stems at least in part from its accessibility to traditional psychological techniques of investigation.

Another example of a traditional experimental approach to studying conversation is to be found in Section 2, Chapter 4 by Derek Roger. In the first experiment discussed in this chapter, the role of simultaneous speech in conversation was investigated by initially classifying all simultaneous speech as either interruptive or non-interruptive. The rate of occurrence of these events was then compared in three different conditions in which dominance predispositions of the dyadic partners had been manipulated on the basis of a prior administration of a personality questionnaire. In this way, the use of experimental techniques made it possible to test predictions about the relationship between personality characteristics and interruptions.

One feature common to both of these examples is that they attempt to relate aspects of communication to features that are external to the communicative context: medium of communication in the case of the studies by Rutter, and personality in the case of the experiments by Roger. Duncan (1969) has called this the 'external variable' approach, and he maintains that this is typical of work carried out using traditional psychological techniques. Duncan contrasts this with what he calls the 'structural' approach, where behaviour is analysed in terms of its sequential and hierarchical organisation. A good example of a structural approach is conversation analysis, which is discussed below.

## Conversation analysis

Conversation analysis (CA) has developed over the past 15 years within the framework of ethnomethodology. The term 'ethnomethodology' was coined by Garfinkel (1974). In combining the words 'ethno' and 'methodology', Garfinkel was influenced by the use of such terms as 'ethnobotany' and 'ethnomedicine' to refer to folk systems of botanical and medical analysis. What is proposed is that any competent member of society (including the professional social scientist) is equipped with a methodology for analysing social phenomena; the term 'ethnomethodology' thus refers to the study of the ways in which everyday common-sense activities are analysed by participants, and of the ways in which these analyses are incorporated into courses of action. The most prominent development within ethnomethodology is undoubtedly that which has become known as conversation analysis, which examines the procedures used in the production of ordinary conversation. The influence of conversation analysis is being increasingly felt in disciplines outside sociology, notably psychology, linguistics and anthropology.

In Chapter 2, Heritage discusses the development of conversation analysis in relation to three fundamental assumptions made by exponents of this approach. The first of these is that all conversations are structurally organised according to certain social conventions; this means that social action and interaction can be studied independently of the psychological or other characteristics of the particular participants involved. The second assumption is that contributions to interaction are both 'context-shaped' and 'context-renewing'. Contributions are said to be context-shaped in the sense that they cannot be fully understood without reference to the context in which they occur, especially the immediately preceding conversation. Since each utterance forms the immediate context for the conversation that follows it, each contribution is also said to be context-renewing. As a consequence of these two assumptions, Heritage argues that every detail of the conversation is potentially significant, and hence cannot be dismissed 'a priori as disorderly, accidental or irrelevant'.

Heritage then reviews recent developments in conversation analysis under five main headings: preference organisation, topic organisation, the use of non- or quasi-lexical speech objects, the integration of vocal and non-vocal activities and 'institutional interaction'. Preference organisation refers to the seeking or avoidance of alternative courses of action. For a variety of 'first' actions (e.g. invitations, offers and requests), there are 'second' actions (e.g. refusals, rejections and denials) which can be seen as 'dispreferred': these are routinely avoided, withheld or delayed in many different social contexts. The term 'topic organisation' is to some extent self-explanatory, referring to the initiation, maintenance and change of topic in conversation.

Heritage regards these two themes as significant guidelines for the organisation of conversation-analysis research. Of the remaining three topics, under non- or quasi-lexical speech objects he discusses the organisation of laughter and the use of what he calls 'response tokens' (e.g. 'mm hm', 'uh huh', 'yes', 'oh', etc.). The integration of vocal with non-vocal activities has been studied particularly with regard to the role of non-vocal cues (such as gaze) in the management of turn-taking. Finally, Heritage discusses the application of conversation-analysis techniques to the study of social interaction in different institutional settings, such as law courts, schools, and medical consultations.

## A comparison of conversation analysis and the experimental approach

Whereas conversation analysis is based on a number of assumptions about communication, psychologists typically start from a belief in the importance of experimentation and quantification, that it is only through the systematic control and manipulation of variables that a rigorous body of scientific knowledge can be established. Thus, research carried out using traditional psychological techniques differs from conversation analysis in a number of important respects.

The first of these is that the conversations studied by psychologists are typically arranged to take place in a laboratory, where the control and manipulation of variables can be systematically implemented. In contrast, in conversation analysis every detail of interaction is regarded as potentially significant; hence, conversation analysts avoid manipulating variables and prefer to make their observations on the basis of naturally occurring situations. Indeed, a sceptic might say that conversation analysts will use any situation as a source of data with the exception only of experiments which have been carried out in social psychology laboratories! The advantages and disadvantages of different research settings are discussed in detail in the Introduction to Section 2.

A second feature of the experimental approach is a belief in the importance of quantification and the value of inferential statistics for the analysis of the data. By contrast, the approach in conversation analysis is essentially descriptive and qualitative. For example, in Section 2, Chapter 5, Paul Drew discusses examples of the way in which people respond to enquiries; each case is discussed individually and there is no attempt at any form of statistical analysis. In Section 4, Chapter 11, Tony Wootton presents a theoretical justification for why conversation analysts prefer to use this kind of qualitative approach.

A major implication of a quantitative approach to the study of communication is the need for categorisation. If the experimenter wishes to compare communication under different experimental conditions he needs to establish independent categories into which different communicative events can be classified. Hence, a third distinguishing feature of the psychological approach has been a preoccupation with the development of scoring systems; a number of such systems are discussed by Peter Bull in Chapter 7, which appears in Section 3.

A good illustration of the way in which experimental and conversation analytic approaches to transcription differ is to be found in the study of 'back-channels'. Yngve (1970) introduced this term to refer to brief utterances (such as 'mmm', 'uh huh', 'yes', etc.) which are used to signal to the speaker the continued interest and attention of the listener. Duncan (1972) identified five forms of back-channel — sentence completions, requests for clarification, brief phrases such as 'uh huh' and 'right', and head nods and head shakes. Duncan (1969), although critical of what he calls 'external variable' approaches, none the less makes extensive use of this classification of back channels as the basis for subsequent quantitative analysis (see Duncan & Fiske, 1977). Heritage, in Chapter 2, takes issue with the conventional treatment of 'back-channels' as signals of continued attention, arguing that the role of what he calls 'response tokens' has been substantially underestimated by the use of this classification. Response tokens, Heritage maintains, may serve a whole variety of communicative functions, such as indicating a desire to shift topic (Jefferson, 1981b), acknowledging receipt of information (Heritage, 1984) or to promote the telling of 'news' (Jefferson, 1981a).

This disagreement over the functions of back-channels can be seen as stemming at least in part from differences in methodology. Psychologists studying communication typically classify events into discrete categories in order to provide a sufficient number of observations for reliable statistical analysis. Researchers working in the framework of conversation analysis are certainly not opposed to categorisation as such; however, since this approach is essentially descriptive and qualitative, there is not the same constraint of having to provide sufficient cell frequencies for the use of inferential statistics.

Both these approaches suffer from different kinds of problem. The categories used by psychologists in order to satisfy the requirements of particular statistical tests are often heterogeneous, lumping together a variety of different behaviours under the same label, which may lead to an oversimplified version of communication (as Heritage is clearly arguing in the case of back-channels). In the same way, certain events may perform different functions in different contexts. If the researcher is concerned solely with the frequency with which they occur, their functional significance may not be demonstrated by an overall statistical analysis. However, without any form of quantification, the interpretation put forward may rest on single idiosyncratic examples whose functional significance is clear but whose occurrence is rare.

In this sense, exponents of both approaches can be seen as having something to learn from each other, psychologists in refining the sensitivity of their classification systems, conversation analysts in avoiding the risks of generalising too much from single instances without sufficient justification for doing so. In this context, it is interesting that a recent paper (Heritage & Greatbatch, 1986) comprises an extensive quantitative analysis of the rhetorical formats identified by Atkinson (1984) in evoking applause during political speeches. The analysis is based on descriptive rather than inferential statistics; none the less it marks a significant shift from conventional conversation analysis.

In making these distinctions between conversation analysis and social psychology we are not suggesting that the two approaches are irreconcilable. Indeed, the editors' view (expressed both here and in subsequent chapters) is one of cautious optimism that practitioners of both conversation analysis and social psychology can learn a great deal from each other. However, as can be seen from Chapter 3, not everyone shares this cautious optimism. Robert Hopper argues that one must 'take sides'; his choice — and, by implication, the position taken up in his chapter — is clearly that of conversation analysis.

In making this comparison between conversation analysis and social psychology, Hopper tends, in the editors' view, to exaggerate their differences. He argues that the key distinction between them is that of repeated listening. Whereas conversation analysts continually re-examine their transcripts and their recordings, Hopper maintains that social psychologists, once they have coded conversations into appropriate categories, from then on proceed to ignore the recordings on which their codings have been based. In the editors' view, Hopper's comparison does not adequately reflect the diversity of approaches within social psychology itself. As one of the editors argues in a subsequent chapter (Chapter 7), the category systems used by social psychologists have been developed and refined over time: through repeated examination of transcripts and recordings (in other words, through repeated listening) the category systems become progressively more detailed and sophisticated. In this sense, the two approaches arguably have far more in common than Hopper acknowledges, in that they are both trying to develop adequate modes of description, which are progressively refined through repeated listening and analysis.

Whereas conversation analysis is based on a number of assumptions about communication, psychologists typically proceed from a belief in the value of a particular method. This in turn determines the way in which psychologists study communication, with a heavy reliance on laboratory-based experimentation, quantification and categorisation. By contrast, conversation analysts typically prefer to study naturally occurring situations, using qualitative methods of analysis. However, conversation analysis could benefit from the rigours of quantification and inferential statistics to avoid the risks of generalising too much from single examples, while psychologists could benefit from the rigours of close textual analysis in refining the sensitivity of their classification systems. It is the editors' contention that these different approaches are not necessarily incompatible; open-mindedness could be to the advantage of all!

**References**

ATKINSON, M. 1984, *Our Masters' Voices: The Language and Body Language of Politics*. London: Methuen.

DUNCAN, S. 1969, Non-verbal communication, *Psychological Bulletin*, 72, 118–37.

— 1972, Some signals and rules for taking speaking turns in conversations, *Journal of Personality and Social Psychology*, 23, 283–92.

DUNCAN, S. & FISKE, D.W. 1977, *Face-to-face Interaction: Research, Methods and Theory*. Hillsdale, N.J.: Lawrence Erlbaum.

GARFINKEL, H. 1974, The origins of the term 'ethnomethodology'. In R. TURNER (ed.), *Ethnomethodology*. Harmondsworth: Penguin, 15–18.

HERITAGE, J. 1984, A change-of-state token and aspects of its sequential placement. In J. M. ATKINSON & J. HERITAGE (eds), *Structures of Social Action: Studies in Conversation Analysis*. Cambridge: Cambridge University Press, 299–345.

HERITAGE, J. & GREATBATCH, D. 1986, Generating applause: a study of rhetoric and response at party political conferences, *American Journal of Sociology*, 92, 110–57.

JEFFERSON, G. 1981a, The abominable 'ne?': a working paper exploring the phenomenon of post-response pursuit of response. University of Manchester, Department of Sociology Occasional Paper no. 6. (A shortened version appears in P. SCHRODER (ed.), *Sprache der Gegenwart*, Mannheim, 1981.)

— 1981b, 'Caveat speaker': a preliminary exploration of shift implicative recipiency in the articulation of topic. Final report to the (British) SSRC. Mimeo.

YNGVE, V.H. 1970, On getting a word in edgewise. *Papers from the Sixth Regional Meeting of the Chicago Linguistic Society*. Chicago: Chicago Linguistic Society.

# 1 The social psychological approach to interpersonal communication

PETER BULL and DEREK ROGER
*University of York*

## Introduction

The belief in the value of the experimental method is in itself the distinctive theoretical perspective of psychology, and this approach has characterised much of the work on interpersonal communication carried out by social psychologists. A typical psychological experiment comprises independent and dependent variables. The independent variables are those which are experimentally manipulated to produce two or more conditions, e.g. high versus low scorers on personality questionnaires, or male and female subjects. The effects of these manipulations are then observed on one or more dependent variables, such as interruption rate or speech hesitations.

Social psychological research on interpersonal communication is frequently conducted in a laboratory setting, where the control and manipulation of independent variables can be systematically implemented. Associated with this is a belief in the importance of quantification and the value of inferential statistics for the analysis of the data. Hence, another important feature of the psychological approach is that the significance of a particular behaviour rests on a statistical criterion, i.e. whether it occurs at a level which is significantly above what would be expected by chance.

A major implication of a quantitative approach to the study of communication is the need for categorisation. If the experimenter wishes to compare communication under different experimental conditions, he needs to establish independent categories into which different communicative events can be classified. Thus, an additional feature of the social psychological approach has been a preoccupation with the development of scoring systems.

Each of these distinctive features of the social psychological approach to the study of interpersonal communication will be discussed in more detail below.

## The social psychology laboratory

Much of the experimental work in social psychology is conducted in laboratories equipped with sophisticated recording apparatus. Naturalistic studies also play an important part in social psychological research on interpersonal communication; however, the advantages of using technically sophisticated equipment in purpose-built laboratories are considerable. For example, there is an extensive psychological literature on the role of eye-contact in interpersonal communication; however, the measurement of eye-contact involves serious technical problems. The angle between one person's gaze towards and away from the other becomes progressively finer at greater conversational distances, thus making it increasingly difficult to measure eye-contact accurately. This was demonstrated empirically by Stephenson & Rutter (1970), who arranged for conversations to take place between pairs of subjects at three different distances (2 feet, 6 feet and 10 feet). The first subject was told to gaze continually into the eyes of the other, while the second subject engaged in eye-contact only when instructed to do so by a light signal which was not visible to the first subject. The results showed that observers from behind a one-way screen did in fact mistakenly judge more mutual gaze as occurring at greater distances.

On the basis of these findings, Stephenson & Rutter argued that a camera with a zoom lens should be used in preference to observers behind a one-way screen, so that a close-up image of the speaker's face can be recorded irrespective of distance. Rimé & McCusker (1976) have provided empirical evidence to support this view. They carried out a study which was intended to assess the validity of different methods of measuring eye-contact, in which the gaze sender had to look into the gaze receiver's eyes each time he received a prerecorded signal through earphones. Observations of mutual gaze were made under three conditions: one-way mirror observer, direct-sight observer (an observer who was in the same room as the subjects), and television observer (an observer who saw a close-up of the gaze sender's face). The results showed that the duration of eye-contact was overestimated at greater conversational distances with the exception only of the television observer; even the gaze receiver, who was participating in the conversation, tended to overestimate the extent of mutual gaze. Hence, Rimé and McCusker's study clearly illustrates the value of zoom-lens video-recording for making accurate measurements of mutual gaze, and indicates at the same time that observations made of eye contact in naturalistic settings may be highly unreliable.

Eye-contact is not the only social behaviour which can be measured more easily by the use of zoom-lens video-recording techniques; in the case where the experimenter is attempting to classify facial movements, its use is absolutely essential. Ekman & Friesen (1978) have devised a procedure called the 'Facial Action Coding System' (FACS), which is intended to give a detailed description of all of the movements which are possible from the facial musculature. Facial movements are highly varied and often subtle and intricate; hence, if this system is to be used, it is essential to have the fine detail which can only be obtained by using zoom lens video-recording.

Another major advantage of using technically sophisticated equipment to study interpersonal communication is that the conversation between two subjects can be recorded using independent cameras, and the separate images can then be mixed onto a single videotape using split-screen techniques. This represents a considerable improvement over recording both participants with a single camera: the angle of the cameras can be manipulated independently, providing a full view of both participants simultaneously. If this technique is combined with the use of a zoom lens, a detailed recording can be obtained of one member of the pair while preserving a full image of the other; alternatively, one participant can be shown with a detailed image on one side of the screen and a full image on the other.

The transcription of speech is greatly facilitated by the use of multi-track tape recorders which, combined with the use of tie-microphones, provides an independent vocal signal for each subject. This procedure has a number of advantages over the use of a single microphone. One of the shortcomings of a single microphone is that the sound quality is often inadequate for an accurate transcription to be made of the whole conversation; certain passages, especially those involving simultaneous speech, cannot be accurately transcribed and have to be omitted from the analysis. Using multi-track recordings the independent vocal signals allow an unambiguous transcription to be made of each participant's contribution. In addition, it is possible to obtain measures of pitch, amplitude and speech rate separately for each of the participants, which can then be used to assess the influence of these variables on, for example, the success of interruption attempts. This could not be done from a recording made with a single microphone.

Although it is possible in principle to use such recording equipment in naturalistic settings, the practical problems of doing so outside a purpose-built social psychology laboratory are enormous. A particular advantage of the laboratory is that all the apparatus can be concealed in specially designed cabinets, so that the subjects remain unaware that their behaviour is being recorded: what is in fact a recording studio may appear to be just an ordinary room. Concealment is important because it can never confidently be assumed that the awareness of being recorded does not have a marked effect on interpersonal communication.

Whether this deception can be justified on ethical grounds is of course another issue. It is the authors' view that when people volunteer to take part in a psychology experiment they must expect their behaviour to be monitored in some way, and would not anticipate being told about the details of the experiment beforehand. In the authors' own experimental research, the subjects are routinely provided with a detailed explanation of the true purpose of the study, and may also have the videotape record of their conversation erased if they so wish. This is certainly a far more ethical way of carrying out research than eavesdropping on people in naturally occurring situations. For example, in a widely quoted study of sex differences in interruptive behaviour, Zimmerman & West (1975) surreptitiously tape recorded conversations between men and women in a university cafeteria; their subjects had neither consented to take part in the study nor given their permission to being recorded. Thus social psychology laboratories not only provide technical sophistication but can also be defended on ethical grounds.

## Quantification

Another distinctive feature of the experimental approach is a belief in the importance of quantification and the use of inferential statistics. Quantification is usually achieved through some kind of classification system, which is discussed further in the next section. The advantage of classification is that it allows the experimenter to reduce observed behaviour to frequencies or rates of occurrence, rather than attempting detailed descriptions of each event. These data can then be subjected to statistical analysis, which provides the researcher with an objective criterion for determining whether an observed effect occurs at a level significantly above what might be expected by chance.

The researcher can decide how conservative this criterion should be by varying the level (referred to as the $\alpha$ level) which must be exceeded for a particular statistical test to be accepted as significant. Conventionally, most researchers use an $\alpha$ value of 0.05, which in practical terms means that there is a 5% chance that the decision to accept the results of a statistical test as true will be incorrect. Accepting a false hypothesis as true is referred to as a Type I error, and this can be avoided by using a more stringent $\alpha$ level; for example, the researcher may wish to take only a 1% chance of accepting an incorrect hypothesis as true. However, adopting too stringent an $\alpha$ level can result in what is referred to as a Type II error, in other words, deciding to reject a hypothesis which is in fact true. As a rule, researchers typically adopt a level which minimises the likelihood of committing a Type I error: thus, a significance level of 10% is very seldom used in experimental research. However, one reason for using a less stringent criterion might be where the researcher is exploring a novel idea. These innovative or 'data-snooping' exercises might be based on a 10% confidence limit in order to preserve potentially interesting findings that might otherwise have been lost if a more stringent criterion had been used. By contrast, a more conservative criterion (based on an $\alpha$ level of 0.05, 0.01 or even 0.001) might be adopted for a more rigorous test of a previously reported finding.

Statistical analysis is thus a tool which allows the researcher to arrive at an objective decision about the importance of a particular aspect of behaviour. For example, men may appear to interrupt women more than women interrupt men, but to what extent is this true? A statistical analysis of interruptions of men and women enables the researcher to ascertain whether this is an effect which occurs at a level significantly greater than would be expected by chance alone. In a more general sense, quantification permits the researcher to present his results far more concisely than a description of each individual case would allow; in addition, the use of a large sample means that the results are more likely to be representative of the population as a whole.

Conversation analysis, in contrast, typically relies on the detailed examination of a few individual cases alone. An interesting exception to this is the work of Heritage & Greatbatch (1986) on political speeches. Initially, Atkinson (1984) used standard techniques of conversation analysis in the study of political rhetoric, presenting a number of excerpts to demonstrate that particular rhetorical formats (such as the contrast or the three-part list) are highly effective in evoking audience applause. Subsequently, in response to the criticism that Atkinson's observations may be unrepresentative of political speeches in general, Heritage & Greatbatch (1986) studied 476 televised speeches delivered at the three annual British party political conferences held in 1981. With such a large sample of data, the approach which they adopted was to use a system of classification in which they identified different rhetorical formats, counted the frequency of those formats and determined how successful they were in evoking applause. The level of analysis employed in this study was thus much more similar to that typically used by psychologists: it could be regarded as a natural consequence of the demands of large-sample analyses.

Social psychologists often use more complex statistical designs such as analysis of variance, which have the advantage of allowing the researcher to ask more sophisticated questions about the way in which two or more independent variables interact to influence behaviour. In the example given above, the researcher might be interested not only in the effects of sex differences on interruptions, but also in the interaction between the sex and the personality of the subjects. Thus, men and women could be selected for participation in an experiment on the basis of their scores on the extroversion/introversion questionnaire. Such a design would allow the researcher to investigate, for example, whether only men with a certain type of personality interrupted women more than they allowed women to interrupt them, or alternatively whether women of a certain personality type allowed themselves to be interrupted more by men. Problems of this kind can only be addressed using research designs which allow an analysis of the interactive effects of independent variables such as sex and personality.

Other complex statistical techniques have been developed specifically for the analysis of sequences of behaviour, and these are particularly useful for the study of interpersonal communication. In Section 4, Chapter 10, Peter Collett describes a number of such procedures; these may be referred to collectively as stochastic techniques, where the occurrence of an event depends to a variable extent upon the events preceding it. Instead of attempting to predict precisely what behaviour will follow from any particular event, the analysis provides a distribution of possible outcomes, each with an associated probability of occurrence. Such techniques can be used, for example, to investigate whether informal conversation has a discernible structure and what are the implications of this structure for gaining, maintaining and relinquishing the speaking turn (Thomas, Roger & Bull, 1983).

Thus, quantification and the use of inferential statistics provide a parsimonious and economical account of a complex data base, as well as allowing an objective decision to be made about the significance of a particular finding. In addition, complex statistical procedures such as analysis of variance allow the researcher to investigate the interactive effects of a number of independent variables simultaneously.

## Classification/transcription

A major implication of a quantitative approach to the study of interpersonal communication is the need for categorisation. If the experimenter wishes to compare communication under different experimental conditions, he needs to establish independent categories into which different communicative events can be classified. Hence, a third consequence of the experimental method for psychologists studying communication has been a preoccupation with the development of scoring systems for the transcription of both speech and non-verbal behaviour. In contrast, conversation analysts rely on the transcripts themselves rather than constructing detailed classification systems. One interesting exception to this is the study by Heritage & Greatbatch (1986) described above, in which a category system was employed for coding rhetorical devices in a comprehensive sample of political speeches. The use of such classification systems can thus be seen as a natural response to the demands of large-scale sampling, rather than representing an exclusive preoccupation of social psychologists.

A satisfactory classification system allows a comprehensive and precise assessment of communicative behaviour which takes full account of its complexity. An excellent example of this is to be found in the Facial Action Coding System (FACS) for categorising facial expression developed by Ekman & Friesen (1978). A number of systems have been developed for coding facial expression; Ekman (1979) has identified 14 such systems (including his own). However, FACS is distinguished from other scoring procedures in a number of important respects. The aim of FACS is to describe visible facial movements in terms of their underlying anatomical basis; the scoring manual provides a description of the muscular changes which are responsible for producing particular facial expressions. The coder's task is to describe a facial expression in terms of what are called 'action units', since in some cases several muscles may be responsible for one particular facial movement, while in other cases the same muscle may be responsible for more than one facial movement.

There are two main advantages to this system. The first is that it is essentially descriptive; it does not attempt to assert what particular facial expressions mean. This distinguishes it from a number of other scoring procedures; for example, Grant (1969) talks about the 'aggressive frown', while Blurton Jones (1971) describes the 'lower lip pout', thus confounding description of the movement with inference about its meaning. The advantage of separating description from inference, as Ekman & Friesen have done, is that inferences about the meanings of particular expressions can be tested independently from the procedures employed to describe those expressions.

A second advantage of the system is its comprehensiveness. Ekman & Friesen's main aim was to develop a system that was comprehensive, and to do this they rejected a purely inductive approach, whereby categories are developed on an *ad hoc* basis to describe instances of movement as they are observed; by concentrating on the anatomical basis of facial movement, they claim it is possible to describe any facial expression in terms of the system. Ekman (1979) maintains that all the facial movements described by other investigators can be described in terms of his own scoring procedure, as well as many more facial movements which have been neglected by other investigators; in fact Ekman & Friesen's system is widely accepted as the main technique available for coding facial expression.

In its entirety, FACS represents a comprehensive coding system for the classification of facial movement. It may be questioned whether a system is required which is so exhaustive, so comprehensive and so detailed. Ekman & Friesen (1976) make the point that it is perfectly possible to use FACS selectively. For example, in preliminary observations or pilot studies, the investigators might wish to use FACS as a comprehensive measure, and then, based on these results, select out certain action units which may be of particular interest in their main study.

Ekman & Friesen (1976) quote a correlation of 0.83 for FACS between the codings of independent observers (0.75 is usually regarded as acceptable for demonstrating adequate reliability). Reliability is an essential pre-requisite of any classification system, since it needs to be demonstrated that the system is sufficiently objective for other investigators to replicate the observations. Thus, a reliability study is typically carried out in which independent observers use the system to score a segment of behaviour, and the scores are then compared in order to assess inter-rater consistency. The use of reliability studies is a characteristic feature of the psychological approach, but should in fact form an integral part of the construction of any coding procedure. In addition to establishing objectivity, reliability studies also help to focus the investigator's attention on the categories used in the system, and in this way add both precision and rigour to its development.

Coding systems may undergo many modifications in response to shortcomings which emerge in subsequent investigations, which is clearly illustrated in the development of systems for the content analysis of speech. One of the earliest of these systems was Interaction Process Analysis (IPA) devised by Bales (1950). Bales's system was designed for use with problem-solving groups, and comprised 12 categories concerned with either *task* or *social-emotional* behaviour. Task behaviour may be 'given' or 'asked for', and includes categories such as 'gives suggestion' or 'asks for opinion'; social-emotional behaviour comprises 'positive reactions' or 'negative reactions', and includes categories such as 'agrees' and 'disagrees'. Bales describes the basic unit to be scored as the smallest discriminable segment of verbal (or non-verbal) behaviour to which a category can be assigned. However, as Morley & Stephenson (1977) point out, Bales provides no detail as to how the division into units should be achieved. In devising their own coding system, called Conference Process Analysis (CPA), Morley & Stephenson's solution to the problem of the unit of interaction is to adopt what they call a 'psychological unit', in which they take a single psychological idea as the basic unit of analysis. In addition, they provide a detailed set of rules on how this division into act units is to be accomplished.

A more important shortcoming of Bales's IPA is that the categories fail to distinguish between the function of the information exchanged and the way in which that information is made salient in the exchange. So, for example, Bales's category 'gives orientation' both describes what information is given and the way in which information is exchanged in social interaction, whereas Bales's category 'disagrees' only describes the way in which information is being exchanged. Morley & Stephenson's solution to this problem is to separate out what they call a 'mode' dimension (indicating how information is being exchanged) from a 'resource' dimension (indicating what sort of information is being exchanged). Hence they have a list of mode categories (e.g. offer, accept, reject, seek) and a list of resource categories (e.g. point of procedure, settlement point, or point of information). They also distinguish a third dimension, the 'referent' dimension, which is used to indicate who is being explicitly described in the interaction (e.g. no referent, self, or other).

One limitation of the Morley & Stephenson system is that it was devised specifically for analysing industrial negotiations. Thomas, Bull & Roger (1982) used CPA as the basis for a more general system of classification called Conversational Exchange Analysis (CEA), where conversation is classified along three dimensions: activity, type and focus. Activity corresponds to Morley & Stephenson's mode dimension and refers to how information is being exchanged (e.g. offer, request). Type corresponds to Morley & Stephenson's resource dimension and refers to what sort of information is being exchanged (e.g. attitude, belief), while focus, which corresponds to their referent dimension, indicates who is being talked about (e.g. self, other).

The advantage of CEA in contrast to CPA is that conversation can be classified along dimensions that are both general and specific: the activity dimension is applicable to a wide range of conversations, whereas type and focus are more specific to particular social contexts. For example, Bull (1986) used a modified version of the type dimension in a content analysis of a political speech. Coding systems may thus undergo a number of modifications in the course of their development: Morley & Stephenson's CPA represents a substantial advance on Bales's IPA, while CEA provides an extension of Morley & Stephenson's system which can be used across a whole range of different social situations.

## Conclusions

The social psychological approach to the study of interpersonal communication is typically associated with the use of the experimental method. Such research characteristically takes place in social psychology laboratories; it also relies heavily on the use of quantification and inferential statistics, as well as on classification systems for the transcription of behaviour.

The main advantage of laboratory research is the technical sophistication which it affords, such as the use of independent video cameras, split-screen video-recording and multi-track audio-recording. All these techniques enable the researcher to make more precise and accurate observations of interpersonal communication; they do not readily lend themselves to research outside the setting of the social psychology laboratory. Quantification and the use of inferential statistics enable the researcher to arrive at an objective decision about the significance of a particular behaviour; in addition, the more advanced statistical designs permit an examination of complex interactions that may exist amongst the independent variables. Quantification in turn depends upon the development of coding procedures by means of which behaviour can be classified into discrete categories; in this way, the behaviour in question is exhaustively and comprehensively examined. These psychological coding systems are not fixed and inflexible entities that are simply imposed upon the data; they can be progressively revised and refined with the development of a more sophisticated understanding of interpersonal communication, and as such serve as invaluable aids to the perception of events.

## References

ATKINSON, J.M. 1984, *Our Masters' Voices: The Language and Body Language of Politics*. London: Methuen.

BALES, R.F. 1950, *Interaction Process Analysis: A Method for the Study of Small Groups*. Reading, MA: Addison–Wesley.

BLURTON JONES, N.G. 1971, Criteria for use in describing facial expressions in children, *Human Biology*, 41, 365–413.

BULL, P.E. 1986, The use of hand gestures in political speeches: Some case studies, *Journal of Language and Social Psychology*, 5, 103–18.

EKMAN, P. 1979, Methods for measuring facial behaviour. Lecture delivered to NATO Advanced Study Institute, 6 September.

EKMAN, P. & FRIESEN, W.V. 1976, Measuring facial movement, *Environmental Psychology and Nonverbal Behavior*, 1, 56–75.

— 1978, *Facial Action Coding System*. Palo Alto, CA: Consulting Psychologists Press.

GRANT, E.C. 1969, Human facial expression, *Man*, 4, 525–36.

HERITAGE, J. & GREATBATCH, D. 1986, Generating applause: A study of rhetoric and response at party political conferences, *American Journal of Sociology*, 92, 110–57.

MORLEY, I. & STEPHENSON, G. 1977, *The Social Psychology of Bargaining*. London: George Allan & Unwin.

RIME, B. & MC CUSKER, L. 1976, Visual behaviour in social interaction: The validity of eye-contact assessments under different conditions of observation, *British Journal of Psychology*, 67, 507–14.

STEPHENSON, G. & RUTTER, D. 1970, Eye-contact, distance and affiliation: a re-evaluation, *British Journal of Psychology*, 61, 385–93.

THOMAS, A.P., BULL, P.E. & ROGER, D. 1982, Conversational Exchange Analysis, *Journal of Language and Social Psychology*, 1, 141–55.

THOMAS, A.P., ROGER, D. & BULL, P.E. 1983, A sequential analysis of informal dyadic conversation using Markov chains, *British Journal of Social Psychology*, 22, 177–88.

ZIMMERMAN, D.H. & WEST, C. 1975, Sex roles, interruptions and silences in conversations. In B. THORNE & N. HENLEY (eds), *Language and Sex: Difference and Dominance*. Rowley, MA: Newbury House.

# 2 Current developments in conversation analysis[1]

JOHN HERITAGE
*University of Warwick*

Conversation analysis[2] has developed over the past 15 years as a distinctive research stream of the wider intellectual programme of ethnomethodology — the study of the common-sense reasoning skills and abilities through which the ordinary members of a culture produce and recognise intelligible courses of action.[3] Throughout the period of its public existence,[4] the perspective has been distinctive both in its commitment to the study of naturally occurring interaction and in its avoidance of idealised theoretical and empirical treatments of its chosen research materials.

The following discussion will give a brief account of some aspects of conversation-analytic research as it has developed since 1975 and may be viewed as a supplementary sketch to the published summary outlines of the perspective which are presently available (Atkinson & Drew, 1979:34–81; Heritage, 1984a:233–92; Levinson, 1983:284–370; Zimmerman, 1988). Although the last few years have witnessed the publication of a substantial number of monographs and collections of studies (Schenkein, 1978; *Sociology*, 1978; Psathas, 1979; Atkinson & Drew, 1979; Zimmerman & West, 1980; C. Goodwin, 1981; Atkinson & Heritage, 1984; Van Dijk, 1985; Button, Drew & Heritage, 1986; Heath, 1986; Button & Lee, 1987) together with numerous individual articles, there remains a substantial backlog of completed papers which will not be exhausted by collections which are currently in preparation or forthcoming.[5] For space reasons, the present discussion will largely concentrate on 'structural' aspects of conversation-analytic research rather than substantive topic areas (e.g. interaction among children, cf. M. Goodwin, 1982a,b; Maynard, 1985a, b) to which it has made a considerable contribution.

## Background

The basic orientation of conversation analytic studies may be summarised in terms of four fundamental assumptions: (1) interaction is structurally organised; (2) contributions to interaction are both context-shaped and context-renewing; (3) these two properties inhere in the details of interaction so that no order of detail in conversational interaction can be dismissed a priori as disorderly, accidental or interactionally irrelevant; and (4) the study of social interaction in its details is best approached through the analysis of naturally occurring data.

The initial and most fundamental assumption of conversation analysis is that all aspects of social action and interaction can be examined in terms of conventionalised or institutionalised structural organisations which analysably inform their production. These organisations are to be treated as structures in their own right which, like other social institutions or conventions, stand independently of the psychological or other characteristics of particular participants. It is this 'structural' assumption which links conversation analysis both to the linguistics of Harris (1951) and to the Durkheimian sociological tradition (Durkheim, 1982)[6] and it is the successful application of this structural assumption to the fine details of social interaction which has characterised conversation-analytic research from the outset.

Second, it is assumed that the significance of any participant's communicative action is doubly contextual, in that the action is both context-shaped and context-renewing. It is *context-shaped* because its contribution to an ongoing sequence of actions cannot be adequately understood except by reference to the context in which it participates. The term 'context' is here used to refer both to the immediately local configuration of preceding activity in which an utterance occurs, and also to the 'larger' environment of activity within which that configuration analysably occurs. This contextual aspect of utterances is significant both because speakers routinely draw upon it as a resource in designing their utterances and also because, correspondingly, hearers must also draw upon the local contexts of utterances in order to make adequate sense of what is said.[7] Communicative action is also *context-renewing*. Since every current utterance will itself form the immediate context for some next action in a sequence, it will inevitably contribute to the contextual framework in terms of which the next action will be understood. In this sense, the context of a next action is inevitably renewed with each current action. Moreover each current action will, by the same token, function to renew (i.e. maintain, adjust or alter) any broader or more generally prevailing sense of context which is the object of the participants' orientations and actions.

Third, the methodological assumption that no order of detail in interaction can be dismissed a priori as insignificant has had two major consequences for conversation-analytic researchers. One has been a general retreat from premature theory construction in favour of a strongly empirical approach to the study of social action. There has thus been an avoidance of the abstract theoretical constructs which have been characteristic, for example, of traditional sociological treatments of social actions and institutions (see Parsons's 1937 analysis of the 'unit act') in favour of the study of 'actual, particular social actions and sequences of them' (Schegloff, 1980:151). A methodological corollary of this stance is that findings will ultimately be answerable, not merely to statistical treatments of aggregates of data, but also to the detailed explication of singular instances.[8] The other consequence is the adoption of a similarly stringent view towards the analysis of the cultural competences which are employed in the production and recognition of activities. In particular, every effort is made to render empirical analyses responsive to the specific details of research materials and to avoid idealising the latter. In their attitudes towards empirical materials, conversation analysts converge with other proponents of 'context analysis' (Kendon, 1979, 1982) in assuming that the data of interaction will, in all their aspects and until proved otherwise, exhibit systematic and orderly properties which are meaningful for the participants and hence that the idealisation of data will tend, unavoidably, to damage the prospects for a fully coherent and satisfactory analysis.

Finally, the stress on the value of naturally occurring data as the central medium of research emerges in relation to two interrelated considerations. First, without recorded data which can be repeatedly examined, it is simply impossible to gain access to the detail necessary for the analysis of conversational interaction. Neither the intuitive invention of data, nor the use of stenographic notes, nor the on-the-spot coding of behaviour allows the detail of actual conversational behaviour to be recovered and the use of these methods must inevitably compromise the value of the observations made as reliable evidence (cf. Sacks, 1984). Similarly role-plays and experimental techniques are apt to restrict both the range and the authenticity of the activities which are elicited through their use.[9] A second consideration arises from the fact that language, as Schegloff, Jefferson & Sacks (1977:381) have noted, 'is a vehicle for the living of real lives with real interests in a real world'. From the outset, conversation analysts have aimed at grasping the organised procedures of talk as they are employed in real-worldly contexts between persons in real relationships whose talk has a real consequentiality and accountability. The investigation of such procedures will ideally embrace a wide variety of real contexts — many of which may be impossible to replicate in even the most approximate fashion in a contrived situation. For these reasons, conversation analysts have approached their topics by treating the 'real world' as their laboratory. This has involved the cumulative collection of the widest possible array of naturally occurring data. The collection of such data — although sometimes slow and time-consuming by comparison with other methods — has two outstanding advantages. First, because the data constitute samples of the social world which have, as it were, been 'bottled', they can be analysed and reanalysed in the light of different research questions and, in the process, very detailed understandings of particular corpora of data can be established. Second, the data can be used in a process of comparison the scope of which accumulates over time with the cumulative expansion of data corpora. Thus although the process of analysis — which is primarily focused on internal 'structural' issues — may begin with a relatively low level of control over explicitly formulated external variables, a steady accretion of such control can confidently be expected to manifest itself over time.

These basic assumptions were developed to handle the phenomenon of the contextual determination of indexical speech activities. In various ways, they found early expression in the analyses of particular lexical formulations which recur in Sacks's (1964–72) unpublished lectures and in published papers on category use, puns, location formulations and other topics (Sacks, 1972a,b, 1973a, 1975; Schegloff, 1972). Simultaneously, however, related interests in the sequential organisation of interaction assumed a prominence which steadily increased over time.

The latter interests first appeared in the published literature in a focus on the management of conversational turn-taking (Sacks, Schegloff & Jefferson, 1974) and related issues concerning co-ordinated entry into, exit from, and suspension of the turn-taking procedures for conversation (Schegloff, 1968; Schegloff & Sacks, 1973; Sacks, 1974). These studies demonstrated in great detail that turn-transfer is interactionally managed through recursive procedures which enable very precise real-time co-ordination between speakers (Jefferson, 1973; Ervin-Tripp, 1979).[10] Moreover the studies of greetings, closings and the like also intimated a variety of ways in which the turn-by-turn 'context-renewing' character of interaction involved the provision both of a *directionality* for subsequent talk and an architecture for the maintenance of *intersubjective understanding* within talk.

Both these latter aspects received an elementary specification in the context of discussions of the *adjacency pair* concept (Schegloff, 1968, 1972;

Schegloff & Sacks, 1973). Here a basic directionality in talk was provided for in the observation that the production of the first member of a pair of actions (for example, a greeting or a question) empirically projects and normatively requires the relevant occurrence 'next' of a complementary second action to be produced by another speaker. This conceptualisation was important in a number of ways. First, it suggested a systematic basis on which speakers (and 'overhearing' analysts) could determine that particular relevanced next actions were noticeably or non-trivially absent (Schegloff, 1972:75–79). Second, it indicated ways in which the production of subsequent next actions that were unrelated to, or not projected by, the first could be heard to be misaligned. Third, it intimated how, under the latter circumstances, second speakers could be treated as normatively accountable for failures to respond, faulty responses and other interactional mishaps — thus establishing a 'built-in' motivation for competent conversational performance (see also Sacks *et al.*, 1974:727–28). Finally, although the adjacency pair concept was initially developed in discussions of actions that dealt with turn-taking contingencies, it was clear that the concept had a wider applicability and that the underlying generic concept of adjacent positioning was of crucial significance in handling a range of more complex speech activities.

In relation to the maintenance of intersubjectivity, the concept suggested ways in which speakers would, through the production of next actions, unavoidably display a particular public understanding of the prior talk. Thus in so far as a second speaker's utterance performed an action which could be found, with whatever degree of interpretative latitude (Garfinkel, 1963, 1967; Grice, 1975), to be fitted to its prior, it would be treated as displaying an understanding of its prior which was appropriate to that fit (Sacks, 1973b). Thus second pair parts not only accomplish (or fail to accomplish) some relevant next action, they also display some form of public understanding of the prior utterance to which they are directed. In turn, the public understanding of a prior turn's talk that is displayed in a current turn becomes available for 'third turn' comment, correction, etc., by the producer of the initial turn in the sequence. In this way, adjacent positioning generically provides a framework for the continuous updating of public, intersubjective understandings. And it is by means of adjacent positioning, as Schegloff & Sacks (1973:297–98) observed, that various forms of failures can be recognised and that appreciations, corrections, etc., can be understandably attempted.[11]

Thus by 1975, when Sacks was killed in a road accident, much of the basic conceptual scaffolding for subsequent developments in the field was already in place in the literature. Interactants were viewed as simultaneously engaged in fine-grained real time co-ordination of speaking turns tracked predominantly in terms of surface structural features and as organising their actions in terms of publicly accountable normative expectations bearing on the nature and design of their turns at talk. Since 1975, developments in conversation analysis have ranged over a large number of substantive topics. In reviewing them, I will group them loosely under the following sub-headings: preference organisation; topic organisation; the use of non- or quasi-lexical speech objects; the integration of vocal and non-vocal activities; and interaction in institutional settings.

**Preference organisation**

The concept of 'preference' was developed to characterise basic differences in the ways that alternative 'second' actions (for example, accepting or rejecting an invitation) are routinely accomplished. The term itself is potentially misleading in that it does not refer to the personal desires or psychological dispositions of individual speakers, but rather to recurrent and institutionalised features of the turn and sequence structures in which the alternative actions are carried out. In this context, the term gains its currency from the fact that these features tend to maximise the likelihood that 'preferred' actions will occur and, correspondingly, to minimise the occurrence of 'dispreferred' actions.

Research into preference organisation has shown that for a variety of first actions — e.g. assessments (Pomerantz, 1975, 1984a); invitations, proposals and offers (Davidson, 1984, forthcoming) and requests (Wootton, 1981) — particular dispreferred second actions (usually disagreements, rejections and refusals) are routinely avoided, withheld or delayed in many different types of social context involving a great variety of speakers. In terms of design features, preferred actions are overwhelmingly performed directly and with little or no delay. Dispreferred actions, by contrast, exhibit the following features either singly or in combination: (1) the action is delayed within its turn or across a sequence of turns; (2) the action is commonly prefaced or qualified within the turn in which it occurs; (3) the action is commonly accomplished in mitigated or indirect form and (4) the action is usually accounted for (see Atkinson & Drew, 1979; Heritage, 1984a, 1988; and Levinson, 1983, for extensive summaries).[12]

The role of preference organisation in relation to a wide variety of conversational actions appears to be strongly associated with the avoidance of threats to 'face' (Goffman, 1955; Brown & Levinson, 1987) and ultimately the avoidance of outright conflict. Thus Pomerantz (1984a) has shown that the preference for agreement with a prior assessment is reversed when the latter is a self-deprecation. Here, where it is agreement that would constitute the face-threatening act, there is a preference for disagreement.[13] More complex still are the face considerations which inform responses to assessments which are complimentary to the respondent (Pomerantz, 1978; Mulkay, 1984). Conflict avoidance has been proposed by Schegloff *et al.* (1977) to be a significant outcome of the preference for self-correction in conversation (see also Jefferson, 1983a) and the forestalling of conflict has also been demonstrated by Pomerantz (1984a, b) and Davidson (1984, forthcoming) to be an empirical outcome in sequences involving assessments and invitations.[14]

A similar forestalling role is also played by a variety of *pre-sequence* objects (a prototypical instance of which is 'Are you doing anything tonight?'). Very often these are ground-clearing devices directed at establishing the appropriateness or relevance of a projected subsequent action such as telling a joke (Sacks, 1974), making a 'news' announcement (Terasaki, 1976), making an invitation (Drew, 1984) and the like. In each of these cases, the face-threatening rejection of some activity proposed by the speaker can be avoided by the recipient's indication, in advance of the projected action, that the latter is not appropriate, relevant, possible, desired or whatever.

This analysis of pre-sequences has had considerable pay-off in a new and compelling account of indirect speech acts. Drawing on work by Goffman (1976), Merritt (1976), Schegloff (1979a), Heringer (1977) and others, Levinson (1983) has constructed an elegant analysis of indirect speech acts which treats them as the product of contracted sequence packages which, in extended form, would comprise two interconnected two-part sequences (pre-sequence + target sequence). In such cases, he proposes, the contraction of the sequence package is often marked as aimed for by the use of conventionalised features of turn design (e.g. the inclusion of such markers as 'would', 'could' and 'please'). In this way, considerations having to do with the normal design and trajectory of *sequences* can be shown to inform the design and interpretation of conventionalised *turns*. Moreover, through this analysis, the phenomenon of 'indirect speech acts'[15] can be explained by reference to the simple facts of conversational sequence in the place of more tortuous attempts to work solely at the level of the syntax and semantics of sentences (see Levinson, 1983:243–84 for an overview of such accounts).

**Topic organisation**

The domain of topic in conversation was originally proposed by Sacks[16] to be organised by procedures that work to ensure that topics 'flow' into one another without discrete boundaries. These procedures, he suggested, were the product of a pervasive conversational orientation to produce each current utterance so as to display its relatedness to its prior. This relatedness, Sacks insisted, is always an *achieved* relatedness which is not given by simple co-referentiality (or even the sharing of concepts) across turns at talk.

Unfortunately, it has not proved easy to move from these statements to a more specific characterisation of the procedural bases of topic maintenance and topic shift. The achievement of 'relatedness' between turns is so complex and multi-faceted that it can appear that no general principles of topic organisation can be developed because everything is, in principle, both potentially related — and unrelated — to everything else.

In this context, one major development in the analysis of topic organisation has originated in the domain of *boundaried* topical movement in which the closure of one topic is followed by the discrete initiation of another. Thus Button (1987) and Button & Casey (1984, 1985) have described several distinct methods of boundaried topic initiation and identified different sequentially organised procedures for the introduction of new topical material for each type. They have also suggested ways in which these procedures may vary in their suitability for use in various structural locations in conversation and in their sensitivity to a variety of particular needs and objectives which may be held by participants. Jefferson (1984a) has developed the analysis of boundaried topic movement with respect to a very specific conversational environment — new topic beginnings occurring immediately after an episode in which one of the participants has been describing a 'trouble'. Here, Jefferson finds, the initiators of new topics overwhelmingly begin by addressing the concerns of the other speaker — a technique which Jefferson characterises as 'other attentive'. In the same paper, Jefferson also discusses the exploitation of 'stepwise' topic flow in the immediate aftermath of 'troubles talk' and identifies a patterning in this exploitation which is both subtle and suggestive.

In a related monograph-length study, Jefferson (1981b) has discussed a variety of recipient activities — ranging from the choice between 'yes' and 'mm hm' as acknowledgement tokens to recipient assessments, commentaries and enquiries — which may be produced, and understood to be produced, as adumbrative or implicative of some attempt at topic shift (see also Jefferson, 1983b, 1984c). This study clearly shows the extent to which the course of on-topic talk may be strongly influenced by relatively 'small-scale' recipient activities.

Although the domain of topic organisation might appear to be a relatively straightforward and high-priority area for the employment of conversation-analytic techniques, research has in fact proceeded relatively slowly and cautiously thus far. The obstacles to research in this domain are substantial. Topic maintenance and shift are exceptionally complex matters and, as many of the above cited studies indicate, there are no simple routes to the examination of topic flow. On the contrary, all manner of conversational procedures are implicated in the management of topic. Thus, at the present time, it appears that any satisfactory and coherent approach to this domain will depend on extensive prior knowledge of a substantial mass of conversational procedures which, in combination, are employed in its management. In this way, the analysis of topic organisation may prove to be among the most long-term projects of conversation-analytic study.

## The use of non- or quasi-lexical speech objects

In this section a growing corpus of research on the interactional use of non-lexical speech objects will be summarised. Leaving aside the analysis of sound stretches, cut-offs and other perturbations of the speech stream (cf. Jefferson, 1974; Jefferson & Schegloff, 1975; Schegloff *et al.*, 1977; Goodwin, 1981) whose role in relation to repair, overlapped talk, etc., may be variously exploited, the focus of this section will fall on the analysis of a variety of 'back-channel' response tokens and on the organisation of laughter in interaction.

### *Response tokens*

It is not surprising that conversation analysts should have taken some interest in response tokens — such objects as 'mm hm', 'yes', 'oh', and 'really'. Not only are these objects exceptionally prevalent in ordinary conversational interaction (though, interestingly, less so in talk in many institutional settings, see Atkinson, 1982; Heritage, 1985a), they are also objects whose role in interaction is almost purely sequential. In many cases these objects are non-lexical and they gain much of their interactional significance from their specific placements in sequences of talk. Thus the preoccupations of conversation analysts, which are focused on sequential considerations, are perhaps uniquely fitted to shed light on the role of response tokens in talk.

Research in this domain has shown that the role of these objects is very substantially underestimated by the conventional treatment of them merely as 'back-channels' or as 'signals of continued attention'. In fact, their variety and differentiation is indicative of the range of tasks they perform in talk. Research in this area has shown that the organisation and progression of the events of talk are the object of much more fine-grained organisation and control than was previously believed to be the case. Thus, as Schegloff (1982) has shown, it is the precise placement of such items as 'uh huh', 'yes', etc.,[17] by reference to the boundaries of turn-constructional units within a segment of talk which permits them to be heard as 'continuers', 'acknowledgements', 'agreements', etc. Comparing the production of 'yes' and 'mm hm' as responses in the context of extended speaker turns, Jefferson (1981b, 1983b, 1984c) has shown that, while 'mm hm' is a token of 'passive recipiency', the production of 'yes' commonly adumbrates some topic-shifting or topic-curtailing activity by its producer. Heritage (1984b) has shown that 'oh' is distinctive in being used to indicate that its producer has undergone some change of state of current knowledge, information, orientation or awareness and hence that it is extensively used specifically as an 'information receipt' in conversation. Jefferson (1981a) has further shown that such objects as 'really', 'did you', 'you did', etc., function as 'newsmarks', that is, objects which are used to promote the telling of 'news'. However, these objects are by no means equivalent in such contexts and Jefferson has distinguished the various degrees to which they typically promote such tellings. The prevalence of these response tokens in talk is such that a majority of papers in conversation analysis will contain one or more comments *en passant* about their functioning. The above-cited papers, however, have, in various ways, made these objects a central subject-matter.

### *Laughter*

From a distance laughter may appear a rather uninviting candidate for sequential analysis. As Jefferson (1985) points out, not only is laughter never reported 'verbatim', it is also rarely transcribed. Moreover laughter is apt to be regarded as an out-of-control activity and not as a phenomenon which is strongly structured in its occurrence, organisation and tasks. However, Jefferson's detailed transcriptions of laughter have made available a rich corpus of data from which substantial findings are emerging. Among these are that laughter is specifically 'invited' by a variety of techniques and becomes 'due' from recipients at isolable recognition points

(Jefferson, 1979) at which recipients may recognisably accept, or decline, invitations to laugh (see also Jefferson, Sacks & Schegloff, 1987). Jefferson (1984b; Jefferson *et al.* 1987) and, more recently Drew (1987), have investigated particular sites at which invitations to laugh may occur. Jefferson (1984b) has shown that invitations to laugh may occur in the course of 'troubles-telling' sequences where they may be used to exhibit 'troubles resistence' by the teller. In such contexts, recipients rarely join in the laughter and, when they do, special tasks are commonly being accomplished. Drew (1987) has examined the role of teasing as a form of interpersonal sanction and discusses the ways in which the recipient of a tease may use laughter in dealing with it. Finally, in an extended paper, Jefferson *et al.* (1987) have considered the role of laughter in the context of improprieties or 'improper' talk. Here, they propose, relevantly positioned laughter may be used to exhibit appreciation of the impropriety to which it responds and thus establish an environment in which the impropriety may be further escalated. Conversely, laughter may be withheld to forestall such an escalation. In all of these studies, laughter is shown to be systematically and precisely placed and calibrated with respect to the range of interactional tasks which its producer will be understood to be accomplishing. Rather than being the out-of-control expression of inner sentiments, its provenance is thereby shown to be strongly socially organised and geared to the interpersonal environment in which it occurs.

It has already been suggested that the sequentially oriented research techniques of conversation analysis are well fitted to illuminate the interactional uses of the range of objects described above and, indeed, a number of important and exciting results have been achieved. These are, of course, significant in their own right. However knowledge of the systematic features of the non-lexical speech objects is also proving valuable in generating more sophisticated analyses of the larger interactional undertakings in which they are embedded. And this is of particular value because their participation in such undertakings is virtually ubiquitous.

## The integration of vocal with non-vocal activities

Although early conversation-analytic research gave little attention to the role of non-vocal behaviour in interaction, this circumstance arose neither from oversight nor from the failure to appreciate the significance of such behaviour. On the contrary, the pervasive interpenetration of vocal and non-vocal activity in interaction proved to be so significant, and yet so complex, that it threatened to overwhelm the fledgeling analysis of conversation with insuperable complications. In this context the early and extensive use of telephone conversations as data served two objectives. It provided a substantial source of data which was fully naturalistic, while being simplified by the automatic elimination of non-vocal conduct as an object of participants' orientations. In this way the additional complexities of handling non-vocal conduct could legitimately be postponed in favour of an exclusive focus on the details of talk. The findings which have emerged from the use of these procedures have stood up remarkably well in the face of a mass of video data from face-to-face interactions which is increasingly being used by practitioners in the field.

More recently, however, a considerable body of work has emerged from studies which have examined the relationship between speech, gaze and body movement in interaction. A substantial body of research has been focused on the ways in which non-vocal conduct is organised with respect to the management of turn-allocation and turn-construction.

A basic reference point in this field is C. Goodwin's (1979, 1981) demonstration that the production of a turn at talk is itself the object of active management in which the interactants engage in fine-grained 'negotiations' over speaking and hearing roles. Gaze is central to these processes and Goodwin (1981) has shown both that the addressee's gaze towards the speaker is central in establishing hearership and that in the normal course of a speaking turn the addressee should bring his/her gaze to the speaker before the speaker's gaze arrives at the addressee. On occasions in which this does not occur and the speaker is thus gazing at a non-gazing recipient, hesitations and dysfluencies (including turn restarts) may occur. These latter constitute the primary resources by which speakers can solicit the gaze of their recipients. In the same volume, Goodwin shows some ways in which interactants can collaborate in maintaining and altering different states of engagement which are centrally displayed through the disposition of the participants' bodies (see also Heath 1984, 1986). Goodwin's studies vividly show that the turn cannot be regarded as a monolithic 'unit' of discourse. Rather it is the object of continuous management and adjustment contingent on a range of non-vocally displayed states of interaction between speaker and hearer (see also Schegloff, 1987b).

Goodwin's initiatives have been developed in a variety of ways. M.H. Goodwin (1980) has described procedures by which speakers may solicit non-vocal activities (such as nods and head-shakes) which appear to function in similar ways to vocal acknowledgement tokens such as 'mm hm' and 'really'. Heath (1984, 1986) has built on Goodwin's findings by examining the interactive organisation of gaze and body posture during a variety of phases of medical consultations. Finally, Goodwin himself has analysed, *inter alia*, the ways in which non-vocal behaviour is adjusted to different participant roles during a story-telling (C. Goodwin, 1984), and the ways in which agreement sequences are characterised by interlocking activities at the non-vocal as well as the vocal level (cf. Goodwin & Goodwin, 1982).

As in other areas of conversation-analytic research, work on the integration of non-vocal with vocal activities has concentrated on descriptions of the 'architecture' of interaction: the structural organisations through which interactants collaborate and/or compete in the construction of conjoint courses of action. Here the analytic outlook that was developed through the analysis of telephone conversations has proved strikingly adaptable to the analysis of video-recordings. The integration of vocal conduct with non-vocal activity has been shown to be both intimate and the object of delicate and nuanced orientation by interactants. In the process, the production of talk has been shown to be the object of complex interactional co-ordination both within and across turns and sequences.

### Interaction in 'institutional' settings

In the final section of this overview, we turn to examine some studies which, while using conversation-analytic concepts and techniques as their primary resources, are concerned with the analysis of interaction in a range of 'institutional' settings involving strongly defined social roles. Such settings — including interaction in classrooms, the courts, news interviews, medical settings and the like — involve rather different patterns of interaction from those found in ordinary conversational encounters. The studies described in this section aim to describe these patterns and, where possible, to describe and assess the significance of the ways in which they differ from the characteristic features of ordinary talk.

The work done on institutional settings exhibits some important differences from the foundational work in conversation and this requires some preliminary comment. The work in 'pure' conversation is inspired by the realisation that ordinary conversation is the predominant medium of interaction in the social world. It is also the primary form of interaction to which, with whatever simplifications,[18] the child is initially exposed and through which socialisation proceeds. There is thus every reason to suppose that the basic forms of mundane talk constitute a kind of bench-mark against which other more formal or 'institutional' types of interaction are recognised and experienced. The more recent studies of institutional interaction do indeed show systematic variations and restrictions on forms of action relative to ordinary conversation, thus confirming the supposition that mundane conversation represents a broad and flexible domain of primary interactional practices. Given this, it is clear that the primary study of mundane conversation, preferably casual conversation between peers, offers a principled approach to determining what is distinctive about interactions involving, for example, the specialisms of the school or the hospital or the asymmetries of status, gender, ethnicity, etc.

However, while 'pure' conversational interaction has been shown to be organised in terms of formal principles which permit cumulative findings of considerable abstractness and power, studies of interaction in institutional settings presently exhibit a more 'piecemeal' aspect. As noted above, institutional interaction seems to involve specific and significant narrowings and respecifications of the range of options that are operative in conversational interaction. These narrowings and respecifications are *conventional* in character: they are culturally variable, they are sometimes subject to legal constraints, they are discursively justifiable and justified by reference to considerations of task, equity, efficiency, etc., in ways that mundane conversational practices manifestly are not. Associated with these conventions are differing participation frameworks (Goffman, 1979) with their associated rights and obligations, different footings and differential patterns of opportunity and power.

A basic point of departure for some of the more recent studies in institutional interaction has been the discussion by Sacks *et al.* (1974:729–30) of different turn-taking systems. Since then analyses by McHoul (1978), Mehan (1979, 1985), Atkinson & Drew (1979) and Greatbatch (1985, 1988) have detailed the forms of turn-taking which are characteristic in classroom, courtroom and news-interview interactions. These studies converge in suggesting that the relatively restricted patterns of conduct characteristic of these settings are primarily the product of turn-type pre-allocation (Atkinson & Drew, 1979). Here the incumbents of particular roles (e.g. doctor, teacher, lawyer, interviewer) ask questions and, where relevant, select next speakers, while others (e.g. patients, pupils, witnesses, interviewees) are largely confined to answering them. These studies also suggest that this form of question- and answer-mediated turn-taking has a pervasive influence both over the range and design of the interactional activities which the parties routinely undertake and on the detailed management of such encounters.

A second dimension of conversation-analytic research in this domain has focused on the attempt to characterise and explicate the ways in which a broad variety of social roles and their associated tasks are managed through the medium of the question and answer sequence in various different institutional settings. This research has involved explicit analyses of the ways in which particular institutional contexts are recursively evoked and maintained in and through the talk of the interactants (Atkinson & Drew, 1979; Drew, 1985; Heritage, 1985a; Zimmerman, 1984). Detailed studies maintain this overall view while focusing in on specific institutional tasks such as the management of accusations and defences in criminal (Atkinson & Drew, 1979) and small-claims courts (Pomerantz & Atkinson, 1984), plea bargaining (Maynard, 1984), or particular activities in classroom (Mehan, 1978; McHoul, 1978, 1979), news interview (Greatbatch, 1985, 1986, 1988) and medical encounters (Heath, 1986; West, 1984). A number of these studies have been characterised by an interest in the impact of gender on institutional interaction which has been stimulated by the work of West and Zimmerman (West, 1979; West & Zimmerman, 1977, 1983; Zimmerman & West, 1975). And a further input into research on institutional interaction derives from a continuing interest in the categorisations and related typifications (Sudnow, 1968; Cicourel, 1973) which are invoked in institutional contexts (cf. Watson, 1978, 1987). This focus not only preserves Sacks's early concern with membership categorisation in interaction but also represents a significant strand of continuity with sociological studies of organisations which have focused on the creation and negotiation of organisational categories and the labelling of individuals. A final dimension of conversation-analytic research on institutional settings has been developed by Atkinson and focuses upon conduct in large-scale settings — courtrooms, church services, political rallies, etc. — which involve a high proportion of talk directed to a mass audience. Here Atkinson has focused on procedures by which the attention of audiences can be attracted (Atkinson, 1979, 1982) and co-ordinated responses to speaker activities can be secured (Atkinson, 1984; Heritage & Greatbatch, 1986). These procedures, which appear to involve adaptations of ordinary methods of speaking to large-scale public settings, also carry over into written discourse (Atkinson, 1983; Mulkay, 1985).

In this section, we have stressed the value of maintaining a comparative focus between the specifics of particular forms of institutional interaction and the ways in which parallel or related activities are managed in ordinary talk. In this context, it is appropriate to conclude by referring to a large-scale analysis of 'troubles talk' conducted by Jefferson (1980) and Jefferson & Lee (1981). This study develops an analysis of a basic trajectory for 'troubles telling' in ordinary conversation which, Jefferson proposes, is marked by a number of stages and is systematically subject to a variety of contingencies. Since 'troubles telling' is an endemic feature of many forms of institutional interaction which involve members of the 'caring professions' (doctors, social workers, health visitors, etc.), this study is of particular value in sensitising researchers studying interactions between such personnel and their clients to a variety of issues which may be being negotiated over their course.

Taken as a whole, the studies of institutional interaction discussed in this section presently exhibit a 'patchwork' quality which reflects both the diversity of the institutions under investigation, the variety of interactional phenomena which are addressed and the range of research interests (both 'pure' and 'applied') which are being fulfilled through their study. None the less, there is an underlying coherence of perspective and a commonality of approach to data which augurs well for the field. This is based on the recognition that the creation and maintenance of institutional roles is ultimately realised through specific sequences of conversational actions. This recognition functions as a significant prophylactic against the tendency identified by Goffman (1964) for students of communication to treat interaction as merely marking 'the geometric intersection of actors making talk and actors bearing attributes'. As a result, the specifics of institutional interaction are becoming better documented and more fully understood.

## Conclusion

The past decade has seen substantial developments in the field of conversation analysis. Most obviously it has seen the extension of conversation-analytic techniques from the analysis of relatively simple 'ritualised' sequences to an ever increasing range of interactional phenomena. During the same period, the perspective has also come to exert a substantial influence — both methodological and substantive — in a number of areas in the related disciplines of linguistics, social psychology, sociology, anthropology and cognitive science.

At the present time, the field remains strongly orientated towards the systematic description of the details of interactional phenomena. While this orientation may be criticised as resulting in an atheoretical taxonomy, no apology is made for it here. Conversation analysis emerged as part of a reaction within sociology to shortcomings resulting from the premature imposition of inadequate theoretical categories and frameworks on complex empirical data. Prior to the inception of conversation analysis, little was known about the natural organisation of social interaction. Since the currently available and cumulative stock of such knowledge is due in very substantial measure to the efforts of conversation analysts, this pervasive empirical orientation has issued in real and permanent gains.

None of this is to suggest that conversation analysis is in fact atheoretical. Conversation-analytic writings have, from the outset, plainly incorporated a variety of insights (for example, those severally attributable to Garfinkel, Goffman and Grice) within the framework of a coherent, working empirical programme. Moreover, many could be found who would probably assent, for example, to the basics of Levinson's (1981) and Brown & Levinson's (1987) characterisation of a rational speaker. However, it is also likely that the kinds of observation which are presently being made will both require and stimulate new theoretical work and it may well be that, since the ultimate object of investigation is a major dimension of social organisation, the explanatory theory will not be reducible without residue to the properties of rational agents. It may, after all, be unwise to exclude a Durkheimian sociological perspective from the analysis of what he himself pronounced as a prime instance of a 'social fact' and from a domain in which institutionalised conventions are so intricately tied to the exercise of human agency.

### Notes to Chapter 2

1. This paper is a revised, shortened and thoroughly updated version of Heritage (1985b). The latter source contains a considerably larger bibliography of conversation analysis.
2. The term 'conversation analysis' is preferred to the sometimes used 'conversational' analysis since, within this field, conversation is the object of investigation rather than a research methodology. Levinson (1983:286–94) has usefully distinguished between 'conversation analysis' and 'discourse analysis' as alternative research traditions.
3. The classic statement of this orientation remains that of Harold Garfinkel (1967:1), who proposes that the production and recognition of courses of action are the accountable products of a common set of procedures. As he puts it: 'the activities whereby members produce and manage the settings of organised everyday affairs are identical with members' procedures for making those settings "account-able"'.
4. The public existence of conversation analysis may be dated either from the publication of Schegloff (1968) or from the earlier widespread circulation of Sacks' unpublished lectures (Sacks, 1964–72).
5. These collections include Boden & Zimmerman (forthcoming); Drew & Heritage (forthcoming); Psathas (forthcoming), and Helm *et al.* (forthcoming).

6. See Kendon (1979, 1982) for further discussion of conversation analysis in the context of related traditions of investigation in social psychology.
7. See Schegloff (1984) for an exemplary discussion of this issue.
8. See Schegloff (1987b) for a discussion and empirical exemplification of this point.
9. Anyone who, like the present author, has had the opportunity to compare naturally occurring data with interactional data generated from experimentally or role-play-induced contexts, will appreciate the relatively impoverished character of the latter. And, of course, it is extremely unlikely that certain kinds of conversation analytic study — such as those on laughter in relation to intimacy (Jefferson, Sacks & Schegloff, 1987) or on 'troubles telling' (Jefferson & Lee, 1981) could conceivably be based on such data.
10. Relatedly, these studies showed that the turn-taking system for conversation exerts a considerable pressure on sentence design and hence on syntax (cf. Sacks *et al.*, 1974; Schegloff, 1979b; C. Goodwin, 1981; and, more generally, Levinson, 1983, and the contributions to Givon, 1979).
11. The present discussion should not be read as implying that it is *only* strictly defined second pair parts which show a public understanding of a prior turn's talk. Such an implication would be quite unwarranted. Many other turn types display their producer's understanding of a prior, though not all do so.
12. While many preference studies show that the structural features identified under this heading hold across random collections of speakers and contexts, two interesting studies show the persistence of these features into specific social relationships where it might be anticipated that they would be relaxed. Thus Wootton (1981) shows that the standard preference features characterise request sequences involving very young children and their parents, and McHoul (1979) has arrived at similar findings for the case of teachers' corrections of schoolchildren in classroom interaction.
13. Similarly, there appears to be a preference for the rejection of accusations (Atkinson & Drew, 1979:60) and for avoiding the telling of 'bad news' (Terasaki, 1976; Levinson, 1983:350).
14. It is significant that both Pomerantz and Davidson have demonstrated that speakers, attending to such features of dispreferred actions as delay, and/or the production of 'uh' or 'well' prefaces, may revise their utterance-in-progress so as to forestall anticipated rejections and disagreements. These findings demonstrate that the design of a turn-in-progress can be the result of *interaction* rather than of the intentions of the speaker pure and simple. And the influence of preference considerations which inform the design of a *next turn* thus demonstrably operate processually and retroactively on *current turn*.
15. Since conversation analysts do not work with the contrast between 'literal meaning' and 'indirect meaning' that is exploited in, for example, Searle (1975), the concept of an indirect speech act plays no role in conversation-analytic research.
16. See in particular Sacks's lectures of 9 March 1967 and 17 April 1968. See also Spring 1970, lecture 5; Winter 1971, 19 February and Spring 1971, 9 April.
17. Cf. M.H. Goodwin (1980) for a parallel discussion of head-nods.
18. See, for example, Bruner (1983); Ochs & Schieffelin (1979); and Snow & Ferguson (1977) for accounts of some aspects of the simplifications which accompany mothers' speech to young children.

**References**

ATKINSON, J. M. 1979, Sequencing and shared attentiveness to court proceedings. In G. PSATHAS (ed.), *Everyday Language: Studies in Ethnomethodology*. New York: Erlbaum. 257-86.

— 1982, Understanding formality: notes on the categorisation and production of 'formal' interaction, *British Journal of Sociology*, 33, 86–117.

— 1983, Two devices for generating audience approval: a comparative study of public discourse and texts. In K. EHLICH *et al.* (eds), *Connectedness in Sentence, Text and Discourse*. Tilburg, Netherlands: Tilburg Papers in Linguistics, 199–236.

— 1984, *Our Masters' Voices: The Language and Body Language of Politics*. London: Methuen.

ATKINSON, J. M. & DREW, P. 1979, *Order in Court: The Organisation of Verbal Interaction in Judicial Settings*. London: Macmillan.

ATKINSON, J. M. & HERITAGE, J. C. (eds) 1984, *Structures of Social Action: Studies in Conversation Analysis*. Cambridge: Cambridge University Press.

BODEN, D. & ZIMMERMAN, D. H. (eds) forthcoming, *Talk and Social Structure*. Cambridge: Polity Press.

BROWN, P. & LEVINSON, S. 1987, *Politeness: Some Universals in Language Usage*. Cambridge: Cambridge University Press.

BRUNER, J. 1983, *Child's Talk: Learning to Use Language*. Oxford: Oxford University Press.

BUTTON, G., 1987, Moving out of closings. In G. BUTTON & J. R. E. LEE (eds), *Talk and Social Organisation*. Clevedon, Avon: Multilingual Matters.

BUTTON, G. & CASEY, N. (1984), Generating topic: the use of topic initial elicitors. In J. M. ATKINSON & J. C. HERITAGE (eds), *Structures of Social Action: Studies in Conversation Analysis*. Cambridge: Cambridge University Press. 167–90.

— 1985, Topic nomination and topic pursuit, *Human Studies*, 8, 3–55.

BUTTON, G., DREW, P. & HERITAGE, J. (eds) 1986, *Interaction and Language Use*, special double issue of *Human Studies*, 9, 2–3.

BUTTON, G. & LEE, J. R. E. (eds) 1987, *Talk and Social Organisation*. Clevedon, Avon: Multilingual Matters.

CICOUREL, A. 1973, Interpretive procedures and normative rules in the negotiation of status and role. In A. CICOUREL, *Cognitive Sociology*. Harmondsworth: Penguin.

DAVIDSON, J.A. 1984, Subsequent versions of invitations, offers, requests and proposals dealing with potential or actual rejection. In J.M.

Atkinson & J. C. Heritage (eds), *Structures of Social Action: Studies in Conversation Analysis*. Cambridge: Cambridge University Press. 102-28.
— forthcoming, Modifications of invitations, offers and rejections. In G. Psathas (ed.), *Interactional Competence*. New York: Erlbaum. 149-80.
Drew, P. 1984, Speakers' reportings in invitation sequences. In J. M. Atkinson & J. C. Heritage (eds), *Structures of Social Action: Studies in Conversation Analysis*. Cambridge: Cambridge University Press. 129-51.
— 1985, Analysing the use of language in courtroom interaction. In T. Van Dijk (ed.), *Handbook of Discourse Analysis (Vol. 3: Discourse and Dialogue)*. London: Academic Press. 133–48.
— 1987, Po-faced receipts of teases, *Linguistics*, 25: 1, 219–253.
Drew, P. & Heritage, J. (eds) forthcoming, *Talk at Work*. Cambridge: Cambridge University Press
Durkheim, E. 1982, *The Rules of Sociological Method* (trans. W. D. Halls). London: Macmillan.
Eglin, P. & Wideman, D. in press, Inequality in professional service encounters: verbal strategies of control versus task performance in calls to the police. *Zeitschrift für Soziologie*.
Ervin-Tripp, S. 1979, Children's verbal turn-taking. In E. Ochs & B. Schieffelin (eds), *Developmental Pragmatics*. London: Academic Press. pp.391–414.
Garfinkel, H. 1963, A conception of, and experiments with, 'trust' as a condition of stable concerted actions. In O. J. Harvey (ed.), *Motivation and Social Interaction*. New York: Ronald Press, 187–238.
— 1967, *Studies in Ethnomethodology*. Englewood Cliffs, N.J.: Prentice Hall.
Givon, T. (ed.) 1979, *Syntax and Semantics 12: Discourse and Syntax*. New York: Academic Press.
Goffman, E. 1955, On face work, *Psychiatry*, 18, 213–31.
— 1964, The neglected situation, *American Anthropologist*, 66: 6/2, 133–36.
— 1976, Replies and responses, *Language in Society*, 5, 257–313. (Reprinted in E. Goffman, *Forms of Talk*, Oxford, Basil Blackwell, 1981.)
— 1979, Footing, *Semiotica*, 25, 1–29. (Reprinted in E. Goffman, *Forms of Talk*, Oxford, Basil Blackwell, 1981.)
Goodwin, C. 1979, The interactive construction of a sentence in natural conversation. In G. Psathas (ed.), *Everyday Language: Studies in Ethnomethodology*. New York: Erlbaum. 97–121.
— 1981, *Conversational Organisation: Interaction between Speakers and*

*Hearers*. New York: Academic Press.
— 1984, Notes on story structure and the organisation of participation. In J. M. Atkinson & J. C. Heritage (eds), *Structures of Social Action: Studies in Conversation Analysis*. Cambridge: Cambridge University Press. 225–46.
Goodwin, C. & Goodwin, M. H. 1982, Concurrent operations on talk: notes on the interactive organisation of assessments. Paper presented to the 77th Annual Meeting of the American Sociological Association, San Francisco.
Goodwin, M. H. 1980, Some aspects of processes of mutual monitoring implicated in the production of description sequences. In D. H. Zimmerman & C. West (eds), *Language and Social Interaction*, special Double Issue of *Sociological Inquiry*, 50; 303–17.
— 1982, Processes of dispute management among urban black children, *American Ethnologist*, 9, 76–96.
— 1983, Aggravated correction and disagreement in children's conversations, *Journal of Pragmatics*, 7, 657–77.
Greatbatch, D. 1985, The social organisation of news interview interaction. Unpublished PhD dissertation, University of Warwick, England.
— 1986, Aspects of topical organisation in news interviews: the use of agenda shifting procedures by interviewees, *Media, Culture and Society*, 8, 441–55.
— 1988, A turn taking system for British news interviews, *Language in Society*, 17, 3.
— forthcoming, The management of disagreement between news interviewees. In P. Drew & J. Heritage (eds), *Talk at Work*. Cambridge; Cambridge University Press.
Grice, H. P. 1975, Logic and conversation. In P. Cole & J. L. Morgan (eds), *Syntax and Semantics 3: Speech Acts*. New York: Academic Press, 41–58.
Harris, Z. 1951, *Methods in Structural Linguistics*. Chicago: University of Chicago Press.
Heath, C. 1984, Talk and recipiency: sequential organisation in speech and body movement. In J. M. Atkinson & J. C. Heritage (eds), *Structures of Social Action: Studies in Conversation Analysis*. Cambridge: Cambridge University Press. 247-65.
— 1986, *Body Movement and Speech in Medical Interaction*. Cambridge: Cambridge University Press.
Helm, D., Anderson, W. T. & Meehan, A. J. forthcoming, *New Directions in Ethnomethodology and Conversation Analysis*. New York: Irvington.

HERINGER, J. T. (1977), Pre-sequences and indirect speech acts. In E. O. KEENAN & T. L. BENNETT (eds), *Discourse Across Time and Space*. Southern California Occasional Papers in Linguistics 5, University of Southern California, 169–180.

HERITAGE, J. 1984a, *Garfinkel and Ethnomethodology*. Cambridge: Polity Press.

— 1984b, A change of state token and aspects of its sequential placement. In J. M. ATKINSON & J. C. HERITAGE (eds), *Structures of Social Action: Studies in Conversation Analysis*. Cambridge: Cambridge University Press. 299–345.

— 1985a, Analyzing news interviews: aspects of the production of talk for an 'overhearing' audience. In T. VAN DIJK (ed.), *Handbook of Discourse Analysis* (*Vol 3: Discourse and Dialogue*). London: Academic Press. 95–119.

— 1985b, Recent developments in conversation analysis. *Sociolinguistics*, 15:1, 1–19.

— 1988, Explanations as accounts: a conversation analytic perspective. In C. ANTAKI (ed.), *Analysing Everyday Explanation: A Case Book of Methods*. London: Sage.

HERITAGE, J. & GREATBATCH, D. 1986, Generating applause: a study of rhetoric and response at party political conferences, *American Journal of Sociology*, 92, 110–57.

JEFFERSON, G. 1973, A case of precision timing in ordinary conversation: overlapped tag-positioned address terms in closing sequences, *Semiotica*, 9, 47–96.

— 1974, Error correction as an interactional resource, *Language in Society*, 2, 181–99.

— 1979, A technique for inviting laughter and its subsequent acceptance/declination. In G. PSATHAS (ed.), *Everyday Language: Studies in Ethnomethodology*. New York: Erlbaum. 79–96.

— 1980, The analysis of conversations in which 'troubles' and 'anxieties' are expressed. Final report to the (British) SSRC, report nos HR 4805/1–2.

— 1981a, The abominable 'ne?': a working paper exploring the phenomenon of post-response pursuit of response. University of Manchester, Department of Sociology, Occasional Paper no.6. (A shortened version appears in P. SCHRODER (ed.), *Sprache der Gegenwart*, Mannheim, 1981.)

— 1981b, 'Caveat speaker': a preliminary exploration of shift implicative recipiency in the articulation of topic. Final report to the (British) SSRC. Mimeo.

— 1983a, On exposed and embedded correction in conversation, *Studium*

*Linguistik*, 14, 58–68. (Reprinted in BUTTON & LEE 1987: 86–100.)

— 1983b, Two papers on 'transitory recipientship', *Tilburg Papers in Language and Literature*, no. 30, Tilburg University, Tilburg, Netherlands.

— 1983c, Issues in the transcription of naturally occurring talk: caricature versus capturing pronounciational particulars. *Tilburg Papers in Language and Literature*, no.34, Tilburg University, Tilburg, Netherlands.

— 1984a, Stepwise transition out of topic to inappropriately next positioned matters. In J. M. ATKINSON & J. C. HERITAGE (eds), *Structures of Social Action: Studies in Conversation Analysis*. Cambridge: Cambridge University Press. 194–222.

— 1984b, On the organisation of laughter in talk about troubles. In J. M. ATKINSON & J. C. HERITAGE (eds), *Structures of Social Action: Studies in Conversation Analysis*. Cambridge: Cambridge University Press. 347–69.

— 1984c, Notes on a systematic deployment of the acknowledgement tokens 'yeah' and 'mm hm', *Papers in Linguistics*, 17, 197–206. (Part publication of a revised version of JEFFERSON 1983c.)

— 1985, An exercise in the transcription and analysis of laughter. In T. VAN DIJK (ed.), *Handbook of Discourse Analysis* (*Vol.3: Discourse and Dialogue*). London: Academic Press. 25–34.

JEFFERSON, G. & LEE, J. R. E. 1981, The rejection of advice: managing the problematic convergence of a 'troubles telling' and a 'service encounter', *Journal of Pragmatics*, 5, 339–422.

JEFFERSON, G., SACKS, H. & SCHEGLOFF, E. A. 1987, Notes on laughter in pursuit of intimacy. In G. BUTTON & J. R. E. LEE (eds), *Talk and Social Organisation*. Clevedon, Avon: Multilingual Matters.

JEFFERSON, G. & SCHEGLOFF, E.A. 1975, Sketch: some orderly aspects of overlap in natural conversation. Paper presented at the Meeting of the American Anthropological Association, December.

KENDON, A. 1979, Some theoretical and methodological aspects of the use of film in the study of social interaction. In G.P. GINSBURG (ed.), *Emerging Strategies in Social Psychological Research*. New York: Wiley, 67–91.

— 1982, The organisation of behaviour in face-to-face interaction: observations on the development of a methodology. In K. R. SCHERER & P. EKMAN (eds), *Handbook of Methods in Nonverbal Behaviour Research*. Cambridge: Cambridge University Press. 440–505.

LEVINSON, S. C. 1981, Some pre-observations on the modeling of dialogue, *Discourse Processes*, 4, 93–110.

— 1983, *Pragmatics*. Cambridge: Cambridge University Press.

McHoul, A. 1978, The organisation of turns at formal talk in the classroom, *Language in Society*, 7, 183–213.

— 1979, Notes on the organisation of repair in the classroom. Unpublished mimeo, Murdoch University, Western Australia.

Maynard, D. 1984, *Inside Plea Bargaining: The Language of Negotiation*. New York: Plenum.

— 1985a, How children start arguments, *Language in Society*, 14, 1–29.

— 1985b, On the functions of social conflict among children, *American Sociological Review*, 50, 207–23.

Mehan, H. 1978, Structuring school structure, *Harvard Educational Review*, 5, 311–38.

— 1979, *Learning Lessons: Social Organisation in the Classroom*. Cambridge, MA: Harvard University Press.

— 1985, The structure of classroom discourse. In T. Van Dijk (ed.), *Handbook of Discourse Analysis* (*Vol. 3: Discourse and Dialogue*). London: Academic Press. 120–32.

Merritt, M. 1976, On questions following questions (in service encounters), *Language in Society*, 5, 315–57.

Mulkay, M. 1984, The ultimate compliment: a sociological analysis of ceremonial discourse, *Sociology*, 18, 531–49.

— 1985, Agreement and disagreement in conversations and letters, *Text*, 5, 201–27.

Ochs, E. & Schieffelin, B. (eds) 1979, *Developmental Pragmatics*. New York: Academic Press.

Parsons, T. 1937, *The Structure of Social Action*. New York: Free Press.

Pomerantz, A. M. 1975, Second assessments: a study of some features of agreements/disagreements. Unpublished PhD dissertation, University of California, Irvine.

— 1978, Compliment responses: notes on the co-operation of multiple constraints. In J. N. Schenkein (ed.), *Studies in the Organisation of Conversational Interaction*. New York: Academic Press. 79–112.

— 1984a, Agreeing and disagreeing with assessments: some features of preferred/dispreferred turn shapes. In J. M. Atkinson & J. C. Heritage (eds), *Structures in Social Action: Studies in Conversation Analysis*. Cambridge: Cambridge University Press. 57–101.

— 1984b, Pursuing a response. In J. M. Atkinson & J. C. Heritage (eds), *Structures in Social Action: Studies in Conversation Analysis*. Cambridge: Cambridge University Press. 152–63.

Pomerantz, A. M. & Atkinson, J. M. 1984, Ethnomethodology, conversation analysis and the study of courtroom interaction. In D. J. Muller, D. E. Blackman & A.J. Chapman (eds), *Topics in Psychology and Law*. Chichester: Wiley, 283–94.

PSATHAS, G. (ed.) 1979, *Everyday Language: Studies in Ethnomethodology*. New York: Erlbaum.

— (ed.) forthcoming, *Interactional Competence*. New York: Erlbaum.

SACKS, H. 1964–72, Unpublished transcribed lectures, University of California, Irvine (transcribed and indexed by G. Jefferson).

— 1972a, An initial investigation of the usability of conversational data for doing sociology. In D. SUDNOW (ed.), *Studies in Social Interaction*. New York: Free Press. 31–74.

— 1972b, On the analyzability of stories by children. In J.J. GUMPERZ & D. HYMES (eds), *Directions in Sociolinguistics*. New York: Holt, Rinehart and Winston, 325–345. (Reprinted in R. TURNER (ed.), *Ethnomethodology*, Harmondsworth, Penguin, 1974.)

— 1973a, On some puns with some intimations. In R.W. SHUY (ed.), *Sociolinguistics: Current Trends and Prospects*. 23rd Annual Round Table Monograph Series on Languages and Linguistics. Washington, D.C.: Georgetown University Press, 135–144.

— 1973b, Lectures at the Linguistics Institute, Ann Arbor, MI.

— 1974, An analysis of the course of a joke's telling in conversation. In R.BAUMAN & J. SHERZER (eds), *Explorations in the Ethnography of Speaking*. Cambridge: Cambridge University Press, 337–53.

— 1975, Everyone has to lie. In M. SANCHES & B. G. BLOUNT (eds), *Sociocultural Dimensions of Language Use*. New York: Academic Press, 57–80.

— 1984, Notes on methodology. In J.M. ATKINSON & J.C. HERITAGE (eds), *Structures in Social Action: Studies in Conversation Analysis*. Cambridge: Cambridge University Press. 21–27.

— 1987, On the preferences for agreement and contiguity in sequences in conversation. In G. BUTTON & J. R. E. LEE (eds), *Talk and Social Organisation*. Clevedon, Avon: Multilingual Matters. 54–69.

SACKS, H., SCHEGLOFF, E. A. & JEFFERSON, G. 1974, A simplest systematics for the organisation of turn-taking for conversation, *Language*, 50, 696–735.

SCHEGLOFF, E. A. 1968, Sequencing in conversational openings, *American Anthropologist*, 70, 1075–95. (Reprinted in J. J. GUMPERZ & D. HYMES (eds), *Directions in Sociolinguistics*, New York, Holt Rinehart and Winston, 1972, 346–80.)

— 1972, Notes on conversational practice: formulating place. In D. SUDNOW (ed.), *Studies in Social Interaction*. New York: Free Press. 75–119. (Reprinted in P.P. GIGLIOLI (ed.), *Language and Social Context*, Harmondsworth, Penguin, 1972, 95–135.)

— 1979a, Identification and recognition in telephone openings. In G.

PSASTHAS (ed.), *Everyday Language: Studies in Ethnomethodology*. New York: Erlbaum. 23–78.
— 1979b, The relevance of repair to syntax-for-conversation. In T. GIVON (ed.), *Syntax and Semantics 12: Discourse and Syntax*. New York: Academic Press. 261-88.
— 1980, Preliminaries to preliminaries: 'can I ask you a question?'. In D. H. ZIMMERMAN & C. WEST (eds), *Language and Social Interaction*. Special Double Issue of *Sociological Inquiry*, 50: 104–52.
— 1982, Discourse as an interactional achievement: some uses of 'uh huh' and other things that come between sentences. In D. TANNEN (ed.), *Analyzing Discourse, Text and Talk*. Georgetown University Roundtable on Languages and Linguistics. Washington, D.C.: Georgetown University Press, 71–93.
— 1984, On some questions and ambiguities in conversation. In J. M. ATKINSON & J. C. HERITAGE (eds), *Structures in Social Action: Studies in Conversation Analysis*. Cambridge: Cambridge University Press. 28–52.
— 1987a, Between macro and micro: contexts and other connections. In J. ALEXANDER *et al.* (eds), *The Micro–Macro Link*. Berkeley: University of California Press.
— 1987b, Analyzing single episodes in interaction: an exercise in conversation analysis, *Social Psychology Quarterly*, 50, 101–14.
SCHEGLOFF, E. A. JEFFERSON, G. & SACKS, H. 1977, The preference for self correction in the organisation of repair in conversation, *Language*, 53, 361–82.
SCHEGLOFF, E. A. & SACKS, H. 1973, Opening up closings, *Semiotica*, 7, 289–327.
SCHENKEIN, J. N. (ed.) 1978, *Studies in the Organisation of Conversational Interaction*. New York: Academic Press.
SEARLE, J. 1975, Indirect speech acts. In P. COLE & J. L. MORGAN (eds), *Syntax and Semantics Vol. 3, Speech Acts*. New York: Academic Press, 59–82.
SNOW, C. & FERGUSON, C. A. (eds.) 1977, *Talking to Children: Language Input and Acquisition*. Cambridge: Cambridge University Press.
*Sociology* 1978, *Special Issue: Language and Practical Reasoning*, 12: 1.
SUDNOW, D. 1968, Normal crimes, *Social Problems*, 12, 255–76.
— (ed.) 1972, *Studies in Social Interaction*. New York: Free Press.
TERASAKI, A. K. 1976, *Pre-Announcement Sequences in Conversation*, Social Science Working Paper no. 99, School of Social Science, University of California, Irvine.
VAN DIJK, T. (ed.) 1985, *Handbook of Discourse Analysis* (*Vol 3: Discourse and Dialogue*). London: Academic Press.

WATSON, D.R. 1978, Categorisation, authorisation and blame negotiation in conversation, *Sociology*, 12, 105–13.
— 1987, Doing the organisation's work: an examination of aspects of the operations of a crisis intervention center. In S. FISHER & A. TODD (eds), *Discourse and Institutional Authority*. Norwood, N.J.: Ablex, 91–120.
WEST, C. 1979, Against our will: male interruptions of females in cross-sex conversations. In J. ORSANU, M. K. SLATER & L. L. ADLER (eds), *Language, Sex and Gender*, Annals of the New York Academy of Sciences, Vol. 327, 81–97.
— 1984, *Routine Complications: Troubles with Talk between Doctors and Patients*. Bloomington: Indiana University Press.
WEST, C. & ZIMMERMAN, D. H. 1977, Women's place in everyday talk: reflections on parent–child interaction, *Social Problems*, 24, 521–29.
— 1983, Small insults: a study of interruptions in cross-sex conversations with unacquainted persons. In B. THORNE, C. KRAMARAE & N. HENLEY (eds), *Language, Gender and Society*. Rowley, MA: Newbury House, 102–17.
WOOTTON, A. 1981, The management of grantings and rejections by parents in request sequences, *Semiotica*, 37, 59–89.
ZIMMERMAN, D. H. 1984, Talk and its occasion: the case of calling the police. In D. SCHIFFREN (ed.), *Meaning, Form and Use in Context: Linguistic Applications*. Georgetown Roundtable on Languages and Linguistics. Washington, D.C.: Georgetown University Press.
— 1988, On conversation: the conversation analytic perspective. In *Communication Yearbook 11*. Beverly Hills: Sage.
ZIMMERMAN, D. H. & WEST, C. 1975, Sex roles, interruptions and silences in conversation. In B. THORNE & N. HENLEY (eds), *Language and Sex: Difference and Dominance*. Rowley, MA: Newbury House, 105–29.
— (eds) 1980, Language and Social Interaction, Special Double Issue of *Sociological Inquiry*, 50: 3–4.

# 3 Conversation analysis and social psychology as descriptions of interpersonal communication[1]

ROBERT HOPPER
*University of Texas, Austin*

Several chapters in the present volume show alignment to research traditions of social psychology (SP) and conversation analysis (CA). *Social psychologists* emphasise variable-based theoretic models, experimental research designs and quantified cross-tabulations of message variables with other variables. *Conversation analysts*, typically describe message phenomena through repeated listening to tape-recordings, through transcription, and through example-driven analytic induction. These schools of thought are alike in seeking empirical descriptions of message phenomena from a base of tape-recorded data. Nevertheless, CA and SP appear distinct in approach and practice, and the present chapter contrasts these two paradigms.

CA is exemplified in the present volume in work by Heritage (Chapter 2), Drew (5), Jefferson (8) and Wootton (11); while SP describes methods employed by Roger (Chapter 4), Huls (6), Bull (7), Thomas (12) and Rutter (13). Notice that not all chapters are classified, and that this particular scheme is only one way in which these chapters might be coded.[2]

The editors of the present volume relate CA to SP in their connective essays. These pieces show background in SP, and display interest in the promise of CA. The reader will have noted that I have coded the editors as social psychologists (according to the perspective of their chapters).

I articulate in the present chapter a stance closer to CA than that of the editors. Still, this chapter is *not* conversation analysis. This should offer you, the reader, some exciting conceptual dialectic.

I agree with the editors that CA and SP, since they investigate related phenomena, may accomplish tasks of mutual benefit from time to time. At the end of the day, however, the usefulness of CA–SP collaboration depends on how we accomplish 'it', that is, how we face certain recurrent problems blocking collaboration.

Interpersonal communication, the intended focus of the present volume is one major subdivision of my 'home' academic discipline: speech communication. Speech communication is a populist discipline strongest at state-supported universities in the USA and dedicated to improving citizens' speaking and listening skills. Speech communication may have no precise equivalent in Britain or Europe.

Interpersonal communication is a sub-area of speech communication, and its concerns include the description of two-party and small-group encounters. Interpersonal communication considers human interpersonal speaking-relationships, and signing practices (messages) in face-to-face and telephone talk.

Interpersonal communication historically has its roots in social psychology. My own education featured SP along with linguistic approaches to interpersonal communication. Initially (in the 1970s) I perceived CA as one sociolinguistic method that could be assimilated into my eclectic toolbag. At that time I was optimistic about CA–SP complementarity. Nowadays, however, my enthusiasm for combining CA and SP has faded. For the moment one must, perhaps, take sides and concentrate on consistency and clarity within each paradigm. Let us examine SP and CA in turn.

Social psychologists display orientation to being experimental and theoretical. Social psychologists predict message details or communicative outcomes from features of participants or settings. Independent variables are conceptualised as existing before interaction and more or less causing message features. SP chapters in the present volume recurrently construct these independent variables around individual differences: predisposition toward dominance, physical handicap, social class, sex, and so on. Communicative outcomes, either message-feature counts or judgements of effectiveness or satisfaction, may be tabulated in SP as dependent variables. This provides interpersonal communication with experimental and statistical standards, and with procedures for relating message to non-message variables.

Conversation analysts conceptualise interpersonal communication as displays of orientation speakers offer to each other in interaction. Participants manage interaction in response to problems that arise; and with respect to certain systemic constraints on turn-taking, sequencing and the like. The conversation analyst's task is to describe how these procedures are accomplished. Communication is thus seen as emerging in participants' displays, and conversation analysts typically examine in great detail aspects such as timing and sequential placement occurring in actual instances. This emphasis on the details of message phenomena holds promise for interpersonal communication.

## An example of the CA–SP contrast

We illustrate the CA–SP contrast by contrasting Chapter 4 of this volume with Chapter 11 in terms of their respective discussions of the term 'back-channels'.

Chapter 4 treats speakers' sex and personality 'dominance' as independent variables. Dependent measures are codings of message features: interruptions for example and 'back-channels'. Such coding procedures claim that sex, dominance and the like constitute characteristics whose consequences include certain message features. For instance, Chapter 4 argues that women emit more 'back-channels' than men. Notice that this finding is formulated in a way that pays little specific attention to the details of any particular instance in which these particles occur. Rather, instances are grouped within a plural-sounding single category, and conclusions are reached about 'back-channels'.

CA distinguishes between a variety of forms related to instances coded in SP as 'back channels' (see Jefferson, 1981; Heritage, 1984). Wootton, in Chapter 11, distinguishes between 'uh huh' and 'oh'. He also notes that particles such as 'oh' or 'uh huh' may be used in different ways when spoken in different sequential positions in talk.

SP may praise CA's descriptions by using them to improve details in coding categories. An SP investigator, for instance, may distinguish between the codings given to 'uh huh', 'oh' and 'yeah'. But this increased specification does not speak to Wootton's second point. SP decisions about variable specification are difficult, detailed decisions. For example, in Chapter 4 Roger distinguishes between successful and unsuccessful interruptions, and also attempts to account for timing and sequence by comparing aggregates of feature counts appearing in the early minutes of an encounter with those occurring later in the encounter.

A CA response might be to ask why the investigator selected these features to ask about, *and no others*. Are there not an indefinitely large number of such formulations that may apply? Should we not describe what features the participants themselves *use*? (Heritage, 1984; and Chapter 2 in the present volume.)

> 'All sorts of conversational, linguistic, so-called non-verbal, and other interactional behavior have been related to such classical dimensions of social organization as class, race, ethnicity and gender. Although one may choose to proceed along the lines of such a strategy in order to focus on important aspects of social structure in a traditional sociological sense, the risks of underspecification of the interactional phenomena should be made explicit . . .' (Schegloff, 1987).

What is gained by grouping somewhat diverse particles under a term 'back-channel' and what is lost to underspecification?

To summarise: Instances of CA and SP offer contrasting approaches and treatments of 'back-channels'. In SP 'number of back-channels' is counted, lumped together, and treated as a consequence of sex or personality. In CA 'uh huh' has been compared to other particles such as 'yeah' and 'oh' as contrastive signs that can be arrayed in similar sequential positions — and the use of these items is further adapted to their local (sequential) occasion of occurrence.

## Conversation analysis and discourse analysis

Levinson (1983) distinguishes conversation analysis (CA) from discourse analysis (DA). DA and SP are not the same, but for our purposes here we may substitute SP when Levinson writes DA. Both CA and DA, he writes, describe coherence and sequential organisation in talk. Both approaches study these phenomena with reference to tape-recordings of interpersonal communication. However, according to Levinson, 'the two approaches have distinctive and largely incompatible styles of analysis'.

Discourse analysts seek coding procedures for dividing talk into categorised segments; and this is done by formulating 'a set of concatenation rules stated over those categories'.

In contrast, *conversation analysis* as practised by Sacks, Schegloff, Jefferson, Pomerantz and others, is a rigorously empirical approach which avoids premature theory construction . . . The methods are essentially *inductive*; search is made for recurring patterns across many records of naturally occurring conversation, in contrast to the immediate categorization of (usually) restricted data which is the typical first step in DA work. Secondly, . . . we have an emphasis on the interactional and inferential consequences of the choice between alternative utterances. (Levinson, 1987: 286–7).

Levinson rejects DA as 'fundamentally misguided' while citing CA as the outstanding empirical tradition in pragmatics. He expresses pessimism about combining the two traditions. Perhaps a review of 'how the work of science gets done' in each of these traditions will clarify some problems.

We may contrast CA with SP as descriptions of interpersonal communication by listing some steps in typical inquiries in each.The pair of lists in Figure 3.1 accents initial affinities between two approaches to interpersonal communication. Comparing CA with SP we find columns of like words describing 'steps' in the everyday research acts of practitioners of each school: recording, transcription, analysis, writing. However, these similarities shrink under scrutiny. In the next few pages I describe my own studies in SP and in CA.

*Social psychology*

1. Theory
2. Tape recording
3. Transcription
4. Coding
5. Analysis
6. Writing

*Conversation analysis*

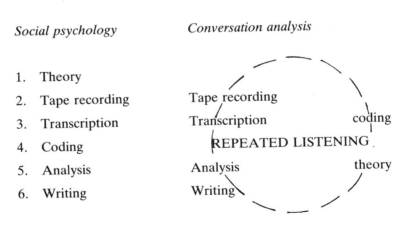

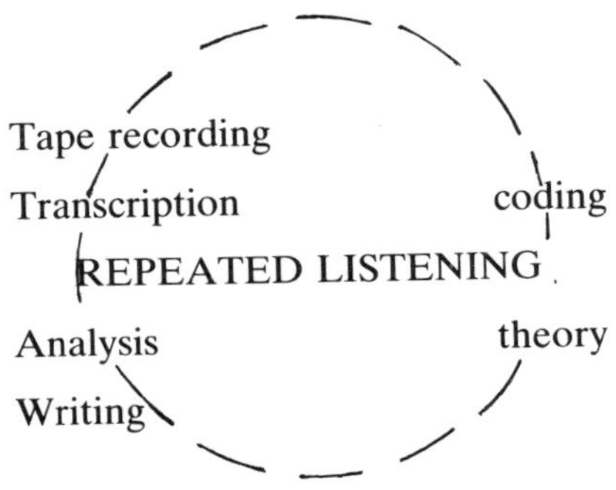


FIGURE 3.1 *Two approaches to describing interpersonal communication*

Throughout the discussion of Figure 3.1, consider that SP's methods provide discrete, ordered procedures. This is shown in Figure 3.1 by numbering the words corresponding to stages in 'doing a research project'. Conversation analysts also make recordings, transcriptions and analyses — but these working activities all continue alongside one another. This can perhaps be represented by a circle connecting these various activities.

Notice that in the CA column of Figure 3.1, the words 'theory' and 'coding' (which appear in definite sequential positions in social psychology) are represented aside from the other words, hovering in no particular sequential position. This placement marks the intermittent use of theory and coding in CA.

At the centre of the CA model in Figure 3.1, in capital letters, is the procedure that to date most typifies CA: repeated listening to tape-recordings.[3]

We may compare CA and SP by describing activities indexed by words that appear in both models. What activities do these words gloss in each school of thought?

## Theory

Social psychologists produce studies that are based on theoretical and empirical literatures. To study 'accounts', you read research reports to learn how other investigators have conceptualised 'accounts', and what covariates occur in previous research. One may write a literature review concluding with propositional hypotheses. Data are tested for quantitative disconfirmation of hypotheses.

CA's descriptions and activities rarely begin with theory; hence the word 'theory' is not at the top of the CA column in Figure 3.1. Rather, CA practitioners attempt to begin with data. This stance derives from phenomenology, and especially ethnomethodology. The conversation analyst resists premature theory. Rather, the methodical routine includes occasions of 'unmotivated'[4] listening to tape-recordings, encounters holding no particular goal except disciplined decoding.

Conversation analysts do pay respects to theory (see Heritage, Chapter 2, this volume). There are now hundreds of programmatic research reports that array findings around such notions as turn-taking, repair, and speech overlap. However, individual investigators are not encouraged to begin work by grinding particular theoretical axes.

**Tape recording**

Both social psychologists and conversation analysts may make tape recordings during the research process. How are these recordings accomplished? SPs who tape-record speech 'construct' settings in which pre-selected variables are subject to 'control' to prepare data to be arrayed in experimental or quasi-experimental designs. Prototypically, unacquainted college students converse or argue on a specified topic, or else 'just get acquainted'. Investigators may try to maximise occurrence of particular features. For example, to examine interruptions, ask subjects to argue a controversial topic.

Some SP recordings exhibit excellent production values — high fidelity sound, split-screen video and the like. Disadvantages involve the questionable ecological validity of the talk, and its homogeneity from study to study. SP tolerates narrow data to achieve experimental control of extraneous variance.

Conversation analysts argue that the best tape-recordings are not those made in carefully controlled circumstances, but upon the stages of everyday life: 'naturally occurring' speech events. CA recordings have included phone calls, dinner-table conversations, medical interviews, sales calls, courtroom cross-examination, radio talk shows, and SP initial encounters.

Conversation analysts make use of a wide variety of recordings. Social psychologists find it difficult to understand why in CA it is sometimes unimportant what recordings you examine (see Sacks, 1984, for one explanation). One should examine diverse recordings, of course, but one rarely encounters in CA a list of the number of minutes or hours of recording (or of listening) that justify any description. In fact the CA dictum advising 'unmotivated listening' flies in the very conceptual face of practices to control variance. The important thing in CA is to get started listening. Recording is something that continues throughout an analyst's work, and rarely occupies a specific sequential position in a research project. Rather, each analyst builds a collection of recordings and transcripts. Although I list tape-recording as a chronological 'first' step toward doing CA, no particular study need begin with making new recordings.

**Transcription**

Social psychologists may create written transcripts connecting recordings with data reduction. SP transcription may be completed by assistants and stenographers. Upon completion these transcriptions become primary texts for the coding process; the recordings may be set aside. Transcripts may include all the spoken words, but transcribers may not note vocalisations like 'um', and details of pauses or restarts. SP practices for transcribing vary with the investigator.

Conversation analysts transcribe to display speech sounds emitted by participants and related actions. Conversation analysts transcribe using ordinary writing supplemented by special typographic symbols coined by Jefferson. CA transcription emphasises occurrence of pauses, dysfluencies, restarts, sound stretching, and events near turn-boundaries. Jefferson's procedures display details of how participants solve problems and give accounts for action. These transcription procedures are useful for showing timing and reciprocity in ritual moments such as those in greetings and in exchanges of 'how are you?'. Much of the developing theory in CA concentrates precisely on timing and turn-related issues (see the list of these symbols at the end of Chapter 8.)

Conversation analysts use transcripts primarily *in conjuction with tape-recordings*. It is in the repeated paired use of transcription and recording that analysis derives its fuel.

Analysts may use special-purpose transcription systems, especially for accurate sound representation enabling phonetic analyses. No CA transcript is regarded as complete; like poems, transcripts are 'abandoned' rather than 'finished'. In a useful contribution to the present collection, Kelly & Local (Chapter 9) reflect upon transcription process with special reference to both phonetic transcription and Jefferson's system. As these authors indicate, there can be no one complete system of transcription that does justice to the richness of conversational data. Kelly & Local display some analytic leverage that may be gained by close phonetic transcription.

Given CA's openness to new detail, certain readability problems may arise in the presentation of CA transcriptions to readers of written research. Phonetic renderings also bring readability problems; and any transcription system may face trade-offs between specifications sufficient for professionals and readability by laypersons. See transcriptions in this volume by Drew (Chapter 5) and Jefferson (Chapter 8); compare with those by Kelly & Local. In each system special signs supplementing the writing display how the passage was spoken.[5]

Some CA practitioners use transcript markings as aids to read these passages aloud. Any reader may learn the Jefferson conventions in a few hours of practice with a teacher who is a CA transcriber. After two hours of classroom instruction and tutorial on two to four short assignments, students can read these symbols with comprehension and transcribe with surprising accuracy. Students who learn CA transcribing in my classes indicate that it teaches them to be more accurate listeners.

To summarise, in SP, transcribing occurs right after tape-recording and consists of 'writing down the words'. In CA transcribing is done by each investigator as an ongoing part of analysis. This description of transcribing oversimplifies considerably.

**Coding**

This stage follows transcribing in most SP studies of interpersonal communication. The goal of SP coding is to reduce or simplify messages into numerical or categorical instances. This can be done by giving each segment (say, each 'turn') a value, like 'one-up' or 'request' or 'successful interruption', or 'back-channel cue'. At this stage of research coding becomes mass-production operational-defining using categories derived from theory. The goal of coding procedure is to array instances in order to test hypotheses. My own actual experiences of SP coding have been rich with *ad hoc* considerations — on-the-spot decisions about how to code problem cases (Garfinkel, 1967: Chapter 1). These decisions seem inconvenient to the SP coder at the coding station, who displays orientation towards making rapid and rule-conforming decisions that another coder, working independently, can replicate.

To certify coding work as objective (i.e. reasonably free from the taint of the *ad hoc*) most social psychologists adopt reliability measures of separately taken coder's judgements (as indicators of construct validity). Coders, like transcribers, are often novice practitioners. SP coders may treat the issue of *ad hoc* coding decisions as matters of 'noise' that needs to be winnowed from signal in any message analysis. Here social psychologists may miss the direction of Garfinkel's critique of coding studies. Garfinkel argues that *ad hoc* coding decisions are in fact what communicators actually do when interpreting speech and other social action. Ironically, social psychologists' attempts to minimise *ad hoc* considerations may accidentally fail to describe those very processes by which humans understand and interact:

> 'Ordinarily researchers treat such *ad hoc* procedures as flawed ways of writing, recognizing, or following coding instructions . . . [which] is very much like complaining that if the walls of a building were only

gotten out of the way one could see what was keeping the roof up. Our studies showed that *ad hoc* considerations are essential features of coding procedures' (Garfinkel, 1967:21–22).

SP coding assumes that what makes a speech act work is that it performs 'an X' where X might be 'account', 'interruption' etc. These X items are conceptualised as interchangeable parts for interaction. This formulation neglects animals' rich *ad hoc* decision-making during interaction. A five-second human turn-at-talk displays fantastic bricollage. Yet in SP each speech act is considered an interchangeable part — just another brick in the wall.

When coding is complete, social psychologists set the transcript aside (with the recording). Subsequent analyses utilise primarily the categorical or numerical specifications that are outcomes of coding.

In SP, coding comprises a discrete phase of experimental work. When coding is complete, analysis may begin. In CA, there is no phase of coding; rather, coding is ongoing. If an analyst codes an action as a 'request', that counts as a provisional judgement to guide analysis, not as a category to hold fast. CA describes how participants bring off speech accomplishments. If a conversation analyst claims 'this is a request', the claim does not become a final portrait of an utterance; but rather codings become probes to guide description. Consider Example 1:

(1) [UTCL D10]

**A:** Hang on one second okay?
**B:** Okay.

It makes sense to 'code' what speaker A says as: 'Speaker A is making a request'. In SP, that might be the final interested glance at this instance. But in CA this is a beginning. How do these participants display 'requesting' to one another? One way is that B provides 'Okay', which in this sequential location, provides agreeing/granting to A's speech act. In other words, part of the grounds for coding A's turn as 'requesting' (in Example 1) are displayed by speaker B's acts in the next turn. Commonly, conversation analysts describe talk by displaying and highlighting the analysis of that turn that next speaker provides in the subsequent turn. That is one thread of adjacency-pair research. In sum, coding in CA is a prelude to description of instances. A coded instance in CA is not a fact, but a gesture toward some paths for analysis, an invitation to dialectic.

**Analysis**

SP displays cross-tabulations of code-item counts with dimensions of setting and individual difference (e.g. measures of dominance, sex, social status, communication apprehension, field dependence, or cognitive complexity). The investigator is taken to know, from the literature, what the important analytical categories are. These should be written as hypotheses before data collection.

SP produces results of hypothesis tests by treating every coded segment in a category just like every other instance of that category, regardless of when it occurs or how it is accomplished. Variables, like potatoes, become uniform mash when compressed. The mash is easy to chew, but its conceptual value depends upon the validity of the assumption that all instances of X are equivalent. To the extent that each speech act of 'requesting' is like all others, this sort of coding may produce distributional information about speech features. If, however, each request is individually tailored by its participants to the specifics of occasioned use, SP coding and analyses introduce error into sums of squares.

From a CA view, social psychologists filter phenomena through a number of simplifying processes: simulations of interaction are tape-recorded, then the recordings are simplified to transcripts of words, which become further effaced to tabulations of instances of coded categories that provide numerical specifications suitable for hypothesis testing. These activities, CAs might argue, squander empirical purchase.

Conversation analytic practices are less easy to describe than those of social psychology. Most conversation analyses take shape as inductive proofs structured around exemplars. Analysts utilise extracted exemplars somewhat as linguists and sociolinguists do. CA exemplars differ from those of many linguists in being subject to this methodical restriction: *that the action has actually occurred*. Linguists, by contrast, commonly admit any possible or plausible exemplar.

Analysts glean evidence about what participants are doing; inspecting action for its displays of orientation. Participants' categories take precedence over theorists' categories. As Schegloff & Sacks (1973:290) write: 'insofar as the materials we worked with exhibited orderliness, they did so not only for us, indeed not in the first place for us, but for the coparticipants who had produced them'. CA practitioners display in transcriptions and describe in analysis those empirical sense details displayed by and available to participants. This focus on participants' productions pushes CA toward strict textual empiricism, supported by the recurrent appeal to replay of recordings. Description is methodically restricted to details displayed in recordings. Recordings are at best incomplete copies of actual talk, but they seem relatively rich and replayable representations of many speech details. If a feature is audible (or visible) in recordings, it is likely to have been available to participants.[6]

To repeat: This textual empiricism involves *methodical* restrictions, not an epistemological claim that everything important about 'context' is invariably displayed in talk; nor a claim that every actor in every scene perceives everything that gets displayed on recordings. The limiting of evidence in CA to displays in the talk is a methodical prescription to allow other investigators to verify any description. As such, the limit to details of the talk is a procedure akin to SP procedures for calculation of $p < 0.05$, or those for deciding whether a sample is normally distributed.

Conversation analysts do resist typifying speakers' a priori characteristics (e.g. those based on 'dominance') unless grounds for these are specifically indexed or displayed in talk. This restriction to what is displayed in the talk provides one of the rigours responsible for the cumulativeness of CA theory.

In the present account I cannot take you very far towards understanding why or how conversation analyses work. (In the present volume, see Heritage (Chapter 2) and Wootton (Chapter 11) for description; Drew (Chapter 5) and Jefferson (Chapter 8) for exemplification.) The goals are to describe how communicators do things with and in talk. These goals allow considerable investigator autonomy.

Mostly, analysts listen for nothing, returning repeatedly to recordings, and to writing descriptions of speakers' accomplishments. Repeated listening is the daily work of analysis. The rest of analysis hinges on skills developed in repeated listening.

CA is diverse as well as programmatic. Some analyses argue points of linguistic theory such as 'questions' or 'ambiguities' (Schegloff, 1984), or 'the sentence' (Goodwin, 1979). Other analyses take the form of case studies (Sacks, 1974), or descriptions of a feature in talk (Jefferson, 1979).

CA provides fine-grained descriptions of speech action in *single* actual cases. Conversation analysts require descriptions to be accurate in accounting for each actual occurrence. How can investigators display description of naturally occurring message details as CA prescribes and still use standard SP tools like self-report questionnaires, or a priori specifications of institutional setting or individual difference? SP's approach to characterological causation of messages aims to account for precisely what is not accomplished on the scene by the participants. SP glosses communicative accomplishment that occurs on the scene, and therefore bypasses description of the most message-laden communicative phenomena. These problems complicate a wedding of insufficiencies between SP and CA. SP insists on, but CA resists a priori constructs.[7]

To this point, our discussion of what CA and SP scientists do has concerned itself with 'backstage' activity: what happens in the lab, the office, and the classroom. In the final step of any present-day inquiry, research reports display in writing the orientations of CA and SP.

**Research reporting**

Most readers come to know research traditions less in the context of discovery (which we have discussed till now) than in their contexts of justification — that is, in articles, monographs, and textbooks. Both SP and CA essays appear in distinctive recognisable formats across several disciplines. Usual trappings of SP research reports are reflected in the publication guidelines of psychological associations: a literature review, hypotheses, a method section, tabular presentation of statistically appraised results, and discussion.

Conversation analysis essays are recognisable by the appearance of transcribed examples: with p*ar*tial words emphasised and sound stre::tches shown by colons; with detailed display of speech overlap, cut-offs and the like. Beyond that the essays are diverse. Rarely does one find a section called literature review or method (but see Mandelbaum, 1987). Rather, these materials are found larded throughout the essay. You must understand something about ethnomethodology to realise how this works, which is a further bar to an easy combination of CA and SPP. Ethnomethodology seldom finds a priori postulation of theoretical dimensions to be useful; rather, investigators are asked to display reflexivities both in their subject matter, and between subject matter and investigation.

**Empirical methods**

Might an investigator collect a hundred instances of a conversational feature? Yes, analysts customarily make such collections. Indeed it is a common practice to justify a description of a conversational feature with the presentation of sets of transcript fragments (and if possible) recordings from such collections.

For these reasons, it may be tempting, yet mistaken in principle, to characterise CA as 'qualitative' and SP 'quantitative'. CA inquiries sometimes provide frequency counts for phenomena (see Jefferson, Chapter 8, this volume). Similarly, a number of social psychological inquiries resist counting (see Collett, this volume, Chapter 10). Conversation analysts do not oppose use of quantification, merely its premature use. Quantification may aid study of interpersonal communication; but certain central mysteries (say, 'play' or 'interruption') must be thoroughly described in terms of empirical phenomena before recourse to counting. Empirical verifiability of description is a more important standard for science than is quantification. Which is the more empirical, CA or SP?

Conversation analysis has to date made sparing use of numbers and statistics, yet it provides the outstanding empirical tradition in pragmatics. CA descriptions are made available to readers, both by inspection of transcriptions, and through listening to recordings. As with examples in linguistics, counter-examples may invalidate or extend an analysis. CA offers the most cumulative empiricism in the present marketplace of human studies. But does CA empiricism mix with SP empiricism?

## Conclusions

How can we promote the usefulness of conversation analysis and social psychology to each other? I urge students interested in either school to study the other for at least three (US) semester courses. But I temper this advice with caution about paradigm-specific use of concepts and methods.

How can one focus on the study of individual differences, and simultaneously inquire into probable sequential universals? That is part of the future's challenge. The conversation analyst might claim that, in the absence of theory about conversational universals, studies of individual differences are left rudderless. Individual differences in what? What kind of difference makes a difference? It might be like constructing a theory of the Jaguar v. the Buick v. the Toyota in the absence of a construct like 'automobile'.

**SP researches displaying CA influence**

Since about 1975 researchers in social psychology and communication have utilised terminology and (sometimes) transcribing format borrowed from conversation analysis (Ragan, 1983; Zahn, 1984; Zimmerman & West, 1975, 1983; Bell, Zahn & Hopper, 1984; Morris, 1985; reviews in Haslett, 1987; McLaughlin, 1984). This scholarship does not always utilise these concepts and methods in ways that make it cumulative with or even compatible with their use in CA.

Each of these studies make some use of CA terminology (e.g. repair; adjacency pair, pre-sequence), yet most of them show orientation to SP by offering operational definitions and coding procedures, and the cross-tabulation of occurrence of defined items with psychological variables, for instance sex of subject, length of acquaintance, speaker dominance, or age. A number of SP studies undertake similar moves. These studies offer little that is newsworthy to CA. Details of interest to CA are bypassed in SP.

Certain of the best articles in speech communication in recent years also combine CA with 'speech-act' theories and other influences (Nofsinger, 1975; Jackson & Jacobs, 1980; Beach & Dunning, 1982). To discuss the opportunities and problems rising from those treatments is outside our scope here. These studies are mentioned to show that CA–SP problems may be similar to those faced by other combined inquiries.

Conversational phenomena yield insights to a variety of perspectives, and the phenomena of conversation may display unities to emerge from our muddled scientific groping. However, as Brown (1970) wrote, it is easy for the interdisciplinary to degenerate to the undisciplined. We may pay later for early optimism about combinations of paradigms. The penalty may involve belated discoveries of type 1 error.

Data from divergent paradigms may become valuable beyond original circumstances of collection. But this does not happen routinely in the human studies. Furthermore, misuse of CA concepts may lead to illusions of advanced knowledge. The penalty is also acted out in groundless advice given by well-intentioned teachers and parents who consume our instructional wares.

I still practise SP, especially in the area of speech evaluation, an area in which the use of semantic differential techniques bypass some problems of operationalisation (Zahn & Hopper, 1985). I am attempting to learn CA (Hopper, Koch & Mandelbaum, 1986) and I am optimistic about this paradigm — especially in the study of telephone talk, an area in which an audio-tape-recording may bear striking resemblance to the participants' own conversational resources.

During the years ahead, let us carefully document our presumptions and methods. We had best keep our accounts straight about the kind of work we do, where we derive our concepts, and how deeply our findings reflect speech phenomena. Let us respect CA and SP as left and right branches of the description of interpersonal communication.

## Notes to Chapter 3

1. This chapter was composed after others in the volume. The original intention was to place it last in the collection. However, in the judgement of the editors, its focus on methodological issues made its inclusion in Section 1 more appropriate. It offers comments on chapters in subsequent sections and should be read in conjunction with them. It is not intended that any comments and claims contained in it should be taken to apply to 'social psychology' as a whole.
2. The CA–DA coding decision as introduced in this chapter, for instance, is more like the work of SP practitioners than of CA practitioners.
3. I am not sure this feature is a necessary condition for CA but it seems a useful fallible sign for the presence of CA practitioners.
4. Unmotivated listening does not entail the claim of bias-free or project-absent perception; rather it is a bracketing operation, an applied phenomenology.
5. CA writing should not be evaluated from reading alone, but from reading and inspecting recordings. I favour increasing use of publication outlets in which tapes may be included to accompany print. I advise CA investigators to make tapes of extracts used in a publication, and to make these available to readers at a nominal cost.
6. Similarly, participants are presumed to display to each other evidence of their present orientations and alignments. Conversation analysts describe participants' ways of accomplishing these interactive displays.
7. But do a priori forces not influence speaking? Should these not be major foci of conversation analyses? asks Thompson in *Studies of the Theory of Ideology:* '*which* interpretation is to count, and *which* participant is to succeed in holding or usurping the right to speak, depends upon *who* the participants are and how much *power* they respectively have in the situation concerned.' Thompson's attack on CA concludes a review lauding CA's descriptions. Thompson's evidence for the argument that conversation analysis does not account for communicator power is limited to the claim that one of Sacks' analyses of a dirty joke did not include a discussion of links between sexuality and patrimony. Perhaps Thompson did not read Sacks' (1979:9) analysis of Oedipus: 'People regularly talk about an Oedipus complex as though what Freud says about the Oedipus plays are perfectly obvious, wheras if you read them without first starting with Freud's way of looking at them, it seems to me at least it's perfectly obvious that they're just about the exact opposite of what's proposed. They're perfectly clearly about infanticide, not parricide.'

**References**

BEACH, W. & DUNNING, D. 1982, Pre-indexing and conversational organization, *The Quarterly Journal of Speech*, 68, 170–85.

BELL, R., ZAHN, C. & HOPPER, R. 1984, Disclaiming: A test of two competing views, *Communication Quarterly*, 32, 28–36.

BROWN, R. 1970, *Psycholinguistics*. New York: The Free Press.

GARFINKEL, H. 1967, *Studies in Ethnomethodology*. Englewood Cliffs, NJ: Prentice-Hall.

GOODWIN, C. 1979, The interactive construction of a sentence in natural conversation. In G. PSATHAS (ed.), *Everyday Language*. New York: Irvington, 97–122.

HASLETT, B. 1987, *Communication: Strategic Action in Context*. London: Erlbaum.

HERITAGE, J. 1984, A change-of-state token and aspects of its sequential placement. In J. M. ATKINSON & J. HERITAGE (eds), *Structures of Social Action*. Cambridge: Cambridge University Press, 299–345.

HOPPER, R., KOCH, S. & MANDELBAUM, J. 1986, Conversation analysis methods. In D. ELLIS & W. DONOHUE (eds), *Contemporary Issues and Discourse Processes*. London: Erlbaum, 169–86.

JACKSON, S. & JACOBS, S. 1980, Structure of conversational argument: Pragmatic bases for the enthymeme, *Quarterly Journal of Speech*, 66, 251–65.

JEFFERSON, G. 1979, A technique for inviting laughter and its subsequent acceptance declination. In G. PSATHAS (ed.), *Everyday Language*. New York: Irvington, 79–96.

— 1981, On the articulation of topic in conversation. Final Report of the (British) Social Science Research Council.

LEVINSON, S. 1983, *Pragmatics*. Cambridge: Cambridge University Press.

MCLAUGHLIN, M. 1984, *Conversation: How Talk is Organized*. Beverly Hills: Sage.

MANDELBAUM, J. 1987, Couples sharing stories, *Communication Quarterly*, 35, 144–70.

MORRIS, G. 1985, The remedial episode as a negotiation of rules. In R. STREET & J. CAPPELLA (eds), *Sequence and Pattern in Communicative Behaviour*. London: Arnold, 70–84.

NOFSINGER, R. 1975, The demand ticket, *Speech Monographs*, 42, 1–9.

RAGAN, A. 1983, A conversational analysis of alignment talk in job interviews. *Communication Yearbook 7*, 502–16.

RAGAN, S. & HOPPER, R. 1984, Ways to leave your lover, *Communication Quarterly*, 32, 310–17.

ROGER, D. & SCHUMACHER, A. 1983, Effects of individual differences on dyadic conversation strategies, *Journal of Personality and Social Psychology*, 45, 700–5.

SACKS, H. 1974, An analysis of a joke's telling in conversation. In R. BAUMANN & J. SHERZER (eds), *Explorations in the Ethnography of Speaking*. London: Combridge University Press, 337–53.

— 1979, Hotrodder: a revolutionary category. In G. PSATHAS (ed.), *Everyday Language*. New York: Irvington.

— 1984, Remarks on methodology. In J. ATKINSON & J. HERITAGE (eds), *Structures of Social Action*. Cambridge: Cambridge University Press.

SCHEGLOFF, E. 1984, On some questions and ambiguities in conversation. In J. M. ATKINSON & J. HERITAGE (eds), *Structures of Social Action*. Cambridge: Cambridge University Press.

— 1987, Between micro and macro: Contexts and other connections. In J. ALEXANDER *et al.* (eds), *The Macro–Micro Link*. Berkeley: University of California Press.

SCHEGLOFF, E. & SACKS, H. 1973, Opening up closings, *Semiotica*, 30, 289–327.

WEST, C. & ZIMMERMAN, D. 1983, Small insults: a study of interpretations in cross-sex conversations between unacquainted persons. In B. THORNE, C. KRAMARAE & N. HENLEY (eds), *Language, Gender and Society*. Rowley, MA: Newbury House, 103–118.

ZAHN, C. 1984, A re-examination of conversational repair, *Communication Monographs*, 51, 56–66.

ZAHN, C. & HOPPER, R. 1985, Measuring language attitudes: the speech evaluation instrument, *Journal of Language and Social Psychology*, 4, 113–23.

ZIMMERMAN, D. H. & WEST, C. 1975, Sex roles, interruptions and silences in conversations. In B. THORNE & N. HENLEY (eds), *Language and Sex: Difference and Dominance*. Rowley, MA: Newbury House.

# SECTION 2: Methods of observation

## Introduction

A major methodological issue in the study of interpersonal communication concerns the context in which the data are collected, whether through controlled laboratory experimentation or through observation in more naturalistic settings. Traditionally, social psychologists have employed an experimental approach, in which the aim is to exert as much control as possible over independent variables such as sex or personality. The effects of these manipulations are observed on dependent variables, such as rate of interruption, and the data are then subjected to some form of statistical analysis. By contrast, sociologists carrying out research within the framework of conversation analysis employ naturally occurring conversations as the basis for their research and are not interested in manipulating variables. They proceed by first identifying systematic patterns in conversations, which are then examined in detail in order to establish their role in social interaction; the analysis is typically qualitative rather than quantitative.

These methodological differences have created divisions between researchers from different disciplines — for example, conversation analysts such as Heritage (1984) typically argue that experimental work is contrived and that the conversations obtained in laboratory settings are artificial. Heritage maintains that the problem of experimenter effects is so serious that it is better to work with data derived only from naturally occurring situations. An additional advantage claimed for the naturalistic approach is that some social situations (involving, for example, intimate conversations) may be difficult or even impossible to create in a laboratory setting. By contrast, experimental psychologists tend to regard this kind of research as lacking in control and consequently always leaving the results open to a variety of alternative interpretations.

There has been no real attempt to distinguish these different approaches to interpersonal communication in a systematic way. What the editors propose here is a framework for comparing them which is based on an examination of three interrelated features of conversation: the selection of participants; the setting in which it takes place; and the reason for engaging in the conversation. The discussion that follows will be based upon each of these three aspects in turn, with particular reference to the three chapters presented in this section.

## The selection of participants

In experimental research, the participants are often preselected on the basis of independent variables. For example, in the first experiment discussed by Derek Roger in Chapter 4, subjects were pre-tested for dominance predispositions by means of a personality questionnaire. The subjects then met one another in pairs representing three experimental conditions; in two of these the subjects were either both high or both low on dominance, while in the third condition one subject was high on dominance and the other low on dominance. The purpose of this experiment was to investigate the effects of personality on interruption rate during the course of conversation. The advantage of using an experimental procedure was that the subjects could be allocated to the dominance conditions, in order to test the hypothesis that interruption rate would increase over time in pairs where both partners were high on dominance, but not in pairs where either one or both partners were low on dominance. This hypothesis could only effectively be tested using experimental procedures.

By contrast, Paul Drew's contribution (Chapter 5) is based primarily on a detailed analysis of a video-recording of one naturally occurring conversation. The participants in this conversation were the members of a family, two of whom — Betty and Uncle Victor — had not seen one another for some years. In this study, there was no attempt to pre-select the participants for observation; conversation analysts typically assume that the phenomena which are of real interest occur independently of factors such as gender, personality or acquaintanceship. They are interested in these factors only to the extent that interactants can be shown to orientate to such categories in their dealings with each other; Drew's analysis, for example, reveals how age categories are orientated to by interactants through the minutiae of their conduct.

In the contribution by Erica Huls (Chapter 6), the data presented were not obtained in an experimental setting. However, since she was interested in the effects of social class on conversational style, the participants in this study were pre-selected. Her observations were based on conversations that took place in two families, one in which the husband's occupation was described as unskilled, the other in which the husband was a factory director. In the former case, neither parent had been educated beyond elementary school, whereas in the latter both parents had completed a course in higher education.

To some extent the research described in these three chapters represents a continuum, ranging from Paul Drew's study, where there was no explicit attempt to pre-select the participants, to Derek Roger's experiments, where there was a very careful pre-selection of participants in order to test a specific hypothesis. Nevertheless, pre-selection of participants is not the essential feature dividing experimental and naturalistic approaches to the study of interpersonal communication, since there is no reason why this procedure should be confined to laboratory research; the study by Erica Huls is interesting in this respect because she uses pre-selection of participants in a naturalistic setting. In terms of the framework proposed by the editors, experimental and naturalistic research can also be contrasted in terms of the setting in which the observations are made and the reason for the conversation taking place; these additional features are discussed below.

## The setting

A major advantage of social psychology laboratories is that they can be equipped with sophisticated apparatus which enables the experimenter to obtain high-quality recordings of social interaction. For example, conversation can be recorded by tie microphones which provide independent vocal signals for each subject. This procedure has a number of advantages over the use of a single microphone. One of these is that the sound quality from a single microphone is often inadequate for an accurate transcription to be made of the whole conversation; certain passages cannot be accurately transcribed and have to be omitted from the analysis. This is particularly true during simultaneous speech, where the independent vocal signals allow an unambiguous transcription to be made of each participant's contribution. Using this procedure, it is possible in addition to obtain measures of pitch, amplitude and speech rate separately for each of the participants, which can then be used to assess the influence of these variables on, for example, the success of interruption attempts. This could not be done from a recording made with a single microphone. Similarly, there are advantages in using laboratory procedures for studies of non-verbal communication: problems in the measurement of eye-contact were discussed as an example of this in Chapter 1.

Despite the greater technical sophistication which using a social psychology laboratory allows, critics (especially conversation analysts) have argued that this creates an unnatural situation in which to observe interpersonal communication. However, this kind of research actually has important implications for non-experimental approaches. For example, conversation analysts have frequently made use of telephone conversations, on the grounds that this eliminates the intrusion of non-verbal communication and allows access to what they regard as the 'simplest' form of conversational data (see, for example, Chapter 2 in this volume). But research in experimental social psychology carried out by Rutter *et al.* (1981) has demonstrated important differences between telephone and face-to-face conversations in content, style and outcome. They interpret these effects in terms of what they call 'cuelessness', the number of social cues which are available through a particular medium of communication. Their findings show that the fewer the number of social cues available, the more conversation becomes depersonalised in content and formal in style, which in turn affects outcome. For example, studies of bargaining have repeatedly shown that the side with the stronger case tends to do better over a more 'cueless' medium of communication, where the opportunities for influencing outcome through introducing extraneous personal considerations are restricted.

Hence, the results of psychological studies do have important implications for non-experimental research. However, experimentalists have often been criticised on the grounds that laboratory-based research on communication is contrived and artificial: for example, it may be argued that in an experiment, the spontaneity of conversation is lost once people are aware that they are being observed. In the editors' view this is not a problem peculiar to laboratory situations — whatever the setting, the researcher is still faced with the problem of concealing the recording equipment. In the conversation analysed by Paul Drew, no attempt was made to conceal the recording apparatus, although he recognises this as a potential problem. Erica Huls also made no attempt to conceal the recording apparatus, but instead adopted a role as a member of the family (home-help) in the hope that people would become accustomed to her presence. Thus, the participants' awareness of being observed or recorded does not enable us to specify what is 'unnatural' or 'artificial' about social psychology experiments.

## The reason for the conversation

It has been argued above that it is neither the presence of recording apparatus nor the pre-selection of participants which distinguishes naturalistic from laboratory-based research; instead, it is proposed here that the critical difference lies in the *reason* for the conversation taking place. When people take part in social psychology experiments on communication, it is of course for the purpose of providing data for analysis. For the experimenter, this creates a problem. If the participants become aware that their communication is the focus of interest, this may significantly alter the way in which they converse. Indeed, any invitation to participate in an experiment implies that some aspect of one's behaviour is being monitored, which may as a consequence affect the way in which one responds to that situation. Experimenter effects have been demonstrated empirically in a variety of contexts by Rosenthal and his colleagues (for example Rosenthal, 1976) and may well confound the results of experiments on interpersonal communication.

The problem of experimenter bias in this context can best be illustrated by a discussion of some of the procedures which have been used in laboratory-based research on interpersonal communication. When people take part in an experiment in a social psychology laboratory, they are sometimes asked simply to talk and get to know one another (see, for example, Kendon, 1967). The difficulty with this approach is that subjects will naturally be curious about the reason for the conversation; this may as a consequence affect the way in which they communicate. An alternative procedure is to give the participants an explicit task to perform, such as first completing an attitude questionnaire and then discussing those items on which they have disagreed. This procedure was adopted in both experiments discussed by Derek Roger in Chapter 4: the participants were instructed to try and convince their partners of their own point of view in order to maximise the frequency of interruptions. Informal debriefing after the discussion indicated that most participants believed that the experiment was about attitude change rather than about communication. Nevertheless, they may also have thought that the experimenter was assessing their skill in debate or their ability to maintain their own point of view in the face of contrary arguments; this might actually have increased the extent to which simultaneous speech occurred in these conversations.

Another problem with both procedures discussed above is that the participants are *instructed* by the experimenter to talk to one another, which may make their conversation stilted. One way of avoiding this problem is to use the so-called 'waiting-room' technique. This involves bringing participants together in what they believe to be a waiting-room prior to the start of the experiment in which they will both be taking part; in fact their conversations in this situation are recorded without their knowledge. This allows the experimenters to monitor spontaneous conversations while at the same time retaining the advantage of being able to pre-select the participants. For example, LaFrance & Ickes (1981) used this procedure to investigate the effects of sex-role attitudes on postural mirroring in dyadic conversations. Subjects were selected for participation in the study on the basis of their responses to the Bem Sex-Role Inventory. The results showed a significant relationship between sex-role attitudes and postural mirroring, but the authors also report low correlations between postural mirroring and other measures of verbal and non-verbal behaviour. This they attribute in part to a range artefact, since in the sex-typed dyads very little conversation took place. This is a general problem affecting waiting-room studies; there is always the risk that the subjects simply may not talk to one another, perhaps because they see it as inappropriate to converse before the 'experiment' takes place.

Consequently, the basic disadvantage of the waiting-room procedure is that the experimenter loses control over the interaction which takes place. But if the advantages of experimental control are to be retained, experimenters must devise situations which are sufficiently ingenious to evoke the style of communication they wish to study while at the same time disguising from the subjects the true purpose of the investigation. A good example of this approach is the study by Edelmann & Hampson (1979), which was intended to investigate non-verbal encoding of embarrassment. In this study, a structured interview was arranged consisting of 15 questions concerning a painting which the subject had selected prior to the interview as the one which he or she liked least from a collection of paintings. In the eighth question, the interviewer revealed that he himself was the artist (he had in fact painted all of the pictures in the original collection). After the interview was over, each subject was shown a video tape of the interview and asked to rate his or her response to the eighth question on a list of 19 emotion categories which included embarrassment. Edelmann and Hampson were then able to investigate the encoding of embarrassment by comparing the behaviour of the group who reported themselves as embarrassed in response to the critical eighth question with the behaviour of those who did not report themselves as embarrassed. Their results showed that embarrassment was associated with speech disturbances, reduced gaze and increased body movement.

By using this imaginative procedure the authors were able to create a potentially embarrassing situation and to check from their post-experimental questionnaire that some of their subjects had indeed been embarrassed. This has the advantage over a naturalistic study in that the judgement of embarrassment is not based on the researchers' intuitions but stems from the self-reports of the subjects themselves. The conversations which occurred may also be seen as far less artificial or contrived than other experimental procedures which involve instructing subjects to converse on a given topic for no apparent reason.

The issue of artificiality can thus be seen to revolve around the reason for holding the conversation rather than the setting in which it takes place. From the point of view of the experimental social psychologist, the crucial problem is to devise situations which evoke the sort of communication he wishes to study without alerting his subjects to the true purpose of the experiment. The study by Edelmann & Hampson goes some way to resolving this problem, but it is, none the less, open to criticism. For example, why was it that for seven out of the total of 22 participants the experimental manipulation apparently failed to arouse embarrassment? One possible explanation is that simply being invited to participate in an experiment was sufficient to arouse suspicions about the procedure in some subjects, particularly since in this case the participants had been forewarned that they were to be video-taped.

Clearly, both the experimental and naturalistic approaches to the study of communication have their advantages and disadvantages. Experimental approaches at their best allow an effective manipulation of variables while at the same time disguising from the participants the true purpose of the investigation. Nevertheless, people are still always aware that they are participating in an experiment, and the experimenter can never be entirely sure that their behaviour has not been affected as a consequence. The only way this can be corroborated is to confirm the observations in naturalistic settings. Here spontaneity is retained but experimental control is relinquished, and the researcher can only reliably draw conclusions about observed behaviour if they are confirmed in both settings.

## Summary

The main concern of this section is with the methods of observation and data collection used in different approaches to the study of interpersonal communication. A broad distinction has been drawn between experimental and naturalistic approaches, which the choice of the three chapters presented in this section is intended to illustrate. These approaches the editors propose can be contrasted along three main dimensions: the selection of participants; the setting in which the observations are made; and the reason for the conversation taking place. On the basis of the discussion, the editors conclude that it is neither the participants nor the setting but the reason for the conversation which essentially distinguishes experimental from naturalistic approaches. Nevertheless, it is also contended that these two approaches are not incompatible. Irrespective of which approach is used, the confirmation of the data in an alternative setting can only strengthen the force of the conclusions: data obtained in experiments need to be confirmed in naturalistic settings, while naturalistic settings may also provide a fertile source of ideas for controlled experimentation.

## References

EDELMANN, R. J. & HAMPSON, S.E. 1979, Changes in non-verbal behaviour during embarrassment, *British Journal of Social and Clinical Psychology*, 18, 385–90

HERITAGE, J. 1984, *Garfinkel and Ethnomethodology*. Cambridge: Polity Press.

KENDON, A. 1967, Some functions of gaze direction in social interaction, *Acta Psychologica*, 26, 22–63.

LAFRANCE, M. & ICKES, W. 1981, Posture mirroring and interactional involvement: sex and sex-typing effects, *Journal of Nonverbal Behavior*, 5, 139–54.

RIME, B. & MCCUSKER, L. 1976, Visual behaviour in social interaction: the validity of eye-contact assessments under different conditions of observation, *British Journal of Psychology*, 67, 507–14.

ROSENTHAL, R. 1976, *Experimenter Effects in Behavioral Research*. New York: Irvington Press.

RUTTER, D. R., STEPHENSON, G. M. & DEWEY, M.E. 1981, Visual communication and the content and style of conversation, *British Journal of Social Psychology*, 20, 41–52.

STEPHENSON, G. M. & RUTTER, D.R. 1970, Eye-contact, distance and affiliation: a re-evaluation, *British Journal of Psychology*, 61, 385–93.

# 4 Experimental studies of dyadic turn-taking behaviour

DEREK ROGER
*University of York*

## Introduction

Conversation typically proceeds by a more or less orderly exchange of speaker turns, but it is also characterised by periods of simultaneous speech. These simultaneous speech events are sometimes referred to as 'speaker-switch non-fluencies' (Ferguson, 1977), a term which emphasises the mutually exclusive nature of talking and listening. Defined in this way, simultaneous speech is seen as having a disruptive effect on the flow of the speaker's utterance, which is certainly the case where the listener attempts to take the floor by ignoring turn-taking rules. However, simultaneous speech also comprises signals which are intended to convey to the speaker that the listener is attending to what is being said, and a number of non-verbal cues such as head-nods and smiles are thought to serve a similar monitoring function in conversation (Duncan & Fiske, 1977; Brunner, 1979). These verbal and non-verbal signals have been referred to collectively as listener responses (Dittman & Llewellyn, 1967), accompaniment signals (Kendon, 1967) or back-channel behaviours (Yngve, 1970).

Interruptive utterances have been more difficult to classify. Mishler & Waxler (1968) distinguished between successful and unsuccessful interruptions, but Ferguson (1977) has argued that so broad a classification combines interruptive behaviours that are empirically discriminable. She has presented an alternative system comprising overlaps and simple, butting-in and silent interruptions, but Ferguson's categories do not provide a significant improvement over the system originally suggested by Mishler & Waxler. For example, simple and butting-in interruptions correspond closely to successful and unsuccessful interruptions, respectively, and although overlaps are potentially disruptive, they may simply reflect lapses in turn-change synchrony common in animated conversation. Ferguson's final category, silent interruptions, presents special problems, since it is based on the assumption that the speaker intended to continue; as the author will argue later in this chapter, apparent pauses may in fact signal turn-completion. The problem of scoring silent interruptions is particularly acute when the researcher is obliged to work from a transcript of the conversation. In these cases the judgement of incompleteness is based largely on grammatical criteria, and in ordinary conversation grammatical rules are not necessarily observed.

Roger, Bull & Smith (1988) have recently devised a more comprehensive system for the classification of simultaneous speech, but in the experiments described in this chapter the classification is based mainly on the more conventional distinction between interruptive and non-interruptive simultaneous speech. The first of these categories is further divided into successful and unsuccessful interruptions, and the term 'back-channel' is used to refer to non-interruptive simultaneous speech. Apart from problems of classification, the present chapter is also concerned with the role that personality dispositions and sex differences might play in determining conversational strategies. The personality variable most likely to affect turn-taking is dominance, since floor-holding may be seen as a way of exercising influence in groups; indeed, the frequency with which an individual interrupts has been shown to be related to the attribution of influence (Scherer, 1979), and interrupting has widely been used as an index of dominance, particularly in studies of family interaction (Jacob, 1974). However, dominance has seldom been adequately defined in these studies, and few researchers have systematically investigated the relationship between dominance and turn-taking. Two studies which have attempted to do so are those by Ferguson (1977) and Rogers & Jones (1975).

Ferguson employed a questionnaire and a behaviour rating to measure dominance in her study of dyadic conversations, and a relationship was predicted between these measures and the four speaker-switch non-fluencies described in her classification system. In fact, marginally significant correlations were found only between the questionnaire scores and her index of overlaps and between the behavioural ratings and silent interruptions, but the correlation between the questionnaire and the behaviour ratings themselves was extremely low. Furthermore, since each subject interacted with a single confederate dominance was manipulated in only one member of the dyad, and the dominance behaviour rating was based on the confederate's subjective rank-ordering of the subjects.

Rogers & Jones (1975) also investigated the effects of personality dominance on interruptive behaviour, but in contrast to Ferguson these authors pre-tested all their subjects for dominance using two well-validated questionnaires. Only those subjects whose scores were consistent on both scales were used to create single-sex dyads comprising one high-dominant and one low-dominant member. The results of this study showed that subjects scoring high on dominance held the floor for longer, and attempted more interruptions than their low-scoring counterparts did. Although there was a trend for males to interrupt more than females, this difference was not statistically significant.

In the first experiment reported in this chapter, a procedure similar to that used by Rogers & Jones was implemented by pre-testing subjects for dominance using a standardised questionnaire. The dependent variables were interruptive and non-interruptive simultaneous utterances, expressed as a function of the dyadic partner's speaking time. In addition to the high–low dominance condition, high–high and low–low combinations were also tested, yielding one dyadic condition in which the dominance predispositions of the partners were complementary to each other — the high–low pairs — and two conditions in which they were non-complementary. The dyads were again single-sex, and the aim of the study was to investigate the relationship between dominance complementarity and patterns of turn-taking during dyadic conversations (see Roger & Schumacher, 1983, for an extended report).

The effects of complementarity rather than simple dominance are particularly interesting in the light of the 'accommodation' theory proposed by Giles (1973) and Giles & Smith (1979), who showed that conversational partners may accommodate to one another by displaying convergent speech styles, which encourages further interaction by reducing perceived differences between them; alternatively, speech styles may diverge when the partners wish to emphasise differences between themselves (Bourhis & Giles, 1977). Bearing these findings in mind, repeated measures on the dependent variables were included in the design of the experiment by dividing the conversations into two equal segments. The partners were unacquainted prior to participation, and since turn-taking between strangers is likely to be governed initially by shared norms about the appropriateness of turn-taking, it was expected that the interruption rates would be similar for members of the dyads in all three dominance conditions during the first half of the conversation. These rates were expected to remain more or less constant over the two halves of the conversation in the high–low combination, where the partners would accommodate to each other's dominance needs, but it was predicted that the rate would increase significantly in the non-complementary pairs during the second half.

Non-complementarity was not expected to affect interruption rates among low–low pairs, since they would not be competing for the floor. With regard to back-channels, the opposite trend to that predicted for interruptions was expected: since competing partners would be unwilling to provide cues designed to encourage floor-holding by their partners, significantly fewer back-channels were expected over time in the high–high dyads compared with the complementary high–low pairs. Again, the rates for the low–low condition were expected to remain more or less constant, since neither partner would be competing for the floor.

Although Rogers & Jones (1975) reported a trend for males to interrupt each other more than females did, the effect was not statistically significant. This is a surprising finding, in view of earlier research showing that men tend to interrupt more than women do (see, for example, Thorne & Henley, 1975). On the other hand, the studies reported by Thorne and Henley and others were based on mixed-sex interactions, and the results are seen as reflecting sex-role stereotyped behaviour. An experiment by Zimmerman & West (1975) is particularly widely quoted in support of the sex-role hypothesis but, as Beattie (1982) has pointed out, their study suffered from a number of methodological weaknesses. Perhaps the most important of these is that while men used a total of 46 interruptions during the course of 11 conversations, compared with only two used by women, the authors acknowledge that a single male subject contributed 13 of these interruptions — more than a quarter of the total.

Further doubt has been cast on the male dominance hypothesis by other recent studies. For example, McCarrick, Manderscheid & Silbergeld (1981) found that wives in the marital couples they studied not only initiated more of the within-couple interruptions that occurred, but also tended to 'interrupt back' in cross-couple interactions rather than adopt the submissive, silent role suggested by Zimmerman & West (1975). Furthermore, Beattie (1981) reported almost identical interruption rates for men and women participating in mixed-sex discussion groups, and while Aries, Gold & Weigel (1983) obtained positive correlations between dominance predispositions and behaviour such as interrupting in single-sex groups, the corresponding correlations for mixed-sex interactions approached zero.

On the basis of her own and other recent research, Aries (1982) has argued that male-dominant conversational behaviour associated with traditional sex-role stereotypes may be changing. However, comparisons between these findings and those reported earlier may be confounded by a number of factors, including procedural differences between them. In contrast to the Zimmerman & West (1975) study, McCarrick *et al.* (1981), Aries *et al.* (1983) and Beattie (1981) all analysed behaviour in groups larger than dyads, which may significantly have affected the patterns of communication that occurred. The unique character of dyadic interaction processes was noted long ago by Bales & Borgatta (1955), and a number of studies have reported differences in communication patterns as a function of group size (for example, Sacks, Schegloff & Jefferson, 1974). In order to provide a more direct test of the results reported by Zimmerman and West, the subjects in the second experiment reported in this chapter were run in mixed-sex dyads.

The subjects in the second experiment were also pre-tested for dominance predispositions, and their scores were used to create four experimental conditions: high male–high female (HM–HF), high male–low female (HM–LF), low male–high female (LM–HF), and low male–low female (LM–LF). Manipulating dyadic sex composition and individual differences simultaneously in this experiment thus provides a test of dominance effects arising from both sex-role stereotypes and personality. The results obtained in the study by Rogers & Jones (1975) demonstrated that interruptions occurring in single-sex dyads are significantly affected by personality dominance, and in view of Zimmerman & West's (1975) findings with mixed-sex dyads it was predicted that sex and dominance would have interactive effects on interruption rates. Specifically, males were expected to interrupt at a higher rate in the HM–HF, HM–LF and LM–LF dyads but not in the LM–HF dyads, although effects were expected to emerge only in the second half of the conversations. Verbal back-channels were also scored in the present study, in order to investigate their role in mixed-sex interactions.

A major problem in analysing simultaneous speech is that it is often difficult to obtain an unambiguous record of each participant's contribution. In the second experiment, tie-microphones were used to record independent audio signals from each subject, rather than relying only on the video-tape sound-track. Apart from facilitating transcription and scoring, the independent channels also permitted the analysis of speech rate and amplitude for each member of the dyad during simultaneous utterances. Speech rate and amplitude are affected by a wide range of social and personality variables — for example, drawling on final syllables and a drop in loudness are among the turn-yielding cues described by Duncan & Fiske (1977), and Scherer (1979) has reported that perceived influence is associated with loudness by American subjects and with rapid speech by German subjects. However, the role of these para-verbal cues in speaker-switch non-fluencies such as interruptions has not been systematically investigated. Duncan's work suggests that both floor-holding and floor-taking should be associated with speaking louder and faster, so that speech rate and amplitude might be expected to increase for both interruptor and interruptee during interruptive simultaneous speech. Whether or not an interruption attempt succeeds should therefore depend upon relative rate and amplitude, and this was investigated in the second experiment by comparing these indices before and during successful and unsuccessful interruptions.

The classification of speech events is usually carried out by the experimenters themselves, and although inter-rater reliability may be high (see Rogers & Jones, 1975, and the first experiment in this chapter) the judgements are none the less made independently of the participants' own assessment of the interaction. A final procedural modification in the second experiment was that the members of each dyad participated in an extensive debriefing in which they were asked to classify simultaneous utterances that had occurred in their own conversations; the subsequent data analysis was based on their classification of the events. Simultaneous speech was also scored by two experimenters while monitoring the conversations, and differences between observers' and participants' perceptions of these events were investigated by comparing the discrepant and congruent judgements made by experimenters and subjects (see Roger & Nesshoever, 1987, for an extended report of this study).

## Experiment 1

### Method

#### *Subjects*

Subjects for the first experiment were 36 male and 36 female undergraduates from the University of York and the College of Ripon and York St John. The mean age was 19.7 years for the men and 19.9 years for the women.

#### *Procedure*

The 28-item dominance subscale from the Edwards Personal Preference Schedule (EPPS) (Edwards, 1959), combined with 13 buffer items, was used to assess dominance predispositions. The questionnaires were sent to an initial pool of 312 subjects, and the mean scores (out of 28) for the 107 men and 154 women who returned them were 12.03 and 8.96, respectively; the discrepancy in the scores reflects widely reported sex differences in self-assessed dominance behaviour. The 36 highest-scoring and the 36 lowest-scoring males and females from these samples were used to form six male and six female dyads in each of the three dominance conditions: high–high (HH), high–low (HL) and low–low (LL). All questionnaires were returned to an independent scorer, who also assigned subjects to conditions.

Before testing, all subjects completed an opinion questionnaire in which they were asked to indicate agreement or disagreement with 24 statements relating to topical social and political issues. It was suggested to the subjects that the experiment was concerned with opinion change, and after comparing their responses the members of each dyad were told to discuss only those items on which they had disagreed with one another. They were also told to try to convince their partners of their own point of view. These instructions were intended to divert the subjects' attention from the true purpose of the experiment, and to maximise the likelihood of interruption attempts occurring during the discussions. All subjects were debriefed after participating.

The conversations took place in a laboratory equipped with two Hitachi HV17 video-cameras, monitoring two chairs placed about 90cm apart and angled 20° from a face-to-face orientation. The cameras were positioned 4.5m from each chair, and both participants were recorded simultaneously using a split-screen image on a Sanyo 1100SL video-recorder located in an adjoining observation room. The subjects were informed that their conversations were being recorded, and no attempt was made to disguise the cameras. Data from a preliminary pilot study indicated that subjects became accustomed to being filmed within two minutes, a finding which has been confirmed elsewhere (Weimann, 1981). The first two minutes of each ten-minute conversation were consequently regarded as a familiarisation period, and were omitted from the data analysis. The remaining eight minutes were divided into two four-minute segments to allow comparisons to be made over time. Elapsed time, measured in tenths of a second, was superimposed on the top section of the video tape by means of a Digitel timer.

The video tapes were examined in detail by two experimenters, who classified all simultaneous speech events as either back-channel utterances or as successful or unsuccessful interruptions. Successful interruptions were those events in which the first speaker was prevented from completing an utterance by the second speaker taking the floor. In unsuccessful interruptions, on the other hand, the second speaker attempted but failed to take the floor. The first type corresponds to Ferguson's (1977) simple interruptions and the second type to her butting-in interruptions. Speaker-switches occurring during pauses (Ferguson's 'silent interruptions') occurred infrequently, although two of these events were classified as unsuccessful interruptions where the first speaker prevented the second speaker from completing by resuming the original utterance. The remaining cases were ambiguous, and were omitted.

Once the final classification had been agreed the tapes were scored blind by an independent rater; inter-rater reliability coefficients for successful and unsuccessful interruptions were 0.91 and 0.82, respectively. Vocal back-channels, which comprised all simultaneous speech which did not disrupt the speaker's utterance, were easier to code than interruptions, and inter-rater reliabilities were not computed. The data for both interruptive and non-interruptive simultaneous speech were converted to rates by dividing the frequencies by the dyadic partner's total speech duration.

**Data analysis and results**

The mean scores for the three types of simultaneous speech appear in Table 4.1, where the within-subjects variable, time, refers to the two halves of the last eight minutes of the conversations.

TABLE 4.1 *Mean scores for interruptions and back-channels for males and females in the three dyadic conditions*

| *Dyadic condition* | *Successful interruptions* | | *Unsuccessful interruptions* | | *Back-channel utterances* | |
|---|---|---|---|---|---|---|
| | *Time 1* | *Time 2* | *Time 1* | *Time 2* | *Time 1* | *Time 2* |
| *Males* | | | | | | |
| HH | 0.99 | 2.47 | 0.40 | 0.55 | 2.84 | 2.24 |
| HL | 0.81 | 1.04 | 0.35 | 0.44 | 3.35 | 3.94 |
| LL | 0.71 | 0.84 | 0.34 | 0.32 | 4.72 | 3.96 |
| *Females* | | | | | | |
| HH | 0.95 | 1.94 | 0.44 | 0.71 | 3.32 | 4.22 |
| HL | 0.54 | 0.64 | 0.34 | 0.52 | 4.93 | 5.11 |
| LL | 0.59 | 0.62 | 0.40 | 0.38 | 5.13 | 4.43 |

The interruption and back-channel indices were analysed by means of separate 2(sex) × 3(dominance) × 2(time) split-plot analyses of variance. The results showed no significant effects for unsuccessful interruptions, but there were significant main effects for dominance ($F(2,66)=11.70$; $p<0.001$) and time ($F(1,66)=24.42$; $p<0.001$) and a significant dominance × time interaction ($F(2,66)=13.38$; $p<0.001$) for successful interruptions. Simple main effects for the interaction showed that the mean rate for successful interruptions had increased significantly from the first to the second half of the conversation for the HH dyads ($F(2,66)=6.59$; $p<0.01$). Individual contrasts by means of Tukey tests for the significant simple main effect for dominance at level 2 for time ($F(1,66)=11.69$; $p<0.01$) showed that although the mean successful interruption rates for the HL and LL dyads did not differ during the second half of the conversation, the corresponding rate for the HH dyads was significantly greater than that for both HL ($q(2,66)=8.06$; $p<0.01$) and LL ($q(2,66)=8.69$; $p<0.01$) dyads.

Although the successful interruption rates for men and women did not differ significantly overall, there was a significant main effect for sex for back-channels ($F(1,66)=9.88$; $p<0.005$) which showed that women engaged in more verbal back-channel behaviour than men did. The dominance main effect was also significant here ($F(2,66)=6.83$; $p<0.005$), and Tukey tests showed that significantly fewer back-channel utterances occurred in the HH than in the LL dyads.

**Discussion**

The results of this study provide clear experimental evidence for the effects of complementarity or non-complementarity of dominance predispositions on interruptive behaviour. The most important feature of the findings was that the significantly higher rates of successful interruptions in the HH dyads emerged only after an initial period during which the three dyadic conditions did not differ from one another. These results indicate that shared social norms governing turn-taking do indeed constrain potentially offensive interruptive behaviour in non-complementary pairs during the initial stages of acquaintanceship, but that the members of these dyads diverge from one another as the conversation progresses. The absence of significant effects for unsuccessful interruptions may perhaps be attributable to the lower reliability for this index, and there were zero scores for one or both members in all three dominance conditions for these data.

In common with the findings reported by Rogers and Jones, the mean interruption rate was greater for the male dyads than it was for the female dyads. However, the difference was not statistically significant, and the manipulation of dominance had the same effect on interruptive behaviour amongst women as it did amongst men. The women did emit a significantly higher rate of back-channel utterances, which may have resulted from differences in the way men and women respond to competitive instructions. On the other hand, similar sex differences have been reported for other conversational monitoring cues under con-competitive conditions (Aiello, 1973), and an alternative interpretation of these findings is that women employ a more 'empathic' conversational style than men do.

## Experiment 2

### Method

*Subjects*

A total of 56 subjects, 28 male and 28 female, participated in the experiment. All were undergraduates from the University of York, with a mean age of 19.4 years for the men and 20.1 years for the women.

*Procedure*

The procedure for selecting subjects for this experiment was similar to that used in the first study, drawing on an initial subject pool of 265 University of York undergraduates. The mean dominance questionnaire scores for the 93 men and 122 women who returned them were 12.52 and 9.11, respectively, and the 28 highest-scoring and 28 lowest-scoring males and females from these samples were selected to make seven mixed-sex dyads in each of the four dominance conditions (HM–HF, HM–LF, LM–HF, and LM–LF). Members of each dyad again discussed only those opinion questionnaire items where they had disagreed with one another, and they were told to try to convince their partners of their own point of view.

The conversations took place in the same laboratory used in the first study, with the same recording procedure. However, in addition to the video-tape sound-track, each subject wore a Sony ECM-50PB tie-microphone; these were connected to separate channels of a Sony TC-766-2 reel-to-reel audio-tape-recorder located in the observation room. Two observers also monitored the conversations via a one-way panel, noting separately any instances of simultaneous speech that occurred. Upon completion, the members of the dyad were invited into the observation room where they were shown the video tape of their conversation. They were instructed to stop the tape whenever they thought an interruption had occurred. Initially, no specific instructions were given regarding the nature of interruptions, but as each event was identified that section of the tape was replayed and the subjects were asked to clarify the exchange — who had attempted the interruption, and whether or not they had succeeded. Simultaneous utterances regarded as interruptive by the experimenters but not noted by the subjects were then shown, with the request that subjects attempt to classify these events in the same way.

## Data preparation and dependent variables

All segments of simultaneous speech occurring in the last eight minutes of each ten-minute conversation were transcribed from the tapes, using the independent audio-tape channels to clarify indistinct utterances. The tapes and transcripts were then used to extract four dependent variables.

### *Interruptions*

The subjects' judgements were used to identify a total of 81 successful and 24 unsuccessful interruptions during the 224 minutes of conversation that were analysed. The frequencies were divided by partner speech duration to convert them to rates. As with the first experiment, there were no significant effects for unsuccessful interruptions, and these events were therefore analysed only in relation to the measures of speech rate and amplitude.

### *Back-channels*

Verbal and vocal back-channels were identified and combined to form a single index. After excluding ambiguous cases, a total of 141 were extracted and converted to rates using the procedure described above.

### *Speech rate*

This index was based on syllable frequency, expressed as a rate per second of speech duration. Speech rate was assessed for both members of the dyads during each burst of simultaneous speech associated with successful and unsuccessful interruptions, and in each case a similar assessment was made for a period of uninterrupted speech of a corresponding duration immediately prior to the simultaneous speech. The data thus comprised counts of syllables per second for periods of simultaneous speech during successful and unsuccessful interruptions for both interruptor and interruptee, as well as syllable counts for matched periods of uninterrupted speech for each member prior to the interruption attempt; these latter segments comprised 'baselines' for simultaneous speech rates. Some of the interruptions identified in the corpus of data were prolonged or progressed over a series of attempts, and their precise points of onset and completion were consequently difficult to locate. These were excluded from the analysis, which reduced the number of successful and unsuccessful interruptions investigated for speech rate to 71 and 18, respectively.

*Speech amplitude*

For this index, the rectified vocal signal from each channel of the audio tape was analysed by means of a Research Machines 380Z computer, programmed to sample the selected speech envelope at 100-millisecond intervals and extract peak amplitudes. The output was calibrated to assess amplitude increments up to a maximum of 100 units, determined as a linear function of the V/U meter signal. Amplitude was measured for both interruptor and interruptee during successful and unsuccessful interruptions, commencing with simultaneous speech onset and continuing until resolution. The same cases analysed for speech rate were used for the analysis of amplitude.

## Data analysis and results

*Successful interruptions and back-channels*

The mean scores for successful interruptions and back-channel utterances appear in Table 4.2. The scores are expressed as rate per minute of partner speaking time. The dyads in the first experiment were all single-sex, and each pair could therefore be treated as the unit of analysis. In the present experiment the sex of the dyadic partner was of particular interest, and the data for each variable were therefore entered into separate 2 (sex) × 2(dominance of subject) × 2(dominance of partner) × 2(time) split-plot ANOVAs, where time refers to the within-subjects comparison between the first and second halves of the conversation.

For interruptions, there were significant main effects for dominance of subject ($F(1,32)=7.23$; $p<0.05$), dominance of partner ($F(1,32)=13.61$;

TABLE 4.2 *Mean rates for successful interruptions and back-channels in the first and second halves of the conversations for each dyadic condition*

| *Dyadic condition* | *Sex of subject* | *Successful interruptions* *1st half* | *2nd half* | *Back-channels* *1st half* | *2nd half* |
|---|---|---|---|---|---|
| High Male/ | Male | 0.89 | 2.93 | 1.74 | 1.93 |
| High Female | Female | 0.79 | 2.23 | 3.48 | 3.72 |
| High Male/ | Male | 0.97 | 0.84 | 2.18 | 2.02 |
| Low Female | Female | 0.90 | 0.81 | 4.20 | 4.56 |
| Low Male/ | Male | 1.02 | 1.03 | 2.53 | 3.11 |
| High Female | Female | 0.74 | 0.55 | 4.22 | 3.68 |
| Low Male/ | Male | 0.72 | 0.69 | 2.77 | 2.91 |
| Low Female | Female | 0.84 | 0.76 | 4.28 | 4.13 |

$p<0.001$) and time ($F(1,32)=4.78; p<0.05$), and the interaction between the three factors was also significant ($F(1,32)=7.34$; $p<0.05$). Simple main effects computed for the three-way interaction showed that there was a significant between-subjects effect during the second but not the first half of the conversation, and Tukey tests for individual contrasts showed that although the interruption rates for the partners in the HM–HF condition did not differ from each other during the second half of the conversation ($q$ = 1.69; NS), they were significantly different from the rates recorded for members of the remaining conditions. For example, the contrast between the lower mean score for the female members of the HM–HF dyads and the next highest mean score (obtained by the males in the LM–HF condition) yielded a $q$-value of 3.59 (df 2,8; $p<0.01$). The mean scores for members within the remaining HM–LF, LM–HF, and LM–LF conditions did not differ significantly from one another. There was also a significant within-subjects simple main effect, which showed that the interruption rate had increased for both male ($F(1,78)=4.75$; $p<0.05$) and female ($F(1,78)=5.35$; $p<0.01$) members of the HM–HF dyads. None of the remaining within-subjects comparisons was significant. A similar four-way split-plot ANOVA for the back-channel data yielded a single significant effect. This was the main effect for sex ($F(1,32=6.89$; $p<0.01$), which showed that women gave significantly more verbal back-channels than men across all conditions.

The four-way ANOVA design used in these analyses treats subjects rather than dyads as the unit of analysis, allowing computation of the interaction effects upon which the hypotheses in the present study are predicated. However, interactional behaviour between two or more subjects is of necessity *interdependent*, which means that statistical procedures in which individual subjects are used as the unit may produce biased results. This problem has been discussed by Kraemer & Jacklin (1979), who proposed an alternative method of analysis based on matched-pairs procedures. Their technique does not generalise easily to the complex split-plot design demanded by this experiment, but separate analyses for each of the four dyadic conditions based on the matched-pairs method did confirm the results obtained by the ANOVAs. These analyses were based on contrasts between subjects (male versus female) and across time (first versus second half of the conversation) in each condition, and the only significant effect for successful interruptions showed that the rate increased significantly from the first to the second half of the conversation ($Z = 5.72$; $p<0.01$) in the HM–HF dyads. Corresponding analyses for back-channels produced significant main effects between subjects in the HM–HF ($Z = 2.84$; $p<0.05$), LM–HF ($Z = 3.12$; $p<0.01$) and LM–LF ($Z = 2.36$; $p<0.05$) conditions, while the effect approached significance ($Z = 1.81$; NS) in the remaining HM–LF condition; in all cases women gave more verbal back-channels than men did.

### *Speech rate and amplitude*

The mean speech rate and amplitude scores prior to and during successful and unsuccessful interruptions are presented in Table 4.3. The scores for speech rate and amplitude were derived from the same segments of pre-interruptive and interruptive speech, and the mean scores for both interruptor and interruptee are given in the table.

The data for successful and unsuccessful interruptions were analysed separately for speech rate and amplitude, using 2(interruptor/interruptee) × 2(pre-interruptive/interruptive) split-plot ANOVAs. For successful interruptions, there were significant within-subjects main effects for both

TABLE 4.3 *Mean speech rate and amplitude scores for interruptors and interruptees before and during successful and unsuccessful interruptions*

| *Variable* | *Group* | *Period* | *Type of interruption* *Successful* | *Unsuccessful* |
|---|---|---|---|---|
| Speech rate | Interruptor | Before | 1.251 | 1.350 |
| | | During | 3.274 | 2.373 |
| | Interruptee | Before | 1.572 | 1.803 |
| | | During | 2.800 | 2.856 |
| Amplitude | Interruptor | Before | 2.622 | 2.530 |
| | | During | 6.840 | 4.020 |
| | Interruptee | Before | 2.297 | 3.260 |
| | | During | 4.363 | 5.716 |

analyses, indicating that interruptors and interruptees spoke faster ($F(1,69)=32.94$; $p<0.01$) and with greater amplitude ($F(1,69)=48.63$; $p<0.01$) during the interruption attempt than prior to it. The between-subjects main effects were non-significant, but the interaction term was significant in the case of amplitude. An analysis of simple main effects here showed that vocal amplitude was significantly greater for interruptors than it was for interruptees during the interruption ($F(1,280)=3.95$; $p<0.05$).

There were significant within-subjects main effects in the analyses for unsuccessful interruptions as well, showing that both interruptors and interruptees spoke faster ($F(1,69)=4.87$; $p<0.05$) and with greater amplitude ($F(1,69)=5.39$; $p<0.05$) during the interruption attempt than before it commenced. There were no other significant main effects or interactions for these analyses.

**Discussion**

In this second experiment, the analysis of successful interruption rates occurring in the four sex × dominance conditions showed that all subjects interrupted at a similar rate during the first half of the conversations, and that the rate increased to a significant extent during the second half in the groups where two high-dominant subjects were paired. The results fail to provide any evidence for sex-role effects on interruption rates in mixed-sex interactions; instead, they replicate closely the findings obtained in the first experiment, where significant effects were reported involving dominance and time, but not sex, in the analysis of single-sex dyads.

The results thus demonstrate gender equivalence in interruptive behaviour, and in this case the subjects were student dyads similar to those used in earlier work (e.g. Zimmerman & West, 1975) that did report sex differences in cross-sex interrupting. The data were collected in an experimental rather than a naturalistic setting, but this allowed the manipulation of dominance predispositions that have been shown to influence turn-taking procedures. The findings also confirm the effects of acquaintanceship on turn-taking strategies reported in the first study, where it was suggested that potentially offensive behaviour such as interrupting is constrained by social conventions during the initial stages of interpersonal contact. The analysis of back-channel rates shows that the sex difference in the use of these monitoring cues occurs in cross-sex as well as single-sex interactions, and supports the view that women use a more empathic interactional style than men do.

An important procedural modification in this study was the use of tie-microphones, which improved the quality of the recorded data to a significant degree; in fact, the analysis of speech rate and amplitude during simultaneous speech would have been impossible without independent vocal signals for each participant. It could be argued that intrusive recording techniques such as tie-microphones might inhibit or change spontaneous behaviour, but the overwhelming majority of the subjects in the present study said that they quickly became accustomed to them. Most of the subjects felt that because the tie-microphones were attached at lapel level, out of the field of vision, they were considerably less intrusive than the table microphone.

The analysis of speech rate and amplitude was aimed at investigating the role of these variables as turn-taking and turn-maintaining cues. There was a significant interaction in the analysis of successful interruptions for amplitude, which showed that interruptors spoke with greater amplitude than interruptees during, but not prior to, the interruption. Although the interaction in the corresponding analysis for unsuccessful interruptions was not significant, the trend in the data here showed a reversal, with the interruptee speaking with greater amplitude than the interruptor during simultaneous speech. The interaction terms in the analyses for speech rate were both non-significant, but the trends in the data again reveal a similar pattern of scores: interruptors spoke faster than interruptees during successful interruptions, which was reversed during unsuccessful interruptions. Although the interactions were not all significant, these results suggest that increases in speech rate and amplitude relative to conversational partner may serve both turn-taking and turn-maintaining functions.

Turning to the debriefing sessions, their major advantage lay in clarifying the classification of simultaneous utterances. During the course of the conversations, the two experimenters noted independently any periods of simultaneous speech that they regarded as interruptions, and their judgements were virtually unanimous. However, 18 of the events were not detected by the subjects themselves during their initial inspection of the tape-recorded conversations, and when they were subsequently asked to classify the discrepant events they agreed in only three (16.6%) cases that these were interruptions they had missed. Five other events were reclassified as back-channels on the basis of the subjects' judgements, while the remaining ten (55.5%) were regarded as overlaps and omitted from the analysis. The most common reason for disagreeing over the classification of an event as an interruption was that the speaker was 'tailing off', and although these utterances may not have been grammatically complete, the turn-change was not in dispute. The findings demonstrate the value of debriefing sessions of this kind, and argue strongly for their regular use in research where judgements about speech events are to be made.

Finally, the debriefings indicated that current systems for classifying simultaneous speech (e.g. Ferguson, 1977; Mishler & Waxler, 1968) do not adequately encompass the richness and complexity of speaker-turn routines. For example, lengthy back-channels were sometimes interpreted by the speakers as turn-attempts, and resulted in a series of exchanges that were resolved by a resumption of the turn by the speaker, by an unchallenged speaker-switch, or by a turn-change regarded by the speaker as an interruption. Other utterances which appeared to be back-channels were in fact used as initial cues to a turn-attempt; these were often expressed as back-channel queries or disagreements, but formed part of a progressive series of linked utterances that culminated in an interruption. These preliminary data form part of a current programme of research being undertaken by the author, aimed at establishing a more comprehensive and satisfactory system for classifying simultaneous speech events.

## Concluding remarks

Taken together, the results of these two experiments demonstrate clearly the importance of personality dominance in determining dyadic conversational strategies. High dominance was associated with fewer monitoring signals in the first study, and with a greater number of interruption attempts in both studies. These effects occurred in both male and female dyads in the first experiment, and even when mixed-sex dyads were studied it was the dominance level rather than the sex of the dyadic partner which determined interruptive behaviour. It might be argued that the tendency for men to interrupt women more than the reverse is less likely to occur in the student samples used in these experiments. However, other studies on non-student samples have produced comparable results, and Aries (1982) may be correct in concluding that stereotypical behaviour of this kind is changing.

In contrast to the similarities in the interruptive behaviour of men and women, both of the experiments reported here revealed a significant sex difference in the use of verbal back-channels. The term back-channel refers to simultaneous speech that is used by the listener to signal continued attendance to the speaker, such as 'uh huh' or 'yeah'. These utterances serve to extend floor-holding by the speaker, and their role in conversation is thus the opposite of interruptive simultaneous speech. In both experiments women used significantly more of these cues, suggesting that women employ a more empathic conversational style than men do.

The most important feature of the work presented in this chapter is its reliance on experimental methods. The conversations took place in the context of a social psychology laboratory, and the subjects were explicitly monitored throughout their conversations. The sex composition of the dyads and the dominance scores of the members were determined beforehand, and the topics for conversation were dictated by the subjects' responses to an opinion questionnaire. The likelihood of interruptions occurring was maximised by choosing topics on which the members of each dyad disagreed with one another, and they were specifically instructed to try to convince their partners of their own point of view.

All of these experimental manipulations were aimed at allowing the experimenter as much control as possible over independent variables such as the setting, the topics for discussion, acquaintanceship, and dyadic dominance and sex composition. Control of this kind is intended to preclude factors which might confound the behaviour under investigation, such as the effects of random variations in the social setting in which it occurs, and it permits tests of hypotheses about the role of personality in determining turn-taking behaviour that could be carried out only with great difficulty in more naturalistic settings. The data reported in this chapter also show the extent to which conversation is affected by acquaintanceship: the constraining effects of social norms governing interpersonal conduct with strangers were observable even over the brief ten-minute conversations studied here, a finding which could not easily have been demonstrated outside of the laboratory context.

In addition to using mixed-sex rather than single-sex dyads, the procedure for the second experiment was modified in two important ways. The first of these involved the use of tie-microphones, which resulted in a significant improvement in the quality of the recordings. The participants themselves felt that the tie-microphones were less intrusive than the table microphone, and independent vocal signals are essential if an accurate record of both participants' simultaneous speech is to be obtained. The second procedural modification was the inclusion of an extended debriefing during which the subjects evaluated the simultaneous utterances occurring in their own conversations. This technique avoids the subjective biases inherent in the classification of speech by non-participants, and could be used in a wider context to explore in more detail the precise function of simultaneous speech events occurring in conversation.

## References

AIELLO, J. R. 1973, Gaze direction during interaction. Paper presented at the annual meeting of the Eastern Psychological Association, Washington, D.C., May.

ARIES, E. J. 1982, Verbal and nonverbal behavior in single-sex and mixed-sex groups: Are traditional sex roles changing?, *Psychological Reports*, 51, 127–34.

ARIES, E. J., GOLD, C. & WEIGEL, R. H. 1983, Dispositional and situational influences on dominance behavior in small groups, *Journal of Personality and Social Psychology*, 44, 779–86.

BALES, R. F. & BORGATTA, E. F. 1955, Size of group as a factor in the interaction profile. In A. P. HARE, E. F. BORGATTA & R. F. BALES, *Small Groups: Studies in Social Interaction*. New York: Alfred Knopf, 396–413.

BEATTIE, G. 1981, Interruption in conversational interaction, and its relation to the sex and status of the interactants, *Linguistics*, 19, 15–35.

— 1982, Look, just don't interrupt, *New Scientist*, 95, 859–60.

BOURHIS, R. Y. & GILES, H. 1977, The language of intergroup distinctiveness. In H. GILES (ed.), *Language, Ethnicity and Intergroup Relations*. London: Academic Press.

BRUNNER, L.J. 1979, Smiles can be back-channels, *Journal of Personality and Social Psychology*, 37, 728–34.

DITTMAN, A. T. & LLEWELLYN, L. G. 1967, The phonemic clause as a unit of speech decoding, *Journal of Personality and Social Psychology*, 6, 341–48.

DUNCAN, S. & FISKE, D. W. 1977, *Face-to-face Interaction*. Hillsdale, N.J.: Erlbaum.

EDWARDS, A. L. 1959, *Manual for the Edwards Personal Preference Schedule* (revised edition). New York: Psychological Corporation.

FERGUSON, N. 1977, Simultaneous speech, interruptions and dominance, *British Journal of Social and Clinical Psychology*, 16, 295–302.

GILES, H. 1973, Accent mobility: A model and some data, *Anthropological Linguistics*, 15, 87–105.

GILES, H. & SMITH, P. M. 1979, Accommodation theory: Optimal levels of convergence. In H. GILES & R. N. ST.CLAIR (eds), *Language and Social Psychology*. Oxford: Blackwell.

JACOB, T. 1974, Patterns of family conflict and dominance as a function of child age and social class, *Developmental Psychology*, 10, 1–12.

KENDON, A. 1967, Some functions of gaze direction in social interaction, *Acta Psychologia*, 26, 22–63.

KRAEMER, H. C. & JACKLIN, C. N. 1979, Statistical analysis of dyadic social behavior, *Psychological Bulletin*, 86, 217–24.

MCCARRICK, A. K., MANDERSCHEID, R. W. & SILBERGELD, S. 1981, Gender differences in competition and dominance during married-couples group therapy, *Social Psychology Quarterly*, 44, 164–77.

MISHLER, E. G. & WAXLER, N. E. 1968, *Interaction in Families: An Experimental Study of Family Processes and Schizophrenia*. New York: Wiley.

ROGER, D., BULL, P. E. & SMITH, S. 1988, The development of a comprehensive system for classifying interruptions. *Journal of Language and Social Psychology*, 7.

ROGER, D. & NESSHOEVER, W. 1987, Individual differences in dyadic conversational strategies: A further study, *British Journal of Social Psychology*, 26, 247–55.

ROGER, D. B. & SCHUMACHER, A. 1983, Effects of individual differences on dyadic conversational strategies, *Journal of Personality and Social Psychology*, 45, 700–05.

ROGERS, W. T. & JONES, S. E. 1975, Effects of dominance tendencies on floor holding and interruption behavior in dyadic interaction, *Communication Research*, 1, 113–22.

SACKS, H., SCHEGLOFF, E. A. & JEFFERSON, G. A. 1974, A simplest systematics for the organization of turn-taking in conversation, *Language*, 50, 697–793.

SCHERER, K.R. 1979, Voice and speech correlates of perceived social influence in simulated juries. In H. GILES & R. ST.CLAIR (eds), *Language and Social Psychology*. Oxford: Blackwell, 88–120.

THORNE, B. & HENLEY, W. (eds) 1975, *Language and Sex: Difference and Dominance*. Rowley, MA: Newbury House.

WEIMANN, J. M. 1981, Effects of laboratory videotaping procedures on selected conversation behaviors, *Human Communication Research*, 7, 302–11.

YNGVE, V. H. 1970, On getting a word in edgewise. *Papers from the Sixth Regional Meeting of the Chicago Linguistic Society*. Chicago: Chicago Linguistic Society.

ZIMMERMAN, D. H. & WEST, C. 1975, Sex roles, interruptions and silences in conversation. In B. THORNE & W. HENLEY (eds), *Language and Sex: Difference and Dominance*. Rowley, MA: Newbury House.

# 5 Recalling someone from the past[1]

PAUL DREW
*University of York*

The topic of this chapter concerns the difficulty someone has in answering a question. In the data extract on which this investigation will focus, one participant, Betty,[2] is asked by another, Victor, whether she knows him; after some delay, in which Victor repeats his question, Betty admits that she does not remember him. Now it is possible to attribute difficulties or hesitations in answering to various psychological states, particularly cognitive ones, for example 'not knowing' either the answer or what the speaker means, or deciding what to say. And what I shall be attempting to do here is to make a connection between Betty's evident difficulty in answering and something which is indubitably psychological, namely a dilemma — one for which there is a social organisational, and what has come to be called 'pragmatic' (Levinson, 1983: especially Chapter 1), basis. So more generally this is an exercise to show how the analysis of talk in naturally occurring interaction, and of some conventionally organised properties of knowledge, can be brought to bear on and reveal something about the practices of the mind(s) which are at work in interaction.

The target data for this analytic exercise is an extract from a video-recording of a scene which was naturally occurring in so far as the setting is someone's home; the participants gathered in the setting for an occasion which was unconnected with the recording; and although one of the participants made the recording, she did not do so for any pre-formulated investigative or research purposes. So the participants have not been gathered in an experimental setting, given any experimental task, nor told to engage in any specific activity. The setting happens to be the apartment in which two of the participants, Ivy and her teenage daughter,

Betty, live; the others are arriving at the apartment on the morning of Ivy's birthday, having driven over from a nearby city. They are Ivy's sister, Grace; Grace's husband, Jim; their two children, Paula and Rob; and an elderly male relative, Victor, who is visiting them from Germany. The extract begins at the point when Betty has opened the apartment door to admit the guests, with her mother standing a few feet behind her. So Betty is the first to greet each person as he/she enters.

(1) [Birthday Party: 1–2]

((Betty opens door))
**Rob:** Good mor[ning,] =
**Betty:** [Hi :]
**Jim:** =[We did'n know whether-]
**Rob:** [Did we get you o]ut of bed,=
**Betty:** =[N:o:
**Rob:** [Howeyeh Betty hh
**Betty:** u:nh[:
**Ivy:** [Not quite. Come on in.=
**Rob:** =Hi girl.
(0.6)
((Betty and Rob kiss))=
**Rob:** =How are you,
((Rob moves in towards Ivy))
(0.2)
**Grace:** Hi Betty,
**Betty:** Hi
((Betty and Grace kiss))
((Grace moves in towards Ivy))
**Paula:** Hello::.
**Betty:** ( )
((Paula and Betty kiss))
((Paula moves in towards Ivy))
**Betty:** Hi:.
**Victor:** That's Betty.
((Betty and Victor shake hands))
**Jim:** I haven't seen ( [ ) Debbie no w-
**Victor:** [Kennst du mich noch?=Do-
do you- do you know me[:?
**Jim:** [hehh=
**Ivy:** =See hehe[·hh
**Victor:** [°huh? Do you know me?

| | | |
|---|---|---|
| 33 | | (1.9) |
| 34 | **Betty:** | Unh (0.4) I don't know (h) (h) [ (whether I) |
| 35 | **Jim:** | [Uh let's go= |
| 36 | **Betty:** | remember [ (you) |
| 37 | **Jim:** | [=inside 'n close the door. |
| 38 | **Ivy:** | [remember |
| 39 | | ((Victor moves in towards Ivy)) |
| 40 | | (1.0) |
| 41 | **Jim:** | How ye Betty. |
| 42 | **Betty:** | (uhn) ((Betty and Jim kiss)) fine. |
| 43 | | (1.7) |
| 44 | **Jim:** | (Let's-) let's see how <u>ta</u>:ll you got. |

Having greeted her aunt and two cousins, Betty is approached by Victor: and it is then, in lines 24–36, that the difficulty to which I referred earlier occurs. A puzzle in Betty's delay in answering Victor's repeated question 'Do you <u>kn</u>ow me?', and in admitting that 'I don't know (h) (h) (whether I) remember (you)' is that ethnographically there are good grounds for supposing that Betty does know who he is: these relatives are expected to come to celebrate Ivy's birthday, and Betty knows that Victor will be amongst them. Although they have not seen one another for many years, since Victor last visited the United States, it should be straightforward enough for Betty to pick him out as the one who is Victor. So in part the puzzle I will be dealing with is what difficulty she might be having in putting that knowledge to use as a way of answering his question.

I should mention briefly a couple of methodological points about these data. My analysis will focus almost solely on participants' talk in this fragment of interaction, although of course it is a face-to-face interaction in which gesture, expression, movement, gaze, stance, etc., would all undoubtedly have been associated with the talk and monitored by participants. An advantage of the usual practice in conversation analysis of working on recordings of telephone calls is that whatever gestures, expressions, etc., speakers may make, these do not play any part in the interaction between parties to the call. What is available to them, and also to the professional analyst, is just those sounds which can be heard across the line. Non-verbal 'activities' in face-to-face interaction provide participants with a wealth of further interactional resources; in contrast to the largely (but not entirely) quantitative studies by social psychologists, the sequential integration of non-verbal phenomena into the ongoing management of talk has begun to be investigated by some such as Kendon (1982) and more lately within conversation analysis (see especially Goodwin, 1981; Heath, 1986; and papers by Goodwin, Heath, and Schegloff in Atkinson & Heritage, 1984). In what follows I will not be exploring anything of the non-verbal aspects of the scene whose talk is reproduced above, except for the rather grossly apparent actions such as someone's movement towards another and mode of greeting, which are noted in the transcription. There is nothing on the video-recording which would appear to be contrary to my analysis: for instance, throughout lines 24–36 Betty is looking directly at Victor, so that the absence of a reply and his repetition of the question cannot have arisen from her inattention or not realising she was being addressed. There is no sign in her voice or on her face that she is being playful in delaying answering and saying that she does not remember him (as there is on the faces of Jim and Rob as they enter, their turns in lines 4 and 5 being a possibly ironic reference to the fact that they are very slightly late). Of course the analysis of even a simple stretch of conversation cannot hope to be comprehensive (Sacks, 1986: 128), so I do not see the omission of non-verbal phenomena as a disadvantage on the grounds of the (in)completeness of the analysis. However, it most certainly is unfortunate that readers cannot check for themselves whether there is anything in the non-verbal activities of these participants which might in some way alter my analysis.

The other methodological point concerns the video-camera being plainly visible to all participants, one of whom, Betty, is responsible for making the recording: which raises, then, issues to do with the intrusion of the camera into a 'natural' setting, and the extent to which that intrusion might contaminate their behaviour. The point is particularly worth addressing because the extract to be analysed occurs almost as soon as the camera has been switched on and right as one set of participants arrive on the scene, so that no argument could be made for their having 'settled down' and forgotten about the camera; and because the person making the recording is to be one of the principal characters in the analysis. In general my argument about the possible disturbance effect of a camera is that being filmed may indeed alter people's behaviour: it may make them nervous, they may make more jokes, talk more, be more withdrawn, sit in different places, hesitate to say certain things, and so on. So that were an analysis to be based upon frequency counts of the incidence of certain kinds of behaviour, or upon sociometric diagrams or the like, any assessment of the results might need to take into account the possible disturbance effect of a camera's presence. But if instead the focus of one's analysis is not how often they joke but how they joke, not how often they display nervousness but how nervousness is manifest, not how often they pass objects (e.g. vegetable dishes at a family dinner) but how they pass objects — in short not on the frequency of some activity but on the details of its management and accomplishment — then any possible disturbance caused by participants' knowledge of their being filmed becomes unimportant. People cannot think about or control their behaviour at the level of details for which the systematics of the organisation of action (verbal or non-verbal) are being investigated in conversation analysis. So that, for example, in a recent study of teasing (Drew, 1987) it made no difference to the sequential environment or design of the tease, or even to the properties of the responses by tease recipients, whether the data were face-to-face or telephone recordings — and if the latter, which party knew beforehand that they were being recorded. In the particular data at hand here, it might be supposed that Betty is particularly reluctant to make her admission in lines 32–34 in front of the camera. I have no way of testing whether or not that made a difference to the length of her delay (i.e. between lines 13 and 17); and I hope no reader would want to suggest asking Betty, as an informant on her own behaviour.[3] Whether or not her reluctance was the greater for being filmed, the basis for there being any delay in her answering (and here the reader is referred to Jefferson's contribution, Chapter 8, in this volume), that she has any dilemma in answering or is in the position of 'admitting' something in lines 34–36 has still to be explicated.

As a preliminary way of beginning this analysis, it is worth recalling that a very general property of conversation is that its local turn-by-turn organisation — the coherence which turns at talk have with one another — is generated out of participants' understandings of what other participants have just said. That is, speakers are engaged in analysing each other's prior turns at talk and constructing appropriate next turns, responses or whatever, in the light of their analyses. Thus a turn at talk is the product of its speaker's analysis of or understanding about what was meant in some prior turn(s); in it one speaker displays what another speaker meant. This has come to be regarded in conversation analysis as a kind of 'proof procedure' whereby we as analysts have access to the understandings participants have of one another's talk. And the systematic orderlinesses which can be found in conversation are not synthetic constructions, but are the results of the analyses and activities of participants themselves. Part of our goal as professional analysts is to try to uncover the bases on which speakers can have arrived at their particular analyses or understandings. Of course, any given turn at talk is not only the product of an analysis, but also itself becomes the subject of an analysis by next speaker, and thereby has implications for the further sequential development of talk.

An assumption behind this approach to conversation, that turns at talk are fitted together as relevant next actions to (some understanding of) prior actions, is that of the intersubjectivity of speakers. It is assumed that there is a basic symmetry between speakers in so far as 'both the production of conduct and its interpretations are the accountable products of a common set of methods or procedures' (Heritage, 1984:241). By virtue of these common, shared procedures a recipient of talk can make some appropriate analysis of what a speaker meant or intended. This should not be taken to imply that recipients always come up with a 'correct' analysis: the importance of repair in conversation is that it is a means by which mis-analyses can be remedied, either by the one who made what turns out to have been a mistaken analysis, or by the speaker whose talk has been misunderstood (Schegloff, 1984, 1987). For instance, Schegloff (1986a) discusses cases such as the following, in which an enquiry 'Do you know who's going to that meeting?' is initially misunderstood by its recipient.

(2) [Family Dinner]

| | |
|---|---|
| **Mother:** | 'z everybody (0.2) [washed for dinner? |
| **Gary:** | [Yah. |
| **Mother:** | Daddy 'n I have t- both go in different directions, en I wanna talk ta you about where I'm going (t'night). |
| **Russ:** | mm hmm |
| **Gary:** | Is it about us? |
| **Mother:** | Uh huh |
| **Russ:** | I know where you're go'in, |
| **Mother:** | Where. |
| **Russ:** | To the uh (eighth grade )= |
| **Mother:** | =Yeah. Right. |
| →**Mother:** | Do you know who's going to that meeting? |
| →**Russ:** | Who. |
| **Mother:** | I don't kno:w. |
| **Russ:** | Oh::. Prob'ly Missiz McOwen ('n detsa) en prob'ly Missiz Cadry and some of the teachers. (0.4) and the coun[sellors. |
| **Mother:** | [Missiz Cadry went to the- I'll tell you . . . |

Schegloff notes that Russ's first response to his mother's enquiry is to treat it as a 'pre-sequence' item (Atkinson & Drew, 1979:141–48; Levinson, 1983: 345–64): in replying 'Who', he shows that he understood her enquiry to have been not a genuine request for information, but a preliminary to telling him who will be there. Thus he treats 'Do you know who's going to that meeting?' as a pre-announcement, just as enquiries like 'Are you doing anything tonight?' may conventionally be made and recognised as a pre-invitation. However his mother's next turn, 'I don't kno:w.' reveals to Russ that his analysis of her enquiry was incorrect (Schegloff, 1986a:7), that she had not been going to tell him but wants to know who will be there. In his last turn in the extract he remedies his initially mistaken analysis by giving her the information which he now sees she wanted.

Cases such as this illustrate that whilst the intersubjectivity associated with the symmetry between procedures of production and of interpretation does not guarantee that speakers' analyses of one another's utterances are always correct, nevertheless those same procedures enable misunderstandings to be located and repaired. But in addition the sheer transparency of the alternative analyses of the mother's enquiry in this case demonstrates the relevance of such phenomena for a social psychology of human behaviour. In a very real and clear way Russ is engaged in 'reading the mind' of his mother, in analysing what she intends to be doing in making that enquiry. And that is what people do in conversation: they do not necessarily need to 'think about' how to interpret another's utterance, but the organised procedures — whether of reasoning or conversation structure — which underlie this practical lay psychology (Drew, 1986) are at the heart of the mental map which enable people to understand one another and act appropriately.

Something else is evidenced in this extract which is of some direct importance in our consideration of Betty's dilemma in Extract 1. It was noted that Russ first treats his mother's enquiry as having been a pre-announcement: his response 'Who' is designed then to give her the opportunity to make her announcement. About this Schegloff (1986a:7) makes the following point:

> 'this is quite different from saying that he does not know who is going to the meeting. A moment later, when he realizes he is being asked, he shows that he *does* know. Why then does he not say earlier who is going to the meeting? Because he has understood the preceding utterance not to be a request for information, but to be the harbinger of an announcement, and he fits his response to the action he understood to have been done.'

That is to say — and this is the issue to be addressed in analysing Extract 1 — cognitive states are not determinate factors in interaction. What someone says or does in conversation may not match or follow directly from what they know or do not know. The exigencies of what someone may understand the other to be meaning (albeit in Extract 2 mistakenly) may result in their 'suspending' the relevance of what they know. What an interactant knows, and what from an analysis of the other's talk he knows the other is doing, are quite different factors in that person's response. What he knows may not be a determining factor in what he says he knows. And with that theme in mind we can turn to a closer consideration of Extract 1 and Betty's dilemma in answering Victor's enquiry.

A turn at talk can have a structural position; it is a slot in a sequence of moves. However, what fills that slot, what a speaker actually says in that turn, is selected by that speaker from the alternative things which might appropriately go in that slot. For instance, in answering the telephone one might give one's name, phone number, an institutional name ('University of York'), or say 'Hello'; the selection between these is quite clearly context-sensitive, and in rather delicate ways can reflect an orientation by answerers of the phone to who might be calling, whom they would want to reach, etc. (Schegloff, 1986b:123). Similarly Betty fills her greeting slot in line 24 by selecting from a range of possible items which could go there, e.g. 'Hello', 'Hi Uncle Victor', 'Hello, I'm Betty', 'Good morning', 'How are you?', etc., some of which have been used between Betty and her cousins and aunt in lines 3–21. The item she selects has a minimal character; as such 'Hi' may conventionally make a strong claim to know the addressee and to be known by him (Schegloff, 1986b:127). Betty's 'Hi' to Grace (line 17), for example, has that character; it has rising intonation, and plainly orientates to and displays their familiarity with one another.

Of course, being close relatives and living in some proximity, their recognition of one another — at sight — can be taken for granted, treated as unproblematic. However, since Victor is a very rare visitor whom Betty has not seen for many years, since she was a young child, her recognition of him cannot be a similarly routine, unnoticeable, automatic matter. And the position in which she greets him also being a first opportunity for her to identify or recognise him (Schegloff, 1979:63), there is a special kind of work to be done in the slot in line 24: what she selects to say in that slot may be inspected for its recognitional import.

Now in contrast to the 'Hi' with which she greets Rob and Grace (lines 3 and 17 respectively), Betty's 'Hi:.' in line 24 is done with downward intonation (marked with the stop)[4]: and it is done without any facial or other accompanying indication of her recognising him. For instance, very broad smiling and a kiss accompany her greeting to each of her aunt and cousins, whilst these are absent when she greets Victor (she does not move to kiss him, and in line 26 they only shake hands). Thus her 'Hi:.' is not done with the confidence of recognition: neither does she attempt to identify him explicitly with some equivalent for face-to-face interaction of the quasi-interrogative 'try-marked' address term used in telephone openings (Schegloff, 1979:50–51). So whilst Betty does not treat introductions as relevant (e.g. she does not wait for Victor to introduce himself), and whilst she selects a form of greeting between people who are known to each other or even familiar, in other respects her greeting to Victor is at least equivocal as regards claiming or displaying recognition. In the slot where an 'effortless' display of recognition was especially relevant (Schegloff, 1979: 63), it has not been provided.

One can notice in other materials that a similarly equivocal greeting may be treated sceptically by its addressee. For instance, in Extract 3 Marge figures from her analysis of Sam's greeting that he doesn't know to whom he is speaking.

(3) [JG:I:10:1 (Goldberg transcript)]

| | |
|---|---|
| **Sam:** | Hello |
| **Marge:** | Yeah. Hi:::. How are you boyfriend? |
| →**Sam:** | I'm good. How are you. |
| →**Marge:** | ha ha ha You don't know which one of these girls you eh that's talking to you. |
| **Sam:** | Huh? |
| **Marge:** | You do not know which one of your girlfriends is talking to you. |
| **Sam:** | Yes I do. |
| **Marge:** | You do. |
| **Sam:** | Yeah. |
| **Marge:** | And so who. |
| **Sam:** | Is this Mary? |
| **Marge:** | Ahh haa! I knew it, see:, I knew I wasn't the only girl you had on your string. |
| | (1.0) |
| **Marge:** | This is Marge. |
| **Sam:** | Marge! [How are ya honey. |
| **Marge:** | [ha ha |
| **Marge:** | Oh I'm fine. How are you. Listen ..... |

Sam's return greeting 'I'm good. How are you.' occurs in an equivalent slot to that in which Betty greets Victor in Extract 1; that is, it's a first opportunity to identify the caller. From the clues in Marge's first turn (these being the voice sample; absence of a named self-identification; inclusion of the strongly recognition-relevant other-identification 'boyfriend'), Sam can detect that he is being expected to recognise who is calling; an expectation to which he orientates in his return greeting which, in so far as he does not ask who is calling nor check if it is who he thinks it is (e.g. a try-marked 'Hi, Mary?'), *claims* to recognise the caller. But it does not unambiguously *display* that recognition[5]: he does not, for instance, include the supposed recipient's name, as in 'Hi Mary, I'm good. How are you'. Marge correctly analyses the equivocality of his return greeting as indicating that he does not recognise her, and proceeds playfully to test and to expose his lack of knowledge.

Victor embarks upon a similar, but less playful, test in Extract 1 (lines 25–33). Both Betty's greeting to Victor in Extract 1 and Sam's return greeting in Extract 3 are equivocal as regards their recognition of the other; they do not plainly display recognition. In response Victor and Marge, respectively, have the option of leaving the matter of recognition to be handled *en passant*, as the interaction develops: but each chooses instead to make an issue of Betty's and Sam's avoidance of a recognitional display. In particular, in line 25 of Extract 1, Victor withholds a return greeting such as a reciprocal 'Hi' on its own or together with a self-identification ('Hi, I'm your Uncle Victor'). Furthermore his reply 'That's Betty' directly contrasts with her greeting by performing the other-identification (naming her) which she conspicuously failed to do: nor does he mask that identification as being an inference, e.g. 'You must be Betty'. In Extract 3 Marge directly challenges Sam's implicitly claimed recognition, before then testing his explicit claim to know who he's talking to:

| | |
|---|---|
| **Sam:** | Yes I do. |
| **Marge:** | You do. |
| **Sam:** | Yeah. |
| →**Marge:** | And so who. |

Victor does not make any such comparable challenge in Extract 1; but in his testing her by asking 'Kennst du mich noch?=Do do you- do you know me:?' he is making her possible non-recognition of him into something not to be left as hinted at but as a topic to be addressed. If 'That's Betty' was a subtle attempt to elicit a reciprocal recognition of him, it does not achieve that. His 'testing' inquiry in lines 28–29 is equivalent to Marge's 'And so who' in overtly checking whether Betty really knew whom she greeted with 'Hi:.'.

Until now I have been using the words 'know', 'identify' and 'recognise' quite interchangeably. And of course 'know' has just that kind of looseness or possible ambiguity which can be exploited in using it to be heard by the recipient as 'friends with' someone whom one has perhaps only 'met'. Here, when Victor asks 'do you know me:?', he orients to an expectation that Betty might or should know him, not in the way that ageing entertainers or TV personalities might more hope than expect to be recognised by whomsoever, but by virtue of some mutual but past history. So that 'know' here indexes the passing of time since they last met and the ability to identify someone by remembering a face from a long time ago. Victor's enquiry suggests that Betty might be able to do that, to recall him from the past.

Parenthetically, I should like to notice two sorts of asymmetry which may have been occasioned in Victor's turns 'That's Betty' and 'Kennst du mich noch?=Do do you- do you know me:?'. The first is an asymmetry of knowledge: from her greeting it seems likely that she does not remember or recognise him, but he remembers her — and displays that he does so in naming her, and in asking if she knows him (a speaker would only ask someone he recognised if she knew him, since otherwise there would be no grounds for supposing that she might do so — unless of course he is a 'personality'). So these utterances of his bring to attention that he knows something which she, it appears, does not. The second kind of asymmetry concerns something which Sacks (1971a:8–10) referred to as mind control. Sacks is talking about 'questions' which take the form 'Remember that X?', as in 'Remember that car you had?'. He says about them that they are not really questions at all, but commands: the memory which is summoned up had not previously been in mind, but the first thing you know is you remember it. The question/command having been made, it is out of your control; you have been told what to do with your head. 'We go through conversations thinking we're being spontaneous, our own persons . . . when some immense amount of the things we say are cast there by reference to the way the other talked, that they didn't even know they were using' (Sacks, 1971a:10). Furthermore, one cannot complain when one is asked/told 'Remember that car you had?', or opt out (you cannot say 'Go to hell') or try not to remember. This kind of mind control is akin to the position in which 'do you know me:?' places Betty; though what Sacks is pointing to is really both mind and interactional control, neither of which may be being deployed by the speaker (here Victor) intentionally or strategically. Betty has no choice but to put her mind to the exercise of trying to remember him: neither has she any redress, interactionally, against being asked. The sequence having been set up as a test, that is something which she just cannot opt out of. She is stuck with trying to find an answer for it. It is her dilemma in finding this answer to which I now want to turn.

Betty does of course have a way of 'knowing' who is asking 'do you know me:?'. Knowing who will be visiting for this small birthday gathering, knowing that Victor will be among them, she can easily infer that this man is Victor. She can attribute that identity to him on the basis of characteristics such as that he is elderly; that he is male; that he is the only stranger; and that he is German, a clue he gives rather overtly in 'Kennst du mich noch?' in line 28. So she might have no trouble in 'knowing' who he is in the sense of attributing an identity to him, in naming him. But her position is akin to Russ's in Extract 2, in which he knew who was going to the PTA meeting, but did not answer, at first, by giving those names because he treated his mother's enquiry as a different kind of object than just wanting to know. His initial answer, 'Who', to her enquiry was built, not upon a cognitive state (his knowing who), but with an eye to the enquiry's business — or what he first and mistakenly thought was its business. Here, too, in Extract 1 Betty could come up with an answer to Victor's enquiry by naming him: but instead she treats the enquiry's business as one of recalling/remembering Victor, an analysis which she makes explicit in her answer in lines 34–36 that 'I don't know (h) (h) (whether I) remember you'.

Recalling someone from somewhere, including from the past, can involve recognising a face,[6] and then trying to fit an identity to that face. For some persons whose face is recognised, a name may not have been known; in which case a generalised identity may be recalled (e.g. 'Of course, she's the woman who used to serve at the fishshop'). For others, a name may be searched for and found. In either case the basis for an identification is recognising someone from a picture one has in the memory.

With that, it is possible that Victor's identification of Betty may be somewhat contrived or artificial; he has not seen her since she was very young (three or four years old), and the physical changes in her appearance over the intervening 14 or 15 years have presumably been enormous, so that the picture of her which Victor carries around in his mind might bear little relation to the face in front of him. But without needing to get into debates about how people can see one face in another's (e.g. how resemblances are seen between a baby and one or other of its parents),[7] adults have a conventional entitlement to display that they are able to picture someone from the past. They can do this in identifying someone, as Victor does Betty; or in monitoring changes in someone's appearance, as Jim does at the end of Extract 1 (line 44) in remarking to Betty 'let's see how ta:11 you got.'. Such an observation relies upon a comparison between a picture of someone in the past, held in the memory, and that person's appearance now. Thus it displays, as does Victor's recognitional identification, a certain *cognisance* of the recipient back at the time the picture of him was 'fixed' in the memory.

Now in this respect there is a further asymmetry between Victor and Betty which arises from a category attribution. Although Betty is not now a child, she was when she last saw Victor. In order not merely to identify (that this must be) Victor, but to recognise him, she would have to retrieve a picture of him in her memory of the time they last met — when she was a very young child. However in *not* laying claim to recognising/remembering him, and therefore in not claiming to recall that picture of him in her memory, she orients to a conventional attribution to the category 'children' an inability to 'know', and hence to remember, something or someone in the way adults do. The state of cognisance of someone necessary to picture that person in one's mind, which can be claimed and displayed by adults, is not a competence ordinarily attributed to children. Thus Betty's dilemma is that although she is an adult now, and although she can quite easily know/guess/infer who he is, in so far as she treats Victor's enquiry as a test of whether she remembers him, if then she identified him, e.g. 'Yes, you're Uncle Victor', such an identification could be heard as *recognitional*, which would then be to claim just that state of cognisance of him at the time she was a child which children are not 'permitted' to have.

I want it to be clear that I am talking about *attributions* of states of knowledge to categories of persons — not *actual* states of knowledge of either the category as a whole or by individuals who may be so categorised. There may or may not be scientific, professional psychological studies into what, and how, some or all children may know or remember. There may be good grounds for thinking that children know more than that with which they are credited. I am referring not to the psychological reality of cognition or consequent memory, but instead to a social organisation whereby a population may be divided into two classes, 'adults' and 'children': a division which, for the moment setting aside but not forgetting how the boundary is constituted and how membership of one or the other of its categories is achieved or accomplished,[8] may then be used to attribute to persons identified by one category, 'child', the absence of a cognitive competence possessed by the other, 'adult'. An orientation to such a social organisation is evident in practical psychological reasoning of which the following are examples. In psycholinguistic studies of the development of language in children, very young children have been recorded as saying things like 'Mummy, I simply can't get through the day without a cup of coffee'. Such utterances are routinely attributed to *imitation,* on the grounds not only of the child not otherwise demonstrating mastery of the syntactic constructions needed to put the utterances together, but more particularly because a child cannot be supposed to appreciate the apprehensions or tribulations a day can bring or how drinking coffee might help — and hence cannot know what such an utterance 'means'. Secondly, parents frequently tell anecdotes about asking a young child if they remember something (e.g. the day they visited a castle), and the child replying, maybe hesitantly, that he does: rightly or wrongly, the anecdote is told as being about not a feat of memory by the child, but the child's willingness to please the parent, which assumes that the child does not really remember but recognises what the parent wants to hear, what the 'right answer' is to the parent's enquiry. Finally, sociological studies report a reluctance by coroners to come to a finding of 'suicide' in cases where young children have been found hanged, or dead from wounds from a shotgun found next to the body (Atkinson, 1978:119, 152–53): although an adult found dead in similar circumstances would almost certainly be found to have committed suicide, coroners will routinely come to the conclusion that children have died 'accidentally' because, even though they may have pulled the trigger, they cannot be supposed to know what they were doing, to suffer the anxieties of life, or to know the full meaning of (the release of) death — they may just have been imitating, or trying something out. To repeat, the issue is *not* whether the suppositions about or attributions to children embodied in such reports are correct or are 'scientifically' unfounded. The point is that they have in common a social organisation for knowledge and states of awareness to which psycholinguistic researchers, parents, and coroners orient in deciding that children did not do something which they appear to have done. Were an adult to have done those things, the 'appearance' would be taken to correspond with 'reality'. In noticing the disjuncture between appearance and reality in such cases of children's conduct, adults employ practical reasoning about the psychology of children, specifically the absence of some requisite cognitive competence. It is just this to which Betty, an adult, orientates in not attributing to herself, as a child, the kind of cognisance or awareness of Victor which would have enabled her to keep a picture of him in her mind, and hence to remember and recognise him. Underlying her quandary in answering his enquiry, and eventually replying that 'I don't know (h) (h) (whether I) remember (you)', is not her inability to identify him, but a conventional social organisation of knowledge, whereby, were she to say she knows him, that might be heard as an accountably illegitimate claim (the kind of claim she could be teased about) to have fixed a picture of him in her mind back when she was very young, and from that to recognise him now. Something like this could be meant when sociologists and social psychologists talk about the 'internalisation of norms'.

Finally, I just want to go back to the issue of the asymmetry which is managed through Victor's *testing* Betty, to notice that he does not assist her when her difficulty in answering becomes evident. We saw earlier that his initial enquiry in lines 28–29 could be regarded as a test question, and could be so treated by Betty. Now we can further notice that he pursues his testing. When at first Betty does not respond to his enquiry, Victor repeats it in line 32 (the apparently intrusive utterances by Jim and Ivy can be disregarded, as for the present, i.e. until line 35, they are only spectators to the interaction between Betty and Victor). There is then a pause of 1.9 seconds before Betty hesitatingly answers. When a recipient delays a response, for instance delays answering a question or responding to a proposal or invitation, then first speaker (the one who asked the question, or made the invitation or proposal) can analyse that delay as implying a difficulty which the other is having. And 'If a recipient manifests behaviours that indicate he or she is having difficulty or is hesitant to respond, the speaker is in the position of guessing or inferring or determining what the trouble is' (Pomerantz, 1984a:155). Based on his guesses or inferences about the trouble recipient is having, a speaker may clarify something he said (Pomerantz, 1984a:153–56); he may change his position to align with that of recipient (Pomerantz, 1984a:159–61); he may do subsequent versions which in various ways encourage the recipient, for example, to accept an invitation (Davidson, 1984); or he may profer an explicit understanding of the difficulty recipient may be having. A couple of things can be noticed about such remedial actions. The first is that they variously 'read the other's mind': in analysing the difficulty manifested in pauses and hesitation, a speaker figures out what is going through the other's mind in delaying a response. The second is that such actions in various ways *assist* the recipient: for instance, by locating and repairing something which might not have been clear, the speaker obviates the recipient's having to seek clarification or taking a wrong direction. Or by changing his position to align with that which, by virtue of the pause, can now be attributed to the recipient, the speaker manages to save the recipient from overtly disagreeing. Or the speaker may find and state an excuse for the non-response on the recipient's behalf.

This brief overview of the reparative actions which may be engaged in by speakers when recipients display difficulty or hesitation in responding suggests that when Betty does not answer his initial inquiry, an option for Victor would be to find and attempt to deal with the difficulty she was having, and thus assist her. Most straightforwardly he might have abandoned his 'test', and perhaps simply introduced himself. Alternatively he might have accounted on her behalf for her difficulty in recognising him, by saying something like 'It's been a long time since we last met, you were a very little girl'. Or he might have noted changes in his appearance which might account for her not recognising him, e.g. 'I've got a little fatter since

I last saw you'. In conspicuously not assisting her in any of these ways, but instead just repeating 'huh? Do you know me?' in line 32 and then waiting out through the pause in line 33, Victor pursues his testing until she is 'forced' into her admission that she doesn't remember him. 'Testing' can have that quality, of managing to expose something about recipient that was suspected by the speaker all along — in this case, as in Extract 3, that the recipient does not recognise the speaker — and getting the recipient to admit it.

## Conclusion

There is a theme running through this chapter which, whilst essentially simple, begins to throw into relief some quite striking complexities in the relationships between inner psychological states and overt behaviour. These complexities have, I think, important and fascinating significance for the cognitive sciences. The theme may, perhaps, be nicely illustrated by considering how we decline invitations. Research in conversation analysis has shown that, when going to decline invitations, speakers (a) generally preface the rejection with an appreciation, whereas in accepting appreciations are either omitted or follow the acceptance component; (b) do mitigated or 'softened' forms of declining (e.g. 'I don't think I can make it this morning . . . '), whereas acceptances are unmitigated, unhedged; and (c) produce accounts for declining (but not for acceptances) which are constructed as constraints, as reasons for being unable to accept, either implying or overtly expressing that the speaker would rather have accepted and might like to for some future occasion. Now these are quite systematic properties of the way declinations are managed: these properties, and the systematic differences between the design of declinations from that of acceptances, reveal a social organisation with respect to responses to invitations, whereby acceptances are 'preferred' and declinations are 'dispreferred'. 'Preference' does not refer, of course, to the private inclinations, proclivities, or intentions of individuals; that is, in this technical sense it is not a psychological state. Just as we often make invitations that we hope or expect the other will decline, so also we know that on occasions when we have no desire at all to accept an invitation from someone, either now or in the future, nevertheless in declining the invitation we follow the format outlined in (a)–(c) above. That is, we express how valued the invitation is (even when it is not), and that we are unable to accept on this occasion because of some prior commitment, even though we have had to fabricate a quite false account or excuse or had to turn something we were merely going to do into something we *have* to do, and even though we have no intention of accepting such an invitation in the future. So there is a plain distinction to be drawn between an individual's psychological inclination and the conventional, normative social organisation of 'preference/dispreference' manifest in the systematic differences between the design of acceptances and of declinations of invitations (on preference organisation in general, see Atkinson & Drew, 1979:57–61; Heritage, 1984: Chapter 6; and Levinson, 1983: Chapter 6).

The theme to which I am drawing attention, then, is this degree of independence of manifest public behaviour from private inner psychological states: this independence arises from the 'gap' between psychological dispositions or inclinations individuals may have, and their necessary orientation to social organisations for talk-in-interaction. In the data analysis above I have pursued this theme by attempting to show an independence between thought and action — here, in Extracts 1 and 2 between states of cognisance and expressions of those states. In particular my aims have been to show that the former (inner psychological states) are not straightforward determinants of the latter (social actions); and to explicate the social organisational basis — here, especially, the pragmatics of the social distributions of knowledge, memory, etc. (the tie between categories and states of cognisance) — for the speakers 'knowing' but 'not saying' that they know. So the analysis has tried to show how an occasioned gap between thought and action has been generated by a social organisation.

It should be emphasised that such analysis does not deny psychology or diminish its relevance for social action. For instance, I have sought to explicate how social organisation generates a dilemma for Betty in Extract 1, a dilemma surely being an inner psychological state, albeit one which is generated by non-individualistic factors. My point as regards psychology is only that a state of cognition (knowing the answer to a question) does not automatically trigger the behavioural manifestation of that state (i.e. the production of the answer). This is a cautionary note about directly imputing inner states of mind to overt behaviour, and vice versa, and hence about the relationships which are rather generally assumed, in sociology and psychology, to hold between thought/emotion and action. In this respect I am taking an empirical step in the direction suggested by the various theoretical and philosophical strictures of such writers as Coulter (1982) and Ryle (1949) concerning the model of action appropriate for the cognitive sciences.

## Notes to Chapter 5

1. The origins of this paper go back to some data sessions on the materials analysed

here, held at UCLA in 1980. I recall Mike Lynch, Anita Pomerantz and Manny Schegloff being at those sessions. It is possible that I have borrowed not only from the published work of Pomerantz and Schegloff, as cited in the text, but also from remarks they may have made in the sessions, but which are unattributed. But the main lines of the argument here follow and develop the one I began then.

2. As is usual practice, pseudonyms have been used throughout to protect people's anonymity.
3. For two principal reasons. First, people's awareness and memory of their actions simply does not extend to this level of conversational detail; and second, the accounts they might provide are *ex post facto* reconstructions which cannot be cleansed of the work they do to rationalise, justify, exonerate, etc. — as accounts of actions they cannot be separated from accounts *for* actions, and hence have an indeterminate relation to the action as constituted in progress (see Heritage, 1984:135–78).
4. The transcription conventions used here are those which have been developed for conversation analysis. Glossaries can be found in Atkinson & Heritage (1984) and Button *et al.* (1986).
5. Sacks distinguishes between *claiming* an understanding and *displaying* or proving one. The former involves only the claim, for instance that one has understood, e.g. 'Uhuh', or 'Oh yeah, I see'; whereas in displaying an understanding, the next speaker does a sequentially relevant next action to that which the prior speaker's turn is understood to have been. In performing a sequentially implicated next action for one of the understandings available from the prior utterance, the next speaker proves that he has 'correctly' understood. See for example Sacks (1971b:10–11).
6. This assertion, that one can remember someone by recognising their face, is almost certainly rather culture bound, if Goffman (1963) is right.
7. Recently there was a news story about a maternity hospital in Ireland at which two mothers were mistakenly given each other's baby. Unsuspecting, these two mothers returned home with 'their' child, and it was some days before the error was found by the hospital. This caused such distress to the families concerned that at first both sets of parents refused to believe that a mistake had been made; and one set continued to dispute a court order to have the babies swapped back again. Presumably the distress they felt might in part have owed to what is almost a custom among parents and relatives, of finding particular likenesses between the baby and one or the other parent. Indeed, so strong is this sense that a family resemblance should be apparent at even a very early age, that if a resemblance with at least some feature of the father's is not found, this can be the source of ribald jokes or serious doubts about the baby's paternity. At any rate, whilst the hospital's mistake was undetected, it is most likely that in the awestruck way of parents of newly-born children they had discovered and marvelled over, and possibly attributed to previous generations (e.g. 'He's got his grandfather's eyes alright'), a number of family facial likenesses — then to be told they had been duped, with the consequent prospect of doing it all over again with a different baby. And what has once been revealed to have been a sham is not as easy to believe in a second time.
8. Sacks (1964: Lecture 6, 14–15) noticed that there are quite a variety of classes by which a binary categorisation of the population is possible, e.g. sex and race (and to the unanalytical use of which sociologists seem to have developed a

fetishistic attraction). He reflected on whether such two-set classes (rich/poor, young/old, North/South, rural/urban, proletarian/bourgeois, etc.) might have some special kind of interactional and political uses. One issue they pose for their proper appreciation is where the line is to be drawn. Or rather, what kind of contextual matters or reasoning procedures get to be involved in assigning someone as a member of one or the other class. Particularly fascinating in this respect is Garfinkel's discussion of the 'intersexed' Agnes (see Heritage, 1984: 180–98).

## References

ATKINSON, J. M. 1978, *Discovering Suicide: Studies in the Social Organisation of Sudden Death*. London: Macmillan.

ATKINSON, J. M. & DREW, P. 1979, *Order in Court: the Organisation of Verbal Interaction in Judicial Settings*. London: Macmillan.

ATKINSON, J. M. & HERITAGE, J. C. (eds) 1984, *Structures of Social Action: Studies in Conversation Analysis*. Cambridge: Cambridge University Press.

BUTTON, G., DREW, P. & HERITAGE, J. (eds) 1986, *Human Studies*, 9, 2–9: Special Issue on 'Interaction and Language Use'.

COULTER, J. 1982, *Rethinking Cognitive Theory*. London: Macmillan.

DAVIDSON, J. 1984, Subsequent versions of invitations, offers, requests, and proposals dealing with potential or actual rejection. In J. M. ATKINSON & J. C. HERITAGE (eds), *Structures of Social Action: Studies in Conversation Analysis*. Cambridge: Cambridge University Press. 102–28.

DREW, P. 1984, Speakers' reportings in invitation sequences. In J. M. ATKINSON & J. C. HERITAGE (eds), *Structures of Social Action*. Cambridge: Cambridge University Press. 129–51.

— 1986, Individual–society interface: a comment on Taylor and Johnson, *British Journal of Social Psychology,* 25, 195–96.

— 1987, Po-faced responses to teases, *Linguistics*, 25, 219–53.

GOFFMAN, E. 1963, *Stigma: Notes on the Management of Spoiled Identity*. Englewood Cliffs, NJ: Prentice Hall.

GOODWIN, C. 1981, *Conversational Organisation. Interaction between Speakers and Hearers*. New York: Academic Press.

HEATH, C. 1986, *Body Movement and Speech in Medical Interaction*. Cambridge: Cambridge University Press.

HERITAGE, J. 1984, *Garfinkel and Ethnomethodology*. Cambridge: Polity Press.

KENDON, A. 1982, The organisation of behaviour in face-to-face interaction: observations on the development of a methodology. In K. R. SCHERER & P. EKMAN (eds), *Handbook of Methods in Nonverbal Behaviour*

*Research*. Cambridge: Cambridge University Press, 440–505.

LEVINSON, S. 1983, *Pragmatics*. Cambridge: Cambridge University Press.

POMERANTZ, A. M. 1984a, Pursuing a response. In J. M. ATKINSON & J. C. HERITAGE (eds) *Structures of Social Action*. Cambridge: Cambridge University Press, 152–63.

— 1984b, Agreeing and disagreeing with assessments: some features of preferred/dispreferred turn shapes. In ATKINSON & HERITAGE (1984:57–101).

PSATHAS, G. (ed.) 1979, *Everyday Language: Studies in Ethnomethodology*. New York: Plenum.

RYLE, G. 1949, *The Concept of Mind*. London: Hutchinson.

SACKS, H. (1964) Lectures 1–8, University of California, Irvine (edited by G. Jefferson from unpublished lectures Winter 1964–Spring 1965). Mimeo, University of York.

— 1971a, Unpublished lecture (17 May), University of California, Irvine. Mimeo.

— 1971b, Unpublished lecture (no. 3, Fall), University of California, Irvine. Mimeo.

— 1979, Hotrodder: a revolutionary category. In G. PSATHAS (ed.), *Everyday Language: Studies in Ethnomethodology*. New York: Plenum. 7–14.

— 1986, Some considerations of a story told in ordinary conversation, *Poetics*, 15, 127–38.

SCHEGLOFF, E. A. 1979, Identification and recognition in telephone openings. In G. PSATHAS (ed.), *Everyday Language*. New York. Plenum, 23–78.

— 1984, On some questions and ambiguities in conversation. In J. M. ATKINSON & J. C. HERITAGE (eds), *Structures of Social Action*. Cambridge: Cambridge University Press. 28–52.

— 1986a, Presequences and indirection: applying speech act theory to ordinary conversation. Mimeo, Department of Sociology, UCLA.

— 1986b, The routine as achievement. In BUTTON *et al*. (eds), *Human Studies*, 9, 111–52.

— 1987, Some sources of misunderstanding in talk-in-interaction, *Linguistics*, 25, 201–18.

# 6 Family interaction from an interactional sociolinguistic perspective[1]

ERICA HULS
*University of Nijmegen*

## Introduction

In general, it will be readily agreed that it makes a great deal of difference whether you grow up as the daughter of a factory director or as the daughter of a janitor. But where exactly does the difference lie? Are you — discounting the obvious financial advantages — better off as the daughter of a factory director? And if you are better off, what role has verbal stimulation played in establishing this position? Or is it a question of 'different' rather than 'better'?

Such questions are pivotal in the discussions about the causes and the backgrounds of social class differences with regard to educational opportunities (e.g. Bernstein, 1973; Labov, 1972). In this chapter I intend to specify, in pragmatic and conversational terms, a number of differences and similarities in the socialisation of two children, the daughter of a janitor and the daughter of a factory director. Before doing this, I would like to treat some theoretical and methodological considerations that gave rise to this study.

## Theoretical background

The educational sociologist, Basil Bernstein (1973), was a pioneer in the development of a theoretical framework with respect to the problem of the reproduction of social inequality. He suggested, in brief, that the social relationships within the family, and the ways in which these are expressed in language, play a crucial role in the participation of family members in school and societal life. According to Bernstein, the following combination of characteristics in the primary socialisation of children is supposed to improve their chances in school.

1. A person-orientated type of family. In such a family, personal considerations are seen as relevant.
2. An open communication structure. This means that there is ample opportunity for discussion.
3. Explicitness. This notion refers to the tendency to verbalise matters relatively often.
4. Elaborated code. The interaction is based upon the principle that as much as possible is exposed, expressed and put into words.

In accordance with the role relationships inherent in the higher professions, the combination of phenomena as stated above is supposed to be more frequent in the higher social class. The opposite poles of these phenomena (i.e. the position-orientated family type, the closed communication structure, implicitness, and restricted code) are more likely to be found in the lower social class.[2]

In the present study we attempt to elaborate upon Bernstein's ideas about socialisation in the family and social inequality from an interactional sociolinguistic perspective. More specifically, theoretical findings in pragmatics and conversation analysis are applied in an analysis of spontaneous family interaction. The study is aimed at exploring the variation that exists in the communication habits of families from different social classes.

The notion of 'behaviour regulation' is central to the study: to what degree and by what means do family members attempt to regulate each other's behaviour? The study is limited to verbal aspects of behaviour regulation, as these are considered to be especially relevant in the discussions about the causes of social inequality. We attempt to gain access to the general notion of 'behaviour regulation' via many specific analyses, each focusing upon a different aspect of this general notion. These analyses are as follows:

1. The analysis of 'competition' indicates who takes the floor when family members compete for a turn (e.g. interruption, simultaneous starts), thereby limiting the verbal contribution of others.

2. The analysis of 'steering' shows who steers the verbal behaviour of others by asking questions, and whether this steering is successful in terms of receiving replies to these questions.
3. The analysis of 'dependency' indicates who makes a contribution to the conversation dependent upon the consent of others by using special techniques for taking the floor, such as the pre-start (e.g. '*Mom, you know what?*'), thereby giving the other the right to control turn distribution.
4. The analysis of 'listening activity' shows which member-participants stimulate one another's behaviour by giving animating back-channel cues (e.g. '*hm*', '*yeah*').
5. The analysis of 'directives' deals with the attempts of member-participants to regulate one another's non-verbal behaviour. Attention is paid to the choice of directive formulations (e.g. '*Close the door*' against '*Will you please close the door*?', with the former formulation being more direct and explicit and the latter more indirect and orientated to personal considerations).
6. The analysis of 'schoolish speech acts' indicates which member-participants stimulate each other with interaction patterns that fit well into the realm of the school (e.g. positive reinforcements, corrections, achievement-directed continuations).

Through the various specific analyses noted above, we hope to gain a relatively differentiated and encompassing insight into such a general and complex concept as 'behaviour regulation'.

The practical relevance of this study of pre-school children in their home environment is to show some of the variation in conversational style which teachers have to deal with in the classroom.

## Methodological options

As stated in the introduction to Section 2 of this volume, a major methodological issue in the area under discussion concerns the context in which the data are collected. This context can be more or less devised by the researcher. At one end of the continuum there is laboratory experimentation: the researcher pre-selects participants and provides the setting and the topic for conversation. At the other end there is observation in a more natural setting, where participants are not pre-selected, no sophisticated recording equipment is used and the conversation takes place as a matter of course. There are no a priori reasons for choosing either end of this continuum. The approaches are complementary to one another, each having certain advantages that the other does not and each resulting in a particular kind of knowledge. Both the specific conceptualisation of the research question and practical considerations play a decisive role in the choice of a more natural or more experimental approach.

The stance of the present study in this continuum can be characterised as follows: participants are pre-selected to a certain degree and the conversation takes place in a natural setting, i.e. the situation is not created for the sake of carrying out research. Additionally, recording equipment is used openly, although attempts are made to minimise its obtrusiveness. And although the study lacks the rigorous control of most laboratory experiments, we could trace the influence of many relevant variables by specific comparisons in which the variables such as the number of participants in the interaction, the type of activity or the topic of conversation, are held constant or varied. Controls are made after data collection, not before, as is usual in laboratory experimentation.

In the present study, data are collected by participant observation in two families with children from five to six years of age. Thus we have opted for a case approach by studying many different aspects of a few cases. Such a case approach is increasingly being used in research on language use (e.g. Ervin-Tripp & Mitchell-Kernan, 1977; Ochs & Schieffelin, 1979; Gumperz, 1982). The collection and analysis of natural conversation is generally agreed to be necessary but time-consuming.

Although there may be some disadvantages, a case study also has some distinct advantages. First, a case study enables one to carry out an intensive data-collection process in a natural setting. This is especially relevant because the study concerns social class differences in socialisation processes. It is well known from the research tradition (e.g. Ginsburg, 1972; Labov, 1972) that especially socially disadvantaged persons can react defensively to situations solely created for the aim of doing research, resulting in an acknowledgement of existing prejudices towards them as if they were deficient. Through our participation in the natural home environment of the families, we attempt to avoid this problem.

A second advantage of a case study is that one can gain a thorough insight into the social context of the language phenomena. Further, one can study a lot of settings, e.g. during mealtime or during play. And it also enables one to study the embedding of individuals in a group.

Although the study can involve as many as 20 individuals, the main disadvantage is that only some families are studied. A choice has to be made between investigating some families in many respects or many families in some respects. In the preferred in-depth approach it is, of course, not possible to generalise results to broader categories such as social class, or mothers and children. However, this is not the aim of the project. The study aims to give additional insight into the character and the variation in domestic communication patterns in families from different social backgrounds.

## Data collection

Via a family-care organisation, contact was sought with families which needed help and met the criterial demands posed by the investigation. In the role of a home help, the investigator was able to enter the family as a participant observer (naturally with the consent of those involved). In this way the natural character of the family interaction was hardly, if at all, disturbed.

The observation took place daily, between 3.30 and 7.30 p.m., for a period of seven weeks. Following a period of mutual habituation between researcher and family, recordings were made of verbal interaction. In the manner described above, data were collected within two families having widely divergent socio-economic status: the family of a janitor and the family of a factory director.

In the janitor's family neither parent had completed a course of education subsequent to elementary school. Before her marriage the mother had first been employed as an unskilled factory labourer and later as a home help. The family includes five children, all girls. The eldest, Mirjam, is 11 years of age. She attends a boarding school. The next to eldest child is Elise, who is nine. Then comes Mieke, aged six, who is the focal point of the research. In addition, there are two 'little mollies', as their mother calls them: Ingrid, who is about one year old, and baby Elsje. The family lives in a renovated workers' quarters in Nijmegen. Their living situation is somewhat cramped: the children sleep in bunk beds in two small rooms, and when Mirjam is at home she sleeps with her parents. There is little traffic on their street, so the children are able to play there. The financial situation of the family is rather sad; there simply is not enough money to satisfy even the most basic needs.

In the family of the factory director both parents have completed a course of higher education. The father has studied law and the mother is a kindergarten teacher. The family includes three children: Leonard, the eldest, is nine; Wientje, 'the object of the research' (as her mother puts it) is five; Otto is two. The family lives in the suburbs of Nijmegen, a wooded neighbourhood of villas. Each child has a room of its own. The house has a large piece of land attached to it which offers many possibilities. Financially, they can afford almost anything they desire.

Both families are comparable in composition in the sense that they consist of a father who is employed outside the home for more than 40 hours a week, a mother who takes care of the household and the children, a nine-year-old child, a pre-school child, one or two children who are not yet able to speak, and three or four visitors. The eldest child in the janitor's family is, as mentioned earlier, often absent.

The recordings were made with a portable cassette-recorder which was set up in the living room as inconspicuously as possible. By way of trial, supplementary recordings were made in the janitor's family with mobile recording equipment.

From the recorded material a selection of two periods of eight hours each was transcribed. One recording hour took about 60 hours to transcribe. On the basis of these data the linguistic methods of analysis were developed and carried out.

## Data analysis

The data analysis can be divided into three main components: an analysis of turn-taking; an analysis of directive speech acts; and an analysis of so-called school speech acts. The three components of the analysis provide, each in its own way, insight into verbal aspects of regulation of behaviour.

### The analysis of turn-taking

The turn-taking analysis is conducted on the basis of existing theories on turn-taking in conversations (e.g. Sacks *et al.*, 1974; Zimmerman & West, 1975). In the turn-taking analysis, the structure of the conversation and the participation of the different family members in it are examined. It covers phenomena such as interruptions, simultaneous starts, questions, back-channel cues, and pre-starts (for circumscriptions of these last two phenomena, see p. 118). Although there is some discussion on this point (see West & Zimmerman, 1982), we interpret the distribution of these phenomena among interaction participants as giving insight into background social relationships. For example, if, in relation to others present, one person often holds the floor or interrupts, this behaviour may be interpreted as an expression of dominance (Zimmerman & West, 1975). According to Roger & Schumacher (1983), there is a relationship between interrupting behaviour and a high score on a scale of dominance. For a broader discussion of interruptions as an indicator of dominance, see Huls (1984). In this chapter we should like to confine ourselves to the following remarks, however. We do not want to support the notion that every interruption has to be seen as an expression of dominance in social respects. Each interruption contributes to the defining of the positions of the interaction participants in the social network. In the present study it especially comes down to a matter of symmetries and asymmetries in the distribution of linguistic phenomena. The main patterns which stand out in this distribution form the point of departure for conclusions concerning the degree to which interaction participants may be said to have equal status in relation to one another.

Another example of an interpretation: if someone introduces his/her contribution to the conversation with a so-called pre-start (a request for attention and permission to speak), this strategy would indicate, among other things, that he/she presents him or herself as dependent upon his/her speaking partner. This interpretation is in line with that of Sacks (1972): he interprets the use of pre-starts by children as an expression of their limited right to speak. The same sort of nuances introduced in the context of the interpretation of interruptions are valid here as well.

In order to describe the conversational networks within both families in such terms, the transcription of the tape is segmented into 'turns', grossly defined as what someone says between two moments of silence. Within this broad definition, categorisation of, among other things, the following points is necessary: is the utterance a back-channel cue, part of a pre-start, repetition or clarification sequence, an egocentric or act-assisting remark, or a 'standard' turn? The turns are then described in terms of: who the speaker is; who the addressee is; the relation of the turn to the preceding conversation; and the relation of the turn to the following conversation. In the description of the relation of a turn to the preceding and following conversation, patterns such as in Figure 6.1 are used. A speaker (S) interrupts the preceding turn of P after P chooses another participant A as the next speaker. As P chose a speaker other than A we speak of a 'severe' interruption.

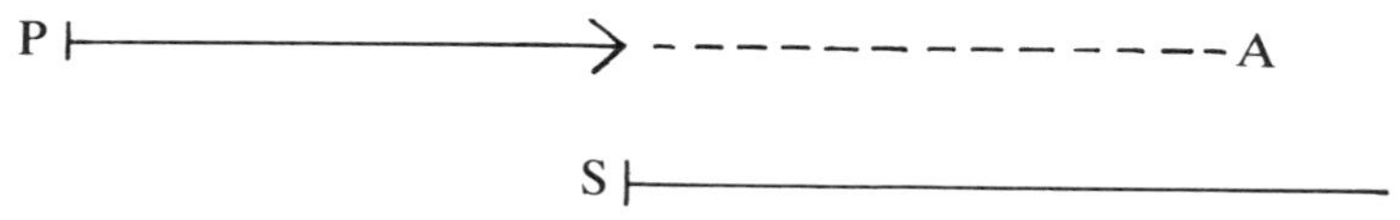


Key:

| | |
|---|---|
| P, A, S, | interaction participants |
| ———————— | successful utterance |
| - - - - - - - - | unsuccessful utterance |
| ————————> | choice of next speaker |

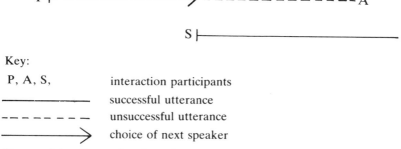

FIGURE 6.1 *Example of a relation of a turn to the preceding conversation*

Variations on the above pattern are easy to conceive. Some 42 patterns which define the turn in relation to the preceding conversation are distinguished in the study. The description of speaker alternation in terms of these patterns is rather formal: the turn-taking sequence forms the core of this description. In an effort to distinguish competitive from non-competitive simultaneousness, criteria which will not be specified here have been used.

Thus, passages of coherent conversation are transformed into a data set of 13,768 turns. The data set also contains information on many extra-lingual variables, such as 'topic' and 'type of activity', so that the influence of these variables can be investigated.

## The analysis of directives

A directive is defined as an effort to steer the non-verbal behaviour of the addressee (cf. Ervin-Tripp, 1976). This effort may incorporate various degrees of power (from strong to weak) and may vary, for example, from invitation to suggestion, from urging to dissuasion, and order to forbid.

In accordance with pragmalinguistic research by Searle (1975), Ervin-Tripp (1976) and Garvey (1975), a typology of directives is developed in Table 6.1. The categorisational principle behind the typology can be summarised as follows: what is the relationship between the actual chosen formulation, the illocutionary force of the utterance (its function as, for example, a directive, representative, or expressive speech act), and its propositional content (an addressee performs an act)? This relationship can vary in directness. Although we cannot treat the entire contents of Table 6.1 now, we will treat three examples as an illustration.

TABLE 6.1 *Overview of directive types and their interpretation*

| *Code* | *Type + example of a formulation* | *Major type* | *Explicitness* | *Strategy* |
|---|---|---|---|---|
| 1 | Imperative<br>'Just run upstairs' | Direct | Yes | None |
| 2 | Explicit performative<br>'I advise everyone not to lay one single finger on it' | Direct | Yes | None |
| 3 | Ellipsis<br>'A plate' | Direct | Yes | None |
| 4 | 'You can'<br>'You can play outside once in a while, can't you?' | Embedded | Yes | Personal (hearer) |
| 5 | 'I want you to'<br>'I want you to play in the bath for a while after supper' | Embedded | Yes | Personal (speaker) |
| 6 | 'You do'<br>'And Wientje, you come with me to get some bread' | Embedded | Yes | None |
| 7 | 'You must'<br>'And your mother must go on sitting here' | Embedded | Yes | Rights, duties, sanctions |
| 8 | 'You may'<br>'Yes, but you may not go on walking around naked like that' | Embedded | Yes | Rights, duties, sanctions |
| 9 | 'Do you want to'<br>'Yeah, look, do you want to get me a serving spoon?' | Embedded | Yes | Personal (hearer) |
| 10 | 'You need to'<br>'No, no, then you don't need to put *those* trousers on anymore either' | Embedded | Yes | None |
| 11 | 'Why'<br>'Can you tell me why you don't want to go to the same school as Walt?' | Embedded | Yes | Personal (hearer) |
| 12 | Another matrix or two matrices simultaneously<br>'When are you going to get the chocolates?' | Embedded | Yes | None |
| 13 | Permission directive<br>'Mom, may I put the bikini on?' | Indirect | No | None |
| 14 | Question directive<br>'Do you want me to get angry?' | Indirect | No | Rights, duties, sanctions |
| 15 | Hint<br>'We're not in the Dutch Indies here' | Indirect | No | None |
| 16 | Other | — | — | — |

With the imperative '*Just run upstairs*' (code 1), the illocutionary force as well as the propositional content of the directive is formulated, so this type is relatively direct. With the formulation '*Do you want to get me a serving spoon?*' (code 9), the propositional content is stated (you get a serving spoon for me), but a misunderstanding is possible concerning the directive aspect of the formulation (one can simply take it as a question about the addressee's willingness). The propositional content is, in this case, couched in a frame (a 'matrix' in the terminology used by Garvey, 1975), which brings up the question of the addressee's willingness. This type is therefore of an intermediate directness. The last example, code 15 ('*We're not in the Dutch Indies here*'), is typically Dutch. The situation finds a child sitting naked at the table while her parents want her to get dressed. In this formulation neither the desired act (getting dressed), nor the agent (the child), nor the illocutionary force of the utterance (a directive), is literally formulated. So this type is relatively indirect.

The left-hand half of Table 6.1 contains the types; in the right-hand half, the types are grouped together under more general headings. The last two types found in Table 6.1, the question directive and the hint, show immense diversity in content. For these types a subdivision is made concerning 'theme': what reason or condition does the speaker supply in order to move the addressee to the desired act? The speaker can, for example, call attention to his own feelings, a sanction, or a general norm. Table 6.2 provides an overview of the distinctions that are made for 'theme'. Analogous to Table 6.1, this table also gives an overview of the interpretation under more general headings.

A directive analysis set up in such a way provides a first step towards a pragmalinguistic access to central concepts from the language disadvantage discussion, e.g. 'degree of explicitness and directness', and 'personal versus positional orientation'. The kind of extralingual variables studied is the same as in the turn-taking analysis.

**The analysis of 'school speech acts'**

In the analysis of 'school speech acts', the distribution of the following speech acts among participants in interaction has been studied:

1. Positive reinforcements, i.e. positive verbal evaluations given in response to the behaviour (verbal or non-verbal) of an interaction participant.
2. Known-answer questions. A broad definition of known-answer questions was used. Not only was the type of question aimed at testing the reasoning power of another (usually a child) considered

TABLE 6.2 *Overview of the themes distinguished within the directive types 'question directive' and 'hint', and their interpretation*

| *Code* | *Theme + example of a formulation* | *Major type* | *Explicitness* | *Strategy* |
|---|---|---|---|---|
| 1 | Need or feelings of the speaker<br>'I know I was always scared to death when I saw the plumber climbing through the window' | Indirect | No | Personal (speaker) |
| 2 | Necessity<br>'It's not at all necessary' | Indirect | No | General |
| 3 | (Im)possibility<br>'It's not possible, dear' | Indirect | No | General |
| 4 | (In)ability of the speaker<br>'I can't have you on my lap the whole time, can I?' | Indirect | No | Personal (speaker) |
| 5 | Norm or rule<br>'It's not proper to sit naked at the table' | Indirect | No | General |
| 6 | Sanction<br>'Alright, then I'll walk bare-arsed' | Indirect | No | Rights, duties, sanctions |
| 7 | Consequence<br>'The spoon is going to get in there again, isn't it?' | Indirect | No | None |
| 8 | Statement about behaviour<br>'Come on, you're naughty' | Indirect | Yes | None |
| 9 | Address-term and/or attention-getter<br>'Hey, little one' | Indirect | Yes | None |
| 10 | Other<br>'And we're not in the Dutch Indies here' | Indirect | No | None |

a known-answer question, but questions which nearly feed the answer, or those to which the speaker already knows the answer but poses them anyway in order to stimulate speaking, were also referred to as such.

3. Corrections, i.e. the responsive steerings of verbal behaviour.
4. Achievement-directed continuations, i.e. continuations of the conversation which imply that someone can/cannot do something, is/is not good at something, can already/cannot yet do something, is clever/stupid, and so on.

## Results

As it is not possible to treat all results here, we have limited ourselves to the following selection:

1. With regard to the turn-taking analysis, we present the networks of competition and dependency.
2. With regard to the directive analysis, we treat the composition of the directive repertoires of the families, the mothers and the pre-school children with regard to major type, explicitness and strategy.
3. With regard to the analysis of so-called school speech acts, we treat an overview of the absolute and relative frequencies of the school speech acts in the repertoires of the interaction participants. For a full treatment of results, see Huls (1982).

### Turn-taking analysis: competition

The analysis of competition indicates who takes the floor in competition for a turn (e.g. interruptions, simultaneous starts), and thereby limits the verbal contribution of others. Networks of competition (Tables 6.3 and 6.4) were obtained by cross-tabulation.

The comparison of the families starts with the main total. In the family of the factory director (hereafter the High family), 606 cases of competition were found; in the family of the janitor (hereafter the Low family) 269. These absolute numbers form respectively 7.8% and 4.6% of the total of turns. This difference is significant[3] ($p<0.001$) and is not brought about by only one or some participants in the interaction: a look at the column 'RC' indicates that every participant in the High family surpasses his or her counterpart in the Low family.

Within the Low family, the parents and children are rather well-matched in relative competition (RC). The winning chances reflect a

Table 6.3 *The network of competition in the Low family*

| | *Loser* Mother | Father | Elise | Mieke | Mirjam | Ingrid Elsje | Others unknown | *Total* | *W+L* | *RC* | *Winning chance (%)* |
|---|---|---|---|---|---|---|---|---|---|---|---|
| *Winner* | | | | | | | | | | | |
| Mother | | 17 | 27 | 21 | 30 | 12 | 27 | 134 | 183 | 10.1 | 73.2 |
| Father | 6 | | 2 | 10 | 2 | 4 | 2 | 26 | 49 | 10.4 | 53.1 |
| Elise | 6 | 1 | | 7 | 9 | 1 | 2 | 26 | 71 | 9.2 | 36.6 |
| Mieke | 7 | 3 | 1 | | 2 | | 1 | 14 | 57 | 10.6 | 24.6 |
| Mirjam | 9 | 1 | 2 | 2 | | 1 | | 15 | 63 | 10.9 | 23.8 |
| Ingrid Elsje | | | 1 | | | | | 1 | 19 | 4.8 | 5.3 |
| Others Unknown | 21 | 1 | 12 | 3 | 5 | | 11 | 53 | 96 | 11.1 | 55.2 |
| Total | 49 | 23 | 45 | 43 | 48 | 18 | 43 | 269 | 538 | 9.0 | 50.0 |

The matrix shows the absolute frequency of instances of competition between different participants in the family interaction. The 'W+L' column gives the total number of instances of competition in which each participant was involved as a winner or loser. To correct for differences in the total number of speaking turns of each participant, the 'RC' (relative competition) column gives the frequency of competition per 100 speaking turns. The chance of winning is computed as W/(W × L) x 100.

Table 6.4 *The network of competition in the High family*

| | *Loser* Mother | Father | Leonard | Wientje | Others unknown | *Total* | *W+L* | *RC* | *Winning chance (%)* |
|---|---|---|---|---|---|---|---|---|---|
| *Winner* | | | | | | | | | |
| Mother | | 11 | 49 | 132 | 72 | 264 | 383 | 16.6 | 68.9 |
| Father | 6 | | 8 | 6 | 6 | 26 | 54 | 32.1 | 48.2 |
| Leonard | 10 | 2 | | 33 | 17 | 62 | 156 | 16.8 | 39.7 |
| Wientje | 45 | 2 | 22 | | 19 | 88 | 320 | 21.6 | 27.5 |
| Otto | | | | 1 | | 1 | 1 | | |
| Others Unknown | 53 | 13 | 15 | 60 | 19 | 165 | 298 | 16.7 | 55.4 |
| Total | 119 | 28 | 94 | 232 | 133 | 606 | 1212 | 18.1 | 50.0 |

For clarification see Table 6.3

hierarchy: mother, father, Elise, Mieke, Mirjam and Ingrid/Elsje (we do not take into account 'others unknown' here). Eleven-year-old Mirjam ends up in a rather low position, which may be related to her position in the family as a 'problem child'. The picture that emerges further is strongly influenced by role and age relationships.

In the High family, the 'RC' column is more erratic. Wientje comes across as not aloof. The winning chances in the High family also reflect a hierarchy: mother, father, Leonard and Wientje (we do not take 'others unknown' into account here). The children's winning chances increase with age.

In both families the mothers have a winning chance of about 70%. Fathers, however, have a winning chance of about 50%, while the eight-year-olds have a winning chance of somewhat less than 40%. Pre-school children Wientje and Mieke are not very successful in getting the opportunity to speak under competing circumstances: their winning chance hovers around 25%.

In the left-hand part of the tables we can look for asymmetries between individuals. Both mothers play a central role in the interaction. They win more often than they lose, no matter which family member they compete with. In both families the children have little opportunity to win while competing with their mothers (between 17 and 25%). The fathers seem to take the position of the eldest child. In competition with the mothers, their chance of winning is low; with the children, however, they win more often than they lose.

In terms of the interaction between the children themselves, the older sibling generally wins more often over the younger one than vice versa. The Mirjam–Elise dyad is the only exception in this respect. Perhaps Mirjam's particular position in the family plays a role here.

If we look more carefully at Mieke and Wientje, we detect some differences which are relevant to our general problem of social inequality. The main difference between them is that Wientje is much more experienced in competition situations. Wientje is an active participant in a family that, as far as competition is concerned, is more exciting than Mieke's family. Compared with Mieke, Wientje obtains more experience in acquiring a place in conversations. This can come in handy for her in the school situations where the opportunity to take the floor is limited.

A second difference concerns the mother–pre-school-child dyad. In the High family this dyad takes on a 'heavy' role in the network. In the Low family there is no such dominant dyad. Thus, Wientje has not only obtained more competition experience, she also has more experience in competing with a superior. This could well be an important asset in climbing the social ladder.

To summarise the conclusions: competition is more marked in the High family than in the Low family. In both families, however, competition relationships show an age and social prestige hierarchy.

Of course one can think of all types of variables which might blur the picture given above, e.g. topic, setting, number of participants, turn density. It has been possible to trace the influence of these variables, but this analysis cannot be presented here. The picture given, however, was not invalidated by this complementary analysis.

### Turn-taking analysis: dependency

Table 6.5 contains the network of dependency in the Low family; Table 6.6 for the High family. It is evident (under DAR) that children especially make use of the pre-start, a technique used to introduce the turn and to guarantee attention in situations where it is not at all certain it will be given. Wientje High takes the prize with her DAR score of 5.3 and her 96 pre-starts, again an indication that she is trying to stand her ground in fast-paced competitive conversation.

The fact that both mothers are usually the recipients of a pre-start (see under DPR) affirms their central position in the family. They are the ones that allocate attention.

In the Low family significantly less use is made of the pre-start ($p<0.001$). Here apparently one can put one's contribution in immediately. In both families the pre-start is predominantly used by younger participants and directed towards older participants.

### The analysis of directives

The number of directives given is the same in both families. As spokeswomen, both mothers take a central position in the directive network: nearly half of the total can be credited to them. As addressee, Wientje stands out. Mieke often plays outdoors, so is away from the attention of adults. Even when Mieke is at home, however, compared with Wientje, she is less regulated by her mother.

TABLE 6.5 *The network of dependency in the Low Family*

| | *Addressee* | | | | | | | | | |
|---|---|---|---|---|---|---|---|---|---|---|
| | *Mother* | *Father* | *Elise* | *Mieke* | *Mirjam* | *Others* | *Total* | *DAR* | *DPR* | *S/A* |
| Speaker | | | | | | | | | | |
| Mother | | 1 | | | | | 1 | 0.1 | 1.4 | 0.1 |
| Father | | | | | | | 0 | 0.0 | 0.9 | 0.0 |
| Elise | 2 | 1 | | | 1 | | 4 | 0.5 | 0.2 | 4.0 |
| Mieke | 5 | | 1 | | | 1 | 7 | 1.2 | 0.3 | 7.0 |
| Mirjam | | | | 1 | | | 1 | 0.2 | 0.7 | 0.5 |
| Ingrid Elsje | 6 | 1 | | | | | 7 | 2.0 | 0.0 | ∞ |
| Others unknown | | | | | 1 | 2 | 3 | 0.4 | 0.1 | 1.0 |
| Total | 13 | 3 | 1 | 1 | 2 | 3 | 23 | 0.4 | 0.4 | 1.0 |

The matrix shows the absolute frequency of utterances of dependency between different participants in the family interaction. The 'DAR' column gives the amount of dependent turns (percentages) in the active turn repertoire; the 'DPR' column gives the amount of dependent turns (percentages) in the passive repertoire. S/A is the participation as speaker divided by the participation as addressee.

TABLE 6.6 *The network of dependency in the High Family*

| | *Addressee* | | | | | | | | |
|---|---|---|---|---|---|---|---|---|---|
| | *Mother* | *Father* | *Leonard* | *Wientje* | *Others* | *Total* | *DAR* | *DPR* | *S/A* |
| Speaker | | | | | | | | | |
| Mother | | | 3 | 8 | 7 | 18 | 0.7 | 5.7 | 0.2 |
| Father | | | | | | 0 | 0.0 | 4.7 | 0.0 |
| Leonard | 23 | 4 | | 2 | 9 | 38 | 3.5 | 0.9 | 5.4 |
| Wientje | 75 | 2 | 1 | | 18 | 96 | 5.3 | 1.0 | 7.4 |
| Others | 3 | | 3 | 3 | 1 | 10 | 0.6 | 1.0 | 0.3 |
| Total | 101 | 6 | 7 | 13 | 35 | 162 | 2.1 | 2.1 | 1.0 |

For clarification see Table 6.5

A comparison qua types and themes gives nuanced insight into the choices which are made in the formulation of directives, but we will not give a detailed treatment of these results at this time. Instead, we will present results in the light of interpretative categories related to the language disadvantage discussion. The right-hand sides of Table 6.1 and 6.2 contain the operationalisation of these categories.

Table 6.7 shows results concerning major type. The families are different in this respect ($p<0.001$). In the Low family the style is relatively indirect; in the High family the agent and the act are embedded in a frame or matrix.

TABLE 6.7 *Structure of the directive repertoire of the families, the mothers and the pre-school children regarding major type (percentages)*

| | *Major type* | | | |
|---|---|---|---|---|
| | *Direct* | *Embedded* | *Indirect* | *N* |
| Low family | 35.9 | 17.8 | 46.3 | 2110 |
| Mother as speaker | 27.8 | 17.4 | 54.8 | 984 |
| Pre-school child as speaker | 41.9 | 17.4 | 40.7 | 243 |
| Mother as addressee | 34.9 | 26.0 | 39.0 | 153 |
| Pre-school child as addressee | 29.4 | 25.2 | 45.4 | 342 |
| High family | 32.7 | 28.1 | 39.2 | 2106 |
| Mother as speaker | 33.9 | 24.4 | 41.7 | 978 |
| Pre-school child as speaker | 35.2 | 33.9 | 30.9 | 374 |
| Mother as addressee | 27.9 | 31.3 | 40.8 | 252 |
| Pre-school child as addressee | 34.0 | 23.6 | 42.4 | 622 |

The mothers also vary from one another ($p<0.001$). Mrs Low stands out in giving 'real' indirect directives. The scores of Mrs High are higher on the other two points. Mieke is either direct or indirect. Wientje makes relatively frequent use of forms in between ($p<0.001$). The passive repertoire of the mothers as well as the children has the same structure.

Table 6.8 shows results concerning explicitness. Neither the families nor the mothers are different in this respect. The children do not differ as addressee, but do as speakers ($p<0.001$). Wientje is relatively explicit.

Table 6.9 contains results regarding strategy.The families are different ($p<0.001$). In the Low family a formulation of rights, duties and sanctions is more frequently chosen; in the High family it is the considerations of the addressee that are frequently opted for.

TABLE 6.8 *Structure of the directive repertoire of the families, the mothers and the pre-school children regarding explicitness (percentages)*

| | Explicitness | |
|---|---|---|
| | *Explicit* | *Implicit* |
| Low family | 67.1 | 32.9 |
| Mother as speaker | 62.9 | 37.1 |
| Pre-school child as speaker | 64.3 | 35.7 |
| Mother as addressee | 62.2 | 37.8 |
| Pre-school child as addressee | 64.9 | 35.1 |
| High family | 66.9 | 33.1 |
| Mother as speaker | 63.5 | 36.5 |
| Pre-school child as speaker | 75.6 | 24.4 |
| Mother as addressee | 62.7 | 37.3 |
| Pre-school child as addressee | 64.0 | 36.0 |

Numbers in the directive repertoires are as in Table 6.7

TABLE 6.9 *Structure of the directive repertoire of the families, the mothers and the pre-school children regarding strategy (percentages)*

| | Strategy | | | | |
|---|---|---|---|---|---|
| | *Personal (speaker)* | *Personal (addressee)* | *General* | *Rights, duties, sanctions* | *None* |
| Low family | 3.3 | 2.5 | 3.8 | 13.5 | 77.0 |
| Mother as speaker | 3.6 | 2.6 | 4.9 | 14.2 | 74.7 |
| Pre-school child as speaker | 5.3 | 2.1 | 4.9 | 15.2 | 72.4 |
| Mother as addressee | 5.9 | 4.6 | 2.6 | 15.0 | 71.9 |
| Pre-school child as addressee | 1.2 | 3.5 | 7.0 | 16.7 | 71.6 |
| High family | 3.7 | 4.7 | 4.0 | 10.7 | 76.9 |
| Mother as speaker | 2.2 | 6.4 | 4.3 | 7.6 | 79.4 |
| Pre-school child as speaker | 7.0 | 4.3 | 3.7 | 16.3 | 68.7 |
| Mother as addressee | 8.7 | 8.3 | 5.6 | 11.5 | 65.9 |
| Pre-school child as addressee | 3.7 | 3.9 | 3.7 | 10.5 | 78.3 |

Numbers in the directive repertoires are as in Table 6.7

The active repertoire of the mothers is also different ($p<0.001$). Mrs High refers relatively often to considerations of the addressee while Mrs Low refers to rights, duties and sanctions.

Wientje and Mieke do not differ in regard to strategy, although Wientje and her mother do ($p<0.001$). In comparison to her mother, Wientje makes more use of her own personal considerations. Furthermore, she frequently makes use of rights, duties and sanctions.

Although the passive repertoire of the mothers does not differ in regard to strategy, the children's does ($p<0.01$). Compared with Wientje, Mieke is more often regulated with reference to rights, duties, sanctions and general rules. Wientje is regulated more often with reference to personal considerations of the speaker.

### The analysis of so-called school speech acts

Table 6.10 presents a picture of the differences that can arise between families in regard to the use of school speech acts. In every school speech act that we studied, the High family yields a higher score than the Low family. This is true in an absolute (see the frequencies under 'S') as well as relative sense (see under 'AR'). The application of a test leads in all four cases of school speech acts to a significant result ($p<0.001$).

It does not appear that schoolishness chiefly emanates from the parents: the children participate whole-heartedly in achievement-directed continuations. They also make use of corrections. Of all children, Wientje High is by far the most active in the use of schoolish speech acts.

The absolute frequencies are especially an important factor in the life of the pre-school children. It is there that we see great differences. Wientje receives 89 positive reinforcements; Mieke only two. Wientje receives 26 known answer questions; Mieke only one. Wientje is corrected 91 times to Mieke's 35 times. Achievements are mentioned to Wientje 56 times, yet only twice to Mieke. It is clear that the children are growing up in thoroughly different atmospheres.

## Concluding remarks

The present study must primarily be considered a methodological exercise aimed at opening the question raised by Bernstein — how social

TABLE 6.10 *Overview of the 'school speech acts' in the families*

| | *Positive reinforcement* | | | | *Known-answer question* | | | | *Correction* | | | | *Achievement-directed continuation* | | | |
|---|---|---|---|---|---|---|---|---|---|---|---|---|---|---|---|---|
| | *S* | *A* | *AR* | *PR* | *S* | *A* | *AR* | *PR* | *S* | *A* | *AR* | *PR* | *S* | *A* | *AR* | *PR* |
| *Low Family* | | | | | | | | | | | | | | | | |
| Mother | 16 | 8 | 0.5 | 0.2 | 1 | 1 | 0.0 | 0.0 | 52 | 7 | 1.4 | 0.4 | 6 | 2 | 0.2 | 0.1 |
| Father | | | 0.0 | 0.0 | | | 0.0 | 0.0 | 7 | 3 | 1.0 | 0.9 | | | 0.0 | 0.0 |
| Elise | 6 | 2 | 0.2 | 0.4 | | | 0.0 | 0.0 | 14 | 18 | 0.2 | 0.6 | 4 | 6 | 0.5 | 1.0 |
| Mieke | 9 | 2 | 0.2 | 0.3 | 1 | 1 | 0.0 | 0.0 | 10 | 35 | 0.3 | 4.4 | 8 | 2 | 0.8 | 0.5 |
| Mirjam | 1 | | 0.2 | 0.0 | | | 0.0 | 0.0 | 9 | 18 | 1.4 | 4.8 | 4 | 3 | 0.6 | 1.0 |
| Ingrid/Elsje | | 14 | 0.0 | 0.9 | | | 0.0 | 0.0 | | 11 | 0.0 | 0.9 | | 1 | 0.0 | 0.1 |
| Others | 5 | 11 | | | | | 0.0 | 0.0 | 14 | 14 | | | 8 | 16 | | |
| Total | 37 | 37 | 0.3 | 0.3 | 2 | 2 | 0.0 | 0.0 | 106 | 106 | 0.9 | 0.9 | 30 | 30 | 0.4 | 0.4 |
| *High family* | | | | | | | | | | | | | | | | |
| Mother | 90 | 68 | 2.6 | 3.3 | 11 | 2 | 0.2 | 0.1 | 92 | 19 | 2.3 | 0.8 | 46 | 40 | 1.3 | 1.3 |
| Father | 6 | 4 | 2.6 | 2.3 | 3 | | 1.3 | 0.0 | 10 | 4 | 3.9 | 3.1 | 2 | | 0.9 | 0.0 |
| Leonard | 5 | 21 | 0.3 | 2.2 | 2 | 6 | 0.2 | 0.4 | 36 | 42 | 2.6 | 4.1 | 33 | 21 | 1.6 | 1.5 |
| Wientje | 15 | 89 | 0.8 | 5.1 | 3 | 26 | 0.1 | 1.7 | 48 | 91 | 1.6 | 4.7 | 67 | 56 | 2.3 | 3.2 |
| Otto | | 6 | 0.0 | 2.6 | | | 0.0 | 0.0 | | 9 | 0.0 | 5.3 | | | 0.0 | 0.0 |
| Others | 116 | 44 | | | 21 | 6 | | | 24 | 45 | | | 53 | 84 | | |
| Total | 232 | 232 | 2.3 | 2.3 | 40 | 40 | 0.4 | 0.4 | 210 | 210 | 1.8 | 1.8 | 201 | 201 | 1.6 | 1.6 |

Absolute frequencies as speaker are given under 'S', as addressee under A. The 'AR' and 'PR' columns give the percentage frequencies of the speech act in the active and passive turn repertoires respectively.

relations and linguistic form are related — to empirical research based on concepts from pragmatics and conversation analysis. The results illustrate the research methodology.

It was our intention in this chapter to specify in pragmatic and conversational terms a number of differences and similarities in the socialisation of two children, the daughter of a factory director and the daughter of a janitor. Important differences seem to exist in the communication habits with which these children grow up.

In turn-taking analysis we find that within the Low family there is more chance that one will be able to take and hold the floor; within the High family one is more often pushed aside. In the High family the style is more assertive. In the Low family the interaction is coloured less by power differences. In the High family the mother is in charge and Wientje is especially kept in line. Mieke can go her own way to a greater extent. A rate of competition which is 'normal' for Wientje is abnormally high for Mieke. In their respective homes they become accustomed to a different base rate. Wientje attempts to obtain attention by making use of the pre-start, thereby making her contribution to the conversation dependent upon the consent of others. In Mieke's family the necessity to do so is much less.

The results of the directive analysis conflict with the stereotyped characterisation of the directive style within families from lower social classes as 'imperative', 'direct', and 'commanding' (see Hess & Shipman, 1967). On the dimension of 'person-orientated versus status-orientated control' (the variable 'strategy' in this study) the picture which appears in the literature on class-specific styles of socialisation is confirmed here: considerations of a personal character play a more important role in the higher-class family than in the other family. In contrast, in the latter family people more often appeal to rights, duties, sanctions and general rules. As far as directness is concerned (the 'major type' variable), our results offer an instructive contradiction of the expectations expressed in the literature: people are more direct in the higher-class family in the sense that the agent and the action are more often specified. The results also disagree with expectations concerning explicitness, as it appears that no differences exist on this point. Thus, some results support the picture found in the literature; others refute it.

In the school speech act analysis, the High family yields higher scores then the Low family on all four of the variables that were coded. Although interaction in school was not actually examined in the present study, the results from the turn-taking analysis and the analysis of so-called school speech acts appear to indicate that communication habits within the High family correspond more closely to those of the school than do the communication habits in the Low family. The communication habits in Wientje High's family are not better or worse of themselves, but at school she will be at an advantage in relation to Mieke Low.

For an interpretation of the analysis of directives in the light of participation in school interaction, it would be necessary to analyse more aspects of the question than was possible in this brief report.

As we mentioned previously, results cannot be generalised to broader categories of children; this in any case is not the goal of this study. It is the aim of this study to derive a better understanding of the possible variation in communication habits with which children grow up. The children are chosen from different socio-economic backgrounds for heuristic reasons; not to permit generalisations about social class. The study of these two children, in respect to variables about which very little was known until recently, constitutes a starting point for the development of a typology of interaction styles. The practical relevance of the study is to show some of the variation in conversational style with which teachers have to deal in the classroom.

## Notes to Chapter 6

1. The investigation has been carried out in the Department of General Linguistics, University of Nijmegen, Nijmegen. Financial support was obtained from the research pool of the University of Nijmegen. Thanks are due to J. Niskie, P. Stringer and H.M. Buunk-Kleiweg for their contribution to the translation of this paper.
2. This dichotomy is not meant to be an adequate description of reality. It is a conceptualisation of the problem that needs to be nuanced by empirical research.
3. When we applied a test, it was the $\chi^2$ test. This test only makes sense when the observations are independent from one another. By means of a technique called 'autocorrelation' we investigated whether the data met this condition (see Huls, 1982). The results did not give reason to apply a modified $\chi^2$ test (analogous to Altham, 1979). I am grateful to Dr M.A. van't Hof for his contribution to the statistical analysis of the material.

## References

Altham, P.M.E. 1979, Detecting relationships between categorical variables observed over time: a problem of deflating a chi-squared statistic, *Applied Statistics* 28:2, 115–25.

Bernstein, B. 1973, *Class, Codes and Control Vol. 1, Theoretical Studies towards a Sociology of Language*. St. Albans, Herts: Paladin.

Ervin-Tripp, S., 1976, Is Sybil there? The structure of some American English directives, *Language in Society*, 5, 25–66.

Ervin-Tripp, S. & Mitchell-Kernan, C. (eds) 1977, *Child Discourse*. London: Academic Press.

Garvey, C. 1975, Requests and responses in children's speech, *Journal of Child Language*, 2, 41–63.

Ginsburg, H., 1972, *The Myth of the Deprived Child; Poor Children's Intellect and Education*. Englewood Cliffs, NJ: Prentice Hall.

Gumperz, J. (ed.) 1982, *Language and Social Identity*. Cambridge: Cambridge University Press.

Hess, R. D. & Shipman V. C. 1967, Cognitive elements in maternal behavior. In J. P. Hill (ed), *Minnesota Symposia on Child Psychology*, Vol.1. Minneapolis: University of Minnesota Press, 57–81.

Huls, E. 1982, Taalgebruik in het gezin en sociale ongelijkheid; een interactioneel sociolinguistisch onderzoek. PhD dissertation, Nijmegen.

— 1984, Man en vrouw: gelijkwaardige gesprekspartners? *Nederlands tijdschrift voor de psychologie*, 39, 385–95.

Labov, W. 1972, *Language in the Inner City*. Philadelphia: University of Pennsylvania Press.

Ochs, E. & Schieffelin, B. B. (eds), 1979, *Developmental Pragmatics*. New York: Academic Press.

Roger, D. B. & Schumacher, A., 1983, Effects of individual differences on dyadic conversational strategies, *Journal of Personality and Social Psychology*, 45:3, 700–05.

Sacks, H. 1972, On the analyzability of stories by children. In J. Gumperz & D. Hymes (eds), *Directions in Sociolinguistics*. New York: Holt, Rinehart and Winston, 325–45.

Sacks, H., Schegloff, E. A. & Jefferson, G. 1974, A simplest systematics for the organisation of turn-taking for conversation, *Language*, 50, 696–735.

Searle, J. R. 1975, Indirect speech acts. In P. Cole & J. R. Morgan (eds), *Syntax and Semantics Vol. 3: Speech Acts*. New York: Academic Press, 59–82.

Sinclair, J. McH. & Coulthard, R. M., 1975, *Towards an Analysis of Discourse: the English used by Teachers and Pupils*. London: Oxford University Press.

West, C. & Zimmerman, D. H. 1982, Conversation analysis. In K. R. Scherer & P. Ekman (eds), *Handbook of Methods in Nonverbal Behaviour Research*. Cambridge: Cambridge University Press, 506–42.

ZIMMERMAN, D. H. & WEST, C. 1975, Sex roles, interruptions and silences in conversation. In B. THORNE & N. HENLEY (eds), *Language and Sex: Difference and Dominance*. Rowley, MA: Newbury House, 105–29.

# SECTION 3: Transcription procedures

## Introduction

Most studies of interpersonal communication are based on a transcription made from either an audio-tape or video-tape record. Making a valid transcription which will adequately reflect the complexity of human communication presents researchers from diverse disciplines with a common problem. In this section, three chapters on transcription are presented by a psychologist, a sociologist and two linguists.

## The psychological approach

In Chapter 1 of this volume, Roger & Bull described the distinctive approach of experimental social psychologists to research on interpersonal communication, with its heavy emphasis on experimentation, quantification and the use of inferential statistics. A natural consequence of a quantitative approach to the study of communication is the need for categorisation. If the experimenter wishes to compare communication under different experimental conditions, he needs to establish independent categories into which different communicative events can be classified. Thus, an additional feature of the social psychological approach to the study of interpersonal communication has been a preoccupation with the development of scoring systems. In order to illustrate the psychological approach to transcription, Peter Bull discusses in Chapter 7 a number of coding systems which he and his colleagues have devised for classifying both speech and non-verbal behaviour.

In the first section of this chapter, two systems are described for the transcription of speech: one a form of content analysis, the other a system for categorising interruptions and simultaneous speech. The first of these, entitled Conversational Exchange Analysis (CEA) (Thomas, Bull & Roger, 1982) is coded along three dimensions, referred to as activity, type and focus. Activity describes the way in which information is exchanged in conversation (e.g. whether it is offered or requested); type describes the sort of information which is exchanged (e.g. beliefs, personal details); focus is used to indicate who is being described and from whom the description emanates (e.g. self, other). The system for describing interruptions and simultaneous speech (Roger, Bull & Smith, 1988) enables the observer to distinguish between interruptions and listener responses, and also to distinguish between 14 different types of interruption.

In the second section of the chapter, Bull describes a system for coding non-verbal behaviour (the Body Movement Scoring System; see Bull, 1981, 1987). In this system, a basic distinction is made between movements which involve contact with an object or part of the body and those movements which do not involve any such contact. Non-contact acts are described in terms of the various movements which are possible from each of the major joints of the body. Body-contact and object-contact acts are described in terms of the way the contact is made (e.g. touching, grasping, scratching), the part of the body which makes the contact and the part of the body or object with which contact is made.

In describing these systems, Bull points out a number of features which they share in common. Thus, they have all been developed from earlier coding procedures; for example, CEA was based in part on a system devised by Morley & Stephenson (1977) entitled Conference Process Analysis (CPA). It can also be argued that each of the three coding systems described in this chapter possesses a number of advantages over its predecessors. CPA was specifically designed to investigate bargaining in industrial settings, whereas CEA provides a more general system which can be applied in a much wider range of social situations. Similarly, the system for coding interruptions and simultaneous speech (Roger, Bull & Smith, 1988) distinguishes between many more types of interruption than any of its predecessors (e.g. Ferguson, 1977).

However, although coding procedures become progressively more sophisticated and detailed over time, they do not necessarily have to be used at a fine-grained level of analysis. For example, the Body Movement Scoring System enables the observer to make extremely detailed descriptions of movement, but can also be used in a much more general way. If the researcher is interested in hand movements, he might simply classify them into contact or non-contact hand movements, or he might further classify non-contact movements just according to the point of articulation involved (shoulders, elbow, wrist, fingers) and contact movements just according to the type of activity employed (touch, grasp, rub, scratch, etc.). The three coding systems described in Bull's chapter are all hierarchical: they can be used at a general level if the observer is interested in categorising broad classes of events, but can also be used to provide highly detailed descriptions if the observer considers this more appropriate.

Nevertheless, the advantage of using a fine-grained level of analysis is that it serves as an invaluable aid to the perception of events. For example, the system for classifying simultaneous speech and interruptions enables the researcher to distinguish between 14 different types of interruption, which are by no means readily apparent to the untrained observer. This in turn enables the researcher to pose questions about the relative effectiveness of different types of interruption strategies, which both enhances our understanding of interpersonal communication and has immediate practical applications for training in communication skills. Bull concludes that typologies are essential if we are to be able to generalise about the fine details of interpersonal communication: such typologies must be both sophisticated and sensitive to the data which they are intended to represent if we are to acquire a sophisticated understanding of the intricacies of interpersonal communication.

## The approach of phonetics and conversation analysis

In contrast to the psychological approach, the two remaining chapters in this section are concerned not with classifying conversation into pre-existing category systems, but with ways in which the details of conversation (including sound, content and structure) can be represented as faithfully as possible in transcription. To this end, conversation analysts have developed extremely detailed conventions for making transcriptions. One primary reason given for this approach is that it provides readers with an opportunity to check for themselves the adequacy of the claims being made. Thus, Sacks, Schegloff & Jefferson (1974) devised a number of conventions to indicate the sequential structure of utterances in conversation: a double oblique sign (//) indicates the point at which a current speaker's talk is overlapped by the talk of another, while an equals sign (=) refers to what they call 'latching', where there is no interval between the end of one person's utterance and the start of another. Another convention is that punctuation markers are not used as grammatical symbols, but to represent intonation. For example, a colon indicates that the prior syllable is prolonged; underscoring indicates various forms of stress; a short dash indicates a 'cut off' of the prior word or sound. A glossary of these symbols appears at the end of Chapter 8.

The most striking feature of transcriptions produced by conversation analysts is that standard spelling is ignored in order to reproduce on paper as exactly as possible the way the conversation sounds. For example, 'back in a minute' becomes 'back inna minnit', while 'lighting a fire in Perry's cellar' becomes 'lightin' a fiyuh in Perry's celluh' (Sacks, Schegloff & Jefferson, 1974). Jefferson has even been concerned to devise highly detailed ways of representing different kinds of laughter; in one excerpt, a laugh is transcribed as 'ihh hh heh heh huh', while in another excerpt a different form of laughter is transcribed as 'hhhhHA HA HA HA' (Jefferson, 1984). Sacks, Schegloff & Jefferson (1974:734) write that their aim is 'to get as much of the actual sound as possible into our transcripts, while still making them accessible to linguistically unsophisticated readers'. Whether this aim is actually achieved is very much open to question; for example, one of their extracts reads 'I'd a' cracked up 'f duh friggin (gla-i(h)f y'kno(h)w it) sm(h)a(h) heh heh', which in the editors' opinion seems totally inaccessible, even with reference to the glossary of symbols which Jefferson provides.

The conventions used by conversation analysts for transcribing speech are amply illustrated in the contribution of Gail Jefferson (Chapter 8), which presents a number of excerpts transcribed in conversation-analytic orthography, as well as a glossary of transcript symbols. In this chapter, Jefferson attempts to uncover what she calls a 'standard maximum' of one second for silences occurring during conversation. To do this, she carries out a series of analyses on a large corpus of data, extracting all silences with a duration of at least nine-tenths of a second. What her results show is that the majority of these pauses — 75% in one particular analysis — conform to the 'standard maximum' duration of approximately one second; Jefferson sees this standard maximum as the outcome of the variable significance which people attach to pauses of different length in conversation.

Jefferson's analysis is based on transcripts of conversations, but she also refers to the differences in pause lengths typically occurring in reading. She concludes in her chapter that while the duration of silences is more variable in conversation than in reading, the metric is none the less present in both forms of speech. However, it is less strictly adhered to in conversation, and Jefferson proposes that there may be an 'alternate metric' where speakers will typically commence with one-second pauses but then modify the duration of their subsequent pauses in a variety of ways.

The final contribution in this section (Chapter 9) is by two linguists, John Kelly and John Local. They show a similar concern with achieving as accurate a representation of speech as possible. Kelly and Local put forward the principle that transcription should allow the analyst to register 'all the discriminable matter in the spoken medium of language', including such features as muscular contractions of the cheeks, or larynx movements, together with the dynamics of amplitude, rhythm, and so on. However, they are extremely critical of existing systems of phonetic notation, such as the International Phonetic Association (IPA) alphabet. The IPA alphabet segments speech into phonemes, with the consequent tendency for people to assume that phonemes 'reside inside the material as registered, much like the statue in the marble'. Kelly and Local maintain that this segmentation of speech into phonemes is arbitrary and selective; the IPA alphabet is not useful for their purposes, because it is the result of a particular kind of analysis rather than a tool for describing speech.

Kelly and Local's own work can be seen as an attempt to implement one of the basic assumptions of conversation analysis, namely, that 'no order of detail in conversational interaction can be dismissed a priori as disorderly, accidental or irrelevant' (Heritage, Chapter 2 of this volume). They praise conversation analysts for the close attention that they pay in their transcripts to pausal phenomena, to audible respiratory activity and to the points at which overlapping talk begins and ends. In other respects however, they find the transcriptions inconsistent, arbitrary and sporadic, for example, in reflecting features of tempo, pitch, loudness, vowel quality and voice quality. Kelly and Local's procedures constitute an attempt to overcome what they see as shortcomings in both conversation analysis and conventional phonetic transcription. They claim that their own techniques can make available to the analyst aspects of talk which other transcription procedures are unable to reflect.

## A comparison of different approaches to transcription

Comparing these different approaches to transcribing conversation, an important distinction that emerges is the degree to which researchers from different disciplines attempt to represent the sound as well as the content of speech. Phoneticians by the nature of their discipline are concerned to represent vocal sounds; conversation analysts are also preoccupied with achieving as faithful as possible a depiction of all the potentially significant features of speech, including sound, content and structure. However, as Kelly and Local have pointed out, conversation-analytic transcriptions do not adequately reflect features such as tempo, pitch, loudness, vowel quality and voice quality.

Psychologists, in contrast, have been less concerned with achieving a precise account of vocal and verbal utterances than with classifying utterances into predetermined category systems. When making this classification, the researchers do make use of phonetic and structural information, but typically do not attempt to incorporate it into the transcript. Because this involves a substantial element of judgement on the part of the researcher, a reliability study is normally carried out in which another observer independently scores a segment or segments of tape. The protocols of the two observers are then correlated to determine the level of inter-observer agreement, and the research does not proceed until a satisfactory level of agreement had been established. As was discussed in Section 1, psychologists' concern with classification can be seen as reflecting their belief in the value of quantification as a corner-stone of psychological science.

The analysis of non-verbal behaviour has been primarily the province of psychologists; a striking feature of this work is that psychologists have shown the same attention to fine detail in the representation of non-verbal communication as conversation analysts have with speech. Thus, it should be possible to reconstruct faithfully the visual appearance of a sequence of movement from a transcript of non-verbal behaviour derived from a system like the Body Movement Scoring System. In contrast, conversation analysts have tended to pay relatively little attention to the study of non-verbal behaviour. Indeed, much of their earlier work was based on the study of telephone conversations, in order to simplify the work of analysis through 'the automatic elimination of non-vocal conduct as an object of participants' orientations' (see Chapter 2 of this volume).

Where conversation analysts have attempted to include non-verbal behaviour in their research, they have done so seemingly in ignorance of much of the extensive psychological literature on this topic. For example, Goodwin (1981) includes an analysis of what he calls 'gaze' in the research reported in his book. In fact, Goodwin's observations are actually based on head orientation rather than on the detailed orientation of the eyes, on the grounds that it was frequently impossible accurately to monitor individual eye movements (Goodwin, 1981:53). Goodwin further justifies this on the grounds that for participants, orientation of the head is one of the central components of the activity of gazing. Nevertheless, given the attention conversation analysts typically pay to the minutiae of verbal interaction, it is surprising that Goodwin should treat head orientation as indicative of gaze, when clearly they are not actually interchangeable. Moreover, studies in experimental social psychology laboratories have demonstrated that it *is* possible to achieve an accurate representation of eye contact, with the aid of the techniques of close-up video-recording (Rime & McCusker, 1976; see also Section 2 of this volume).

There are clearly substantial differences between the transcription procedures employed by the exponents of different disciplines, but it is the editors' view that these differences are not necessarily irreconcilable. Instead, these procedures might be placed along a continuum depending upon the detail of analysis desired by the investigator. For example, the systems which psychologists have developed for the transcription of non-verbal behaviour can be used at different levels of analysis. In the case of the Body Movement Scoring System, it is possible to divide hand gestures simply into contact and non-contact movements, or to classify them further according to the type of activity for contact movements and the type of hand shape for non-contact movements. At a still finer level of analysis, information can be included on the various movements which are possible from each of the major joints of the body, or for contact acts on the part of the body which makes the contact and the object or part of the body with which contact is made. Similarly, the transcription procedures used by conversation analysts could be implemented at differing levels of analysis: in either case, it simply depends on the level of detail which is required by the investigator.

The level of detail is in turn related to the issue of sampling. Conversation analysts regard individual cases as representative of the language community from which they are drawn, hence they are content to carry out detailed analyses based on excerpts from one or two conversations. Psychologists, because of their greater concern with the validity of any generalisations that might be made from the analysis, have tended to employ a lower level of detail in order to sample a greater number of conversations.

In fact, the level of analysis typically used by psychologists almost inevitably follows from any attempt to achieve more extensive sampling. This point can be illustrated by some recent research on political speeches carried out within the framework of conversation analysis. Initially, Atkinson (1983, 1984) used standard techniques of conversation analysis in the study of political rhetoric, presenting a number of excerpts to demonstrate that particular rhetorical formats (such as the contrast or the three-part list) are highly effective in evoking audience applause. Subsequently, in response to the criticism that Atkinson's observations may be unrepresentative of political speeches in general, Heritage & Greatbatch (1986) studied all 476 speeches delivered at the three British annual party political conferences held in 1981. With such a large sample of data, the approach they adopted was to use a system of classification in which they identified different rhetorical formats, counted the frequency of those formats and determined how successful they were in evoking applause.

In fact, a similar point might be made about the chapter by Jefferson in this section: in order to discover whether there was any regularity in the duration of pauses occurring in conversation, Jefferson was obliged to examine all cases occurring in her data. The level of analysis employed in both of these studies was thus much more similar to that typically used by psychologists, and it may be regarded as a natural consequence of the demands of large-sample analyses.

## Conclusion

There are clearly substantial differences between the transcription procedures employed by the exponents of different disciplines. For example, psychologists and conversation analysts differ in the level of detail they employ in the transcription of speech. Psychologists have been criticised for oversimplifying conversation in order to fit it into their preconceived category systems, but this can be seen at least in part as reflecting differences in the level of sampling typically used in these two approaches. On the other hand, conversation analysts have been criticised by phoneticians for being arbitrary and selective in their representation of vocal sounds, and they can also be criticised for not taking sufficient account of non-verbal communication. In fact, in the analysis of non-verbal communication, psychologists typically produce transcriptions as fine-grained as conversational analysts do in their transcription of speech.

In spite of the differences that emerge between the transcriptions made by psychologists, phoneticians and conversation analysts, it is the editors' view that they are not irreconcilable. Instead, they can be seen as reflecting different levels of analysis, and can be placed along a continuum depending upon the level of detail desired by the analyst.

**References**

ATKINSON, M. 1983, Two devices for generating audience approval: a comparative study of public discourses and texts. In K. EHLICH *et al.* (eds), *Connectedness in Sentence, Text and Discourse*. Tilburg: Tilburg papers in Linguistics.

— 1984, *Our Masters' Voices: The Language and Body Language of Politics*. London: Methuen.

BULL, P. E. 1981, Body movement scoring system. In The Social Functions of Speech-related Body Movement, SSRC end-of-grant report, HR 6404/2, pp. 1-16.

— 1987, *Posture and Gesture*. Oxford: Pergamon.

FERGUSON, N. 1977, Simultaneous speech, interruptions and dominance, *British Journal of Social and Clinical Psychology*, 16, 295–302.

GOODWIN, C. 1981, *Conversational Organization: Interaction between Speakers and Hearers*. New York: Academic Press.

HERITAGE, J. C. & GREATBATCH, D. L. 1986, Generating applause: A study of rhetoric and response at party political conferences, *American Journal of Sociology*, 92, 110–57.

JEFFERSON, G. 1984, On the organisation of laughter in talk about troubles. In J. M. ATKINSON & J. C. HERITAGE (eds), *Structures of Social Action: Studies in Conversation Analysis*. Cambridge: Cambridge University Press.

MORLEY, I. E. & STEPHENSON, G. M. 1977, *The Social Psychology of Bargaining*. London: George Allen & Unwin.

RIME, B. & MCCUSKER, L. 1976, Visual behaviour in social interaction: The validity of eye-contact assessments under different conditions of observation, *British Journal of Psychology*, 67, 507–14.

ROGER, D., BULL, P. E. & SMITH, S. 1988, The development of a comprehensive system for classifying interruptions. *Journal of Language and Social Psychology*, 7.

SACKS, H., SCHEGLOFF, E. A. & JEFFERSON, G. 1974, A simplest systematics for the organization of turn-taking for conversation, *Language*, 50, 696–735.

THOMAS, A. P., BULL, P. & ROGER, D. 1982, Conversational exchange analysis, *Journal of Language and Social Psychology*, 1, 141–55.

# 7 Psychological approaches to transcription

PETER BULL
*University of York*

## Introduction

In Chapter 1 of this volume, Bull & Roger described the distinctive approach of experimental social psychologists to research on interpersonal communication, with its heavy emphasis on experimentation, quantification and the use of inferential statistics. A natural consequence of a quantitative approach to the study of communication is the need for categorisation. If the experimenter wishes to compare communication under different experimental conditions, he needs to establish independent categories into which different communicative events can be classified. Thus, an additional feature of the social psychological approach to the study of interpersonal communication has been a preoccupation with the development of scoring systems. The purpose of this chapter is to illustrate psychological approaches to transcription with reference to a number of systems which the author and his colleagues have devised for the transcription both of speech and of non-verbal behaviour.

## Speech

### Content analysis

In psychological approaches to the transcription of speech, a distinction can be drawn between systems which are generally applicable to conversations that occur in any context and those which are restricted to specific situations. An example of a specific system is Conference Process Analysis (CPA), which was developed by Morley & Stephenson (1977). CPA involves dividing transcripts of negotiations into 'acts', which are defined as psychological units each conveying a point, proposition or single thought. Each unit is coded in terms of three dimensions: mode, resource and referent. One category and only one category is attributed to it from a list of categories for each dimension. The mode dimension indicates how information is being exchanged (e.g. offer, seek, etc.); the resource dimension indicates what sort of information is being exchanged (e.g. procedure, settlement point etc.); the referent dimension indicates who is being talked about (e.g. one's own party, opponent, etc.).

CPA was specifically designed to investigate bargaining in industrial settings. However, Thomas, Bull & Roger (1982) used CPA as the basis for a more general system of classification called Conversational Exchange Analysis (CEA). This system is also coded along three dimensions (referred to as activity, type and focus); these dimensions correspond to those devised by Morley & Stephenson, but are intended to be applicable to a wider range of social situations. Thus, the activity dimension refers to how information is made salient in the interaction, such as whether the information is requested or given. Type refers to the sort of information exchanged, such as beliefs or past experiences. Focus describes the referent of the information: for example, one may be referring to one's own opinions or the opinions of a third party. A full list of the speech categories can be found in Thomas, Bull & Roger (1982).

The advantage of CEA is that conversation can be classified along dimensions that are both general and specific: the activity dimension is applicable to a wide range of conversations, whereas the type and focus dimensions are more specific to particular social contexts. For example, the activity dimension of CEA was used by Thomas, Roger & Bull (1983) in a study intended to investigate the sequential structure of informal conversation, employing a Markov chain analysis. (Markov analysis is one of a number of statistical procedures for investigating the sequential organisation of behaviour; issues concerning the analysis of sequencing in conversation are discussed in greater detail in Section 4). The results of this study showed that informal conversation conformed to a first-order Markovian process, in which information concerning the immediately preceding speech act is sufficient to predict the current speech act without requiring further information on earlier speech acts. In addition, the results showed that the offer, reply and dissent categories tend to perpetuate themselves (i.e. an offer is typically followed by another within-turn offer), thereby maintaining the turn for the speaker, whereas the consent, reaction and request categories typically relinquish the speaker turn. Thus, if a listener wishes to retain the listener state, he should use either a reaction, a consent or a request; if he wishes to take the turn, he should use either an offer or a dissent.

Thomas (1985) has also used Markov procedures in a study of informal conversation employing the type dimension of CEA. He found that six type categories — belief, personal experience, explanation, active recognition, example and listener response — formed the basic core of the conversations he studied. In addition, he found that these categories played a significant role in the process of floor apportionment. Thus, if a speaker-switch occurred, the loss of the speaking turn tended to be transient if associated with an active recognition or listener response, but more permanent if associated with any of the other major speech states.

Thomas goes on to point out a number of interesting regularities which may form useful strategies and routines for improving conversational skills. For example, revealing personal details increases the likelihood that the other person will reciprocate with similar information. This forms a useful social strategy, as in the process of getting to know someone: by initially demonstrating a willingness to give personal information about oneself, one predisposes the other person to respond with information of a similar nature. Again, completions, which are acts whereby the listener completes what the other person is saying, have a tendency to act as a subtle method of taking the turn from the other person. In 18% of the cases in Thomas's sample, they led to an immediate long-term change of speaker, and in an additional 31% of cases they led to the first speaker recognising the completion with an active recognition, followed by an immediate switch of speaking turn to the second speaker.

Bull (1986) has used a modified form of the type dimension in a study of the role of hand gesture in political speeches. This investigation was based in part on the work of Atkinson (1983, 1984a, 1984b), who has argued that certain rhetorical devices (such as three-part lists and contrasts) are consistently effective in evoking audience applause. Atkinson has also proposed that skilled use of these devices is characteristic of 'charismatic' speakers (Atkinson, 1984a: 86–123) and that such devices are often to be found in those passages of political speeches which are selected for presentation in the news media (Atkinson, 1984a: 124–63).

An obvious problem with Atkinson's research is the role of speech content; after all, it may be the content of a speech which determines whether or not it is applauded rather than the rhetorical devices which the speaker employs. In the study by this author, a modified form of the CEA type dimension was devised in order to content-analyse a speech by Mr Arthur Scargill (President of the British National Union of Mineworkers). Applause was categorised into sustained and isolated applause: sustained applause refers to clapping from a substantial proportion of the audience, whereas isolated applause refers to claps from just one or two people. The importance of this distinction is that if rhetorical formatting is effective in signalling to the audience when applause is appropriate, then it should be associated with sustained rather than isolated applause.

The results of the content analysis were clearly consistent with the argument that rhetorical devices are effective in evoking applause. A large proportion of the speech by Arthur Scargill was made up of statements critical of other political parties and other external groups, referred to as external attacks (58% of the total number of speech acts). Eighty-six per cent of rhetorically formatted external attacks received sustained applause, in contrast to only 13% of non-formatted external attacks. All the other types of speech act which evoked sustained applause received more sustained applause when rhetorically formatted with the exception only of replies to heckling, of which there were only three examples in the whole speech. In contrast, isolated applause occurred more frequently in response to non-formatted than to formatted types of speech act, again with the exception only of replies to heckling. What the results showed is that although applause is clearly related (not surprisingly) to certain types of speech content, nevertheless the chance of speech receiving sustained applause is greatly increased if it is expressed using appropriate rhetorical devices, thus providing strong support for Atkinson's observations. This content analysis also provided the framework for a detailed study of the role of hand gesture in relation to the content of political speeches, which is discussed later in this chapter with reference to the transcription of non-verbal behaviour.

Thus, CEA can be applied to widely differing social situations, but the type dimension can always be modified to take account of the specific kinds of information which are exchanged in particular social contexts. At the same time, findings from different social situations can be evaluated within a common conceptual framework, leading both to a greater understanding of conversation and to a progressive refinement of the classification system.

### Interruptions and simultaneous speech

Another system has been devised by the author and his colleagues specifically for the purpose of classifying simultaneous speech and interruptions (Roger, Bull & Smith, 1988). Just as CEA represents an elaboration on earlier systems of content analysis, so this typology has been developed from previous systems for classifying interruptions. Thus, Mishler & Waxler (1968) made a distinction between successful and unsuccessful interruptions, but Ferguson (1977) argued that so broad a classification combines interruptive behaviours that are empirically discriminable. She presented an alternative system, comprising four categories: simple, butting-in and silent interruptions, and overlaps.

Each of these categories may be contrasted with what she calls a perfect speaker-switch, which occurs when a change in speaker is effected in such a way that there is no simultaneous speech and the first speaker's utterance appears to be complete in every way. Thus, a simple interruption differs from a perfect speaker-switch because it involves both simultaneous speech and a break in continuity as the second speaker prevents the first speaker from completing an utterance. In an overlap, the first speaker completes the utterance, but the second speaker starts speaking just before the first speaker has finished, so that simultaneous speech occurs. In a butting-in interruption, simultaneous speech occurs, but in contrast to a simple interruption, the interruptor does not take the floor, but instead breaks off before completing the utterance. In silent interruptions, the first speaker's utterance is incomplete, but there is a pause before the second speaker takes over, so there is no simultaneous speech: hence, this non-fluency is called a 'silent interruption'.

However, despite her claims, Ferguson's categories do not provide a significant improvement over Mishler and Waxler's typology. Simple and butting-in interruptions correspond closely to Mishler and Waxler's successful and unsuccessful interruption types; they do not represent any substantial modification of their work. Overlaps, although potentially disruptive to the smooth flow of conversation, may also simply reflect speaker enthusiasm or involvement, and so should not necessarily be seen as intrinsically interruptive. Ferguson's final category, silent interruptions, presents special problems, since it is based on the assumption that because an utterance is incomplete, the speaker intended to continue; however, conversations do not strictly follow the rules of standard grammar, and a speaker may tail off simply because he has finished what he wants to say.

The limitations of these interruption typologies led the author and his colleagues to devise a new system for classifying interruptions and simultaneous speech (Roger, Bull & Smith, 1988). This system takes the form of a binary flow chart (Figure 7.1), and the simplest way to present it is to work through each level of the chart in sequence.

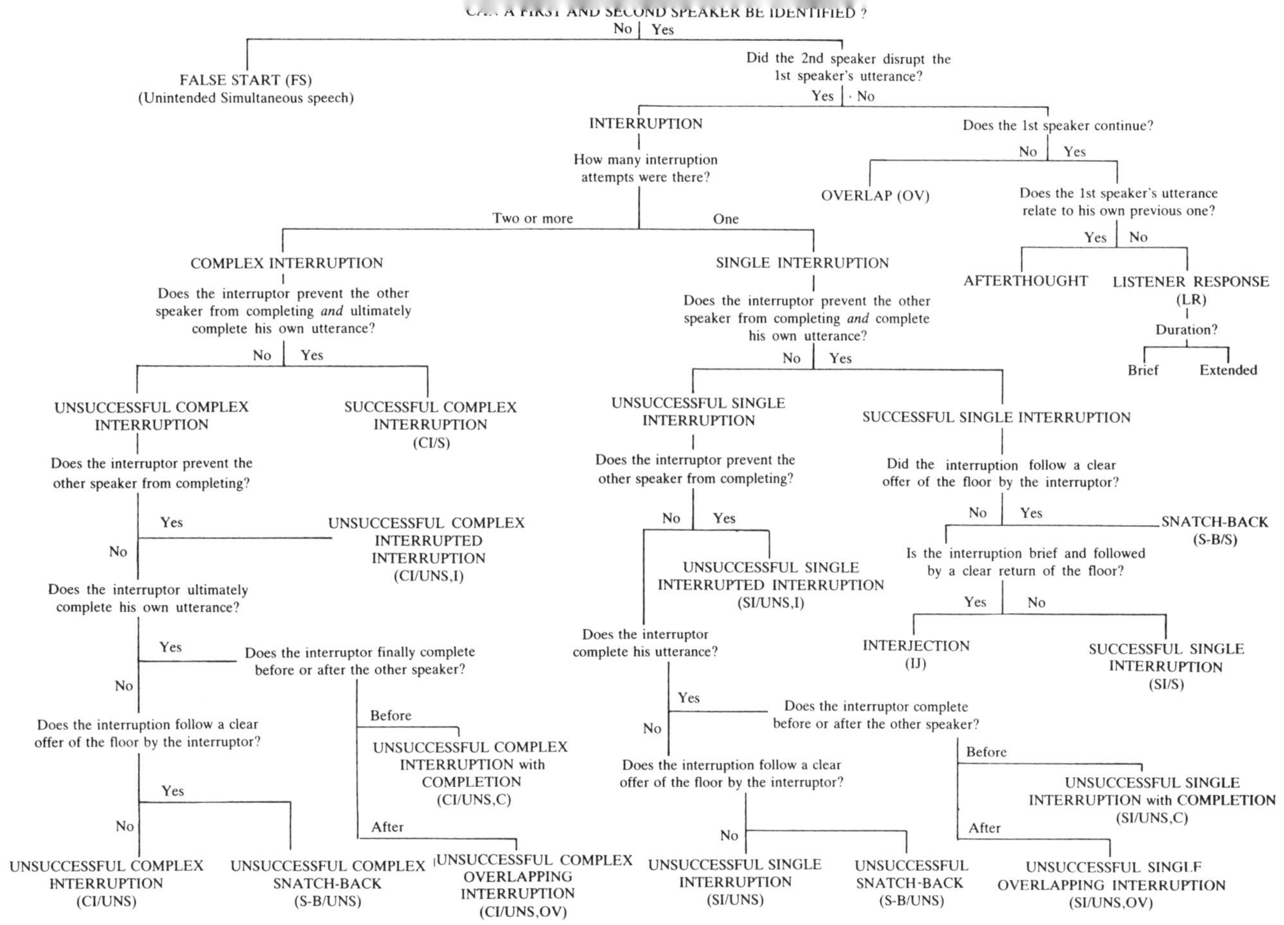


FIGURE 7.1 *Classification of interruptions and simultaneous speech*
*Source*: Roger, Bull & Smith (1988)

The initial question asked is whether a first and a second speaker can be identified. If the answer to this question is no, then the event is labelled a false start, or unintended simultaneous speech. Such events are typically followed by some form of repair, for example, a pause followed by apology and a sequence of mutual floor-offering.

If a first and second speaker can be identified, then the next step is to ask whether the second speaker disrupted the first speaker's utterance. If the answer to this question is no, then the chart leads into non-interruptive simultaneous speech, the form of which is determined by whether or not the first speaker continues with his utterance. If the first speaker does not continue, then the event is classified as an overlap; if the first speaker does continue, then the event is classified as either a listener response (brief or extended) or as an afterthought. Listener responses are simply acknowledgement or attention signals on the part of the listener; an afterthought represents a sort of coda attached to the first speaker's utterance in the form of phrases such as 'or something' or 'well, anyway'. The second speaker's utterance is not regarded as interruptive if he starts to speak before or during the afterthought, because the first speaker is regarded as having effectively completed his turn before the afterthought occurs.

If the observer considers the second speaker did disrupt the first speaker's utterance, then the event is classified as an interruption. Interruptions are further subdivided according to the number of interruption attempts: whether there is only one attempt (a single interruption) or whether there are two or more attempts (a complex interruption). For single interruptions, the first question is whether the interruptor prevents the other speaker from completing his utterance and ultimately completes his own utterance. If the answer to this question is yes, the event is classified as a successful interruption. Successful single interruptions are then clarified by the question whether the interruption followed a clear offer of a turn by the interruptor. If the answer to this question is yes, then the interruption is categorised as a snatch-back (because the interruptor offered the other person a speaking turn, and then literally snatched it back!). If the answer to this question is no, then the interruption is classified either as an interjection (if the interruption is brief and followed by a clear return of the floor), or as a straightforward successful single interruption.

A number of distinctions are also made between different types of unsuccessful single interruption. If the interruptor prevents the first speaker from completing his utterance but fails to complete his own utterance, then the event is classified as an unsuccessful single interrupted interruption (because the interruptor's attempted interruption is in turn interrupted by the other speaker!). If the interruptor fails to prevent the other speaker from completing his utterance, but does succeed in completing his own utterance, then the event is classified either as an unsuccessful single overlapping interruption (if the interruptor completes after the other speaker) or as an unsuccessful single interruption with completion (if the interruptor completes before the other speaker). If the interruptor neither prevents the first speaker from completing his utterance nor completes his own utterance, then the event is classified as an unsuccessful single interruption, unless it followed a clear offer of the turn by the interruptor, in which case it is classified as an unsuccessful snatch-back.

For complex interruptions, the first question is also whether the interruptor prevents the other speaker from completing his utterance and ultimately completes his own utterance. If the answer to this question is yes, then the event is classified as a successful complex interruption. If the interruptor prevents the first speaker from completing his utterance, but does not succeed in completing his own utterance, then the event is classified as an unsuccessful complex interrupted interruption (because the interruptor's attempted complex interruption is in turn interrupted by the other speaker!). If the interruptor does not succeed in preventing the first speaker from completing his utterance, but does succeed in completing his own utterance, then the event is classified as either an unsuccessful complex overlapping interruption (if the interruptor completes after the other speaker) or as an unsuccessful complex interruption with completion (if the interruptor completes before the first speaker completes). Finally, if the interruptor neither prevents the other speaker from completing nor completes his own utterance, the event is classified as an unsuccessful complex interruption, unless it follows a clear offer of the floor by the interruptor, in which case it is classified as an unsuccessful complex snatch-back.

Compared with the typology devised by Ferguson, this system allows the researcher to make many more distinctions between different types of interruption. For example, in Ferguson's system, there is no way of distinguishing between single and complex interruptions. Repeated attempts at interruption have to be treated as independent events, which fails to capture the fact that such events are related and constitute part of a sequence. In the system devised by Roger, Bull & Smith, single and complex interruptions are distinguished, and distinctions are also made between a number of different types of both complex and simple interruption. The advantage of making these distinctions is that it then becomes possible for the researcher to investigate different types of interruptive strategy. For example, in Roger, Bull & Smith's system, three types of successful single interruption are distinguished: interjections, snatch-backs and successful interruptions. Using this scoring procedure, it is possible to investigate the relative effectiveness of these different types of interruptive strategy. The system has already been used in a detailed study of interruptions in political interviews (Bull & Mayer, 1988). Far from being a Procrustean bed into which the data are arbitrarily forced, the system allows the researcher to make fine distinctions between different types of interruption and hence to acquire a greater understanding of the role of interruptions in conversation.

## Non-verbal behaviour

The author has also been involved in devising systems for transcribing and classifying non-verbal behaviour. Most contemporary studies of non-verbal communication have used either film or video tape as the main technique of observation. Studies have also been carried out where an observer takes a 'live' record of behaviour, often concealed from subjects behind a one-way screen, which permits the observer to see without being seen. But this approach has a number of real disadvantages in comparison with recording on video tape or film. If the observer misses any behaviours, there is no way of going back to rectify the omission. Moreover, a number of bodily movements (especially, for example, movements of the hands and arms) are simply too rapid to be noted by an observer without the aid of repeated viewing of a particular behavioural sequence, or sometimes without the use of slow-motion replay facilities. Another advantage of film or tape is that the duration of a particular behaviour can be timed much more precisely from frame numbers superimposed on the recording. Frame numbering is useful both as a method of referencing particular sequences of behaviour through the unique number given to each frame and as a method of measuring the duration of any given behaviour in real time; it is certainly far more accurate than timing movements with a stop-watch.

However, the main disadvantage of all visual methods of analysing body movement is that they rely on a human observer to code that behaviour accurately into different categories. It is customary to check an observer's scoring by carrying out a reliability study in which his coding of behaviour is correlated with that of an independent observer. Nevertheless, the procedure of coding behaviour from film or tape is still exceedingly time-consuming and fatiguing, and it would clearly be desirable if fully automated systems of recording behaviour were available.

Unfortunately, where such systems do exist, they usually raise different kinds of problems. For example, Hadar *et al.* (1983, 1984) have used a polarised-light goniometer as a way of studying head movement. This operates by projecting strong light from a single source through a plane polariser material and a rapidly rotating disc on to a photosensor (or photosensors) attached to the subject. The reflected light is automatically processed by the goniometer to provide immediate information on properties of movement such as its rate, duration, range and speed. One particular advantage of this apparatus is its sensitivity to small movements, which a human observer working from video tape might miss or find very difficult to classify. Another advantage is its precision — by taking direct readings of speech amplitude, it is possible to make fine measurements of the relationship between head movements and speech. A disadvantage of the system is that it does not allow a detailed description to be given of the visual appearance of particular movements. An additional problem is of course the intrusiveness of attaching photosensors to the body. In certain circumstances where one might wish to make observations of body movement, this may simply not be possible; there is also the further difficulty that their use (even when practical) may in some way affect people's social behaviour, through making them aware that it is their body movement which is the focus of the investigation.

Other techniques for measuring posture and gesture involve making a behavioural record through tape or film and analysing that record through some kind of coding system. For example, Friesen, Ekman & Wallbott (1980) describe a relatively simple system for classifying hand movements, which distinguishes between emblems, illustrators and manipulators. Emblems are symbolic hand gestures with a verbal meaning known to the members of a particular social group. Illustrators are hand movements which follow the rhythm and content of speech, and typically do not involve contact with an object or part of the body. Manipulators can be divided into those movements which satisfy self or bodily needs (self-manipulators) and those movements in which some instrumental task is performed (object-manipulators). The system also records which hand is involved in the activity and which part of the body is manipulated. One major problem with these distinctions is that the observer is asked to make an inference concerning the function of a particular aspect of behaviour, for example, to judge whether a movement does actually follow the rhythm and content of speech and hence is in fact an illustrator. While it is certainly clear that some hand movements involve touching the body, that others involve touching objects and others neither, it would be much simpler to refer to these movements as 'body-contact', 'object-contact' and 'non-contact' movements, rather than to ask the observer to make any judgements about their hypothesised social or psychological functions. A more fundamental problem with this system of categories is that no attempt is made to describe the visual appearance of particular movements, a feature which is important if we are to discuss visual communication.

Mehrabian (1968) has described a slightly more elaborate procedure for coding bodily posture. For example, he proposes that relaxation of the legs can be coded on a four-point scale ranging from a symmetrical stance of the legs with insteps touching to an asymmetrical stance of the legs with both feet resting flat on the floor. The main problem with Mehrabian's system is that it is highly selective and omits many common forms of bodily posture.

Much more elaborate systems have been proposed by Birdwhistell (1971) and Frey & von Cranach (1973). Birdwhistell's system has a very detailed range of categories, but it is not clear how these categories were derived nor how they should be applied in practice. For example, it is not clear whether the categories refer to movements or to positions or both. Nor is it clear whether the categories are intended to be independent of one another, or whether one behavioural unit can be described in terms of more than one category. Finally, no reliability data are reported for the system, so it is not clear how successfully it has been applied in practice.

Frey & von Cranach (1973) are much more explicit with regard to these questions. They describe a system whereby the positions of the body are scored at different time intervals. The positions of the head and trunk are defined in relation to three main axes, dissecting the body from front to back, side to side and top to bottom. Hand positions are classified according to whether 11 spatial areas (e.g. head, hand or desk) are touched by the hands. Foot positions are classified according to whether four parts of the foot (heels, toes, inner and outer edge) are touching one of five areas (floor, chair, thigh, lower part of leg or foot). Movements are scored by assessing the position of the body at different time intervals, so that the system is essentially static, characterising all body movements in terms of a series of positions. The main difficulty with this approach is that it destroys the natural structure of body movement. For example, in Frey & von Cranach's system it would not be possible to describe a head nod as a single behavioural unit; instead, it would have to be described in terms of three positions (head upright, head dropped, head upright) and hence the basic unity of the movement is lost.

In the Body Movement Scoring System devised by this author (Bull,

1981, 1987), the basic unit of analysis is the single movement act. Hence, the system is dynamic, not static; it describes gestures as a series of movements rather than as a series of positions. Where static positions (postures) do occur, these are described in terms of the body movements which bring about those changes in posture. A basic distinction is made between those movements which involve contact with an object or part of the body and those movements which do not involve any such contact. Body-contact and object-contact acts are described in terms of the way the contact is made (e.g. touching, grasping, scratching), the part of the body which makes the contact (e.g. palm of hand, back of hand, fingertips) and the body part or object with which contact is made (e.g. thigh, chair arm). Any change in one of these three elements is regarded as starting a new movement act.

Non-contact movements are described in terms of the various movements which are possible from each of the major joints of the body (neck, spine, hips, knees, ankles, toes, shoulder girdle, shoulders, elbows, wrists and fingers). For example, the forearm can flex, extend, rotate inwards and rotate outwards. The head can lower, raise, nod (lower and raise), tilt to one side, rock (tilt from side to side), turn, shake (turn from side to side) and rotate. Some of these movements can occur in combination from the same point of articulation; for example, the forearm may be extended and rotated outwards simultaneously. Some movements may be embedded in other movements; for example, a person may nod his head while turning it away from another person. The basic unit of analysis for non-contact acts is movement along one axis; if the axis of movement is changed, then a new movement act is scored. A full list of the body movement categories is to be found in Bull (1981, 1987).

This system has been used in the study of the role of gesture both in informal conversation (Bull & Connelly, 1985), political speeches (Bull, 1986) and in television news broadcasts (Bull, 1987). In the study by Bull & Connelly, inter-observer reliability was tested, showing a *k*-coefficient of agreement of 0.81 between the main scorer and the project investigator for the arms/hands (based on 120 behavioural categories from three different subjects) and of 0.75 for the head (based on 68 behavioural categories from four different subjects). Since comparatively few observations were made of trunk and leg/feet movements, these were all scored by both scorers, disagreements being resolved by discussion. An analysis was also carried out of the way in which body movement is related to vocal stress: video tapes were made of opposite-sex pairs of students in conversation with one another, and body movements related to tonic stress were selected for each subject from the first 15 of such movements occurring in the first, second and final third of the conversation. For the 12 subjects so observed, a mean 90.5% of the tonic stresses within the segments of tape scored were accompanied by body movement (the total number of tonic stresses within the segments of tape scored being 277). The results also showed that it is not just movements of the hands and arms which accompany tonic stress, but movements of all parts of the body. Of the total number of 540 movements observed in relation to tonic stress, 35% were movements of the head, 15% movements of the trunk, 34% movements of the hands/arms and 16% movements of the legs/feet.

These results were of interest for a number of reasons. The finding that most tonic stresses are accompanied by body movement suggests that body movement may constitute a fourth component (in addition to pitch, loudness and duration) of the way in which stress is communicated in speech. Research workers (e.g. Condon & Ogston, 1966; Freedman & Hoffman, 1967) have frequently commented on how certain body movements appear to be closely related to the rhythm of speech, but the analysis reported here suggests much more specifically one way in which body movement is related to speech, namely, in terms of its relationship to tonic stress.

The Body Movement Scoring System was also used in the study of political speeches described above (Bull, 1986) and in a study of news broadcasts (Bul!, 1987). The study of news broadcasts showed that two television newsreaders frequently employed characteristic changes of posture when they moved on to a new item of news, thus showing that body movement can be used to mark out higher-order semantic units such as topic change. The study of political speeches showed that hand gesture is closely related to intonation, both in terms of vocal stress and tone group boundaries. The analysis of the speech by Mr Arthur Scargill also showed that gesture was closely synchronised to rhetorical devices used to arouse applause, while he also frequently used hand gesture to quell the applause. In fact, he actually seemed to conduct his audience: his gestures both accompany rhetorical devices which evoke applause and curtail the applause once it has been aroused.

The Body Movement Scoring System is intended to provide a comprehensive system for describing posture and gesture in the context of seated conversations. In contrast to the procedure of Frey & von Cranach (1973), the Body Movement Scoring System uses movements rather than positions as the basic unit of analysis; hence, it is possible through these categories to capture the natural structure of body movement. In contrast to the system described by Friesen, Ekman & Wallbott (1980), no assumptions are made regarding the social functions of body movement; the system is intended simply to describe the physical appearance of particular movements, their social significance to be ascertained by empirical research. The main problem with the system is the time-consuming and laborious nature of transcribing movement descriptions from video tape. Nevertheless, it retains the advantage of being unobtrusive, in contrast to polarised-light goniometry which, although technically highly sophisticated, still requires the attachment of light reflectors to the limbs; this is impracticable in many of the naturally occurring situations where one might wish to observe body movement.

## Conclusions

In this chapter, three systems devised by the author and his colleagues for classifying different aspects of communication have been described. One feature which these systems have in common is that they have all been developed from earlier coding procedures; in each case, they also possess a number of advantages over their predecessors. Thus, Conversation Exchange Analysis is applicable to a wider range of situations than Conference Process Analysis, while the interruption typology allows one to discriminate between many more different types of interruption than in the earlier systems of Ferguson (1977) and Mishler & Waxler (1968). Again, the Body Movement Scoring System is a comprehensive coding procedure which enables the observer to describe the natural structure of movement through categories which make no assumptions about the social significance of body movement.

However, although these coding procedures have become progressively more sophisticated and detailed over time, they do not necessarily have to be used at this fine-grained level of analysis. Thus, the Body Movement Scoring System enables the observer to make extremely detailed descriptions of movement, but can also be used in a much more general way. For example, if the researcher is interested in hand movements, he might simply classify them into contact or non-contact hand movements, or he might further classify non-contact movements just according to the point of articulation involved (shoulder, elbow, wrist, fingers) and contact movements just according to the type of activity employed (touch, grasp, rub, scratch, etc.). The coding systems presented here are hierarchical: they can be used at a general level if the observer is interested in categorising broad classes of events, but can also be used to provide highly detailed descriptions if the observer considers this appropriate.

Nevertheless, the advantage of using a fine-grained level of analysis is that it serves as an invaluable aid to the perception of events. For example, the system for classifying simultaneous speech and interruptions enables the researcher to distinguish between a number of different types of interruption, which are by no means immediately apparent to the untrained observer. This in turn enables the researcher to pose questions about the relative effectiveness of different types of interruption strategy, which both enhances our understanding of interpersonal communication and has immediate practical applications for training in communication skills. Typologies are essential if we are to be able to make generalisations about the fine details of interpersonal communication: such typologies must be both sophisticated and sensitive to the data which they are intended to represent if we are to acquire a sophisticated understanding of the intricacies of interpersonal communication.

## References

ATKINSON, J. M. 1983, Two devices for generating audience approval: a comparative study of public discourse and text. In K. EHLICH *et al.* (eds), *Connectedness in Sentence, Text and Discourse*. Tilburg: Tilburg Papers in Linguistics.

— 1984a, *Our Masters' Voices: The Language and Body Language of Politics*. London: Methuen.

— 1984b, Public speaking and audience responses: some techniques for inviting applause. In J. M. ATKINSON & J. HERITAGE (eds), *Structures of Social Action: Studies in Conversation Analysis*. Cambridge: Cambridge University Press.

BIRDWHISTELL, R. L. 1971, *Kinesics and Context*. London: Allen Lane.

BULL, P. E. 1981, Body movement scoring system. In The social functions of speech-related body movement. SSRC End-of-grant report, HR 6404/2, 1–16.

— 1986, The use of hand gesture in political speeches: some case studies, *Journal of Language and Social Psychology*, 5, 103–18.

— 1987, *Posture and Gesture*. Oxford: Pergamon.

BULL, P. E. & CONNELLY, G. 1985, Body movement and emphasis in speech, *Journal of Nonverbal Behaviour*, 9, 169–87.

BULL, P.E. & MAYER, K. 1988, Interruptions in political interviews: a study of Margaret Thatcher and Neil Kinnock, *Journal of Language and Social Psychology*, 7.

CONDON, W. S. & OGSTON, W. D. 1966, Sound film analysis of normal and pathological behaviour patterns, *Journal of Nervous and Mental Disease*, 143, 338–47.

FERGUSON, N. 1977, Simultaneous speech, interruptions and dominance, *British Journal of Social and Clinical Psychology*, 16, 295–302.

FREEDMAN, N. & HOFFMAN, S. P. (1967), Kinetic behaviour in altered clinical states: approach to objective analysis of motor behaviour during clinical interviews, *Perceptual and Motor Skills*, 24, 527–39.

FREY, S. & VON CRANACH, M. 1973, A method for the assessment of body movement variability. In M. VON CRANACH & I. VINE (eds), *Social Communication and Movement*. London: Academic Press, 389–418.

FRIESEN, W. V., EKMAN, P. & WALLBOTT, H. 1980, Measuring hand movements, *Journal of Nonverbal Behaviour*, 4, 97–113.

HADAR, U., STEINER, T. J., GRANT, E. C. & ROSE, F.C. 1983, Head movement correlates of juncture and stress at sentence level, *Language and Speech*, 26, 117–29.

— 1984, The timing of shifts of head postures during conversation, *Human Movement Science*, 3, 237–45.

MEHRABIAN, A. 1968, Inference of attitude from the posture, orientation and distance of a communicator, *Journal of Consulting and Clinical Psychology*, 32, 296–308.

MISHLER, E. G. & WAXLER, N. E. 1968, *Interaction in Families: An Experimental Study of Family Processes and Schizophrenia*. New York: Wiley.

MORLEY, I. & STEPHENSON, G. M. 1977, *The Social Psychology of Bargaining*. London: George Allen & Unwin.

ROGER, D. B., BULL, P. E. & SMITH, S. 1988, The development of a comprehensive system for classifying interruptions, *Journal of Language and Social Psychology*, 7.

THOMAS, A. P. 1985, Conversational routines: a Markov chain analysis, *Language and Communication*, 5, 287–96.

THOMAS, A. P., BULL, P. E. & ROGER, D. B. 1982, Conversational exchange analysis, *Journal of Language and Social Psychology*, 1, 141–55.

THOMAS, A. P., ROGER, D. B. & BULL, P. E. 1983, A sequential analysis of informal dyadic conversation using Markov chains, *British Journal of Social Psychology*, 22, 177–88.

# 8 Preliminary notes on a possible metric which provides for a 'standard maximum' silence of approximately one second in conversation

GAIL JEFFERSON
*University of York*

## Introduction

For most of the 18 years that I have been producing transcripts for the analysis of naturally occurring conversation, I have been timing silence in tenths of seconds. While I try to be accurate, I have not givenparticular attention to the phenomenon of silence *per se*, and have been content with rough timings. (So, for example, I started out using a stop-watch but in 1968 it broke and instead of replacing it I switched over to the method favoured by amateur photographers, simply mumbling 'no one thousand, one one thousand, two one thousand . . .') And while many regularities have emerged from more or less unmotivated scanning of the materials, over the years I have not noticed any of particular interest by reference to the silences.

One possible reason that unmotivated scanning did not turn up any silence-relevant regularities is that silences in conversation occur in a wide range of lengths. For example, in the following array of intra-utterance silences following an 'uh', i.e. in the same sort of environment, there are silences ranging from approximately 0.2s to approximately 3.4s.

(1) [GTS:I:2:3:R:3:SO] ((face-to-face))

**Ken:** And then I work (.) I work at Jake's Jug and I go in there
→ and I: uh (0.2) put all the ↓bottles in ba:ck,

(2) [Rah:A:1:(6):1-2:SO] ((telephone))

**Mr F:** Got them sorted out the: tent's: the tent's up and everything,
**Jessie:** Ye:s,
**Mr F:** → A:nd uh:m (0.6) uh I've just given them a mea:l so: (.) they're gonna be uh it'll keep them warm for awhile,

(3) [PB:3-4:22:SO] ((face to face))

**Merle:** It was so depressing registering for classes next quarter
→ becau:se, u::m, (1.3) ˙tch! (0.9) I: you know if I don't get through Oh I've got to tell you. You're gonna die
→ laughing. (0.4) Dennis and I were talking a:nd uh (1.3) ˙hh Oh see- in September I'm gonna go over there . . .

(4) [NB:II:2:R:8:SO] ((telephone))

**Nancy:** You know for all of this: u[h: inten]sive thou:ght
**Emma:** [°Oh::.°]
(.)
**Nancy:** bus[iness,h[˙hhhh
**Emma:** [Mm: [hm,
**Nancy:** → A::nd uhm (1.8) ˙tch I can't remember one: (.) one of the f:↓kids had said in his thin:g u-something abou:t . . .

(5) [SF:II:22:SO] ((telephone))

**Mark:** Well who's gonna be at this party Friday night. So I can get excited about coming.
**Bob:** Well the old crew hopefully, °°uh°°
(0.3)
( ): ˙khhh˙hhhhh
**Bob:** → Uh:::: let's see. hYou know:: basic uh::(2.0)uh:::oh:,hh
→ (2.2) cre:w,

(6) [Goodwin:AD:7:R:14–15:SO] ((face-to-face))

**Bart:** → Keegan used to race uhruh- uhr it was uh:m (0.4) used
→ → to run uh::m. (3.4) oh::: sh::it. (0.3) uh::m, (0.4) Fisher's ca:r.

Let me note a potentially problematic feature of my silence-timings.

In Fragments 3 and 4, the silences are counted, not from speech-object to speech-object, e.g. from 'uh' to a word as in Fragments 1, 5 and 6, or from 'uh' to 'uh' as in Fragments 2 and 5, but from 'uh' to either an inbreath, as in Fragment 3, 'Dennis and I were talking a:nd uh (1.3) ˙hh' or a tongue-against-teeth click, as in Fragment 3, 'becau:se, u:m, (1.3) ˙tch!' and Fragment 4, 'A::nd uhm (1.8) ˙tch'.

I have been timing the silences that way, without thinking about it. Now that there is reason to think about it, I would want to continue this kind of timing. Specifically, what can be seen is some sort of shift in activity, whether it be from silence to an utterance's next word, or from silence to another 'pause filler', or from silence to some non-speech (or pre-speech) sound such as an inbreath or click.

There are yet longer intra-utterance silences. I do not happen to have any which fit into the above array, i.e. immediately preceded by 'uh', but here is one that comes close, preceded by 'uhm' (0.3) ˙tch'. And this five-second silence is the longest intra-utterance case I have come across so far.

(7) [SBL:2:1:8:R:7–8:SO] ((telephone))
**Nora:** I thought I knew] ↓ HER you know who: I thought it wa:s?
**Bea:** N[o:,
**Nora:**→ [Uh: i:t I thought it was uh:m
(0.3)
**Nora:** ˙tch
*→ (5.0)
**Nora:**→ Oh::-:↓gee: uhm u-one of the women who's eh: ex president of the woman's clu:b, ˙hhh and one of the most deli:ghtful woman I (.) women: I know in tha:t u-She was OUR:: uh counselor: one year? when I was on the boa:rd.
**Bea:** Oh:. No I duh‹
**Nora:** And she:'s a (.) perfectly deli:ghtful woman and I tell you: uh the light was kind of in my eyes, and I th- I:spoke to her because I thought it was she and I: thought=
**Bea:** =[[M- h m ] hm
**Nora:**→ [[well gee] I didn't know
*→ (1.2)
**Nora:**→ I'll think of her name in a minute well any ↓ wa:y. I thought it was she↓:.

Here, the announcement of a name has been set up as the point of the story. Perhaps because of its special status, the speaker permits herself such a long time to search for it. She then tries a good tactic for remembering, which time to search for it. She then tries a good tactic for remembering, which is to sneak up on the forgotten item by building a sentence in which it will naturally occur. She may be starting on something like 'Well gee I didn't know (NAME) was a friend of Bea's', or 'I didn't know (NAME) played bridge'. This second try also failing, she resumes talk much more rapidly.

The foregoing array provides a glimpse of the range of silences which occur in the materials I've been transcribing over the years; materials in which no silence-relevant phenomena emerged to motivate further investigation and thus greater accuracy in the timings. The following report consists of data which, it seems to me, provide glimpses of such a phenomenon.

## Biography of the phenomenon

Early in 1983 I was reading and making comments on an exercise in conversation analysis by a Dutch colleague, Hanneke Houtkoop. She was working with some problematic interactional bits in materials she had collected, and in commenting on her analyses I would occasionally refer to fragments from my own materials. Thus, a little corpus of a certain 'type' of interaction began to build up. And it was in this little corpus that a possible silence-relevant phenomenon emerged. Here is the pertinent comment (the three Dutch fragments translated by Houtkoop into English).

'Something a bit eerie is beginning to crop up in these materials:

[M-F] ((M phones F, talks to someone else who calls F to the phone. Fragment starts with F's first utterance))
**F:** Hi Mar(t), are you coming too?
→ (1.3)
**M:** Hello: Frank. ((smiling))

[M-S] ((Same situation as the M-F call))
**S:** We:ll van Noort. What's up.
**M:** Hello Sjoerd.
→ (1.2)
**M:** Hey how was your party last night?

[M-P] ((P is the Answerer-Not-Called of the above interchange))
**P:** You're the first one to ring at the new house!
**M:** Yeah.

(0.7)
**M:** Oh yeah?
**P:** Yeah.
→ (1.3)
**P:** Well I'll call Sjoerd.

[DA:2:3-4:SO] ((Two women in the course of a problematic arrangements-making))
**N:** She's going to pick me up Thursday morning.
→ (1.2)
**N:** ˙hh˙t˙hhhhhhh=
**G:** =Uh how early is she gonna pick you up.

Most roughly, these four fragments are pointing to the possibility that the 'tolerance interval' for some problematic interactional bit is just over one second, whereupon one of the participants starts to do some resolutional activity. At this point it's just a curio'.

So went the comment. I began to wonder if this 'curio', this 'tolerance interval' of approximately one second, could conceivably be a real phenomenon. So I undertook a data run, going through my transcripts and pulling out interactional bits in which intervals of more or less one second occurred; bits which struck me as, in various ways, problematic for the participants, where I got a sense that some next action ought to happen 'now'. I ended up with some 320 cases. And those cases strongly increased my sense that there might indeed be something systematic going on with this more-or-less one-second silence.

Roughly, it now seemed to me that there is some sort of interactional 'metric' in which 'approximately one second' operates, where that metric has as one artefact a 'standard maximum tolerance' for silence of more or less one second.

Further, some of the materials with longer silences suggested that there might be an alternative available metric; a 'gearing down' to a pacing which provided for silence-termination at one-second intervals, i.e. at about two seconds, and if not then, then at about three seconds, etc.

As I was going through the materials, focusing on this more-or-less one second silence, it occurred to me that the candidate phenomenon was so easy to see, then if it is indeed a systematic feature of interaction, surely the many people working with silence in interaction must have come across it and written it up. On the other hand, if I were doing some sort of selective observation, noticing the 320 cases of problematic interaction in which the silence just happens to be more or less one second, conveniently ignoring the myriad similar cases in which the silence is longer, then some of the work done on silence would show the non-significance of one second. That is, it seemed to me that I had got myself into something that other work would show to be either redundant or wrong.

So I sent out a request for references to a literature on silences/pauses with a sample collection of the more-or-less one-second silences in problematic interaction. The following are just a few of those sample cases.

(1.1) [SBL:2:2:3:R:30-31:SO] ((telephone))
**Claire:** if I say one club and they say one diamond
[what do you d]o
**Chloe:** [T h a t' s a] BU:S:T. isn't it.
**Claire:** → Ye:h then what do you ↓do:.
*→ (1.2)
**Chloe:** → We:ll to ↑me: they haven't explained it to me and I: don't kno:w . . .

(1.2) [JG:IV:1:1-2:SO] ((telephone))
**Ronald:** I'll get a Ninety Niner. ((a fast-food meal))
**Maggie:** Oh no honey no no no no.
**Ronald:** [Eeyeh-
[No I have to go to the store anyway and get stuff for your lunch and all.
**Ronald:** ((shouting)) NO! We have stuff.
**Maggie:** No we don't Ronald, that's why I didn't have anything to take for my own lunch.
**Ronald:** → So what did you eat.
*→ (1.0)
**Maggie:** → ((edgily)) I ate a sandwich Ronald there was nothing
→ in the hou:se.
*→ (1.0)
**Ronald:** → OH.

(1.3) [SBL:1:1:12:R:15-16:SO] ((telephone))
**Maude:** I says well it's funny: Missi:z uh: ↑Schmidt ih you'd think she'd help‹ ˙hhh W:ell (.) Missiz Schmidt was the one she: (0.2) assumed respo:nsibility for the three specials.
(0.6)

**Bea:** Oh↓*::. °°M-hm, °°=
**Maude:** =Maybe:lle ↑told me this.
**Bea:** Ah ↓hah,
(1.2)
**Bea:** °Uh-hah, ° ˙hh Isn't ↑her name jus:t plain Smi:th?
(0.7)
**Maude:** → Schmidt.h
*→ (1.2)
**Bea:** → Oh I thought it was just S-m-i-t-h:.
**Maude:** No I think it's S-c-h m-i-d-t, something like that it's just Sch↑mi↓:dt.
(0.3)
**Bea:** Ah hah.

(1.4) [Fr:USI:2:R:2:SO] (face-to-face))
**Carol:** Victor
**Vic:** Ye:h?
**Carol:** → Come here for a minute.
*→ (1.0)
**Vic:** → You come he[: r e . ]please?]
**Carol:** [↑You can] come b] a:ck=
**Vic:** =I ↑have to go to the ba:th↓room.=
**Carol:** =°Oh:.°

(1.5) [SPC:IV:6:13-14:SO] ((telephone))
**Mr K:** ˙hhhhh Well somebody thought that you were in danger of killing yourse:lf.=
**Mrs B:** =WELL SUPPOSE I WA:S I: (WEN: WITH) MY: SISTER AND MY SISTER'S (WITHUH VIBBINUB anybody).
**Mr K:** I'm sorry I didn't understand you.
**Mrs B:** SUPPOSE I WA:S. MY SISTER'S IN HEAVEN AND EVERYTHING IS BEAUTIFUL IN HEAVEN, (.) AND I DON'T HAVE TO WORRY ABOUT MONEY OR
→ ANYTHING E:LSE.
*→ (1.2)
**Mrs B:** → HELLO:?
**Mr K:** Yes.
(0.2)
**Mr K:** ˙hhhhh I'm:: I'm still here. I'm trying to figure this situation ou:t.

(1.6) [W:PC:III:1:1] (telephone))

**Sue:** → Hello:?h
*→ (1.0)
**Sue:** → Hello::,hh
(3.0)
**Sue:** H'llo?h

(1.7) [GTS:I:2:38-39:PR:SO] ((face-to-face))

**Roger:** You don't have to tell me what it is, just is there anything
→ wrong with you mentally.
*→ (1.0)
**Dan:** → ↓Uh:::::::,
(0.2)
**Ken:** In other words y-are y- are you a dope addict,
(0.4)
**Ken:** whh!
**Dan:** No↑::
**Louise:** That's not [mental,
**Ken:** [hhh heh heh
(1.5)
**Ken:** It's not?
**Roger:** Can't you [analyze yourself? or-
**Louise:** [( ),
**Louise:** ( )
( ): [°( )°
**Roger:** → ih You're perfectly normal.
*→ (1.2)
**Dan:** → ↑We↓:ll th:↑at word perfectly normal is a wi::[de ]
**Roger:** [acc]ORding
to your psychiatry ↓books.
(0.5)
**(Dan):** hhheh[hh[h
**Louise:** ° [° i[h hih ↑h] ih°=
**(Roger):** [° hih-ih° ]
**Roger:** =˙u[] [˙eh
**Dan:** []huh [huh huh huh huh hu[h °↓hu° ˙hhh]=
**Louise:** [( ) ]
**Louise:** =[]( )]
**Dan:** []NO::: I'm not perfectly normal according to m(h)y
psych(h)iatry books.

(1.8) [Owen:8B15(A):43-44:SO] ((face-to-face))

```
Andrea:       By the way do you  want any lettuces little lettuces?
              because they've come ou:t very we[ll
Bette:                                        [↑Have they,
Andrea:       ↑Yeh
                          (0.4)
Bette:        ↑Oh:.
Andrea:  →    °If you're interested°
        *→                (1.0)
Bette:   →    u:Uh::::m I'm just(tr)- thinking.
```

The request-letter received several responses: bibliographies, articles, and occasionally some encouragement. Glancing through the few articles that had been sent me, I found two pieces which in some way addressed the more-or-less one-second silence. The first is from Kraut (1978). Here are the relevant segments (emphasis added).

> Seventy four subjects listened to a 5-minute excerpt from a simulated interview in which a female applicant applied for a job as a dormitory counselor. When the male interviewer asked if the candidate smoked marijuana, he gave the impression that he either strongly opposed its use or supported its use. The job candidate answered either that she did not smoke it and found its use distasteful or that she smoked it recreationally several times a week. *Her answer was preceded by either a 7-second pause or a 1-second pause*. . . .
> The paralinguistic cue was manipulated by *inserting a 7-second partially filled pause* between the interviewer's marijuana question and the candidate's answer. Four seconds of blank tape, an 'uh' spoken by the candidate and taken from another of her answers, and 3 seconds of blank tape were spliced into the interview, starting at the last sounds of the question. *This length of silence seems to be at the limits of those that appear in normal conversation* . . . Thus, the silence . . . was noticed by virtually all subjects but did not appear unnaturally long to them. *In the other version, no silence was inserted between the question and answer, and the naturally occurring hesitation of approximately 1 second was retained*. . . . The most interesting results involve the pause . . . The 7-second pause increased subjects' suspicion of the candidate when they were already suspicious. Compared to *subjects who heard only the candidate's denial of marijuana*, the subjects who heard a long pause and then the denial thought the candidate had been less candid and lied more in the interview . . . Compared to *subjects who only heard the candidate admit to smoking marijuana*, subjects who heard a long pause and the admission thought she had been more candid.

In the first place I found it interesting that in a simulated interview, the 'naturally occurring hesitation' after a problematic question was 'approximately 1 second'. In effect, another datum for my collection, from an altogether different type of talk. Second, there is some evidence that at least this author did not find anything of particular interest in silences of that length. Over the course of the article the more-or-less one-second silence is relegated from 'a 1-second pause' to 'the naturally occurring hesitation of approximately 1 second', to nothing worth mentioning; i.e. the relevant materials are thereafter described in terms of the subjects hearing 'only the candidate's denial' or admission, in contrast to those 'who heard a long pause'.

The second piece comes from Butterworth (1980).

> *Moreover, between-sentence pauses in reading tend to be roughly of the same length, 1.0–1.24 seconds, whereas in spontaneous speech they vary considerably, with many over 2.50 seconds*, reflecting varying cognitive demands of speech as compared with reading (Goldman-Eisler, 1972, emphasis added).

This statement strongly raises the possibility that I had been engaged in selective observation and was just not attending to the many longer silences in the 'spontaneous' materials with which I work. On the other hand it was interesting that approximately the same silence which I was treating as a possible 'standard maximum' for conversation constituted the standard for 'between-sentence pauses in reading'.

At that point I put the matter aside because the work involved in (dis)proving the possible phenomenon seemed overwhelming.

## A possible complementary approach to the candidate phenomenon

In August 1983 I started typing up several hundred pages of retranscriptions I had done when I first arrived in Holland (careful rehearings for a project on the organisation of overlapping talk). As I was typing up these materials, with several hundred pages passing before my eyes in a concentrated batch, it seemed to me that the longer silences tended to fall into a cluster of about 0.9s to 1.2s independent of any specification of the activities in the course of which the silences were occurring.

Given the obvious 'considerable variation' of silences in conversation (cf. Fragments 1–7 and Butterworth, 1980), it had not occurred to me that 'statistical' procedures would be a fruitful way to develop the possibility of a 'standard maximum' silence. But now I wondered if a simple counting procedure might not after all yield something. So I did another run, through some 168 transcripts, altogether some 1,860 pages, collecting and counting all silences of nine-tenths of a second and longer.

The data run yielded a couple of striking results. For one, there are some 951 occurrences of silence of 0.9–1.2s, i.e. of 'approximately one second', compared to some 328 cases of longer silences. Secondly, if the candidate 'standard maximum' cluster of 0.9–1.2s is compared to the next longest cluster, 1.3–1.8s, there is a tremendous drop-off. The 951 silences of 0.9–1.2s are followed by some 92 occurrences of silence of 1.3–1.8s.

Parenthetically let me note that several months later I did my own timings of the Houtkoop fragments, and came up with shorter intervals than her 1.3s, 1.2s and 1.3s (see p. 169–70 above).

[M-F:GJR]
**F:** Hi Mar(t), are you coming to::?
→ (0.9)
**M:** eh ↑Hello Frank,

[M-S:GJR]
**S:** We:ll van Noort. What's up.
**M:** Hello Sjoe:rd,
(0.3)
→ ( ): (1.0) ehh hh
**M:** He:y how was your party last night?

[M-P:GJR]
**P:** You're the first one to ring the new house!
**M:** Yeh-
(0.7) ((not retimed))
**M:** Oh yeah?
**P:** Yea:h.
→ (1.0)
**P:** [ ˙hhhh ] Well I'll call Sjoerd.
[ (0.3) ]

Among the 328 cases of longer silences there are five especially long ones, of 6.2, 6.5, 6.5, 7.3, and 16.4s. Three of the five, the two 6.5s and the one of 16.4, occur in close proximity in a conversation between two secretaries on a coffee break, examining a train schedule.

(2.1) [Owen:8B15(A):29-30:SO]

Andrea: I think I'm gonna have to get up the night be↑fore
(1.2)
Bette: ˙t˙hh Check with the station and (.) ask them what the fir train that goes on Good Friday is and-
Andrea: ˙hh Wonder if I could advertise in the grad centre for anyone who's going up.
(1.9)
Andrea: Be worth trying,
(1.0)
Bette: Hmm:.
**→ (6.5)
Andrea: If it was an ordinary day.hh
(1.2)
Andrea: They've got really early (.) trains:: (0.2) um other da↑:ys=
Bette: =If it was an ordinary day you'd be alri:ght.=
Bette: =Th[ere's plenty[]
Andrea: [Ye:ah. []Five forty three[:.
Bette: [Ye:h,
(1.0)
Andrea: Well the- (1.3) the fi:ve forty three:, (1.4) Well it would- be- it would be the only matter of- the only possible one in fact.
(0.7)
Andrea: But I mean ih- agai:n if I got up at (0.3) four o'clo:ck to get a train at five forty three I may just as well stay at Heathrow overnight anyway[in fa]:[ct.
Bette: [We:ll] [Ye:s::
(.)
Bette: Ye:s
Andrea: It's not gonna make that much (.) difference to the amount of sleep I get,
(1.9)
( ): °Mm:,°
**→ (16.4)
Andrea: It's the weekend after °next°
Bette: °Oh:,°
(1.0)
Andrea: ↓˙kGu::h (Ihh ho(h)pe), hhhuh[huh huh-uh-↑huh-n
Bette: [hmh-hmh

```
Andrea:      ˙uh˙ih ↑hnh[huh huh ˙hhhh ↑heh ˙he::h
Bette:                  [ehh-heh-heh
         **→        (6.5)
Andrea:      °The latest trai:n down on (.) Thursday,°
```

The 7.3s silence occurs in a conversation between two young women sitting in a sunny corner at a neighbourhood block party.

```
(2.2)  [Goodwin:50:Clacia:7-8:SO]
Donna:   It was pretty ni:ce.It really wa:[s,
Tanzi:                                    [°(Yeh)°=
Tanzi:   =°(it [ w a : s.  Y e h.)° ]
Donna:         [It was nice and it was]clean:,=
Tanzi:  =[]Right.]
Donna:     it was new: and they[(h a : d)]‹you know like made the=
Tanzi:                         [°Right.° ]
Donna:   =be:ds and, (0.5) °fu[rniture (and stuff.)
Tanzi:                        [(You) had (choice) furniture.=
Tanzi:   =Right. Well we had that over in our p- uh, (0.8) u-They
         had bought that for our house. °When they furnished the
         house.°
                   (2.5)
Tanzi:   °(But it was different) there's no dou:bt about it.°
      **→          (7.3)
Donna:   Whose car is that down there[(                        ).
Tanzi:                               [BYE BYE ENJOY YOUR
         BRO::CCOLI PIE::,
                   (0.4)
Donna:   Broccoli pie::,
                   (0.6)
Tanzi:   She's going to her sister's house.
```

In the coffee break materials of Fragment 2.1 the long silences may well be unproblematically occupied by one or another of the women looking through the train schedule. In the block party materials of Fragment 2.2 there is good reason to suppose that the long silence is occupied by both women scanning the surrounding scene, each thereafter speaking by reference to things they noticed in the scan; Donna asking about a car, Tanzi calling to someone.

The remaining longest silence occurs in a telephone call. While face-to-face environments provide more resources for, and recurrently house such unproblematic long silences as the two above, telephone environments do permit of at least a few, such as the following, in which one of the participants is writing down an address given to her by the other.

(2.3) [DA:2:5-6:SO] ((Goldie had started to give her address, 'ten forty two . . .' earlier and had interjected some other matter.))

**Goldie:** Alright now you] take the addre:ss and if she doesn't know how to get here then she can uh-call me.=
**Netty:** =Yah.
(0.3)
**Goldie:** Alri:ght, [(that's)-]
**Netty:** [Ten for]ty two what.hh
(0.4)
**Goldie:** I beg your pardon?=
**Netty:** =Ten forty two what.
(0.2)
**Goldie:** ee-u-ri:ght eh: eh-Sou:th Shenandoah,
*→ (3.0)
**Netty:** Ten forty two: s-Sou:th Shenandoah.=
**Goldie:** =Ye:s,
(0.3)
**Goldie:** A:nd uh you may tell he:r that it is, (0.3) about a half a blo::ck,(.)sou:th, of Olympic.
**→ (6.2)
**Netty:** Is- eh, wha-what part of uh::::=
**Netty:** =[[ul- ]uh-
**Goldie:** [[It's ]Los Angeles it's eh:: (0.4) It is Los Angeles,
(.)
**Netty:** Ye:s,
(1.0)
**Goldie:** I:t's near Beverly ↓Hills.

The silences of from 6.2–16.4s in these three fragments can be seen to be occurring in quite different activity bits than those in which the candidate 'standard maximum' silences tend to occur (see again Fragments 1.1–1.8). Indeed, when such activities as examining a train schedule, scanning the scene, writing down an address are not occurring in these fragments, and the participants are engaged in back-and-forth talk, the longest silences tend to fall within the candidate 'standard maximum'. For example, in Fragment 2.1 there are five of 1.0–1.2s, two of 1.3–1.4s, and then two which suggest the 'alternative metric', of approximately two seconds.

And the 'statistical' run yielded yet a further glimpse of the possible phenomenon of an alternative metric, a gearing down to a slower pace with silence parsed second-by-second rather than in small units culminating at approximately one second (cf. Fragment 2.1 just mentioned, the five-second silence in Fragment 7, and in Fragment 1.6 the three-second silence before the third 'Hello'). For example, a small group of transcripts showed an interesting pattern of silences. In 16 conversations ranging in length from three to 65 pages there are very few silences above the candidate standard maximum of 0.9–1.2s, none at all of 1.5–1.8s, and then a little flurry of silences of 1.8–2.2s duration (Table 8.1).

TABLE 8.1 *A pattern of silences in a small subset of conversations*

| Transcript: | 1 | 2 | 3 | 4 | 5 | 6 | 7 | 8 | 9 | 10 | 11 | 12 | 13 | 14 | 15 | 16 | |
|---|---|---|---|---|---|---|---|---|---|---|---|---|---|---|---|---|---|
| No. of pages: | 6 | 27 | 7 | 3 | 15 | 13 | 7 | 12 | 65 | 29 | 6 | 9 | 6 | 12 | 10 | 61 | |
| Silence(s) | | | | | | | | | | | | | | | | | Total |
| 0.9–1.2 | – | 1 | 2 | 2 | 2 | 3 | 3 | 4 | 19 | 11 | 9 | 7 | 3 | 5 | 2 | 33 | 106 |
| 1.3 | – | – | – | – | 1 | 4 | 1 | – | 2 | – | – | – | – | 2 | 1 | 2 | 13 |
| 1.4 | – | – | – | – | – | – | 1 | – | 2 | – | 1 | – | 2 | – | 2 | 2 | 10 |
| 1.5 | – | – | – | – | – | – | – | 1 | 1 | – | 1 | – | – | – | 1 | 3 | 7 |
| 1.6 | – | – | – | – | – | – | – | – | – | – | – | – | – | – | – | – | 0 |
| 1.7 | – | – | – | – | – | – | – | – | – | – | – | – | – | – | – | – | 0 |
| 1.8–2.2 | 1 | 1 | 1 | 1 | 1 | 1 | 1 | 1 | 2 | 2 | 2 | 2 | 4 | 4 | 4 | 6 | 34 |

And in transcript 16 there is another gap between the six more-or-less two-second silences and the range 2.8–3.2s, where another two silences occur. (The pattern in these materials suggests that perhaps I should in the future treat the 'target cluster' as starting at 0.8s rather than the arbitrarily chosen 0.9s.)

## Continuing exploration

Given the results of the counting procedure, it seemed useful to continue with it. From August to September I worked both 'interactionally' and 'statistically' with the candidate phenomenon; looking at selected activity-types and environments, and going through additional transcripts simply counting up the silences of 0.9s and over.

For example, I collected instances of 'innocuous' occurrences of the 'standard maximum', i.e. in the course of activities which did not recommend themselves as interactionally problematic and thus were not collected in the primary data run.

Having used the phenomenon of intra-sentence silences as an example of the wide range of silences (see again Fragments 1–7 above, with its range of 0.2–5.0s), I decided to explore it for possible consistency. The following are a few cases taken from that second data run.

(3.1) [Owen:8B15(A):34:SO] ((face-to-face))
**Andrea:** → The biggest check I ever wrote out was: (1.0) ˙k two
hundred and thirty fi:ve (.) pounds

(3.2) [SBL:2:1:6:R:1:SO] ((telephone))
**Bea:** ˙hhh I'm jus:t servin:g um
(0.7)
**Bea:** ˙tlk˙hhh[hh
**Tess:** [Dessert[(I imagine),]
**Bea:** [a bowl of ] ice cream and some:::
→ b-little: home made' (1.0) cake cookies or something

(3.3) [Goodwin:DP:38:R:SO] ((face-to-face))
**Beth:** you know what I mean?
**Jan:** True. True.
**Beth:** → We were much younger and, (1.0) lots of stuff you
know, like a lot less settled in a lot of wa:ys?
(0.6)
**Beth:** *→ And uh, (1.7) whereas no:w, you know even with the
→ second one, ˙hh it's it was mo:re, (0.9) u-uh::-uh
→ (1.2) like deliberately.

(3.4) [NB:IV:10:R:14:SO] ((telephone))
**Emma:** M[m h m ? ]
**Lottie:** → [A:nd he c]ame in about ' (1.0) °let's see° five thirty,

(3.5) [PB:3-4:16:SO] ((face-to-face))

**Merle:** JoLee's kind of cranky toni:ght.
(0.4)
**Merle:** Probably 'cause we didn't put her to bed until ten=
**Paul:** =[[hh
**Merle:** → last night hhh But uh:m (1.2) I know JoLee used to get kwan- cranky, you know really bad.

(3.6) [CDHQ:II:100:R:4:SO] ((telephone))

**Opal:** but they said tha(0.2)t uh:::*u:-:-: some way that (0.3)
*→ they would know ho:w uh (2.5) that they were getting in touch with him › you know what I mean?‹
**Josh:** ›Mhm?‹
**Opal:** ˙hh[h
**Josh:** [°M[↓hm.°]
**Opal:** [B u ]t (.) it was the wro:ng number I mean a
→ woman answered an:d uh (0.9) u[h: it was=
**Josh:** [Mhm,
**Josh:** =[[°hm,°
**Opal:** just a ↑re:sidence

The results of this second run, through a corpus consisting of intra-sentence silences, are not as dramatic as those of the primary run, but both the ratio of the 261 cases of the 'target cluster' of 0.9–1.2s to the 109 cases of all longer silences (a ratio of 2.5 to 1), and the drop-off from the target cluster to the next cluster of 1.3–1.8s, from 261 to 67, remains substantial.

I also started retiming and counting the silences in some face-to-face, multi-party conversations, which are drastically underrepresented in the primary data run. And given that there was now good reason to be as accurate as possible with the timings, I bought a digital stopwatch, now timing the silences both 'photographer' fashion and by clock. The timings are fairly consistent, within a tolerance of about a tenth of a second, but still rough.

I took samples of half an hour from each of three multi-party conversations; a group therapy session for teenagers, a dinner party of two married couples and two children, and an afternoon in a neighbourhood upholstery shop where several men are gathered, working, talking, and drinking beer.

I will only touch on these materials. First, I want to note that the longest silences seem to support the notion of an 'alternative metric'. In the therapy session sample, of the three longest silences, one is approximately three seconds long and two are approximately four seconds long.

In the dinner party sample, two of the three longest silences fit the candidate alternative metric, one of approximately four seconds and one of approximately six seconds. The other is a 'nowhere' (5.6s).

In the upholstery shop sample the two longest silences, of approximately three and approximately eight seconds, fit the metric.

I will talk about the possible presence of a standard maximum silence of about one second by incorporating the results of the counting done on these three samples into an overview of the results so far.

None of the materials counted for silences of nine-tenths of a second and over shows as strong a preponderance of the candidate standard maximum silence as did the primary run. Here are the ratios of approximately one second to all longer silences:

| | |
|---|---|
| 1. Primary run: | 951 to 328 (c.3 to 1) |
| 2. Intra-sentence silences: | 261 to 109 (c.2.5 to 1) |
| 3. Group therapy session: | 88 to 42 (c.2 to 1) |
| 4. Dinner party: | 36 to 34 (c.1 to 1) |
| 5. Upholstery shop: | 23 to 10 (c.2 to 1) |

The subsequent runs are rather stronger, although much less dramatic than the primary run, when it comes to the drop-off from the target cluster of approximately 1 second (0.9–1.2s) to the next cluster (1.3–1.8s).

| | |
|---|---|
| 1. Primary run: | 951 to 92 (c.10 to 1) |
| 2. Intra-sentence silences: | 261 to 67 (c.4 to 1) |
| 3. Group therapy session: | 88 to 20 (c.2.5 to 1) |
| 4. Dinner party: | 36 to 18 (2 to 1) |
| 5. Upholstery shop: | 23 to 7 (c.3 to 1) |

The difference in strengths of ratio as between about one second and all longer silences, and as between about one second and the next cluster of silences raises the following possibility: perhaps it is that *when* the 'long' silences are not well beyond standard maximum, not having geared down into the alternative metric or gone off metric (or into some other metric I do not know about), *then* they tend to occur in the target cluster. That is, when the 'base metric' *is* orientated to, it is finely orientated to. So, for example, in the dinner party sample it appears that the base metric is not as strongly orientated to as in the other materials (a 1 to 1 ratio of about one second to all longer silences). But when it *is* orientated to, silences are terminated with a 2 to 1 ratio as between the target cluster and the next cluster.

As to the dramatic difference between the results of the primary run and subsequent runs, there are a number of possibilities. For one, it may be that the phenomenon is most strongly present in inter-utterance silences. The primary run was an aggregate of inter- and intra-utterance silences, while the second run consisted exclusively of intra-utterance silences. For another, the phenomenon may be most strongly present in those 'types' of interaction by which telephone calls are heavily constituted (with such exceptions as writing down some information, as in Fragment 2.3, where then the base metric may be temporarily relaxed), but which in face-to-face environments occur in combination with other 'types' of interaction and other activities. The primary run was taken mostly from telephone calls, while the third to fifth runs were taken specifically from face-to-face talk.

## Further possible manifestations of the candidate metric

In October I began to look into other areas in which an interval of approximately one second recurs. One such area is story-telling (which begins perhaps to converge on the phenomenon, reported on by Butterworth, 1980, of reading aloud). The materials are cumbersome, so I will just show one extended fragment.

(4.1) [Merritt:Egg Story:4-5:SO] ((face-to-face))

| | | |
|---|---|---|
| **Halda:** | | she says can I move <u>in</u> today. |
| **Jean:** | | ˙<u>uhh</u>!˙ |
| **Halda:** | | Uh I said uh, |
| | *→ | (1.3) |
| **Halda:** | | well I just don't <u>know</u> if you can get a- uh:: w-wh<u>a</u>t uh-uh are you gonna- have you- |
| | → | (1.0) |
| **Halda:** | | What are you gonna do about your <u>fur</u>niture. and she said I haven't got a st<u>i</u>ck <u>of</u> furniture! |
| | → | (1.0) |
| **Halda:** | | And ah- a:nd uh I [says well- |
| **Jean:** | | [hhh! |
| **Jean:** | | hhh! |
| **Halda:** | | h(ha)how can you move <u>i</u>:n then. ˙hh <u>She</u> said, |
| | → | (1.0) |
| **Halda:** | | <u>oh</u> haven't you got a little bed. or uh <u>ha</u>ven't you |

| | | |
|---|---|---|
| | | got a bed- I- you're not gonna use or a chest of drawers or something. |
| | | (0.5) |
| **Halda:** | | or a little, uh, card table or, something? and she said this- oh it doesn't matter, hh she says, oh::: she says I don't want to- I'm, I'm through(h)looking, I'm just through looking and I want to ( )- right here. |
| | → | (1.0) |
| **Halda:** | | A:nd she says I intend to furnish this house, in antique furniture. |
| | → | (1.2) |
| **Halda:** | | And so uh, |
| | | (0.7) |
| **Halda:** | | We:ll? huh huh-huh! ˙hhhh I was so swept off my feet, and so was Ira, we were just both aghast. that, |
| **Jean:** | | uhh! |
| **Halda:** | | A:nd uh, [so finally- |
| **Jean:** | | [( ), |
| | → | (1.0) |
| **Halda:** | | uh::m, I said ye::s, I, |
| | → | (1.0) |
| **Halda:** | | I have a chest of drawer:s, that I wasn't gonna use, (and uh, and uh-uh), |
| | | (0.7) |
| **Halda:** | | guess we could bring them up with a- ˙hh |
| | *→ | (1.3) |
| **Halda:** | | a bed? mattress and spring, |
| | → | (1.0) |
| **Halda:** | | Well uh and I said I do have a card table, ye:s, and uhm I said you can, probably use a couple chairs (couldn't you), and so uh. Well, they set up housekeeping |
| | *→ | (1.3) |
| **Halda:** | | A:nd uh |
| | → | (1.0) |
| **Halda:** | | thrilled to death. |
| | → | (1.0) |
| **Halda:** | | Well what I started to say. Talking about your boiled eggs. One day . . . |

Let me note that this is an older transcript and I do not have access to the tape. Given the results of various retimings I have done, it is likely that not all the silences marked as precisely one second are just that, although a surprising number of the silences do come out at precisely one second in the 'photographer' count, perhaps 0.9s or 1.04s by the stopwatch.

Another area in which the interval of about one second recurs is that of intra-sentence inbreaths. I only have some preliminary data here, compiled by spotting a long inbreath in a transcript, finding it on the tape and timing it. Recurrently the long inbreaths fall into the target cluster of 0.9–1.2s, occasionally going over as in Fragment 4.2g. These are all from telephone calls.

(4.2a) [SBL:3:3:R:1:SO]

(1.2)
**Milly:** → but it costs so much to sue: that uh[˙hhhhhhhhhh]
hhe says . . .

(4.2b) [TCI(c):11:2:SO]
**Irene:** See w*e wanted to borrow five hundred dollars: mo:re
→ from[˙hhhhhhhhh] H.F.C:.h
(0.9)

(4.2c) [MDE:60-1:7:3:SO]
**Sheila:** And it- it was] really amazing because if you go to the
realtor::,h
(0.3)
**Sheila:** th:ey s- ˙hh ẹ-have ↓hou:ses and they're about four
→ hundred dollars and[˙hhhhhhhhhh]around the:re,
(1.0)

(4.2d) [DA:2:12:SO]
**Ellie:** she kept getting sicker and sicker and uh::::
→ [˙hhhhhhhhh] uh d-ed even when she said she was . . .
(0.9)

(4.2e) [NB:II:4:R:22:SO]
**Nancy:** he said I'd (.) I'd love to (.) get to the beach and
*I[˙hhh˙hh˙hh˙hhh]he said you live at the beach too . . .
(1.0)

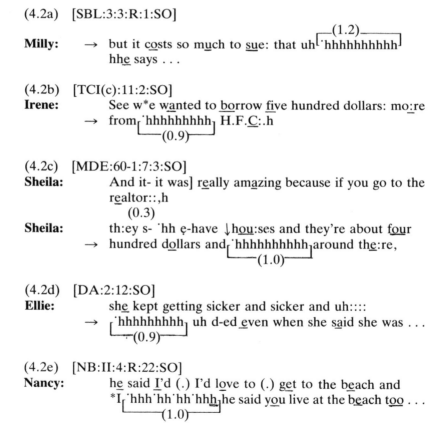

(4.2f) [NB:IV:10:R:26:SO]

**Emma:** He's gonna be very ↓wealthy °some day.° h 'Cause he got a:ll these big co:ntracts with A.B.C: and
→ [˙hh˙hh˙hhuhhh] oh::: General Telephone . . .
—(1.1)°—

(4.2g) [SF:II:15:SO]

**Mark:** ˙hhhh A:nd a:t what point did you find ou:t tha:t uh:
*→ [˙hhhh˙hhhhhh] hhe::r uh hhmhh what shall we call him.
(1.4)
(0.7)

**Mark:** ˙t uh:::m, her[uh::m::,

**Bob:** [Her old boyfriend,

I came across another possibly interesting area, that of prolonged sounds. So, for example, in one conversation, one of the participants tends to produce extended 'uh's. I went through the tape and timed the longer ones. There are some 14 of them running to 0.9s and above, and none of them are longer than 1.2s. Here are several.

(4.3a) [DA:2:8:SO]

**Ellie:** So(w)-uh when she comes over:,
(0.9)

**Ellie:** → I:[uh::::::::] I'll, I'll call you, and tell you . . .
(1.0)

(4.3b) [DA:2:11:SO]

**Goldie:** how did they live uh lately.=

**Ellie:** → =u-They lived[eh::::::::]far better than a lot of . . .
(0.9)

(4.3c) [DA:2:12:SO] ((see Fragment 4.2d. for continuation))

**Ellie:** → But[uh::::::::::]she kept getting sicker and sicker . . .
(1.1)

(4.3d) [DA:2:15:SO]

**Ellie:** because uh ˙hh she left him nothin:g with nothing but a::: a-a-a thing full of uh: probably over his hea:d,
→ [˙hhhhhhhh]in[uh::::::::]
(0.9) (1.2)
(1.0)

**Goldie:** °But uh°[] [But you know]

**Ellie:** []u [W h o knows.]

Akin to the prolonged 'uh's produced by one particular speaker, an interesting little corpus of intra-sentence silences is generated singlehandedly, in this case by a man with a formidable stammer. In the aggregate his 'standard maximum' intra-sentence silences occur at a 4 to 1 ratio as against all longer silences, the longest of which is 1.7s. One gets a strong sense of the possible metric, watching this speaker achieving the termination of his problematic silences within, upon, and rarely beyond the standard maximum. Here are just two fragments from that corpus.

(4.4a) [Her:OI:3:1:SO]

**Barnaby:** → ˙hhh We've agreed (.) agree;d to (.) to go: th-(1.0)
sa:me price, (0.7) which i:s twenty six:, ↑a:n:d
(0.2) ˙hhh if there's going ‹goin:g to be any ek(.)
any sor- sort of (0.5) fuss about oh well we'll: go
an extra five hundred an:d so it goes back to th:em
→ → and ˙hh aw- (1.0) all this: rubbish (0.3) then (1.2)
forget it.

(4.4b) [Her:OI:3:9:SO]

**Barnaby:** The:y s:aid (.) said i-k (.) who it i:s ih-ih-eh-
→ up- appar- apparently it's a Mister:(b) (1.0)
*→ Mister(b) (1.7) Blumford °

## Discussion

The possibility of a metric for conversation which has as one of its artefacts a 'standard maximum' silence of approximately one second emerged via a few fragments of problematic interaction (see pp. 169–70). Ironically, had I transcribed those materials in the first place, then examining them the possibility of such a metric would not have occurred to me (see p. 176; the one-second interval marked in the second fragment would not have been noted in my own transcript; it is there to show the interval that Houtkoop was timing, disregarding an intervening sound. Thus, that fragment would only show 0.3s silence.).

Although I became interested in working up some procedures by which to prove or disprove the presence of such a metric, I have, at least so far, not found a way to make use of the phenomenon in the sort of sequential-interactional analysis I do. However, the possibility of this metric has become an instrument for monitoring data, such that much materials than those from which it emerged, materials such as intra-sentence silences, inbreaths, prolonged 'pause fillers', and stammering, become interesting, not only because they seem to support the notion of such a metric, but they become animated in a way that was heretofore unavailable.

Some of the intra-sentence silences have taken on a particular vividness; for example, those in which a speaker is searching for a word. Sometimes the search extends beyond the candidate standard maximum. (Note that Fragment 5.3 terminates at the 'alternative metric'.)

(5.1) [NB:I:5:5:SO] ((telephone))
**Bud:** *→ And if you can bring uh (1.4) Buster Brown along with you? why bring him along.

(5.2) [Goodwin:84:AD:41-42:SO] ((face-to-face))
**Lenny:** but some guy up in, Ed Shaller or somebody up in,
*→ (1.5) Detroit built this engine and he's got over twelve hundred dollars just in the engine,

(5.3) [Campbell:7:6:SO] ((telephone))
**Mac:** *→ Well it's: it used to be s:: eh::, (1.9) ˙hh only three bo:b to get down there

But recurrently the search is resolved at the proposed edge of the 'tolerance' for silence.

(5.4) [SBL:2:1:6:R:1:SO] ((telephone))
**Tess:** You're only ha]ving six aren't y[ou, ]
**Bea:** [Eh- ]No I'm having
te-e:n.hh˙hhhhhhh (0.3) u-But uh:m hhh (0.3) i-See
→ four for bri:dge and six for: (1.0) ↑Tripoly.

(5.5) [SBL:2:1:8:R:1:SO] ((telephone))
**Nora:** → A:nd uh:*: uh:: she pro:bably wrote a: (1.0) a paper o:n it?

(5.6) [NB:I:1:25:SO] ((telephone))
**Bud:** I've got San Juan Hills phone number here in (my)-
→ in the uh, (1.0) phone book,

(5.7) [TCII(a):14:2:SO] ((telephone))
**EJ:** Is he a ma::le?
(1.0)
**Croff:** → I had him (1.0) demaled.

(5.8) [PB:3-4:20:SO] ((face-to-face))
**Merle:** → But wuh-u-we haven't [seen them since, (1.0) September
**Paul:** [°Mm hm?°

(5.9) [SBL:1:1:12:R:12:SO] ((telephone))
**Maude:** At least I ↓like her↓ I: you know what I mean she's a
→ ↓fo:rthri:ght uh (1.0) HARDWORKING . . .

(5.10) [GTS:I:2:49:R:SO] ((face-to-face))
**Ken:** I thought that was against their uh (0.6) their code of
→ (0.9) eth[ics to uh
**Louise:** [Their code of ethics is not to advertise,

(5.11) [SF:II:16:SO] ((telephone))
**Mark:** hAnd what was your immediate reaction to that.h
(1.3)
**Bob:** Oh:: I guess I was:: uh::hh[hh
**Mark:** [hhhmhhh=
**Bob:** → =Well let me see::. (1.0) Plea::sed?h

See also Fragment 3.1.

Perhaps the most interesting in terms of an orientation to the candidate metric are the word searches which are not *resolved* at the proposed point of 'standard maximum tolerance', but where some activity occurs. Again, there are longer intervals. (Note that Fragments 5.12 and 5.14 terminate at the 'alternative metric').

(5.12) [NB:II:4:R:20:SO] ((telephone))
**Nancy:** e-he's drivin:g his uhm (.) au:nt Hel↓en, up to uh f::
→ (1.9) °*Oh h*ell° where does she ↓live. Up (.) nea:r
Santa(b) not s-uh:m (0.3) ↑Oj*ai.

(5.13) [Goodwin:AD:7:R:14-15:SO] ((face-to-face))
**Bart:** Keegan used to race uhruh- uhr it was uh:m (0.4) used
→ to run uh::m. (3.4) oh::: sh::it. (0.3) uh::m, (0.4)
Fisher's ca:r. [This is Fragment 6]

(5.14) [SBL:2:1:8:R:7:SO] ((telephone))
**Nora:** → I thought it was uh:m (0.3) ˙tch (5.0) oh::-: gee: uhm u-one of the women who's eh: ex president of the woman's clu:b . . . [This is the first part of Fragment 7]

And it is rather interesting that in each of these fragments, selected only by reference to the above 'standard maximum' silences involved in a word-search, the long silence is terminated with a particular type of exclamation in various degrees of 'nicety' ('Oh hell', 'Oh shit' and 'Oh gee').

Recurrently, however, some activity occurs at the proposed edge of the 'standard tolerance' for silence. Fragment 5.15 stands somewhere between resolution and some activity, a possible solution.

(5.15) [Goodwin:84:AD:23:SO] ((face-to-face))
**Bart:** What's his na:me.
(0.5)
**Cal:** → Harry uh, (1.0) Schirmer? ‹Shure?

(5.16) [Owen:8B15(A):41:SO] ((face-to-face))
**Andrea:** → You can ge:t eh:::m (.) grape (1.0) I don't know what they call it grape juice or grape extract=
**Bette:** =[] Mm:,
**Andrea:** or somethi[ng in] Boot's::
**Bette:** [Mm:,]

(5.17) [S:PRP:7-8:SO] ((face-to-face))
**Ann:** I got- uh my- my evening gown was uhm uh crepeback satin. The rea:l hhea:vy sa:tin.
(0.5)
**Ann:** → in the uhm (1.0) ˙tch! uh: what do they ca- princess cut.

(5.18) [NB:II:2:R:15:SO] ((telephone))
**Nancy:** e-He: had uhm (.) ˙t˙hh fi:led a complaint with the schoo:l, (1.0) ˙t[˙hhhhh]hh
**Emma:** [°Mm:,°]
**Nancy:** → that he thought Mister Bradley: (.) was uhm (1.2) ˙tch uh::m(0.5) condoning hhhhh ˙hhhh u[h t h]in:gs . . .
**Emma:** [( )-]

In the following two fragments both participants produce some activity at the edge of the proposed standard tolerance.

(5.19) [NB:III:3:R:2:SO] ((telephone))
**Emma:** We just had a vo:dka Barbara and I: just had a ni:ce great big double vo:dka and we're having a barbequed
→ (1.2)
**Emma:** [[uh :]
**Bud:** [[Some- ]Something?

(5.20) [Her:III:1:5:1:SO] ((telephone))
**Heath:** ˙hhh Ah: he thinks that it's uh as much as anythin:g ah:m a um:
→ (0.9)
**Joan:** ar[:thritis.
**Heath:** [uh

I find myself surprised that this doesn't happen more often, i.e. that recurrently only one participant moves to terminate the silence at the edge of the 'standard maximum'. It may be mere chance but the participants of Fragment 5.19 are husband and wife, and those of Fragment 5.20 are brother and sister. Conceivably there is some organisation or range of organisations which provide for only one participant to terminate the silence in various interactional circumstances, where, then, the fact that the participants here are 'family' to each other may constitute another instance of 'relaxation' of certain 'rules' among intimates.

Another case of 'some activity' occurring at the edge of the proposed 'standard maximum tolerance' can be seen in the second part of Fragment 7. The discussion there refers to the resumption of talk 'much more rapidly'. Perhaps that can be more closely specified as 'at the standard maximum'.

It seems to me that the foregoing series of arrays indicates that the metric which provides for the 'tendency' reported by Butterworth (1980), of inter-sentence pauses in reading to be 'roughly of the same length, 1.0–1.24 seconds', *is* operative in 'spontaneous speech' as well. Clearly it is not as consistently manifest as other systematicities in conversation, for example, the 'tendency' of a first greeting to be followed by a return greeting. And most likely it is not as consistently manifest as is the 1.0–1.24s pause which occurs in reading — otherwise it surely would have been reported.

I am tempted to amend the Butterworth (1980) characterisation of silences in 'spontaneous speech'. It may be that although silences in conversation 'vary considerably' compared to silences in reading, this does not mean that in 'spontaneous speech' the silences are determined by sheer 'cognitive demands' (see, for example, Fragments 5.15–5.20 and Fragment 7 where silence is resolved although the 'cognitive problem' is not). Rather, it appears that the same metric is present in both forms of speaking, perhaps, say, less strictly adhered to in conversation, or perhaps in a more complicated form. For example, the possible 'alternative metric', the gearing down after one second to a parsing which provides for 'next' termination points at two, three and four seconds etc., is one possible 'complication'. There may be others.

**References**

BUTTERWORTH, BRIAN 1980, Evidence from pauses in speech. In B. BUTTERWORTH (ed)., *Language Production, Volume 1, Speech and Talk*. London: Academic Press, 143–54.

GOLDMAN-EISLER, FREIDA 1972, Pauses, clauses, sentence, *Language and Speech*, 15, 103–13.

KRAUT, ROBERT, E. 1978, Verbal and nonverbal cues in the perception of lying, *Journal of Personality and Social Psychology*, 36: 4, 380–91.

## Glossary of transcript symbols

[ A *single left bracket* indicates the point of overlap onset.

] A *single right bracket* indicates the point at which an utterance or utterance-part terminates *vis-à-vis* another.

= *Equal signs*, one at the end of one line and one at the beginning of a next, indicate no 'gap' between the two lines.

[] A *combined left/right bracket* indicates simultaneous onset of the bracketed utterances. It is also used as a substitute for equal signs to indicate no 'gap' between two utterances. This relationship may be shown as:

**E:** Yah,=
**L:** =Tuh hell with im.

or as:

**E:** Yah,[]
**L:** []Tuh hell with im.

(0.0) *Numbers in parentheses* indicate elapsed time in silence by tenths of seconds. For example (1.3) is one and three-tenths seconds.

(.) A *dot in parentheses* indicates a tiny 'gap' within or between utterances. It is probably no more than one-tenth of a second.

_____ *Underscoring* indicates some form of stress, via pitch and/or amplitude. A short underscore indicates lighter stress than does a long underscore.

:: *Colons* indicate prolongation of the immediately prior sound. The length of the colon row indicates length of the prolongation.

::+____ *Combinations of stress and prolongation markers* indicate intonation contours. If the underscore occurs on a letter before a colon, it 'punches up' the letter, i.e. indicates an 'up → down' contour. If the underscore occurs on a colon after a letter, it 'punches up' the colon, i.e. indicates a 'down → up' contour. In the following utterance there are two pitch-shifts, the first, in 'venee:r', an 'up → down' shift, the second, in 'thou:gh', a 'down → up'.

**J:** it's only venee:r thou:gh,

↑ ↓ *Arrows* indicate shifts into higher or lower pitch than would be indicated by just the combined stress/prolongation markers.

.,?? *Punctuation markers* are used to indicate intonation. The combined question mark/comma [?] indicates a stronger rise than a comma but weaker than a question mark. These markers massively occur at appropriate syntactical points, but occasionally there are such displays as:

**C:** Oh I'd say he's about what . five three enna ha:lf?arentchu Robert,

And occasionally, at a point where a punctuation marker would be appropriate, there is none. The absence of an 'utterance-final' punctuation marker indicates some sort of 'indeterminate' contour.

WORD *Upper case* indicates especially loud sounds relative to the surrounding talk.

° The *degree sign* is used as a 'softener'. Utterances or utterance parts bracketed by degree signs are relatively quieter than the surrounding talk.

A subscribed degree sign indicates unvoiced production.

A subscribed degree sign in parenthesis [(b̥)] indicates an 'incipient' sound. For example:

**E:** you couldn'ev'n putcher hand ou:ts:I:DE the CAR ih jiz: (b̥)bu:rn.

And in the speaker-designation column, an empty parentheses plus degree sign [( )°] indicates that an unidentified speaker sounds like a female.

worḍ — A *subscribed dot* is frequently used as a 'hardener'. In this capacity it can indicate, e.g. an especially dentalised 't'. Usually when it occurs under a 'd' it indicates that the 'd' sounds more like a 't'. And, for example, under a possibly ambiguous 'g', it indicates a hard 'g'. Under a possibly ambiguous 'th', it indicates a hard 'th'.

Another sense in which it works as a 'hardener' is to indicate that a sound which is implied in the spelling of a word but is not usually pronounced, is indeed pronounced. For example, in 'diffẹrent' and 'evẹning', which are usually pronounced as 'diff'rent' and 'eev'ning'.

The *subscribed dot* is also frequently used as a 'shortener', for example, in 'the', which is pronounced as 'thee' or 'thuh'; if 'thẹ uh:' is shown, then it is being pronounced 'thuh'.

It can also indicate a trilled 'r'.

‹ — A *pre-positioned left carat* indicates a 'hurried start'; in effect, an utterance trying to start a bit sooner than it actually did. A common locus of this phenomenon is 'self repair'. For example:

| | |
|---|---|
| **C:** | Monday nights we play, (0.3) ‹I mean we go to ceramics, |
| **J:** | y'see it's diffrent f'me:.‹eh f'(.) the othuh boy:s |

A *post-positioned left carat* indicates a 'sudden stop'.

\- — A *dash* indicates a cut-off.

› ‹ — *Right/left carats* bracketing an utterance or utterance-part indicate speeding up.

˙hhh — A *dot-prefixed row of* h*s* indicates an inbreath. Without the dot the *h*s indicate an outbreath.

wohhrd — A *row of* h*s within a word* indicates breathiness.

(h) — A *parenthesized* h indicates plosiveness. This can be associated with laughter, crying, breathlessness, etc.

ƒ — The *florin sign* is, for the time being, used to indicate a certain quality of voice which conveys 'suppressed laughter'. I have not yet settled on a symbol for this phenomenon.

* — An *asterisk* indicates 'creaky voice'

wghord — A *'gh' stuck into a word* indicates gutturalness.

hr — An 'h' *preceding an* 'r' softens the 'r'. This device is used frequently in my transcripts of British talk. Thus, for example, 'part' is shown as 'pahrt', 'court' as 'cohrt', etc.

( ) *Empty parentheses* indicate the transcriber's inability to hear what was said. The length of the parenthesised space indicates the length of the untranscribed talk. In the speaker-designation column, the empty parentheses indicate inability to identify a speaker.

(word) *Parenthesised words* are especially dubious hearings or speaker-identifications.

(∅) A *nul sign* indicates that there may or may not be talk occurring in the designated space.

(( )) *Doubled parentheses* contain transcribers' descriptions rather than, or in addition to, transcriptions.

# 9 On the use of general phonetic techniques in handling conversational material[1]

J. KELLY and J. K. LOCAL
*University of York*

## Problems of transcription

It has become apparent to us during the last few years that the theory and practice of 'transcription' as carried out by linguists leaves a great deal to be desired, especially if applied to conversational material. We want in this paper to discuss why this should be, and to suggest remedies. In addition we present some tentative analyses of conversational material to demonstrate, we hope, that our remedies are worth considering.

The word 'transcription' has many meanings. It is borrowed in, like many terms in linguistics, and has its place in the languages of music and palaeography as well as elsewhere. In linguistic matters, its earliest use was to refer to the reproducing of elements of one script in terms of another. But leaving this aside, it now has an extensive range of meaning. It refers to an activity, to the tools of that activity and to the result of that activity. So that it is possible to say that a linguist at work doing transcription[a] is using a transcription[b] to make a transcription[c]. This way of using our terminology can help no one: and in the remainder of this chapter we shall replace transcription[b] by *notation,* and transcription[c] by *record* or *analysis*. These last two are of course quite different, and for analysis we at York University use notational means not considered in this chapter. But all of these are often conflated under 'transcription' with, as we shall see, serious results for both phonetics and phonology. By *record* we mean here a visual record of the auditory and to some extent visual impressions of a trained phonetician reacting to utterances. The phonetician as observer needs a notational system that is theoretical and, in principle, indeterminately large. The kind of *record* resulting has been called an *impressionistic* transcription. By *analysis* we mean a statement made via a certain notation about patterns, and relationships abstracted at whatever level, out of the language material. Transcription[a] we shall let stand, dropping the superscript. There is nothing startlingly new about this terminological proposal, though the terms, and the notions behind them, are rarely used consistently and seriously.

The standard notation that has been in use amongst the majority of linguists for the making of records and the subsequent presentation of analyses is the 'alphabet' of the International Phonetic Association (IPA). We believe that this 'alphabet', or better, 'symbol stock', has a legitimate use in this application, though ideally, in an extended version. It also has a number of possible worthwhile applications elsewhere. But it is not well suited to work on the systematics of conversation, for instance, or probably for systematic statements in other domains.

As far as extension of the IPA symbol stock is concerned, we should want, in making records of 'talk', to have available ways of notating such things as muscular contractions of the cheeks, or larynx movements, together with the dynamics of loudness, rhythm, and so on. These are relatively easy to supply, at least in an *ad hoc* fashion. And this is why we say that it has a legitimate use in the making of records, even of naturally occurring talk, though one could well imagine better systems. But, as said above, it is less appropriate for the corresponding systematic statement: the reason for this is that it was designed for something quite different.

The modern phase of phonetic transcription in Britain began in the early years of the nineteenth century against a background of Victorian philanthropy, national expansion and public education. The forerunners of the IPA alphabet, of which there were many, were experimental alphabets designed for two main purposes — spelling reform and language teaching. To serve these ends such 'alternative alphabets' had to be designed on the basis of the strictest practicality. They had, for instance, to be readily adaptable to cursive handwritten forms and manageable from the printer's point of view. And they had, of course, to be alphabetic, that is, made up of discrete cumulative segments, that is to say, letters. A.J. Ellis (1848:81), whilst recognising the theoretical justness of an 'analphabetic' representation, rejects it on grounds of practicability: he comments that 'this economy of signs would be a great waste of labour in writing and space in printing . . . Such a proceeding would be so insupportable that we can imagine no nation "philosophic" enough to adopt it.' But Ellis and his successors experimented with many alphabets of various kinds. Some were more detailed than others and designed to preclude any high degree of generalisation; they served to show, say, differences between various regional pronunciations. Writing about his Ethnical Alphabet or 'Alphabet of Nature', Ellis talks of 'distinctions . . . important to the sense', which 'must be made' (viz. in the alphabet): and some alphabets were designed to be adaptable to a number of purposes depending on the extent to which this principle was to be explicit in the selected notation. This notion of necessary distinctions is the forerunner of what later came to be known as the 'phonemic principle'. Ellis distinguishes between an English phonetic alphabet of 66 symbols and, derived from it, a Practical Alphabet of 40: the 66-letter alphabet provides items for more detailed representations of the kinds now called 'allophonic' or 'comparative'. In such a case the items of the larger alphabet are assignable, as groups, to one or other of the items of the lesser alphabet: the items are not different in kind. Ellis carried out a lot of pioneering work in phonetics and produced a large number of alphabets. Some of these were very rich and based upon much aural analysis: but they are all segmental, and none is, of course, indeterminately large. And both Ellis and most of his successors came down in favour of 'practical' style alphabets as the most useful for stating systematicities.

Now, utterances are clusters of phased dynamic events. If one looks at a cine-radiography film of a person talking, the general effect of the movements of the speech organs is of a number of pistons and valves working together but independently in a very complex way. Ellis's phonetic theory, which has served as a general basis for most of our present-day phonetic theory, chooses to treat all this in terms of *configurations* and *transitions* (Ellis, 1848:3). This is clearly not what is *happening*, but is one legitimate way of placing a theoretical framework on perceived events: and it suited Ellis's purpose to use such a framework as it connected directly with his alphabet-making. But it is only one possible framework, and in our phonetic work we have been struck very frequently by the inadequacy of it. In our experience different utterances, which might be transcribed, in our modern equivalent of Ellis's 'practical' mode, as identical at all points but one, do in fact differ at *all* or many points. 'Adam' and 'atom' in the sentences 'say —— again' recorded as part of a randomised list by American male speakers are cases in point. 'Practical'-style transcriptions would offer /aɾəm/ and /aɾ̥əm/ here (or something similar): but there are differences in the release of the initial [ʔ]; the phonatory quality; the vowel qualities throughout; the ballistics and resonance of the intervocalic element; the resonance of the final nasal; and the rhythm. And more and more we have to deal with relativities — with how much 'clearer' one part of a movement is than another, for instance, or with the manners in which prominence variations and articulatory events are phased.

Now, linguists have no institutionalised way of registering some of these things, despite 150 years of 'transcription'. They can improvise bits of notation, but we have nothing standard to hand for the kinds of things we want to attend to. Nor are some of the categories we are recognising generally recognised or institutionalised categories. Nor, most desperately, are the mass of linguists and phoneticians prepared, as far as we can tell, to listen seriously in these terms as a matter of routine. If they are they are seldom prepared to face the implications, but instead edit out as 'predictable', 'irrelevant' or 'unimportant' much of the detail of utterance from the start, by 'listening phonemically', as it were.

The reason for this is that the training of phoneticians and the traditions of their 'transcription' systems have been passed down from Ellis via Sweet's Broad Romic ('My Romic systems were made the basis of the alphabet of . . . l'Association phonétique internationale' (Sweet, 1899)) and the IPA alphabet that is for the most part our present instrument. And, for some, the belief persists that phonemes reside immediately inside the material as registered, much as the statue in the marble.These segmental elements are held to be the basic elements in terms of which sound systems at the word-level work and it is taken for granted that an efficient and proper phonology will get us to them in the run of its analytical procedures as soon as possible, with no dallying along the way to ponder on the status of other bits of material not deemed relevant to this task.

Even when writers pay lip-service to the idea of close observation and recording, in practically all cases they 'abandon this position immediately' (Pike, 1943). Pike himself is not guiltless here: writing a hundred years after Ellis, he advocates close observation, but goes on to say:

> Since the number of segments in a particular continuum approaches the number of phonemes in that continuum . . . an impressionistic phonetic record of a new language proves theoretically legitimate as well as practically valuable as a tool for the phonemicist in his analysis of the phonemic structure of that language.

A similar approach is embodied in textbook after textbook and involves a good deal of unexplained shifting of ground. Here is an example (MacCarthy, 1956):

> Phonetic symbols are conventionally agreed written signs standing for elements of spoken language . . . in dealing with spoken language it is convenient to be able to set down in writing the order in which the essential articulations (or units of sound) succeed one another.

The word 'essential' has appeared here with no explanation, and the word 'elements' above it remains undefined. This shift also involves much exploitation of an ambivalence in the word 'sound' that has been in the literature for over a century. An examination of the use made of this ambivalence would make a fascinating and salutory study, but it is beyond our scope here. A blatant example in an admittedly non-technical book is 'These sounds are all varieties of the same sound' (Lloyd James, 1934). A final example of the kind of muddle that results from such a conflating of *record* and *analysis* can be found in Chao (1968:35):

> In phonetics one tries to anticipate, after a broad survey of the accessible languages of the world, all the necessary distinctions, and set up standard points . . . and then assign the actual sounds of any language under study to the nearest standard points with the appropriate IPA symbols so as to have an accurate representation of the sounds of that language.

This 'accurate' representation is then to be carried out not in terms of some general and indefinitely large framework formed to cover all speech sound production possibilities but in terms of the necessary (to what?) distinctions anticipated after a 'broad' survey of *other* languages. These necessary distinctions are of course the phonemic distinctions. So presumably in working on, for example, Chaga, a linguist following Chao's prescription would carry out his impressionistic transcription *prior to* analysis in terms of what he had set up for other languages *after* analysis. Is it at all surprising that with such astonishing procedures (or pseudo-procedures, see Abercrombie, 1965) as this in operation, linguists have gone no distance along the way of elaborating their notation systems so as to provide a subtle and accurate tool for recording?

This overemphasis on phonology of the phonemic kind has led linguists to regard a specification of the fine detail of utterances as unnecessary or even pernicious. Catford (1972) castigates dialect workers for giving too much detail: 'What is linguistically interesting is surely not the precise quality of the vowel or diphthong in *tail* but whether this is identical (for the informant) with the vowel in *tale*'. Surely *both* are interesting. For instance, the precise quality of the vowel (identical with that of *tale* or not) may have implications for sound-change in progress. The phonetic information and the phonological status are *both* important and interesting, and we could have the best of all worlds by accepting this.

Given these misgivings as to the validity of established systems of notation, our attempts to make accurate records of a (large) number of languages have, then, necessarily led us into a certain amount of experimentation in notation. Our ultimate aim is to develop a multi-layered approach of the kind dubbed 'parametric' by Abercrombie (1965:115–24). Such a notation treats and records variables separately. We are having partly to retrain ourselves to listen impressionistically in these terms, and the actual making of the records is time-consuming because of our lack of skill and the partial and rudimentary nature of the notation we are using; and there are certain disadvantages in such a system. But we believe that by avoiding over-hasty segmental and cross-parametric analysis we can do something to throw light in places till now unlit, particularly in the treatment of conversation. The second part of this chapter attempts to demonstrate this by presenting some preliminary results of detailed impressionistic listening. To close this first section we give, with no further comments, an example of our now evolving 'parametric' notation. We have chosen an utterance in Tongan, rather than a piece of English, so as to highlight the technique as a technique and to avoid the prejudicial effects that looking at English can bring with it. We are not suggesting of course that this kind of display would necessarily be part of any descriptive or analytic statement. Rather it is part of a first-processing technique for handling samples of speech. In the phonetic parts of descriptive statement we might use a 'running' notation which selectively reflected features deemed relevant to the issues at hand.

v = flap    ω̣ = overrounded

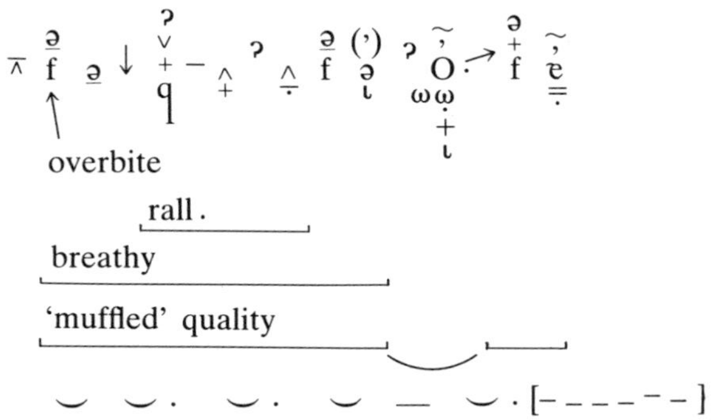

## An impressionistic transcription of conversation

One of the things we have tried to indicate in the first part of this chapter is that there has been a strong tendency for notational systems to be directed in the main towards quasi-alphabet-making rather than towards the making of impressionistic records. Fine phonetic detail when it has been introduced is present as a refinement of superordinate categories; it appears, typically, in dialect work.

But notation systems as commonly established have one further and more important limitation: they are not necessarily suited to the study of conversational matter. Abercrombie (1965:1-9) has distinguished three types of spoken language material that are, or could be, of concern to linguists: conversation, monologue, and spoken prose. He makes a number of important observations: first, that conversation makes up the great bulk of everyday linguistic events; second, that conversation is different *in kind* from spoken prose and monologue; and third, that most linguistic description takes spoken prose as its object of study. As this is so, the usual techniques of linguistic description, including notations, and the constructs they lead to are of a kind best suited to this language activity. Abercrombie goes on to claim that the structures, units, and so on, of spoken prose are derived from those of conversation.

We would agree with Abercrombie's remarks. If his last claim is correct, though, the study of conversation is of prime importance; by studying it we can perhaps gain insights into all three language activities, whereas by studying spoken prose we may never learn very much at all about the phonetic organisation of conversation.

We have suggested above that the IPA system is not best suited to the treatment of conversational material, but rather to the 'spoken prose' mode. But a considerable amount of work has been carried out on the nature of conversations, largely by sociologists working within that sub-area of the discipline dubbed conversation analysis. Such workers routinely use notational devices of a particular kind. Another part of the impetus for writing this chapter came from our attempts to decipher and understand the kind of 'transcriptions' used by practitioners of conversation analysis. We found these transcriptions problematic in a number of ways and were unsure about their status. What was their purpose? Were they supposed to be impressionistic in our sense or were they *post hoc* characterisations of talk which simply included those kinds of things known or supposed to be interactionally relevant? Why did they employ a modified standard orthography? What benefits did that bring over conventional orthography or over impressionistic phonetic transcription? Were the details of pronunciation hinted at by use of the modified orthography ever crucial in the construction of arguments? We saw that in many details — the close attention to pausal phenomena, to audible respiratory activity, to the points at which overlapping talk began and ended, for instance — the CA transcriptions seemed consistent and systematic. At other places, however — in reflecting features of tempo, pitch, loudness, vowel quality and voice quality, for example — the transcriptions seemed inconsistent and arbitrary.

Because we were convinced of the importance of CA work and struck by its honesty and openness we considered it worthwhile to give some thought to the above questions. We therefore found it both interesting and tantalising to discover the following recent statements: the first from Heritage (Chapter 2, this volume): (our italics):

> The basic orientation of conversation analytic studies may be summarised in terms of three fundamental assumptions: (1) interaction is structurally organised; (2) contributions to interaction are both context shaped and *context renewing*, and (3) these two properties inhere in the *details* of interaction so that *no order of detail in conversational interaction can be dismissed a priori* as disorderly, accidental or irrelevant.

the next from Levinson(1983):

> Workers in CA have sometimes used *ad hoc* orthography to represent segmental features, to the irritation of linguists, although no serious theoretical issues seem to be involved (See Goodwin, 1977:120; 1981:47).

We found the Heritage statement uncontroversial, as might be gathered from our comments earlier in the paper. But where, we wondered, did CA transcription stand in the light of his comment on 'detail'? The Levinson remark, however, gave us pause, especially when we looked up the Goodwin references. Goodwin refers to an article by Duncan (1974) in which he says that he did not find *phonemic* transcription revealing in a study of turn-taking behaviour. This is hardly surprising. Phonemic transcription *is not* a tool for description, it is the *result* of a particular kind of analysis, as we have indicated earlier. The lack of usefulness of such a transcription, then, can hardly be used to support a claim that there appear to be no 'theoretical issues' at stake in using a transcription based on modified orthography to deal with *primary material*. This is totally untested ground. No one, to the best of our knowledge, has really tried to do a thoroughgoing impressionistic transcription of conversational data. Therefore, as practising phoneticians, we thought it would be worthwhile to try and do just that. It is in the light of this attempt that we present what follows.

We propose here that if Heritage's statement on 'detail' is taken seriously then it would be well to use the best thing available — impressionistic listening and an impressionistic record which is sensitive enough to capture details of talk in a consistent manner and which has a theoretical base which allows the user to extend the transcription to the point where it reliably reflects discriminable differences. We want to suggest that the impressionistic techniques we use in listening and the records we produce should make available to the analyst aspects of talk which other non-phonetic, or non-consistent, techniques and records are unable to reflect.

In support of this claim we report briefly on some things we have noticed in working on conversational materials. We have not produced detailed, warranted analyses of the aspects of talk we discuss. We have only recently begun to try and handle *conversational* data through the making of impressionistic records. Local, Kelly & Wells (1986), however, do provide a rather more systematic impression of the kinds of findings which emerge from listening to conversation in a particular way and from employing impressionistic phonetic techniques in transcription. The further analytic statements that we make here are, then, preliminary and illustrative. We deal with two phenomena.

**On doing 'well'**

Here we try to indicate some of the things which emerge if the listening and ensuing record pays careful and consistent attention to some so-called 'segmental' aspects of talk. As part of some recent work on turn-structure we have focused our attention on some phonetic aspects of the item 'well'. The following observations are based on a small collection of 'well'-tokens as produced by one speaker. The collection is drawn from a recording of a small claims court proceedings, and includes 34 instances of the item. The speaker is a female from the East London area. The 'well'-tokens serve a range of interactional purposes and have a variety of phonetic shapes. From a phonetic point of view they fall into two gross classes: tokens *without* on-syllable pitch movement (unaccented); and tokens *with* pitch movement (accented). The unaccented tokens are noticeably shorter in duration than the accented tokens and all but one 'run on' to the next word (i.e. they are not pausally separated from the following part of the utterance). We give below our impressionistic records (with a minimum of parametric detail) of the unaccented group [2]:

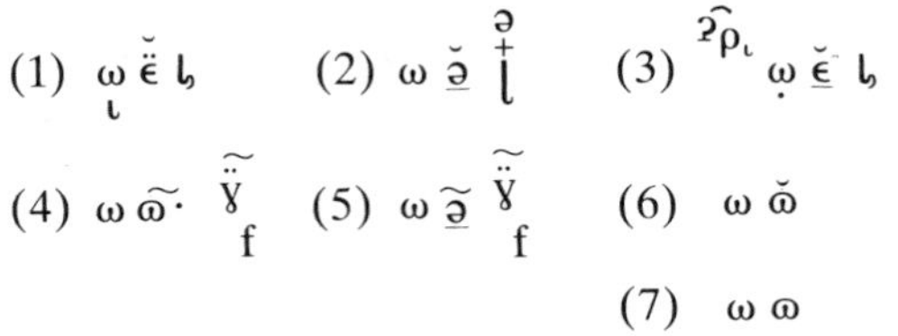

One of the first things to notice about these tokens is the variation in the way that they end. Many varieties of English have a lateral articulation at the end of such words. In the speech of this individual (F) (and other East London speakers, see Wells, 1983) such words end in different ways depending on what follows. That is, such words as 'well', 'material', 'all' and forms such as 'I'll' and 'she'll' have a lateral articulation at their end if they are followed by a vowel. 'Well' -tokens 1-7 above are exemplified in 1–7 below, where we use the quasi-orthographic transcription used by Jefferson for her record of this whole interaction. Line numbers are Jefferson's.

| | | |
|---|---|---|
| (1) | W'l l | (DCD:9.20) |
| (2) | W'l ah think so | (DCD:13.20) |
| | W'l ah think mese:wlf | (DCD:35.14) |
| | No I'm not saying | (DCD:32.9)[3] |
| (3) | Well ah'm: | (DCD:15.5) |

If they are followed by pause or by a consonant they end in a relatively close back vowel which typically is faucalised, sulcalised and accompanied by weak nasality: that is to say that the faucal pillars on each side of the uvula are approximated to each other, the rear part of the tongue is grooved, and the soft palate is slightly lowered.

| | | |
|---|---|---|
| (4) | W'l:this: | (DCD:20.4) |
| | W'l why | (DCD:21.17) |
| | W'l why | (DCD:34.9) |
| (5) | Wul the thing i:s | (DCD:5.20) |
| | Wuwl you | (DCD:32.19) |

Now although these 'positional variants' do occur in F's speech there are also forms with a vocalic ending, not accompanied by faucalisation and not accompanied by a lateral articulation, which occur before *both* vowels *and* consonants:

(6) w'l take ih in (DCD:7.7)

(7) wul 'e sid (DCD:8.20)
wuw look (DCD:15.11)
W'l wi'll (DCD:23.27)
Walt'r (DCD:33.20)[4]

It might be argued that these 'exceptional' forms are simply thrown up by a general phonetic technique which pays nit-picking attention to small, unimportant phonetic details. We would argue otherwise. A close look at the occurrence of these forms (6 and 7) reveals that they have a distributional privilege with respect to their *sequential* placement. These 'well'-tokens, and no others, directly precede (i.e. without pause intervening) reported speech and they do not occur elsewhere. This speaker then has a phonetically distinct 'well'-token which prefaces a particular kind of speaking activity.

Here it seems to us that if close and consistent attention is paid to *phonetic detail*, and no such detail is a priori excluded from consideration as unimportant, it may be possible to uncover unsuspected regularities in the ways in which talk is finely organised. We have not as yet examined other data collections to see whether these features are of general incidence. But it may be that what we have here identified is an instance of a certain kind of phonetic activity which frequently turns up in reporting sequences.

**'Closure pieces' and turn-holding**

One of the interesting things which our transcriptional practices revealed during the course of looking at the 'well'-tokens we have just considered is that 'silent pauses' may be of different types in terms of their phonetic make-up. Although there *are* silences in such sequences it is not the case that these silences are also periods of no activity. In many cases pause is initiated by glottal closure and terminated by glottal release with closed glottis being maintained during the intervening period. Now, this kind of 'closure piece' seems to be deployed by speakers as a resource in interaction. Specifically, we think such 'closure pieces' enter into systems of turn-taking and turn-holding. They appear, for instance, to be able to be used to hold a turn and project further talk by the same speaker.

The issue of taking or holding speakership is considered in some detail in a recent paper by Jefferson (1983). In this paper she discusses the possibility that 'conjunctionals' (such as 'well', 'but', 'so', 'uh') might be 'weak' in terms of taking or holding speakership. In particular, she explores the possibility that such conjunctionals, when followed by pauses, might be 'systematically equivocal' as to whether they are treated as an 'intra-utterance' pause or as a 'trail-off' (i.e. the speaker is 'available for transition'). As part of her discussion Jefferson presents sequences including the following kinds: first, conjunctional + pause + more talk from same speaker ('intra-utterance' pause);

(1.5) [Rah:A:1:(6):2]
**Mr F:** theh'v goht uh sleeping bags end uh:: it's a good ground sheet down en things of this nature,
(0.3)
**Jessie:** ˙t Ye-e[s:
**Mr F:** → [A:nd (0.3) so: uh they should be alright.

(1.3) [SCC:DCD:22]
**Sokol:** it wz a v]ery rude le:ttah.
(0.4)
**Bryant:** My lettuh wz ru:de?
**Sokol:** Oah think so ye:s
(.)
**Bryant:** → W'l (0.3) oll I said in my: (.) °m:.C'n I find it.° I've got it heuh someweh,

Second, conjunctional + pause + 'clean' speaker transition ('trail-off');

(2.4) [NB:III:1:5-6]
**Fran:** I can't be dirdy en do that to um.
(0.4)
**Ted:** → Ne::ah, we-ell,
**Fran:** → We:ll that's th'way it goe:s.
**Ted:** Well one ti:me maybe,

(2.7) [NB:III:3:R:8-9]
**Bud:** ˙hh Hadn'been up t'get iz ch[eck tuh d]eposit=
**Emma:** [Y a : h, ]
**Bud:** → ='n the ba:nk so
→ (0.3)
**Emma:** → ˙t˙hhhh Okay honey well gee tha:nks fer calling . . .

(2.9) [NB:II:1:R:4]

**Emma:** → I jst watched tha:t but
→ (0.3)
**Emma:** [[hhh
**Lottie:** → [[Uh I wouldn'ev'n turn it o:n . . .

And third, conjunctional + pause + overlapping talk.

(3.3) [NB:IV:12:R:3]

**Emma:** ˙t Well ah'll tahlk tihyuh ↓later dear.↓
(0.2)
**Lottie:** → We::ll
→ (.)
**Emma:** *→ [[Ah-
**Lottie:** *→ [[Well ah wz js getti[ng dre:ssed]
**Emma:** [I know yer g ]oin.
**Lottie:** Yeah.

(3.5) [NB:III:3:R:6]

**Emma:** W'l HONEY WIR LOOKIN FORW'R DUH SEEIN YUH. Th' [KIDS SAY=
**Bud:** [(Okay.)
**Emma:** →=when's ↓gra:mpa coming en‹
(.)
**Bud:** *→ [[T h a : t's (n[ice).
**Emma:** *→ [[↑It's really [↑We've hadda n:i:ce time honey

(3.6) [GTS:I:1:69:R:7-8]

**Ken:** cause my father sih now there's g'una be a buncha kids
→ in here'n this routine'n
→ (0.6)
**Ken:** *→ th[is'n that'n the[other] °thing°
**Roger** *→ [Keep yer gua:rd[u(h)u]p ˙he ↑˙hehh↑ ˙hihh Ther g'nna p(h)rainwa(h)sh[yuh

(3.9) [NB:II:5:R:6]

**Lottie:** → We GO:T TWUNNY THREE BENITA but
→ (.)
**Emma:** *→ [[eh hoh]HOH]ho hoh‹.]
**Lottie:** *→ [[GOD we ]had ]mo:re da]:mn fu:n.

Jefferson notes of the cases of overlap here that 'there appears to be no general "rule" for deciding, now, who shall drop out and who proceed'. On listening to some of the extracts cited by Jefferson and to others which seem to exemplify the same kind of sequence we suspect that there *may* be a 'rule' and that in trying to explicate it techniques of impressionistic phonetics need to be brought to bear on the problem. This task is of course greatly aided by a transcriptional record which systematically and consistently reflects the minutiae of phonetic events. We summarise here our preliminary observations which derive from just such a record.

First, in all the instances we have listened to of 'intra-turn' pauses following conjunctionals of the kind discussed by Jefferson our transcriptional records show these to be 'closure pieces' of the kind described above. That is the conjunctional ends in glottal closure which is maintained through silence and is released at the beginning of the following word.

Second, in all the instances we have listened to where, following a conjunction and pause, 'clean' speaker change occurs, the pause is *not* a 'closure piece'. In such cases the transition of the conjunctional into the pause is typically achieved by audible oral and/or glottal release and often by audible breathing which does not terminate in glottal closure. In addition the vowels in these 'trail-off' conjunctionals are noticeably centralised (unlike the vowels in the 'closure piece' conjunctionals) and, in the case of 'uh', this item almost always trails off with brief weak nasality and labiality (either complete labial closure or approximation). The 'trail-off' conjunctionals are also characterised typically by noticeable diminuendo and by slowing down of tempo (see Local, Kelly & Wells, 1986, where some of these features are discussed in detail with respect to turn delimitation).

Third, in all the instances we have listened to where, following the sequence 'conjunctional + pause + overlapping talk', the first speaker does not drop out but proceeds, our impressionistic records reveal that the pause is one which involves the maintenance of glottal closure.

Fourth, in cases where the 'conjunctional + pause' comes off as a 'trail-off' we find the kinds of phonetic event we outlined above (i.e. the pause is *not* a 'closure piece').

There would thus appear to be distinct kinds of phonetic shape for 'closure piece' conjunctionals + pause on the one hand, and 'trail-off' conjunctionals + pause on the other. Of course we have not here addressed the important *interactional* issues which Jefferson deals with in her paper. For instance, why, if our observations have relevance, do speakers come in on occasions after the production by an interlocutor of a 'closure piece' conjunctional? Nor have we yet conducted a large-scale, systematic data run on the phenomena under consideration. Our comments are descriptive in terms of phonetic events and the distributional regularities which accompany them.

## Conclusion

In this paper we have tried to talk about the potentialities of taking seriously the linguist's primary task, namely, that of making accurate and detailed records. We have also discussed the kinds of activity we ourselves are engaging in when we do what we take to be serious impressionistic listening and recording which, for us, are two separate but related activities. We hope we have shown that considerable gains can be made if truly general phonetic techniques of a relatively novel kind are brought to bear on selected aspects of conversational or any other language material.

### Notes to Chapter 9

1. Thanks to Gail Jefferson for making her transcriptions of conversation so readily available. Without them the second part of this paper would never have been written.
2. ? indicates very short duration, F means faucalised.
3. 'No I̠'m not saying' = 'well I'm not saying'.
4. 'W̠alt̄'r' = 'well Theresa'.

### References

Abercrombie, D. 1965, *Studies in Phonetics and Linguistics*. London: Oxford University Press.

Bell, A. M. 1867, *Visible Speech: the Science of Universal Alphabetics* (3rd edition, 1907). Washington: Volta Bureau

Catford, J. C. 1972, Phonetic fieldwork. In T. Sebeok (ed.), *Current Trends in Linguistics*, 12. The Hague: Mouton, 2480–505.

Chao, Y. R. 1970, *Language and Symbolic Systems*. Cambridge: Cambridge University Press.

Duncan, S. 1974, On the structure of speaker–auditor interaction during speaking turns, *Language in Society*, 2, 161–80.

Ellis, A. J. 1848, *The Essentials of Phonetics*. London: F. Pitman.

Jefferson, G. 1983, On a failed hypothesis: 'Conjunctionals' as overlap-vulnerable, *Tilburg Papers in Language and Literature*, 28, 29–33.

LEVINSON, S. 1983, *Pragmatics*. Cambridge: Cambridge University Press.

LLOYD JAMES, A. 1938, *Our Spoken Language*. London: Nelson.

LOCAL, J., KELLY, J. & WELLS, W. 1986, Towards a phonology of conversation: turn-taking in Tyneside English, *Journal of Linguistics*, 22, 411–37.

MACCARTHY, P. 1956, Phonetic transcription. In *Talking of Speaking*. London: Oxford University Press.

PIKE, K. L. 1943, *Phonetics*. The University of Michigan Press.

SWEET, H. 1899, *The Practical Study of Languages*. London: Oxford University Press.

WELLS, J. 1983, *Accents of English*. Cambridge: Cambridge University Press, 2 vols.

# SECTION 4: Data Analysis

## Introduction

Once a transcription has been made from a recorded conversation, the problem arises as to how to interpret the data so obtained. A fundamental issue is whether the corpus of data should be analysed quantitatively or qualitatively. One of the contributions in this section, by Peter Collett (Chapter 10), represents an example of a sophisticated statistical technique used in the sequential analysis of social interaction. The other, by Tony Wootton (Chapter 11), contrasts this approach with those characteristically employed in conversation analysis where qualitative methods are typically preferred.

As was pointed out in Section 1, the most important feature of the psychological approach to the study of interpersonal communication is a belief in the value of the experimental method, which in itself represents the distinctive theoretical perspective of psychology. Duncan (1969) has characterised this approach as the 'external variable' approach, so named because of its basic strategy of attempting to relate aspects of behaviour to features external to the communicative context, such as sex and personality. Duncan contrasts the external variable approach with what he calls a structural approach, which is concerned more with the sequential and hierarchical organisation of behaviour. The problem of adopting the external variable approach is clearly illustrated by the way in which experimental psychologists attempt to deal with time: time is frequently simply ignored, although social psychologists have sometimes attempted to extract sequential information through time-sampling procedures, typically entering successive segments of the conversation into the analysis as levels of a within-subjects variable (Roger, 1986).

The limitations of traditional psychological approaches to the analysis of time are discussed in Chapter 10 by Peter Collett. Collett describes three procedures which can be adopted for describing the sequential ordering of events. The first of these is the time-sampling procedure referred to above. But time-sampling is essentially arbitrary. Collett proposes that slicing procedures may be entirely appropriate for studying the brain, where the solidity and fine grain of cell tissue demand sectional analysis; however, such procedures are quite out of place in the investigation of action where they superimpose arbitrary units on the natural structure of events.

The alternatives to time-sampling described by Collett are to use either a 'time base' or an 'event base' for describing the sequential ordering of events. Instead of imposing some arbitrarily defined interval on the stream of events, the investigator tries to locate the points or junctures at which one unit of action gives way to another. When this is done against a calibrated time continuum, one speaks of a time base; if, however, one is merely concerned with the order in which units follow one another, then one refers to an event base. Thus, while time sampling assumes that the junctures between action units can be exposed by repeatedly sectioning the stream of behaviour, time- and event-base descriptions start by locating the points at which these junctures occur; in this respect, they are more faithful to the character of action.

The time-base and event-base procedures described by Collett may be referred to collectively as stochastic methods, where the occurrence of an event depends to a variable extent upon the events preceding it. Instead of attempting to predict precisely what behaviour will follow from any particular event, the analysis provides a distribution of possible outcomes, each with an associated probability of occurrence. This method in its simplest form allows the estimation of the probability of one event following another (a first-order approximation). However, Collett discusses three other sophisticated methods within the context of transitional probability analysis: lagged probability profiles, the assessment of second- and third-order approximations, and chain analysis. Lagged probability profiles represent the probability with which one type of event follows another, either immediately (i.e. one lag), after one other event (i.e. two lags), after two other events (i.e. three lags) and so forth, depending upon the number of lags being examined. Second-order approximations refer to the extent to which two events are followed by a third; similarly, third-order approximations refer to the extent to which three events are followed by a fourth. Chain analysis attempts to create a hierarchical structure in which the most commonly occurring pairs of events in the initial corpus of data are identified and subsequently treated as a single higher-order event for further analysis. This process is repeated until no further chains can be identified. Chain analysis thus uncovers a chain of influence in which certain higher-order groupings of events lead to others.

Collett then discusses a number of shortcomings in these methods for analysing sequences of events, pointing out that none of them is sufficiently sensitive to uncover the minor transitions between events that may be crucial to a proper understanding of the major ones. The alternative he proposes is his own method of conjoint analysis (Collett & Lamb, 1982). Conjoint analysis is a pictorial description of social interaction, in which the activities produced by one person are arranged along the rows, while the activities of the other person are arranged along the columns of the same matrix. The advantage which Collett claims for this technique is that it is possible to achieve a visual representation of exchanges between two or more individuals along several different modalities, or to depict the interplay between separate modalities within the same individual. However, conjoint analysis does not in itself constitute a form of statistical analysis; rather it is a form of visual transcription, which still leaves the problem of adopting an appropriate form of statistical analysis for coping with sequences of behaviour.

The majority of work in conversation analysis also focuses on sequence and properties of sequences, but the approach taken differs fundamentally from the statistical techniques described by Collett. Whereas these techniques measure the likelihood of occurrence by making transitional probability estimates, Wootton (Chapter 11) writes that one of the main concerns of conversation analysts has been to identify the nature of the constraints existing between utterance pairs such as requests and grantings/rejections, questions and answers, invitations and acceptances/declinings. In both of these approaches, there is an assumption that utterance pairs are linked, but whereas in the stochastic approach the link is purely a statement of a statistical probability, in conversation analysis the link constitutes an expectation that the first part of a pair will be followed by the second.

Wootton claims that this expectation can be traced in a number of ways. For example, if the second part of a pair is not produced, then there may be a follow-up to the first part of a pair which demonstrates that the recipient has not performed an action or a response which might be expected of him. Again, the second part of a pair may be held in abeyance, for example, if the recipient requires further information, Wootton points out that the constraint set up by the first part of a pair can run across a number of intervening utterances. In these and other ways, Wootton claims that one can demonstrate that interactants are influenced by sequential constraints. He goes on to point out that the structural significance of these constraints is essentially independent of the frequency with which they occur: knowing the relevant frequencies alone would not permit one to infer whether or not people actually orientate to such constraints. Moreover, within the framework of conversation analysis, infrequently occurring responses would be as significant as those of frequent occurrence to the task of specifying forms of conversational organisation which are in some sense shared and accessible to members of the society under investigation.

Wootton goes on to describe different sources of evidence that are frequently used by conversation analysts. A number of these types of evidence are concerned with sequential placement, which he illustrates by the use of the particle 'oh'. Thus, 'oh' can be considered in relation to speech preceding its occurrence, to its treatment in subsequent conversation, and in relation to the speaking turn within which it occurs. The distinctive role of 'oh' in conversation might also be assessed by a comparison with the use of other similar particles, such as 'uh huh'. Finally, Wootton points out that in the course of an investigation new phenomena may be discovered which an analysis, as it has been developed up to that point, cannot handle. These deviant cases, Wootton argues, may also constitute a distinctive source of evidence: such instances can lead to a reformulation of the role of the particle, although close investigation may also yield important evidence supporting the analysis which these instances at first appeared to undercut.

## Conclusion

Collett points out that sequence analysis methods come in several shapes and sizes. Although they perform different operations, they are all united in their dedication to the principle that orderly patterns can be uncovered by summarising the way in which events follow one another. They are all founded on the idea that action is orderly, that it has temporal regularities, and that these regularities can be exposed by the analysis of sequence analysis techniques.

Wootton sets conversation analysis apart from the stochastic approach, maintaining that the structural significance of sequential constraints is essentially independent of the frequencies with which particular types of turn or action occupy the position in which the second part is expected: knowing the relevant frequencies alone would not permit one to infer whether or not people actually orientate to such constraints.

Furthermore, within the framework of conversation analysis, infrequently occurring responses would be as significant as those occurring frequently to the task of specifying forms of conversational organisation.

Thus the two approaches to sequential analysis described in this section are essentially different: whereas stochastic analyses are intended to define structure in terms of sequential regularities, conversation analysts are concerned primarily with the interactional significance of structure, and firmly maintain that such information cannot be extracted by charting sequential frequencies.

**References**

Collett, P. & Lamb, R. 1982, Describing sequences of social interaction. In M. Von Cranach & R. Harré (eds), *The Organisation of Human Action*. Cambridge: Cambridge University Press.

Duncan, S. 1969, Non-verbal communication, *Psychological Bulletin*, 72, 118–37.

Roger, D. 1986, Language and social psychology: some thoughts on method, *British Social Psychology Society Social Section Newsletter*, 15, 20–23.

# 10 Time and action

PETER COLLETT
*Oxford University*

There are two broad approaches that the social psychologist can take when studying action, each of which is informed by a totally different attitude to the role of time. The first approach simply ignores time. It proceeds, like all investigations of behaviour, by examining actions as they are produced in real time, but it works towards a characterisation of action which is synchronic and completely devoid of time.[1] The second approach is by nature diachronic. It also begins with observation of actions that are produced in real time, but instead of discarding time at the first available opportunity, it endeavours to capture and summarise the temporal character of action. Let us look at these two approaches in greater detail.

## Ignoring time

The standard methods of the social psychologist are the experiment and the group comparison. In the experiment the psychologist manipulates some variable or variables according to certain accepted procedures, while in the case of the group comparison he merely takes advantage of manipulations that have already been effected by nature. Whether they are conducted in the confines of a laboratory or in the free-wheeling context of a field study, both the experiment and the group comparison tend to place the same atemporal construction on action. For example, when the psychologist manipulates the appearance, proximity or demeanour of a confederate in order to explore its impact on the behaviour of his subjects, or when he compares the activities of people of different ages, personalities or sex, he usually records their responses and then sums them across or within trials. Having, say, manipulated proximity and measured gaze, he may find that people look at each other less when they are sitting closer together, or, having compared the expressive behaviour of males and females, he may discover that the females smile more than males. In so doing he will doubtless have uncovered a regular association between proximity and looking, or between sex and smiling, but his discovery will only have been achieved at the cost of reducing the actions of his subjects to simple aggregates. In other words, looking and smiling will have been expropriated from their natural continuum and summarised in terms of some timeless index.

There are two attitudes which seem to be conducive to the exclusion of time from the study of action. The first is that which conceives of action as being comprised of *variables*, the second that which treats action as though it were *artefact*.

**Action as variable**

The underlying assumption of any discourse which employs the notion of variables is that action consists of parameters which are continuous, infinitely divisible and amenable to summation. This model is borrowed from the physical sciences which deal in quantities like weight, density, temperature and pressure. Once one has conceived of, say, gaze as a variable (even to the point of using the term explicitly) the way is open to talking about the total amount of time that people spend looking at each other, how long they spend looking while listening, who looks more than whom, and so on. There is no doubt that these things can be quantified or that certain people look more than others, but this has nothing to do with the organisation of action in time, or the way in which looks and glances are traded and perceived. By simply calculating the amount of time that people spend looking at each other one does not produce a temporal analysis of their gaze.

Duncan (1969) has distinguished two approaches to the study of behaviour, namely what he calls the 'external variable' approach, where the investigator attempts to relate variable aspects of people's behaviour to something which is external to that behaviour, and the 'structural' approach, where the investigator tries to uncover regularities in the sequential structure of action. The former is exemplified by studies which are concerned with the connection between proximity and gaze or the relationship between sex and smiling, the latter by studies of the sequential organisation of people's activities when they greet or take leave of each other. In considering the relative merits of these two approaches, Duncan expresses the view that they complement each other and that both should be used in the study of social behaviour. But this kind of eclecticism needs to be called into question, for while the external variable approach may be appropriate for certain types of investigation, it is totally unsuitable for the study of human action. It is unsuitable for the simple reason that it ignores the temporal dimension of action and it cannot therefore offer a basis for understanding how actions are organised or how they are interpreted by others. The structural approach, on the other hand, is concerned with the identification of units of behaviour and with their temporal organisation; it attempts, as far as possible, to respect the temporal aspect of action.

Those studies which align themselves with a variable conception of action are prone to overlook the temporal organisation of action. Since they are committed to a view which sees action as parametric in character they are automatically limited to the business of exploring correlations and differences; and since they deny the view which regards action as being comprised of units, they are unable to address themselves to questions about the meaning of action. Meanings necessarily reside in units and combinations of units, and that is why any study which deals in the currency of variables, rather than units, cannot account for the ways in which people behave so as to be understood by others or, for that matter, the ways in which others actually understand them.

## Action as artefact

The other attitude towards action which encourages a neglect of time is that which conceives of action as artefact, as some kind of *thing*. Unlike the variable conception of action, this attitude sees people's behaviour as consisting of discrete and homogeneous units, but as units which are uninformed by time. Of course, sequential analyses of action also regard the flow of behaviour as being reduceable to units. However here the similarity ends, for while the view of action as artefact assumes action to be no more than the synchronic arrangement of its constituent features, sequence analysis is dedicated to the principle that the structure of action is diachronic.

Most contemporary work on the face can be seen as implying a view of action as artefact. When we speak of 'the smile' or 'the frown' we necessarily assume that we are dealing with some object which, although it may consist of several variants, can nevertheless be defined in terms of a synchronic arrangement of facial features. This view of the face is essentially postural. It presupposes that expressions are produced by arranging the face into a static display, and that the task of the investigator is therefore to discover how transfixed displays form categories of expression and how these differ from each other; in other words, what are the variant forms of the smile and in what ways do these differ from those which constitute the frown, and so on. Interestingly, this attitude toward the face also assumes that the information value of facial displays is completely unrelated to the manner in which the various parts of the face are marshalled in time.

The view of action as artefact thus considers that behaviour can be adequately described by simply examining the synchronic arrangement of those features which characterise an action at its most representative moment. It encourages the idea that action can be reduced to a slice of time in which the only sources of variation are configurational, and it therefore fails to allow that actions may vary in the manner in which they are produced in time, or that similar actions which differ in relation to some temporal feature like speed may be designed to serve quite different social ends, or that they may be seen as such by those to whom they are addressed.

## Respecting time

When the investigator analyses action he can either ignore or take account of its organisation in time, just as he can either ignore or take account of its configuration. These options are perhaps made more clear by borrowing the analogy that Saussure (1916) applied to language. Saussure compared language to a plant stem, where the cross-sectional arrangements of cells represented the synchronic structure of language, what Saussure called the *langue*, and the transectional arrangement of cells its diachronic structure, or what he called *parole*. This model also offers a basis for the way in which actions can be studied. If we imagine that action is something like a plant stem, but one in which the cells are arranged in such a way that they do not necessarily extend the full length of the stem, then we see how cross-sections at different points in time may reveal quite different synchronic structures, just as transections in relation to different aspects of action may expose quite different diachronic structures. To describe the overall structure of our hypothetical plant stem we would need to make numerous cuts, either across the stem or along its length. Likewise, in order to gain a proper understanding of action we need to examine its cross-sectional structure as well as its transectional structure, in other words both its configuration and its temporal composition.

Two corollaries follow from this. The first is that both configuration and temporal composition will be revealed by either an infinity of cross-sections or an infinity of transections. The second is that actions with different kinds of structures will be differentially sensitive to cross-sectional and transectional examination. At the extremes this means that an action which is comprised of a single modality which constantly changes its value will be best understood by studying its temporal structure, whereas an action which consists of several modalities which retain a steady state will best be understood by examining its configuration. Of course we seldom, if ever, encounter such extreme cases — we do not, for example, find people switching their gaze to the exclusion of other movements, not do we find them holding a complex facial display for any length of time. Instead we find that when people move their eyes they often move their head as well, and that one facial pattern soon gives way to another. In other words, action is both polymodal and temporally variable, and to that extent its overall structure will always remain intractable to one-shot studies of configuration and to temporal analyses of single modalities.

## Time and action

We are now in a position to return to the point where we began and to gather up the threads of the argument that we have advanced thus far. We started by suggesting that there are two approaches to the study of action — one which simply ignores time and one which endeavours to examine action within some temporal framework. The first of these approaches is again represented by two quite distinct views of action, namely one in which action is conceived of in terms of variables and another in which actions are conceived of as artefacts. In terms of our plant stem analogy it is now possible to see that the conception of action as variable satisfies neither the requirement for a consideration of configuration nor the requirement for a consideration of temporal constitution. It fails to provide an account of configuration because it does not explore the synchronic arrangement of features at any point in time, and it tells us nothing about temporal constitution because it merely regards time as a resource from which aggregate data can be obtained. Likewise, it is apparent that although the conception of action as artefact does address itself to matters of configuration, it fails to offer an account of the way in which configuration depends on time. In other words, the variable conception looks at neither cross-sectional nor transectional aspects of action, and while the artefact conception is based on cross-sectional analysis it too ignores the transectional aspects of action.

## Action in time

When dealing with objects we may distinguish characteristics like temperature and colour from their precise expression. Likewise, when we speak of action, we may distinguish between modalities and their value at a particular moment in time. Just as an object cannot be simultaneously hot and cold, so too the right hand cannot be simultaneously raised and lowered, and just as an object can be concurrently hot and red, so too the hand can be raised and opened. The body is like an object in so far as it accommodates a variety of attributes at any point in time, but it is of course a far more complex entity than most objects because each of its members may be thought of as an object in its own right. The body incorporates numerous modalities such as orientation and elevation of the head, direction of gaze, position of the limbs and so on, and each modality can, in principle, be described as possessing a particular value at any point in time. This polymodal character of action has been nicely illustrated by Scheflen (1973) and Goffman (1972). Scheflen describes how the segments of the body, such as the head, the torso and the limbs, can be orientated in different directions in order to sustain an opening with several people at the same time, and Goffman has drawn attention to the social significance of dysjunction between the orientation of different segments of the body, and the way in which someone can use this technique to distribute his attention between people. For example, when two people are conversing, one of them may be interrupted by a passerby, and he may temporarily detach himself in order to exchange a few words with the passerby. But in so doing he may retain an orientation to his initial interlocutor, or extend an arm in his direction in order to demonstrate his enduring commitment to the initial conversation. By orientating or directing different parts of his body towards both parties he can hold one conversation in play while keeping his options open on another.

The principle of polymodality operates both at the level of body movement and at the level of social function that is served by body movement. Whenever we analyse action we can do so at either level. At the level of body movement we can employ a notation scheme which incorporates those modalities of movement which we regard as important and which enables us to transcribe the various changes that occur in relation to each modality. With the case that we discussed a moment ago, we might, for example, record the changes in orientation, gaze, hand movements, and so on, alongside the speech that is produced when two people are interrupted by a passerby and when one of them temporarily engages a passerby. Such an analysis would be formal in character; it would simply record the movements made by people, not what was being socially achieved by those movements. The other level of analysis is the level of function. Here, instead of recording movements, we might attempt to identify those categories of action, such as engagement or disengagement, which are fulfilled by the movements and speech produced by the various parties. This level would be concerned with the semantic component of action; it would record the various social moves made by people rather than the movements they make with their bodies.

A record of action can therefore be concerned with either movement or function. It can also be concerned with the relationship between movement and function, but this is a subject which we do not have space to discuss here. Aside from being concerned with either movement or function, a record of action can also describe either one modality or several modalities. Clearly, any record which simply addresses itself to one aspect of action remains uncommitted to the possibility that people can move different parts of their body simultaneously, or that they can fulfil several social functions at the same time. As it happens, most analyses of body movement incorporate several modalities, although there are a fair number of studies which have focused on one aspect of movement to the exclusion of all other modalities (e.g. Jaffe & Feldstein, 1970). At the level of function, it is most commonly the case that the record only incorporates one modality — in other words, it usually assumes that someone can only fulfil one function at a time. But as we saw earlier, it is quite within the capacity of individuals to perform several social acts at the same time. This they can do, either by using different parts of their body to perform different functions, or by producing an unfractured performance which they know will be differentially understood by different people. Cryptic teasing often has this type of structure. Here, the teaser can address someone in such a way that the addressee recognises the actual or potential embarrassment of the remark, while others in their presence do not, or in such a way that other people recognise the remark as a tease while the person being addressed does not. When someone fragments his body so that different parts serve different functions, or produces a unified performance that is read differently by different people, he demonstrates that he is capable of doing more than one social thing at a time.[2] Any analysis which aims to capture the essential features of people's actions will need to make provisions for this inherent feature of social action.

If polymodality is an integral feature of action, then it is also the case that the polymodal character of action only finds expression in time. There is now a growing band of psychologists who believe that action can only be understood by describing and then summarising its temporal expression. Their task has been assisted by the development of techniques within psychology and by the importation of techniques developed in other disciplines. At this point, it may be worth our while to distinguish between methods which are designed for *describing* action and those which are designed for *summarising* action. Descriptive methods are usually based on some kind of non-linguistic notation. They provide an alternative language, an orthography which allows the observer to record various aspects of the action being described. It will not be our task to discuss notation schemes in any depth here, except to note that they vary enormously, from those which use simple alpha-numeric symbols for recording strings of events to those which employ synthetic symbols for recording complicated conjunctions of events. With the exception of the home-spun systems produced by Birdwhistell (1970) and people like Kendon (1976), most notation schemes have been developed in the study of dance (cf. Laban, 1956; Eshkol & Wachmann, 1968). These systems are not readily assimilable and they usually require a great deal of practice before they can profitably be employed — which is one of the reasons why they have not found wide currency among psychologists who study action.

Despite the fact that psychologists have been so cautious about adopting dance notation schemes for studying action, they have been far less hesitant about borrowing methods for summarising sequential data from disciplines like ethology and linguistics. Before we turn our attention to the kinds of methods that social psychologists have been using it might be advisable for us to consider some of the requirements that need to be satisfied by any sequence analysis method which sets out to summarise the temporal properties of action.

The first point to be made about sequence analysis methods is that they come in several shapes and sizes. Although they perform different operations, they are all united in their dedication to the principle that orderly pattern can be uncovered by summarising the way in which events follow one another. They are all founded on the idea that action is orderly, that it has temporal regularities, and that these regularities can be exposed by the application of sequence analysis techniques. But beyond their shared commitment to the study of temporal pattern, different techniques entertain rather different assumptions about the nature of action. These differences concern the appropriate time-frame for description, whether action is seen as unimodal or polymodal, the ability of the technique to expose transitive order, and its capacity to take account of repetition in the cycle of events. Let us now look at each of these issues in turn.

*Time frame*

Sequence analysis always proceeds by first identifying the events which are to be entered in the analysis. This requires the specification of what is to count as an event and the articulation of the constitutive rules which enable one to recognise an event as an instantiation of a particular category of events (cf. Clarke, 1979). In ethology this would involve action categories in an ethogram, while in linguistics it might involve either syntactic or speech act categories. The identification of units and their category membership is an essential prerequisite to sequence analysis, if only because sequence analysis offers a means of discovering how one kind of thing leads to another. Without some demarcation of unit boundaries and categories of units — in other words, a discrete conception of action — such analyses would not be possible.

Once the range or vocabulary of units under consideration has been specified, the next step is to describe their order. At this point one of three procedures can be adopted. Each concerns the establishment of a different time-frame within which action units are identified. The first procedure is 'time-sampling', in which the investigator selects a time interval of specified duration during which the stream of behaviour is searched to determine which category of action is being produced. The frequency of this sampling can vary from a few seconds to several hours. As a rule of thumb it is common practice to try and select a time interval which is not so short that notation becomes redundant and unwieldy, nor so long that it misses transitions between action units. The problems with time-sampling are basically twofold: first, it leads to artefactual orderings where one category of action leads on to itself, and, second, it has been shown that the regularities that it uncovers are sensitive to the actual frequency with which action is sampled (Abelson, 1967; Hayes, Meltzer & Wolf, 1970; but see also Arundale, 1977). Time-sampling takes an essentially histological attitude towards action. Although it does not actually place behaviour under the microtome, it does presume that action can only be studied by making cross-sectional slices. Slicing procedures are entirely appropriate for the brain, where solidity and the fine grain of cell tissue demand sectional analysis, but they are quite out of place in the investigation of action where they simply encourage the view that action does not have natural boundaries.

The alternatives to time-sampling are the use of either a 'time base' or an 'event base' (Bakeman, 1978). Here the stream of behaviour is no longer sampled according to some arbitrarily defined time interval. Instead, the investigator tries to locate the points or junctures at which one unit of action gives way to another. When this is done against a calibrated time continuum one speaks of a time base. If, however, one is merely concerned with the order in which units follow one another then one refers to an event base. This means that a time-base description always contains more information than an event-base description. It contains more information because while both kinds of description capture the order of events, a time-base description also captures their actual duration. Consequently, an event-base description can always be derived from a time-base description, but not vice versa. The relative merits of these two kinds of description will usually depend on the demands and requirements of the study in question, but whichever is used it always does far less violence to the material being analysed than does time-sampling. Time-sampling proceeds on the somewhat coy assumption that the junctures between action units can only be exposed by repeatedly sectioning the stream of behaviour. Time- and event-base descriptions, on the other hand, start by locating the points at which these junctures occur, and in this respect they are more faithful to the character of action. A long time ago Plato suggested that nature should always be cut at its joints. Time- and event-base descriptions follow his exhortation; time-sampling does not.[3]

*Polymodality*

We have already observed that action is polymodal, both at the level of movement and at the level of function. In other words, not only is it in the nature of action that it sometimes consists of separate movements which are produced concurrently, but it is also in the nature of action that several functions are sometimes realised simultaneously. Of course, there may be instances where a unimodal description of movement is appropriate, simply because only one feature of movement is being activated, but these are rare to the point of being almost non-existent.

The likelihood of action fulfilling only one function at a time is far greater, and although it is often quite legitimate to offer a unimodal description of function, there are undoubtedly instances where a polymodal description is called for, and where a unimodal description would only serve to obscure part of what is happening.

It is worth noting that, whether they are concerned with movement or function, polymodal descriptions of action can be followed by either polymodal or unimodal summaries of sequential structure. In other words, it is possible to begin with, say, a polymodal description of movement and then proceed to a sequence analysis which either retains the polymodal character of the movement or which reduces it to more manageable unimodal terms. By contrast, unimodal descriptions of action, whether of movement or of function, can only be followed by unimodal summaries of sequential structure. Consequently, sequence analyses can never be more sensitive than the descriptions of action from which they are derived.

*Transitive order*

When we say that time exhibits the properties of succession, transitivity and irreversibility, what we really mean is that time imposes certain relations on events — it ensures, as it were, that one event follows another, that events which follow others also follow their antecedents, and that the order of past events remains invariant. Now, if it is the task of sequence analysis to explore the temporal aspects of action then it is also its task to address the more important relations that time imposes on events. For our purposes, the most important relations are succession and transitivity. Succession concerns the relations between one type of event and its sequitor or sequitors. Here one can either examine how one type of event leads on to another or the way in which one kind of event leads on to various other kinds of event. Either way, one is simply exploring one step in a sequence, or what in certain contexts is referred to as a first-order transition. By contrast, transitivity is concerned with the relations that obtain within strings of events. Here one would examine the way in which one kind of event leads on to various other kinds of event, and how these in turn lead on to other kinds of event, and so on. If studies of succession look at one step in the sequence, then studies of transitivity look at several steps in the sequence of events. That is, they are concerned with *n*th-order transitions, where *n* is greater than one. As we shall see in a moment, some sequence analysis methods are specifically designed to explore the relations between pairs of events, while others are capable of summarising the underlying pattern in fairly long strings of events. It hardly needs to be said that those methods which can handle long strings of events are better suited to sequences of action which contain such strings. They are also more powerful because relations of succession are subsumed by relations of transitivity.

*Repetition*

The final requirement for sequence analysis is that it be capable of handling strings of events in which the same event appears more than once. Broadly speaking, there are two types of sequence — what we might call looped and unlooped sequences. In an unlooped sequence the same event cannot occur more than once. Unlooped sequences are found in stage models, such as that proposed by Piaget, and in fixed action patterns, such as those described by ethologists. The point about a stage model is that it excludes any recycling whereby the individual enters the same stage more than once. Thus, having acquired the ability to conserve liquids, the child may move on to acquire other skills, but it will not return to acquire conservation of liquids again at some later date. Although fixed action patterns differ from stage models, they have in common the feature that events occur in an invariant order. A fixed action pattern is, as it were, wired into the system, so that when, for example, the gull begins to roll an egg along the beach it does so using a stereotyped sequence of movements — so much so that the sequence of movements continues to be run off even when the egg is removed (Hinde, 1982).

In a looped sequence the same event can occur at several points. Everyday conversation offers a case in point, for in conversation there are no proscriptions on the reoccurrence of items like questions, answers, interjections and the like. Much the same is true of leave-taking. Leave-taking is of course notoriously repetitive. When two people negotiate a parting they may engage in several bouts of handshaking, interspersed with attempts by one or both parties to withdraw from the other person. This means that any coding of conversation or leave-taking must make allowances for the repetition that is inherent in the sequence. Or, to put it differently, it should only employ a sequence analysis method which can handle looped sequences.

We have already seen that action can be described using either time-sampling, an event base or a time base. As its title suggests, time-sampling involves the establishment of a series of standard time intervals within which the stream of behaviour is sampled for one of several discrete action types. By contrast, event and time bases are concerned with the location of the boundaries or junctures of action types rather than with whether they are being performed within specified intervals. So, while an event base simply focuses on the order in which action types are performed, a time base looks at both the order of action types and their temporal duration. Action can also be treated as though it is expressed in either one or several modalities. The issue of what constitutes an appropriate time-frame raises questions about the way in which action should be described, while the issue of unimodality versus polymodality raises questions both about the way in which action should be described as well as the way in which its sequential structure should be summarised. The other two issues that need to be addressed in connection with summarising procedures are whether they can reveal transitive relations between events, and whether they can handle the repeated occurrence of event types in the stream of behaviour.

The most commonly employed procedures for summarising sequential structure are those related to transitional probability. Typically the string of event-types is recast in a matrix which summarises the frequency with which each event-type is preceded and followed by every other event-type. The values in the resultant matrix can then be transformed into transitional probabilities and these in turn can be presented in the form of a state transition diagram (Stern, 1974; Bakeman & Brown, 1977; Gottman & Bakeman, 1979). In a state transition diagram each event-type is represented by, say, a circle and the transitional probabilities between each pair of event-types by a labelled arrow, which identifies the frequency with which one type of events leads to another. A state transition diagram is therefore really nothing more than a graphic depiction of a transitional probability matrix, but as with all such depictions, it usually leads itself to more immediate assimilation of the sequential connections between each pair of event types than does a bland matrix of numbers.

State transition diagrams and the transitional probability matrices from which they are derived can summarise both unimodal and polymodal data. They can summarise unimodal data when the coded string of events refers either to single actions produced by an individual or to single actions produced in alternation by the members of a dyad. Correspondingly, a state transition diagram or a transition probability matrix can summarise polymodal data where the coded string of events refers either to concurrent actions produced by the same individual, to single actions produced simultaneously by the members of a dyad, or to concurrent actions produced simultaneously by the members of a dyad. If transitional probability analysis can handle polymodal data, then it can also satisfy the requirement concerning repetition. In fact, it is specifically designed for discrete sequential data which contain iterations of the same event-types and it would have nothing to say about strings without repetition. In this respect lie both its strength and its weakness, for while it can readily be applied to looped sequences it is completely inappropriate for unlooped sequences. For this reason unlooped sequences require alternative modes of analysis. The major issue on which transition probability analysis falters is its awkwardness in exposing patterns of transitive relations within strings of events. Most, but of course not all, transitional probability analysis is concerned with first-order approximations. In other words, it tends to be used for summarising the ways in which certain event-types lead to others. But the point about sequence analysis methods is that they should be capable of showing, not only how one type of event gives way to others, but also how these in turn give way to others, and so on.

There are three ways in which researchers have attempted to satisfy the requirement for transitive ordering within the context of transitional probability analysis: the first is through the assessment of second- and third-order approximations; the second, through lagged probability profiles; and the third, through chain analysis. For example, in a second-order analysis the original matrix would be recast in such a way that, say, the columns contained the initial list of action types while the rows contained sequentially linked pairs of action types. Here, each row would summarise the manner in which a certain event, which was always preceded by a certain other event, was itself followed by various other events, where these included not only its immediate antecedent but possibly also itself. This procedure is a bit like a baby elephant — it is both clumsy and data-hungry. Consequently, the limits of the data corpus very soon place constraints on the number of orders that can be calculated. In addition, transitional probability analysis is liable to what is called the problem of stationarity, which very simply means that it assumes that the cell entries in the matrix remain stable over time. There is some doubt that this assumption can be supported.

Another technique which has been addressed to the question of transitive ordering is the lagged probability profile (Sackett, 1978; Gottman & Bakeman, 1979). This technique represents the probability with which one type of event follows another either immediately (i.e. one lag), after one other event (i.e. two lags), after two other events (i.e. three lags), and so on, depending on the number of lags being examined. Lagged probability profiles can be obtained using either discrete steps in the sequence or discrete intervals of time. In the former it produces a profile of the probabilities with which a certain type of event is followed by another as a function of the number of intervening events, while in the latter it provides a profile of the probabilities with which a certain type of event is followed by another as a function of the amount of time that has passed since it was performed. Although lagged probability profiles do manage to expose the sequential dependencies of certain kinds of events on others under various event or time latencies, these are invariably dependencies of one type of event or another. Because the method focuses in this way on pairs of events it can only reveal relations of succession; and because the method does not specify what events intervene between the criterion event and its lagged sequitor it cannot uncover relations of transitive order.

The third way in which researchers have attempted to summarise transitive relations is through the use of some kind of hierarchical method, such as 'chain analysis'. An example of this technique is found in Dawkins's (1976) study of fly grooming. Here the string of discrete grooming movements are first transformed into a matrix of transitions between each pair of states. Next the matrix is searched for the most common transition, which is treated as though it were a discrete event in its own right. This bracketed or superordinate event is then entered in a new matrix of transitions, and the process is reiterated until the analysis has been exhausted. The picture which emerges from this method is not unlike that which comes out of cluster analysis, except that instead of identifying synchronic groupings, it uncovers a chain of influence in which certain superordinate groupings of events lead to others. This method has the virtue of providing a summary picture of the data corpus, but it does so at the expense of not identifying sequential connections other than those provided by the summary picture. In other words, while it provides a summary picture of the data as a whole, it leaves out those orderings which are not part of the summary picture. This is a shortcoming of chain analysis and transitional probability analysis, to which it is clearly related, as well as lagged probability profiles. In order to discover the transitive relations within a set of events it is necessary to determine not only the major transitive relations but also those minor transitive relations which may be crucial to a proper understanding of the major ones. Large data-crunching operations are seldom sensitive enough for the job.

The only sequence analytic methods which can summarise the entire range of transitive relations within a data corpus are conjunctive analysis and conjoint analysis. Coombs (1964) and Coombs & Smith (1973) have demonstrated how one can begin with, say, a matrix of individuals and attributes, where the latter are not ordered according to any preconceptions, and proceed to a two-dimensional conjunctive display which summarises and exhausts the transitive relations among the attributes. What emerges in the end is a set of overlapping rectangles which define various conjunctions of attributes and the full range of sequences realised by the individuals being studied. Coombs & Smith have presented hypothetical data to show how the method can reveal conjunctions of skills in a developmental sequence which involves both the acquisition and deletion of skills in one of several orders. However the method does not allow that a skill which has been deleted can be re-acquired. Consequently it is unsuitable for representing strings which contain repetition of the same events. Otherwise it offers an attractive means of showing how events in unlooped sequences are related in terms of the ways in which people go through them.

The other sequence analytic technique which satisfies the requirement concerning transitive ordering is conjoint analysis (Collett & Lamb, 1981; 1982). This technique is best suited to summarising exchanges between two individuals, but it can also be applied to more than two individuals or to the interplay between separate modalities within the same individual. Moreover it can be used to chart the progress of several modalities within a dyadic exchange. When it is employed to summarise the exchanges between two people then all the actions performed by one person are listed along the rows and all the actions performed by the other person are listed along the columns of the same matrix. The string of actions performed by the parties is then transferred to the matrix by jointing points in those cells which represent the conjunctions of their actions. In this way the sequence appears as a trajectory through a space which is defined by the actions produced by the two parties. The advantages of this method are several. First, it allows separate interactions to be summarised and compared within the same action space. Second, it is capable of handling repetition, which conjunctive analysis is not. Third, it can incorporate actions which were not performed by one or both parties alongside those which were. And fourth, it can be used to represent either unimodal or polymodal descriptions. Because it is pictorial the method allows the full trajectory of the sequence to be assimilated rapidly, and because it holds the full trajectory in view it automatically reveals the transitive properties of sequences that are represented alongside each other. The disadvantages of the method are basically twofold. First, it is unsuitable for material which is complex to the point where a conjoint display would only serve to confuse the issue.

Second, it is only worth using with sequences which assume simultaneous activity by both parties, and it is quite unsuitable for material which assumes alternation between the parties.

We have seen that there are several requirements that need to be satisfied by any sequence analytic technique, and that different techniques are differentially responsive to these requirements. While transitional probability matrices and profiles are capable of handling polymodal material which contains repetition, they cannot properly reveal transitive relations. Chain analysis goes some way towards uncovering transitive relations, but only in so far as they are major trends in the data. Conjunctive analysis, on the other hand, can expose transitive relations and it is eminently suitable for representing polymodal material, but its weakness lies in its inability to display sequences which contain repetition. Finally, conjoint analysis satisfies the requirements concerning polymodality, repetition and transitivity.

## Conclusion

In this chapter we have explored some of the preconceptions concerning action which encourage a neglect of time. We have identified two such conceptions, namely that which sees action as being composed of variables and that which views action as consisting of artefacts, and have gone on to show how both fail to describe the sequential properties of action, while the former also ignores its configurational properties. Later on we listed several requirements that need to be satisfied by any method which purports to examine the sequential properties of action, and we then considered various sequence analytic methods with these requirements in mind.

There is a loose confederation of social psychologists dedicated to the principle that social behaviour can only be understood by considering its organisation in time. The methods we have developed and helped to refine are still somewhat rudimentary, and it remains to be seen whether more powerful techniques can be devised which reveal the regularities in action without overlooking its intrinsic complexity. In developing new methods we will have to consider how the separate perspectives of interacting parties relate to the sequences of activity that we observe. At the moment our analyses are conditioned almost entirely by our perspective as third party to other people's interactions, and we have yet to see what relationship this bears to what is happening from the point of view of people whose sequences we study. We still take no account of their purviews or their physical location in relation to each other, and consequently we tend to assume that the actions produced by one party automatically inform those produced by another. However there are often good grounds for supposing otherwise, and we need therefore to find a way of incorporating the likely perspectives of those individuals whom we study within our own. Einstein pointed out that space and time cannot be defined absolutely, but only in relation to a particular observer. He was of course addressing himself to the observation of physical events, but perhaps there is also a place for relativity in the study of human action.

## Notes to Chapter 10

1. Neglect of the temporal dimension is by no means exclusive to the study of action. For an interesting review of related arguments in the field of perception, see Johansson *et al.* (1980).
2. In our study of introductions we recorded a fascinating case of parallel performances by the same individual (Collett & Lamb, 1981). In this case someone is presented to two people. He advances towards the first person, grasps his hand and then, while shaking hands, shifts his gaze to the second person and begins to greet her verbally. While he is shaking hands with the first person and greeting the second person verbally he looks back at the first and nods his head. He then terminates his verbal greeting and disengages from the handshake. This case shows how someone can use different modalities to address different people simultaneously, but it also shows how these performances can be nested within each other. In this case the nod to the first person is embedded within the verbal greeting to the second person, which in turn is embedded within the handshake with the first person. Embedding has been discussed at some length by transformational linguists, but the Leviathan character of the body indicates that embedding probably has more complex and interesting properties where social performance is concerned.
3. I am indebted to David Clarke for the point about Plato. The reader who wishes to pursue the discussion about event- and time-base descriptions is referred to the early work of Bakeman and to the treatment of these and related matters by Bakeman & Ginsburg (1983). See also Collett & Lamb (1982) on this topic. For further discussion of time-sampling, see Altmann (1974).

## References

Abelson, R. P. 1967, Mathematical models in social psychology. In L. Berkowitz (ed.), *Advances in Experimental Social Psychology*, Vol. 3. New York: Academic Press.

ALTMANN, J. 1974, Observational study of behaviour: sampling methods. *Behaviour*, 49, 227–67.

ARUNDALE, R. B. 1977, Sampling across time for communication research: a simulation. In P. M. HIRSCH, P. V. MILLER & F. G. KLINE (eds), *Strategies for Communication Research*. Beverly Hills, CA: Sage.

BAKEMAN, R. 1978, Untangling streams of behaviour: sequential analysis of observation data. In G. P. SACKETT (ed.), *Observing Behaviour. Vol. 2: Collection and Analysis Methods*. Baltimore, MD: University Park Press.

BAKEMAN, R. & BROWN, J. V. 1977, Behavioural dialogues: an approach to the assessment of mother–infant interaction, *Child Development*, 48, 195–203.

BAKEMAN, R. & GINSBURG, G. P. 1983, The use of video in the study of human action. In K. KNORR & M. BRENNER (eds), *Methods in the Social Sciences*. London: Academic Press.

BIRDWHISTELL, R. 1970, *Kinesics and Context*. Philadelphia: University of Pennsylvania Press.

CAMPBELL, J. (ed.) 1958, *Man and Time*. London: Routledge & Kegan Paul.

CLARKE, D. 1979, The linguistic analogy or when is a speech act like a morpheme? In G. P. GINSBURG (ed.), *Emerging Strategies in Social Psychology*. Chichester: Wiley.

COLLETT, P. 1980, Segmenting the behaviour stream. In M. BRENNER (ed.), *The Structure of Action*. Oxford: Blackwell.

— in press, Mossi Salutations, *Semiotica*.

COLLETT, P. & LAMB, R. 1981, *The Introduction: Ceremony in Everyday Life*. Unpublished manuscript.

— 1982, Describing sequences of social interaction. In M. VON CRANACH & R. HARRE (eds), *The Organisation of Human Action*. Cambridge: Cambridge University Press.

COOMBS, C. H. 1964, *A Theory of Data*. New York: Wiley.

COOMBS, C. H. & SMITH, J. E. K. 1973, On the detection of structure of attitudes developmental processes, *Psychological Review*, 80, 337–51.

DAWKINS, R. 1976, Hierarchical organisation; a candidate principle for ethology. In P. P. G. BATESON & R. A. HINDE (eds), *Growing Points in Ethology*. London: Cambridge University Press.

DUNCAN, S. 1969, Nonverbal communication, *Psychological Bulletin*, 72, 118–37.

ESHKOL, N. & WACHMANN, A. 1968, *Movement Notation*. Tel Aviv: Movement Notation Society.

Goffman, E. 1972, *Relations in Public*. London: Allen Lane.

Gottman, J. M. & Bakeman, R. 1979, The sequential analysis of observational data. In M. E. Lamb, S. J. Suomi & G. R. Stephenson (eds), *Social Interaction Analysis*. Madison: University of Wisconsin Press.

Hayes, D. P., Meltzer, L. & Wolf, G. 1970, Substantive conclusions are dependent upon techniques of measurement, *Behavioral Science*, 15, 265–68.

Hinde, R. 1982, *Ethology*. London: Fontana.

Jaffe, J. & Feldstein, S. 1970, *Rhythms of Dialogue*. New York: Academic Press.

Johansson, G., Von Hofsten, C. & Jansson, G. 1980, Event perception. In M. Rozenzweig & L. W. Porter (eds), *Annual Review of Psychology*, Vol. 31. Palo Alto, CA: Annual Reviews Inc.

Kendon, A. 1976, Some functions of the face in a kissing round, *Semiotica*, 15, 299–334.

Laban, R. 1956, *Principles of Dance and Movement Notation*. London: Macdonald & Evans.

Sackett, G. P. 1978, The lag sequential analysis of contingency and cyclicity in behavioral interaction research. In J. Osofsky (ed.), *Handbook of Infant Development*. New York: Wiley.

Saussure, F. de. 1916, *Cours de linguistique générale*. Paris: Payot.

Scheflen, A. 1973, *How Behavior Means*. New York: Gordon & Breach.

Stern, D. N. 1974, Mother and infant at play: the dyadic interaction involving facial, vocal and gaze behaviours. In M. Lewis & L. A. Rosenblum (eds), *The Effect of the Infant on its Caregiver*. New York: Wiley.

# 11 Remarks on the methodology of conversation analysis[1]

A. J. WOOTTON
*University of York*

Analysing human action involves at least two considerations. The first is that the recognition procedures employed by the analyst should be explicit, so that others can see how types and units of social action have been identified. In many ways of investigating social interaction, though not in conversation analysis, such explicitness is measured by inter-coder reliability coefficients. But it is clear that any form of investigation, including conversation analysis, needs to be explicit about the way that segments of action are identified and excavated, and that in important ways this contributes to the reproducibility of analyses. But there is a second sense of reproducibility, the second consideration, which requires attention alongside this first one. Bearing on this second aspect is the fact that human beings (and, for that matter, other animals) are required to construct their behaviour so as to be recognisable by others, recognisable as being engaged in some particular form of activity. Our (human) communication system is capable of revealing a wide array of types of interactional involvement and intention. And our presentations of self are mapped on to, and organised so as to display, the relevance of stored knowledge about such matters as context, complex social relationships, social conventions and the like. Furthermore, these issues can be negotiated and renegotiated on a moment-by-moment basis. Mutual intelligibility, in whatever form that empirically exists, requires that we so design our actions that others can discern in them what we intend.

And for others to do this these actions will need to be shaped according to design principles which are available to both parties. Any descriptive investigation of human conduct, therefore, must also be concerned with these shared design principles that people use and orientate to in their dealings with each other.

There are, then, at least two ways in which any analysis can be concerned with the issue of reproducibility. The first relates to the capacity of other investigators to understand and replicate the procedures of analysis that have been employed. The second relates to the fact that members of society are continually organising their conduct so as to have it identifiable by others, and that in the course of this they rely on the capacity of the communication system to reproduce forms of conduct from which systematic inferences can be drawn by other parties involved. And clearly an analysis might be reproducible in the first sense without being so in the second sense. For example, one might develop a sophisticated notation procedure for taxonomising various features of non-verbal communication, a procedure which was conceptually delicate and whose explicitness and clarity was documented through high reliability coefficients. Yet the category system built into the taxonomy might not be isomorphic with the sense-making categories as employed by members of society; *and even if it were then the sense attached to the various categories by them would remain to be explicated.*

Now this is a problem that social psychologists have considered and for which they have developed various kinds of solution.[2] Clarke (1979: 52–56), for example, describes how, in order to decide on a set of equivalence classes for different types of speech act, judges can be asked to make judgements of similarity and dissimilarity. This can be done by giving the judges a number of cards on which are examples 'each representing a speech act or speech act type'. These are then sorted by the judges into piles of related instances, the results being aggregated into matrices from which 'a single set of categories for further use is then formed by setting a certain level of similarity which defines a particular section through the dendrogram, and hence a particular set of clusters' (Clarke, 1979:54). Here, then, the judgements of similarity form one of the important bases for treating the emergent speech act scheme as more than just a reliable instrument. Whether it is claimed that the equivalence classes *duplicate* or *approximate* the speech act categorisation scheme that judges are presumed to share with a wider population is not clear, but it is clear that some form of resemblance is being claimed.

The approach to interaction embodied in the work of conversation analysts is centrally concerned with the second sense of reproducibility as it has been outlined above, and in coming to grips with this they have taken into account various matters that also have a bearing on the way this is handled within social psychology more broadly. But before describing the resulting research procedures within conversation analysis I will first sketch in some of the thinking which lies behind them.

## Considerations bearing on the characterisation of social action

If one is going to make claims about, say, the ways that members of society differentiate and identify various forms of action then the categories employed in such an analysis should themselves be an outcome of the investigation of these processes. Establishing such categories must be a major research objective in its own right. If it is intended that these categories will map on to strips of naturally occurring interaction then an initial complication is introduced by the fact that actions take place in sequences, that they occupy positions within sequences, and that these sequential positions have an important bearing on how acts are understood and treated by their recipients. There is now a wide literature suggesting the importance of this. For example, Schegloff & Sacks (1973), Schegloff (1976) and Levinson (1983) have demonstrated that grammatical, semantic and pragmatic characterisations given of utterances out of sequence will not constitute an appropriate basis for inferring what interactional import these utterances can come to have when employed within particular sequences of interaction. By way of illustration let me turn to pre-invitations as they are one of the speech act types mentioned in the paper by Clarke to which reference has already been made (1979: 53–54). Clarke is aware of the need to introduce some contextual material into the coding processes that he describes. On each card to be sorted a judge would therefore not only be given the utterance in question, but also the surrounding sequence in which it occurs. So when presented with a question like 'What are you doing on Saturday evening?' the judge would be able to identify, from the following sequence, that this question was performing the job of a pre-invitation, and for this reason would be able to group it with other utterances like 'Got any plans for the weekend?' rather than ' What did you do last Saturday night?' (Clarke's examples). But in the light of this consider the following extract:

(1) [Northridge: Frankel] ((D has telephoned N, and N is currently telling D about her new boyfriend, with whom she was out till 3 o'clock in the morning. N lives with her parents and is herself a single parent.))

**N:** I just came home yesterday at three o'clock in the
morni(he)(he)n: = (he) = [(he) = (he)]
**D:** [We::ll ye] yer parents cant
tell you what to do anymore
**N:** They <u>think</u> they ca:- Dot what are you doing right now
**D:** Nothing
**N:** Come over
**D:** ˙hhh Yea:h I kno::w I'm I'm gonna go in a lil- Monty: um
(.) Monty might go to see Ernie (.) so I told them I might
go:

Here N's 'Dot what are you doing right now' looks like a similar pre-invitation device to the one identified by Clarke, indeed D's response 'Nothing' and the subsequent 'invitation' by N, 'Come over', seem consistent with this. But in addition we can note that the pre-invitation is produced by N as a self-interruption within her own turn, and that it occurs at a point where N could have gone on to discuss her relationships with her parents and her boyfriend in more detail. Furthermore the 'invitation' stands as a suggestion as to how the present talk might be best continued, it is constructed as a solution to a problem touched off within the interaction taking place there and then. And as such it stands as a different order of invitation to one where, say, N had phoned D up with the specific purpose of inviting her over. The distinction between these two types of invitation is made by Sacks in a lecture (Lecture 5, Spring 1972), and he stresses both their differential sequential positioning, and the fact that they can be treated by participants as different types of interactional event. To the invitation for dinner on Friday night, for example, a fitted reply might be 'its very kind of you but I have another engagement' whereas to 'Come over' in Extract 1 a counter such as 'No you come over here' would not be amiss.

Three points emerge from this example. First, it is easy to imagine how words such as 'Dot what are you doing right now' would be deemed by a judge as similar to other forms of pre-invitation, yet if that were done we would be confounding in a single equivalence class utterances which on the basis of careful inspection of their sequential placement can be shown to be different interactional events for members of a society. Second, this also suggests that understanding the significance of an action within a given sequential position is not a straightforward process that can be resolved by a simple coding judgement. For example, if we are going to argue that N's 'Come over' is a distinctive type of invitation is it readily apparent from D's next turn, 'Yea:h I know . . .', as to how D is treating it? Third, it can be noted that even if judges did agree with each other that 'Dot what are you doing right now' is a distinct form of pre-invitation, that agreement in itself would be uninteresting in that the basis for the agreement would be unexplicated. Instead of using such agreement as a resource in further analysis one can turn into a topic in its own right the question of *how* people are able to arrive at such similar judgements. And in doing that one would be making explicit the utterance design and sequential positioning features which permitted such judgements to emerge. Conversation analysts would see an explicit account of how any judgement of similarity is arrived at as an integral component of any analysis.

Although this chapter will be primarily concerned with the nature of particular social acts, the majority of work in conversation analysis focuses on sequences and properties of sequences. For this reason characterising the relationship between utterances has been given some attention and in this respect the contrast with such approaches as the sequence analytic techniques described by Collett (Chapter 10 of this volume) is striking. Whereas these techniques are concerned to measure the likelihood of occurrence of next items within the sequence through calculating relevant transitional probability values, one of the main concerns within conversation analysis has been to identify, for example, the nature of the constraints existing between utterance pairs such as requests and grantings/rejections, questions and answers, invitations and acceptances/declinings. Several recent reviews of this literature are available (e.g. Levinson, 1983: Chapter 6; Heritage, 1984a: Chapter 8). An important feature of these pairs is that on the production of the first part of the pair a second part is then expectable. Expectable, that is, on the part of the interactants themselves who are involved in these exchanges. And this expectation can be traced in a number of ways, though here just two will be mentioned. First, on the non-production of a second pair part a follow-up to the first pair part demonstrates the speaker's understanding that his/her recipient had not performed an action, a response, which there was a basis for expecting him/her to do. In Extract 2 A's 'Yes or no' and 'Eh?' document such an expectation:

(2) (Atkinson & Drew, 1979:52)

**A:** Is there something bothering you or not?

|  |  |
|---|---|
|  | (1.0) |
| **A:** | Yes or no |
|  | (1.5) |
| **A:** | Eh? |
| **B:** | No. |

Second, if after the production of a first pair part a turn type is produced in next position which is not recognisable as a fitted second pair part then the second speaker can be understood as holding the production of the second pair part in abeyance. Thus in Extract 3 B's 'Are you twenty one?' is recognisable as an enquiry prior to some action on the part of B which is fitted to A's 'May I have a bottle of Mich?':

(3) (Merritt 1976:333)

|  |  |
|---|---|
| **A:** | May I have a bottle of Mich? |
| **B:** | Are you twenty one? |
| **A:** | No |
| **B:** | No |

Notice also here that the constraint set up by the first part of the pair can run across a number of intervening utterances; indeed it is the ongoing relevance of the constraint which gives the intervening utterances their character as insertions prior to the eventual fitted second pair part — B's 'No' in this case. In these and other ways, then, one can demonstrate that interactants orient to the existence of such constraints. And it is important to note that the structural significance of the constraint is essentially independent of, say, the frequency with which particular types of turn/action occupy the position in which the second part is expected. Knowing the relevant frequencies alone would not permit one to infer whether or not people actually orient to such constraints. Furthermore, within the framework of conversation analysis infrequently occurring responses would be as significant as those of frequent occurrence to the task of specifying forms of conversational organisation which are in some sense shared and accessible to members of the society under investigation.

Perhaps the unifying feature of the above discussion is the concern that conversation analysts have with how people, in their dealings with each other, document for each other what is taking place: document matters such as the character of what has just happened in the interaction, the type of sequence they are engaged in, the kind of action they are now performing and the like. Furthermore, it is from the details of this documentation that conversation analysts seek to discover and evidence (empirically) forms of orderliness existing within interaction. Sacks, Schegloff & Jefferson (1974:729) write that:

> while understandings of other turns' talk are displayed to co-participants, they are available as well to professional analysts, who are thereby afforded a proof criterion (and a search procedure) for the analysis of what a turn's talk is occupied with. Since it is the parties' understandings of prior turns' talk that is relevant to their construction of next turns, it is THEIR understandings that are wanted for analysis. The display of those understandings in the talk of subsequent turns affords both a resource for the analysis of prior turns and a proof procedure for professional analyses of prior turns — resources intrinsic to the data themselves.

In the following sections of this chapter I will briefly exemplify some of the ways in which the details of interaction itself can be drawn on to unravel the question of what turns at talk are occupied with. This will be examined by looking at five types of evidence which are frequently drawn on in the course of such analysis. They will be discussed mainly in relation to words such as 'oh' and 'uhuh', and, as will be plain, my discussion draws heavily on the work of those who have investigated such phenomena. The five types of evidence are: the relationship of the device to just prior turns; co-occurring evidence within a turn; subsequent treatment of the device in question; discriminability of the device; and deviant cases in the use of the device.

## Relationship of the device to just prior turns

Heritage (1984b: 324) has argued that in a variety of sequences '*oh* generically proposes that its producer has undergone some kind of change of state'. One such mental state transition that is displayed through the use of the particle is that from being uninformed to being informed: in certain types of sequence to respond to some item of information with 'oh' is to perform an information receipt; it is a way of receipting something which in effect states that what the speaker has just been told contains information of a kind that alters their knowledge base. One type of occurrence which both leads Heritage to make such a claim, and through which he supports it, are cases where 'oh' is produced in positions in sequences where there is prior sequential evidence that the person producing it is being treated as unaware of information that is being imparted. Thus in Extract 4 we can note that A's 'oh' occurs after A has made an initial enquiry of B (tidju phone yer vicar ye:t); the 'oh' receipts B's information, which A has sought:

(4) (Campbell: 4.1 : cited in Heritage, 1984b:308)

| | |
|---|---|
| **A:** | Well listen, (.) tiz you tidju phone yer vicar ye:t, |
| | (0.3) |
| **B:** | No I ain't |
| **(A):** | :(0.4) (.hhh) |
| **A:** | Oh:. |

In Extract 4, then, there is some evidence of the person who eventually employs 'oh' being earlier unaware of that which the 'oh' receipts. In Extract 5 A's initial 'Hey we got good news' presumes that certain recipients are not aware of that news. On learning that one at least does know, through C's 'I kno:w', A expresses his surprise at this through 'Oh ya do::?'. That is, through 'Oh ya do' A is portraying that he has undergone a change of state from not thinking that C (at least) knew about his news to that of now realising that C does know, the earlier sequential material (i.e. A's 'Hey we got good news') being an important source of evidence for this argument.

(5) (KC: 4 : cited in Heritage, 1984b: 304)

| | |
|---|---|
| **A:** | Hey we got good news. |
| **B:** | [What's the good ne]ws |
| **C:** | [I k n o : w.] |
| | (.) |
| **A:** | Ohya do::? |
| **D:** | Ya heard it? |

One domain of evidence, then, that can be drawn on in characterising a given interactional item concerns how that item stands in relation to the positions that have just previously been taken up both by the speaker and other parties present.

In discussing this use of 'oh' both here and in relation to subsequent extracts I should emphasise that I am not attempting to present a complete or compelling account of the evidence bearing on the character of 'oh'. I am simply using these extracts to illustrate the way that interactional material can be handled so as to generate and support claims concerning the interactional work achieved through the use of particular items. The observant reader will have already noted that in

Extract 4, for example, other forms of response than 'oh' could have been perfectly well employed as a receipt of the prior turn. For example, in Extract 4 informally we might substitute 'good' in the slot that A's 'oh' occupies. But we can note that for A to have there said 'good' would have been to convey the sense that A had a basis for supposing the line of action in question, not phoning the vicar, to be in some way in B's interests. Whereas for A to say 'oh' in that slot conveys more the sense that A had some basis for supposing the reverse to be the case. These, then, are the beginnings of a set of observations that may make it possible to discriminate the interactional work achieved through these two items, though it is important to stress that in making the final case for such a distinction we would need to have recourse to various forms of systematic evidence of the kind addressed in this chapter.

### Co-occurring evidence within the turn

As well as occurring as a free-standing item 'oh' can co-occur with other words in a turn, as in Extracts 6 and 7:

(6) (S:1:1:12:23 : cited in Heritage, 1984b:322)

**A:** Uh, she asked me to stop by, she brought a chest of drawers from um
(4.0)
**A:** What's that gal's name? Just went back to Michigan.
(1.0)
**A:** Hilda, um
→B: Oh I know who you mean,
(1.0)
**B:** Grady-Grady.
**A:** Yeah. Hilda Grady.

(7) (NB:1:2: cited in Heritage, 1984b: 338)

**F:** ((f)) Wul when didju guys go:::.
**S:** Ah: Saturday?hh
**F:** ((f)) Oh: fer, crying out loud. I thought it wz the end'v th'mo:nth you were go::::i:n.

Heritage emphasises how these additional words give a distinctive cast to the overall turn. In Extract 6 'Oh I know who you mean' conveys the sense of B now recollecting what the girl's name is; while in Extract 7 F's 'Oh: fer, crying out loud' claims some form of misapprehension on F's part. Nevertheless in both cases the 'oh' co-occurs with items which suggest that the speaker has just undergone some change of mental state; in Extract 6 as a result of having now remembered what the girl's name is, in Extract 7 as a result of just now being told when S and the others went to wherever they were going. And that can stand as consistent and suggestive evidence concerning the capacity of 'oh' itself to exhibit such mental state transitions. In this way, then, words accompanying the item which is the focus of our analysis, in this case 'oh', can be examined for what they can also reveal about the item in question.

### Subsequent treatment of the interactional device in question

Central to the concerns of conversation analysis is the characterisation of actions in such a way as to capture the significance that they have for those engaged in particular episodes of interaction. Consequently in order to make claims as to the job performed by a turn it is incumbent on the analyst to demonstrate that the person occupying next turn reveals, through the design of his/her action, an analysis of the prior turn which is consistent with that being proposed by the analyst.[3] This is essentially done by exploring the interactional details on a case-by-case basis. Here I will illustrate how this might proceed in relation to a data fragment that has been partially discussed already (see Extract 8, which is a fuller version of Extract 4):

(8) (Campbell 4:1 : cited in Heritage, 1984b:334-5)
**A:** Well lis:ten, (.) tiz you tidju phone yer
vicar ye:t,
(0.3)
**B:** No I ain't.
**(A):**(0.4)(·hhh)
**A:** Oh:.
(0.3)
**(A):** ·hhhhh-
**A:** Ah::-::-[::
**B:** [I w'z gonna wait . . .

In the case of Extract 8 it has been argued that A, in saying 'oh', conveys that there is a basis for supposing that not phoning the vicar was not in B's interests. There could be a number of ways in which such a basis was available to A. A's own view about the situation, in contrast with B's, might be that B should phone the vicar: or B may previously have told

A that he was going to phone the vicar for some reason: these details, though not irrelevant, need not concern us for present purposes. But if, in answering with 'oh', A thereby conveys the sense of a discrepancy between what B has done (not phoned the vicar) and B's suppositions as to what would or should happen (that A would phone the vicar) we would expect to see that discrepancy orientated to in some way in the subsequent turns. Most obviously that could have been done by A directly commenting on the discrepancy at his first opportunity: by saying, for example, 'Oh I thought you said you were going to'. Indeed, if the argument about 'oh' that is being developed is correct then we might expect to find just such turns in just such sequences. But here A does not do this; furthermore from the subsequent evidence in lines 7–9 there is some suggestion that A specifically withholds addressing the discrepancy, if such a discrepancy has been noticeably created through A's use of 'oh'. So the crucial turn which now addresses both the 'oh' and A's withholding of subsequent comment is line 10. Here B begins to construct an explanation of why he decided not to phone the vicar, and in seeing it as necessary to explain this B is orientating to a discrepancy that A has implicitly located. He is in effect treating A as implicitly asking him 'why' he has not phoned the vicar, thereby displaying an analysis of both 'oh' and the subsequent withholding of comment by A which is congruent with the description of 'oh' that the analysis has offered.

In the course of addressing A's 'oh' in Extract 8, and more specifically how that 'oh' is subsequently treated, it has become apparent that this is quite a complex sequence. Indeed some of the sequential evidence discussed by Heritage may seem to distinguish in a clearer and more compelling manner the ways that 'oh' and items like 'yes' are differentially treated by next speakers. Nevertheless it is important to emphasise that in each fragment of data being employed it is necessary for there to be a careful and explicit working through of the interactional details that pertain there. In fact these details are rarely straightforward, to be grasped at a glance, and a thorough acquaintance with these particulars is an essential bedrock for any compelling analysis.

## Discriminability of the interactional device

In the section on 'sequential placement', and specifically in relation to Extract 4, it has been argued that any analysis of the interactional task achieved by some conversational item will involve systematic comparison with other items. In Extract 4 the items in question were 'oh' and 'good'. Such comparison is necessary so as to isolate any distinctive role that some item may play within particular sequences, and the absence of such comparative evidence weakens the discussion of many interactional items in the literature. For example, it is often claimed that a word like 'uhuh' exhibits attention and understanding, but as Schegloff (1981: 79) notes:

> a vast array of types of talk following an utterance by another exhibit an orientation to it: accordingly the claim that *uhuh* exhibits an orientation to, or attention to, preceding talk does not help discriminate *uhuh* from any other talk, or tell us what *uhuh* in particular does or can do, and therefore why a participant might choose to produce it rather than something else.

Given the task of discriminating two interactional devices, a strategy that some interaction analysts might employ is to find gross frequency variations in their production and then to infer their distinctive properties from such variations. This may be done where the interaction is seen as taking place within a given 'context', for example, by noting that 'oh's occur relatively rarely as free-standing items, whereas 'uhuh's occur most frequently as free-standing items. Or it may be done by plotting the incidence of conversational items in what are seen as different contexts; for example, by noting that 'oh's are used very rarely by news interviewers (see Heritage, 1985), 'uhuh's a great deal by certain types of psychiatrist when speaking to their patients. These patternings are of great significance, but in themselves they do not permit one to infer in any rigorous way the distinctive interactional contributions that participants recognise such items as making. Whereas employment of the kinds of evidence that have been discussed in the previous three sections would permit one to construct more compelling inferences.

In the case of 'uhuh', for example, a regular sequential placement (where one person is being informed of something by another) is at a point prior to which the informing may be heard as complete; that is, in a position which thereby suits 'uhuh' to the task of treating the talk it is responsive to as incomplete. In Extract 9, for example, which is an early part of a telephone call to a suicide prevention agency, the doctor asks the patient to 'Tell me about your problems'. In the light of this the patient's 'I've had some therapy' looks to be part of a report of what these problems might be, but not the complete report: and it is at that point that the doctor produces an 'uhuh'[4] :

(9) (New Year's Eve call, 1964: Sacks)

**Dr:** Tell me about your problems

**Pt:** I uh Now that you're here I'm embarrassed to talk about it. I don't want you telling me I'm emotionally immature cause I know I am

**Dr:** Oh I see

**Pt:** Uhm doctor uhm

**Pt:** I've had some therapy

→**Dr:** Uh huh

**Pt:** 'N I haven't had any for about a year or so because I haven't been able to afford it.

**Dr:** Uh huh.

**Pt:** But I have a suicide problem.

Furthermore the treatment of this 'uhuh' in next turn by the patient is also relevant to making a case as it is this which reveals that person's analysis of what kind of interactional device that 'uhuh' is. Here, for example, it is important that the patient immediately starts speaking again after the 'uhuh' and that this talk is constructed as a continuation of what they had been saying prior to the doctor's 'uhuh', this continuation being marked in one way by the turn initial 'N' (i.e. 'and').[5] By collecting together a set of such analysed cases certain generic properties of 'uhuh' as an interactional device (in certain sequential positions) can be identified and these will then permit an informed contrast with the workings of 'oh'. The results of such analysis will then feed back into, and help to reveal the significance of, the various frequency patterns that were mentioned earlier in this section.[6]

### Deviant cases in the use of the device

Any piece of conversation analysis emerges out of the detailed investigation of a series of individual instances as it is only through these means that the types of evidence referred to in previous sections can be gleaned, with a view to both discovering and evidencing systematic features to be found in interaction. In the course of such investigation new cases of a phenomenon may be discovered which an analysis, as it has been developed to that point, cannot handle; cases which suggest, for example, that the kind of constraint held to be existing between two action types seems to break down. Such instances can lead to the reconstitution of an analysis so as to incorporate such deviant cases, the classic example in conversation analysis being the early article by

Schegloff (1968) on summons–answer sequences. But the close investigation of such deviant cases may also yield important evidence supporting an analysis that at first sight they appear to undercut. In the following an instance will be examined where 'uhuh' occurs in a sequential position which appears incongruent in the light of the argument so far. It will be argued that by virtue of occupying this position, and by virtue of the properties of the device that 'uhuh' represents, it can get itself recognised, and treated, in ways which are nevertheless consistent with the analysis of this item that has been emerging.

It has been argued that 'uhuh' is fitted, where it is not an answer to a question, to the task of treating what it acknowledges as incomplete. Part of the basis for claiming this is that 'uhuh's are produced at points where the prior speaker has not yet recognisably completed what he/she was going to say (as in Extract 9). But 'uhuh's can, it turns out, also be produced at recognisable completion points. In the doctor's last turn in Extract 10, which is taken from a later part of the same telephone call as Extract 9, 'uhuh' is produced in a position where it is plain that the patient does not wish to continue with her description of her problems.

(10) (New Year's Eve call, 1964: Sacks)

**Pt:** I've got a date coming in a half hour and I ((sob))
**Dr:** I see
**Pt:** I can't go through with it I can't go through with the evening I can't ((sniffle))
**Dr:** Uh huh
**Pt:** You talk I don't want to talk
→**Dr:** Uh huh
**Pt:** ((laugh sob)) It sounds like a real professional uh huh uh huh uh huh ((sniffle))

If our characterisation of 'uhuh' still works for this occasion then the patient, having come to an end to what she wished to say (with 'you talk I don't want to talk'), on hearing 'uhuh' has a basis for now finding her recipient to be giving her the chance to develop that matter further. And thereby a motivational basis is provided for the patient to find a way of continuing the matter on which she was speaking in spite of having recognisably completed it (see Sacks, 24 May 1971). So that one sequential outcome that could have occurred after the doctor's second 'uhuh' might have been further development of the prior topic by the patient: indeed one might expect to find such instances in transcripts of interaction, and their existence would constitute important evidence for interactants orientating to 'uhuh' in ways that an analysis would predict. Furthermore such evidence, in a case where one party had indicated clearly that he/she did not wish to talk further, would be especially pertinent to documenting the power of 'uhuh' as an interactional object. In our example, however, the patient, instead of choosing to do this, constructs a form of complaint with 'It sounds like a real professional uh huh uh huh uh huh'. It, like many complaints, is a complex and indirect interactional device, but it is constructed so as to exploit a contrast between playing a (professional) role and being a person. In effect the patient, by proffering an explanation for the doctor's behaviour is finding in that behaviour something which, according to some other standard (e.g. the standards of humankind) is in need of explanation. Although the complaint is constructed as removed from exclusive concern with the prior 'uhuh', nevertheless the inappropriateness of that turn in throwing the floor back to her, the patient, after her prior indications to the contrary, is a matter that it indirectly addresses and 'explains'. And that analysis of what the 'uhuh' requires of her is not inconsistent with the one that I have been developing.

In interaction processes we rarely find strict syntactic-like constraints on the occurrence of acts or sequences of acts (cf. Levinson, 1983: Chapter 6, Section 2). Second pair parts of adjacent pairs need not occur after first pair parts, and 'uhuh's can crop up in a variety of unusual interactional positions. This does not mean that utterances occurring in the positions where second pair parts are expectable thereby escape the expectations attached to their position. Nor does it mean that the interactional contributions made by 'uhuh' in their more standard positions of use are irrelevant to the way they work in more unusual positions. Indeed, it has been the argument of this section that the careful analysis of such apparent deviations can reveal evidence especially pertinent to making an argument concerning these devices, just as the analysis of actions occurring where second pair parts would have been expected can reveal important evidence relating to the nature of the constraints existing between adjacent pairs (see p. 243).[7]

## Further remarks

The impression may have been given in previous sections of this chapter that the aim of conversation analysis is to provide empirically grounded descriptions of conversational items such as 'uhuh'. Developing such descriptions is certainly a necessary part of this research strategy, and this is one reason why it has been given prominence here. But even where such an objective appears to be the analyst's primary aim, as in the analysis of Heritage (1984b) that has frequently been referred to, the interest of conversation analysts is not primarily with words like 'oh' as linguistic entities, but with the interactional task that they serve to handle, and, following from that, matters such as other ways in which these tasks can be handled, and the orderly relationships that can be uncovered as between these various devices within particular interactional situations. It follows from this that it is the interactional tasks and problems for which, and to which, language is brought as a solution that conversation analysts are attempting to locate, and which they see as the important organising principles for interaction analysis. So conversation-analytic work comes to be concerned with topics like the solutions that interactants have available to them for solving the interactional problems associated with turn-taking, or the systematic ways through which it is possible for people to infer that their recipients do not agree with them or do not wish to grant their requests (for an overview, see Chapter 2 of this volume).

There is a further way in which what has been written in previous sections may be misleading, but this concerns what has been presumed there rather than further stages of possible analysis that have been omitted. That participants orient to, and use, interactional devices such as 'uhuh' in similar ways is demonstrated through a series of individual analyses of particular data fragments. Therefore the necessary bedrock of an analysis is the attempt, on a case-by-case basis, to unravel the interactional considerations bearing on each exchange. Such analysis, however, is by no means a straightforward process. For example, when confronted by an instance of 'uhuh' many students of interaction might initially describe it as exhibiting attention and understanding, but such a description would have the limitations that have already been identified in the Schegloff quotation on p. 249. And similar problems arise by attempting to describe the item by mapping on to it 'known' technical interactional categories, such as 'back-channel'. And yet here we are dealing with a relatively straightforward type of conversational item — consider again how one might characterise D's turn in Extract 1 :'Yea:h I kno::w I'm I'm gonna go in a lil- Monty: um (·) Monty might go to see Ernie (·) so I told them I might go:'.

The point being made is that recovering the interactional significance that people attach to moves in conversation is complicated. And this is partly bound up with the fact that in interacting we employ highly sophisticated forms of practical inference which even as interactants ourselves we are barely aware of. And as participants we would be as incapable of specifying in any serious analytic way the procedure through which these inferences are made in much the same way that we would be incapable of specifying the orderly linguistic rules which we continually draw on in order to present to others sentences which are intelligible within a given language.[8] Excavating the implicit analyses which parties in interaction make of each other's talk is then a technical task: one which, for example, though it does not preclude consulting with people about what they think they are doing, has to be grounded in close exploration, analysis and documentation from the behavioural details of the exchange in question.

A further complication that has been underplayed in the earlier discussion concerns the ambiguity that turn designs can have, ambiguity in the sense, for example, that they may not be concerned exclusively with one type of business but with several. And if this is the case then a recipient may orient to a device as if it were accomplishing one task when in fact there may be grounds for treating it as designed for another — in which case complexities are involved in taking recipients' analysis of the nature of the device as evidence of what the device, as 'intended' by the speaker, was. Consider, for example, Extract 11, where S's 'What' appears to be analysed by L as requiring a repetition of what he, L, had originally said. Such an analysis of L's turn seems to be shared by E who, on hearing L begin the recycle, interrupts L to locate the error in L's original turn, and in so doing treats S's 'What' as touched off by the error rather than not hearing the words that L originally said.

(11) (Living Room: 97)
**L:** But y'know <u>si</u>ngle <u>be</u>ds 'r <u>aw</u>fully thi<u>n</u> ta sl<u>eep</u> on.
**S:** What?
**L:** Single beds//they're-
**E:** Y'mean narrow?
**L:** They're awfully narrow//yeah

Clearly, then, it is possible for turns to be treated in ways other than those which may have been intended by a speaker; in some cases, as here, this possibility can become transparent through the turns of subsequent speakers. But it is also possible for misunderstandings to be let pass and not exposed in the subsequent interaction. Furthermore even in cases where misunderstanding is not at issue recipients of actions may not formally address certain actions that have patently just taken place

— a matter recently touched on by Drew (1987) in the context of certain teases, where particularly delicate analysis is required to show that in such cases recipients recognise the occurrence of teases even though they do not topicalise them. Such instances clearly recommend both caution and sophistication in examining the way that a turn can evidence and formulate the nature of the action that preceded it.[9]

A point that was stressed earlier was that conversation analysts aim to demonstrate the orderly properties of any given interactional phenomenon that appear to obtain throughout a collection of particular instances of that phenomenon. If, then, we are dealing with a phenomenon like 'uhuh' as it occurs in a particular sequential position in conversation, then this sequential position can define the nature of the relevant collection that the analysis has to come to terms with, and the analysis should aim to reveal properties of 'uhuh' which obtain throughout that collection. In this way the analysis aims to reveal transcontextual properties of the phenomenon in question, properties which inform both its production and comprehension across the variety of particular sequences within the collection. And in this sense the aim is like that of much linguistic enquiry in that what the analysis seeks to reveal are encoding and decoding procedures which are shared by populations of interactants, procedures which are part of our communicative competence. I use the term 'populations of interactants' rather than 'members of a speech community' because there are some suggestions that certain of the organisations located by conversation analysts may be discoverable in societies quite disparate from those in which these organisations were originally located (e.g. Brown & Levinson, 1978).

Following these various remarks, and in the light of the earlier sections of the chapter, it is possible to identify various criteria of adequacy which pertain to any specific piece of conversation analysis. The analysis should be based on thorough and compelling accounts of the data fragments from which it derives, accounts which attend to the unique and context specific features of these interactions as well as their transcontextual properties. If there are known restrictions as to the positions and sequences within interaction in which the analysis holds, then these restrictions need to be clearly stated. Any analytic claims as to the relevance that procedures have for interactants need to be supported by the kinds of evidence to which reference has been made in this chapter. The consequences of falling short of such requirements may, however, be variable. For example, one weakly analysed extract set against powerful patterns demonstrably evident in a set of others may not undercut the central thrust of an analysis. Furthermore it is important to emphasise that the possibility of accumulating knowledge in this domain can be aided by analyses which are less ambitious in their scope than the previous discussion may suggest. The detailed analysis of a single data extract, for example, may yield a specification of interactional considerations bearing on it which can prove valuable in shaping our ideas about the nature of particular phenomena contained within it. Furthermore, detailed analyses of single data extracts can be undertaken with a view to demonstrating how a variety of different forms of conversation organisation intersect in a given instance. There are then, in the last analysis, a variety of ways in which research in conversation analysis can be developed and presented, though each of these ways would attend to the types of concern and evidence that been the focus of this chapter.

## Notes to Chapter 11

1. The author would like to thank the editors of the present volume, as well as Dr J. Heritage and Dr J. Local, for their comments on an earlier draft of this chapter.
2. I recognise, of course, that there are various solutions to these issues that have been adopted by social psychologists working in both experimental and non-experimental ways. The purpose of this chapter is not to address these various solutions, and in particular I do not want to propose that Clarke's work is representative of social psychology as a whole. The motive for discussing it is based partly on the bearing that it has on Collett's argument (Chapter 10 of this volume), and partly out of sympathy with Clarke's aims to explore more closely the connections between linguistic and psychological analysis.
3. The nature of a *turn* is, in itself, of course, a matter that requires detailed investigation, and my use of the term is not intended to presume the viability of adopting a particular analytic definition of a turn. For suggestive discussion see Sacks, Schegloff & Jefferson (1974) and Goodwin (1981: Chapters 1–2).
4. By contrast Heritage (1984b:301) notes that 'oh's tend to occur in sequential positions where informings are potentially complete.
5. The approach to 'uhuh' here draws heavily on Sacks's unpublished lecture of 24 May 1971. For interesting attempts to discriminate objects like [oh + news mark] (e.g. 'oh really?') from [oh + partial repeat of news] (e.g. 'oh did you,') see Jefferson (1981:62–66).
6. For the interconnection between such micro- and macro-level concerns see Heritage (1985) and Schegloff (1987).
7. Sophisticated treatment of how people can exploit the properties of interactional objects and processes in unusual ways can be found in Schegloff (1980) and Jefferson (1983).
8. The limitations of describing the knowledge that we deploy when dealing with others by taking as its index our capacity to represent this knowledge, say to an

experimenter, is, of course, a matter pertinent not only to social psychology. For a clear and coherent account of this issue as it pertains to several areas of developmental psychology, see Cox (1986), especially her discussion of the distinction between practical and representational knowledge.

9. For a fuller discussion of issues to do with ambiguity in conversation, see Schegloff (1976).

## References

Atkinson, J. M. & Drew, P. 1979, *Order in Court*. London: Macmillan.

Brown, P. & Levinson, S. 1978, Universals in language usage: politeness phenomena. In E. Goody (ed.), *Questions and Politeness*. Cambridge: Cambridge University Press.

Clarke, D. D. 1979, The linguistic analogy or when is a speech act like a morpheme. In G. P. Ginsburg (ed.), *Emerging Strategies in Social Psychological Research*. New York: Wiley.

Cox, M. V. 1986, *The Child's Point of View: the Development of Cognition and Language*. Brighton: Harvester Press.

Drew, P. 1987, Po-faced responses to teases, *Linguistics*, 25, 219–53.

Goodwin, C. 1981, *Conversational Organization: Interaction Between Speakers and Hearers*. New York: Academic Press.

Heritage, J. 1984a, *Garfinkel and Ethnomethodology*. Cambridge: Polity Press.

— 1984b, A change of state token and aspects of its sequential placement. In J. M. Atkinson & J. Heritage (eds), *Structures of Social Action*. Cambridge: Cambridge University Press.

— 1985, Analysing news interviews: aspects of the production of talk for an overhearing audience. In T.A. Van Dijk (ed.), *Handbook of Discourse Analysis*, Vol 3. London: Academic Press.

Jefferson, G. 1981, *The Abominable 'Ne?': A Working Paper Exploring the Phenomenon of Post-Response Pursuit of Response.* Occasional Paper no. 6: Department of Sociology, University of Manchester.

— 1983, 'Notes on a systematic deployment of the acknowledgement tokens 'yeah' and 'mmhm'', *Tilburg Papers in Language and Literature*, 30.

Levinson, S. C. 1983, *Pragmatics*. Cambridge: Cambridge University Press.

Merritt, M. 1976, On questions following questions (in service encounters). *Language in Society*, 5:3, 315–57.

Sacks, H. 1967–72, Lecture notes. Mimeo. Department of Sociology, University of California, Irvine.

Sacks, H., Schegloff, E. A. & Jefferson, G. 1974, A simplest systematics for the organization of turn-taking in conversation. *Language*, 50: 4, 696–735.

Schegloff, E. A. 1968, Sequencing in conversational openings. *American Anthropologist*, 70, 1075–95.

— 1976, On some questions and ambiguities in conversation. *Pragmatics Microfiche*, 2, 2, D8-Gl (Reprinted in J. M. Atkinson & J. Heritage (eds), *Structures of Social Action*. Cambridge: Cambridge University Press, 1985).

— 1980, Preliminaries to preliminaries: 'Can I ask you a question?', *Sociological Inquiry*, 50, 104–52.

— 1981, Discourse as an interactional achievement: some uses of 'uh huh' and other things that come between sentences. In D. Tannen (ed.), *Analysing Discourse*. Washington, DC: Georgetown University Round Table in Languages and Linguistics.

— 1987, Between macro and micro: contexts and other connections. In J. Alexander, B. Giesen, R. Munch & N. Smelser (eds), *The Micro–Macro Link*. Berkeley and Los Angeles: University of California Press.

Schegloff, E. A. & Sacks, H. 1973, Opening up closings, *Semiotica*, 7: 4, 289–327.

# SECTION 5:
# Research applications

## Introduction

An important feature of research on interpersonal communication is its potential application in a wide variety of everyday social situations. In this section, three chapters will be presented which focus specifically on applied issues. The first of these (Chapter 12) is by Andrew Thomas, and deals with the problem of social skills deficits amongst disabled patients. Chapter 13 is by Derek Rutter, and is concerned with the effects of medium of communication on tutorial teaching in the Open University. The volume ends with Chapter 14 by Johan Muller; Muller argues that communication strategies are an essential mediating factor in perpetuating educational inequality in South Africa.

In the introductions to the four preceding sections, a distinction has been drawn between the approaches adopted by researchers from different academic disciplines. In this section all three chapters have been contributed by researchers trained in conventional experimental psychology, but they differ markedly in the methods that have been used. For example, Andrew Thomas reviews research on the application of social skills to the treatment of the physically handicapped, where much of the work is based on clinical intervention studies of social skills training programmes. Derek Rutter's work has been carried out within the framework of experimental social psychology, examining under controlled conditions the effects of medium of communication on tutorial teaching. By contrast, Johan Muller has adopted a more descriptive approach, using selected excerpts from recordings of classroom interaction to illustrate the way that science teaching differs for black and white schoolchildren in South Africa. In this sense, Muller's approach is similar to that typically used by conversation analysts. Each of these chapters will be discussed in more detail below.

## Social skills and physical handicap

Chapter 12, by Andrew Thomas, is concerned with social skills problems of the physically handicapped. Social skills training represents one of the main practical applications of research in interpersonal communication, and is based on the so-called social skills model of social interaction. In a highly influential paper, Argyle & Kendon (1967) argued that social skill can be seen as a kind of motor skill, involving the same kinds of process as, for example, driving a car or playing a game of tennis. The advantage of this approach, they maintain, is that we know a great deal about motor-skill processes, and consequently can apply ideas and concepts developed in the study of skills to the study of social interaction.

Argyle & Kendon list six processes which they claim are common to motor skills and social performance: distinctive goals; selective perception of cues; central translation processes; motor responses; feedback and corrective action; and the timing of responses. Social performance can be seen as having distinctive goals — for example, an interviewer has the main goal of obtaining information from the interviewee — and sub-goals, such as establishing rapport. Selective perception of cues refers to the process whereby individuals pay particular attention to certain types of information which are relevant to achieving their particular objectives. Central translation processes prescribe what to do about any particular piece of information; people learn behavioural strategies with which to respond to certain types of perceptual information. Motor responses refer to the actual social behaviours themselves which are implemented as a consequence of the central translation processes. Feedback and corrective action refers to the ways in which an individual may modify his behaviour in the light of feedback from others; Argyle & Kendon argue that non-verbal cues are a particularly important source of feedback. Finally, the timing of responses is of importance, for example, in choosing the right moment to make a point in a group discussion.

One major implication of the social skills model of social interaction is that if social behaviour is seen as a skill, then it is possible for people to increase their social effectiveness through appropriate training procedures. Argyle has in fact argued that certain psychiatric difficulties can be seen as a consequence of lack of social skill leading to rejection and social isolation, resulting in turn in disturbed mental states, which can be alleviated through the use of appropriate social skills training. It is also claimed that such procedures can be employed in non-psychiatric settings, for example, in the training of teachers or interviewers, since the procedure is regarded as a form of training in which new skills are taught, rather than as a therapy in which a 'cure' is provided for an illness.

Thomas points out in his chapter that social skills problems are particularly acute among the physically handicapped, who find difficulty in even the simplest everyday social situations, such as going shopping or eating in public. Most of the chapter is concerned with a review of existing literature on social skills problems of physically handicapped adolescents, but Thomas also presents data of his own, based on self-reported difficulties in situations requiring social skill. The results of this survey showed that 96% of the handicapped adolescents who took part reported experiencing some difficulty in at least one of 14 social situations; 71% of the males and 69% of the females reported difficulties in as many as five or more of the situations.

Despite the widespread incidence of social skills problems amongst the physically handicapped, Thomas's review reveals a general lack of programmes for social skills training of the handicapped. However, it is encouraging that the physically handicapped are beginning to be seen as suitable clients for social skills training. A recent survey of 23 educational establishments run by the Spastics Society indicates that 65% now incorporate the teaching of social skills in their speech therapy programmes (Thomas & Coombes, 1986); these programmes include the encouragement of movement and gesture while communicating, suppression of inappropriate body movements, and teaching conversational skills such as listening and turn-taking.

## An examination of teaching by telephone

Rutter's chapter focuses on the effects of what he calls 'cuelessness' on speech style, content and outcome in telephone tutorials. Cuelessness refers to the number of social cues available to the participants in conversation, ranging from face-to-face interaction, where both visual and auditory cues are presented, to telephone conversations, where only auditory cues are available. This is the kind of topic which lends itself to laboratory research, since it is relatively easy to compare communication under a number of different experimental conditions: face-to-face, via closed-circuit television, or over the telephone. In earlier research, Rutter, Stephenson & Dewey (1981) and Kemp & Rutter (1982) investigated the effects of cuelessness by varying these conditions in a laboratory setting; in the present chapter, Rutter discusses the implications of cuelessness in an applied context, that of telephone tutorial teaching in the British Open University.

Although the study presented in this volume was conducted in an applied setting, the method used by Rutter was, none the less, experimental. In this study, ten Open University tutorial groups were followed throughout the course of one academic year. Each group was scheduled to hold from four to nine face-to-face tutorials during the year and, towards the middle of the year, two telephone meetings were added at the project's expense. The telephone tutorials were scheduled in such a way that at least one face-to-face meeting fell between them. In all, four sessions were recorded from each group, two telephone and two face-to-face, and analyses were carried out comparing content, style and outcome in these two conditions.

In the analysis of content, Rutter predicted that telephone tutorials would be noticeably more task-orientated and depersonalised than face-to-face tutorials. However, contrary to predictions, the results showed that there was more offering of academic information, less responding with personal examples and personal information about study procedures, and less acknowledgement in the face-to-face condition. The second result from the content analysis was that cuelessness served to exaggerate the difference between tutor and students. This, Rutter argues, is shown in the significant interactions between medium and participant, where in every case the data showed a greater discrepancy between tutor and student in the telephone than in the face-to-face condition. Cuelessness, Rutter claims, thus strengthened the way in which the participants fulfilled their roles, making tutors behave even 'more like' tutors and students 'more like' students in the telephone condition.

The second series of analyses examined style and structuring, and here Rutter predicted that telephone tutorials would be less spontaneous than face-to-face tutorials and that they would also be more deliberately structured by the tutors. Both of these predictions were supported by the results: interruptions, laughter and acknowledgement signals were more frequent face-to-face, while filled pauses were less frequent. Questions by the tutor, which Rutter regards as the principal means of structuring the tutorial, were more frequent in the telephone condition, and the sequence of utterances was almost always from tutor to student, with little student–student interaction; by contrast, there were as many switches from student to student as there were between tutors and students in the face-to-face tutorials.

The third series of analyses performed by Rutter was based on the participants' responses to a series of open-ended questions and an adjective checklist that were intended to tap task-orientation, depersonalisation, spontaneity, and overall evaluation of the tutorial. The results showed that telephone tutorials were perceived as more 'formal' and 'tiring' than face-to-face, and also less 'humorous', but in general both forms of tutorial were evaluated very favourably by tutors and students alike.

For the final series of analyses, Rutter first reduced the number of measures used in the study by means of factor analysis; this yielded seven factors for content, three for style, and six for the perceptual measures of outcome. The highest-loading variable on each of the nine style and outcome factors was then selected and entered into regression analyses, where style and outcome for each of the nine measures were regressed sequentially on content. Results showed that all three of the style measures were predicted strongly by content: the less task-orientated and the more personal the content, the more spontaneous the style. Results for outcome provided less support for the predictions: the more task-orientated the tutorial, the less favourable the overall evaluation and the greater the reported anxiety. The final analysis again examined outcome, but this time using style rather than content as the predictor variable. It was predicted that style and outcome would be independent of one another, and the results did indeed reveal that less than 5% of the average variance was explained by the regression.

Rutter goes on to discuss both the practical and theoretical implications of his findings. His main practical conclusion is that the telephone is a perfectly acceptable medium for tutorials, despite the differences between face-to-face and telephone conversations. Content, style and outcome all differ, but tutors and students alike report satisfaction with the technique. The most important limitations of the telephone are technical ones, such as the poor quality of the lines and the problem of accommodating more than a handful of people at a time. Rutter argues that the results of this study provide further support for his model of the effects of cuelessness, which was based on earlier laboratory experimentation.

However, the cuelessness hypothesis is predicated on main effects for medium of communication (telephone versus face-to-face). In Rutter's analysis these main effects were obtained for only four of the 23 measures, and were actually in the opposite direction to what had been predicted by the model — there was more offering of academic information face-to-face, less responding with personal examples and personal information about study procedures, and less acknowledgement. Rutter still claims that these findings support his model, on the grounds that the effect of cuelessness was to strengthen the way in which participants fulfilled their social roles. What he means by this is that the more cueless the setting, the more stereotyped the behaviour becomes: tutors behave more like tutors, and students behave more like students. In fact, this interpretation represents a substantial modification of the cuelessness model, since in its original form it makes no reference to social roles. The effects of social roles in relation to cuelessness is clearly an issue which will have to be addressed in future research, a fact which Rutter himself acknowledges in his concluding remarks.

## An analysis of discourse in two South African science classrooms

In the final chapter in this section, Muller contrasts the distinctive communicative styles occurring in South African science classrooms, one from a white school and one from a black school. However, he argues that these different communicative styles presuppose a social organisation or contract which differs markedly in these two teaching contexts. Muller's analysis of communication is preceded by an account of these differing social organisations in which he points out that the black teaching context is educationally deprived; thus, compared with white schools, black schools are overcrowded and underfunded, and the teachers themselves are less well qualified than their white counterparts.The implications of all this for learning science are not hard to imagine. A poorly trained science teacher with inadequate facilities will find it difficult effectively to 'display' science, since he has never had the opportunity to internalise the grammar of science sufficiently to do so. The best he can do is to 'drill' the pupils along the lines set out in the formal curriculum. Muller points out that it is a commonplace observation that blacks are disposed to rote learning, but that this is not a personal preference and even less is it a cultural one. It is due to force of circumstance, resorted to by people operating within a very particular communicative contract.

Muller then proceeds with an analysis of information exchanges occurring between teachers and pupils in a black as compared to a white science classroom. Excerpts from transcripts of these exchanges are organised into three common patterns of classroom exchange, which Muller refers to as teacher-initiated elicitation exchanges, teacher-initiated confirmation exchanges, and pupil-initiated question exchanges.

In the first two categories, Muller shows that by relying on nominated elicitations (i.e. requesting information from particular pupils rather than the class in general) and by criticising failure to answer correctly, the white teacher exerts significantly more control over the exchanges than the black teacher. Because black teachers fail to authorise knowledge effectively, Muller argues, black pupils come to regard knowledge as 'out there', something which is not available to them in the classroom. Moreover, this view tends to block any sense that failure could be due to personal shortcomings. By contrast, in the white classroom the teacher acts so authoritatively that the pupils never doubt his competence; because of this, pupils can only ascribe their failure to some personal shortcoming of effort or ability. This is succinctly illustrated in a comment from the white teacher quoted by Muller: 'Either you don't hear me or you don't understand or you are lazy.'

Muller's final category differs from the first two in that these exchanges are initiated by the pupils rather than by the teacher. In these cases, the white teacher typically responds in one of two ways: authoritatively if he thinks the question is legitimate, or with personal criticism (with or without directly answering the question) if he judges the question to be foolish. The consequence of this, Muller argues, is that the stronger pupils in the white school 'are authoritatively inducted into the grammar of science, while the weaker ones lapse into silence and lack of understanding'. The pattern in the black classroom is entirely different: whereas factual questions are routinely authorised by the teacher, there are many questions which fall outside the teacher's own competence. For example, in one excerpt quoted by Muller, the teacher is asked how it is possible to form water from hydrogen and oxygen. Her typical response in these cases is to attempt to authorise her reply by comparing the question to self-evident ones, such as whether the earth is round or whether one plus one equals two. However, the pupils do not automatically accept this authorisation because, Muller maintains, they doubt the teacher's authority in a way not possible in the white school. Consequently, the distinction between stronger and weaker pupils which occurs in the white school tends not to occur in the black school, because everyone (including the teacher) feels incompetent.

Muller argues that both teachers contravene what he refers to as the 'contract' appropriate to the teaching context, i.e. the obligation to authorise knowledge and the right of pupils to make mistakes. In the black classroom, the poorly trained and inadequately equipped teacher underauthorises knowledge, thereby reinforcing the view that knowledge is 'out there' and not accessible to the pupils. In contrast, the white teacher overauthorises knowledge by criticising pupils and overreacting to their errors. In this way, the white pupils do not assert their right to make mistakes; they take the teacher and the knowledge he displays for granted, and they develop strategies for avoiding the discomfort of overauthorisations.

In contrast to the experimental approach adopted by Rutter, Muller's research employs a method comparable to that typically used by conversation analysts, based on a detailed analysis of selected excerpts from recorded conversations. The major problem with this approach is its selectivity: the two classrooms which Muller studies are taken as typical of black and white classrooms in general, but we have no evidence that this is in fact the case. A second problem is that, although he claims to validate his conclusions through interviews with the pupils themselves, insufficient detail is given about the conduct of these interviews and about the results which were obtained.

## Conclusions

All three chapters in this section illustrate ways in which research on interpersonal communication might be conducted in applied settings. A major practical application of this kind of work has been in the form of social skills training, which Thomas discusses with particular reference to the problems of the physically handicapped. Thomas's work is based essentially on a literature review and an account of some survey data of his own, in which he describes some of the procedures which are used in social skills training. However, Thomas reports on a general lack of these training programmes for the physically handicapped, and he argues that in view of the obvious advantages of such procedures they should be much more widely implemented.

The effects of medium of communication on social interaction have been investigated in a whole series of studies by Rutter and his colleagues; their findings show that the fewer the number of social cues, the more the conversation becomes depersonalised in content and formal in style, which in turn affects outcome. Rutter's chapter in this section is concerned with the effects of cuelessness in the context of teaching by telephone in the British Open University. His main practical conclusion is that, despite the differences between face-to-face and telephone conversations, the telephone is a perfectly acceptable medium for tutorials. However, some of the findings which Rutter reports are contrary to what would be predicted by the cuelessness model. The problems with Rutter's work have less to do with the method employed than with the way in which he interprets his results: by trying to force his data into pre-existing theoretical concepts, he can be criticised for failing to consider alternative explanations of his results.

Muller investigates in his research the communicative styles occurring in black and white South African science classrooms; he employs a procedure which differs markedly from that used by Rutter. Muller's work eschews statistical analysis, and is based instead on the use of transcribed excerpts from audio-recordings of science classes in one black and one white school. Muller maintains that the contrasting styles observed in these two classrooms are a function of the social organisation or contract underlying them, and the excerpts are used to show how both the black and the white teacher contravene in different ways the contract appropriate to the classroom context. Muller's work uses a research methodology comparable to that typically used by conversation analysts, based on a detailed examination of recorded conversations. Muller may be criticised for his selective use of excerpts to illustrate his arguments, and we have no evidence that his conclusions are representative of the general pattern of classroom exchanges in black and white schools in South Africa. None the less, his work is interesting in an applied context, and shows that science teaching is not concerned simply with the transmission of objective knowledge, but is substantially affected both by the form of communication and the social setting in which it occurs.

## References

Argyle, M. & Kendon, A. 1967, The experimental analysis of social performance. In L. Berkowitz (ed.), *Advances in Experimental Social Psychology 3*. New York: Academic Press, 55–98.

Kemp, N. J. & Rutter, D. R. 1982, Cuelessness and the content and style of conversation, *British Journal of Social Psychology*, 21, 43–49.

Kraemer, H. C. & Jacklin, C. N. 1979, Statistical analysis of dyadic social behavior, *Psychological Bulletin*, 86, 217–24.

Rutter, D. R., Stephenson, G. M. & Dewey, M. E. 1981, Visual communication and the content and style of conversation, *British Journal of Social Psychology*, 20, 41–52.

Thomas, A. P. & Coombes, K. 1986, A survey of the provision of speech therapy services administered by, or affiliated to The Spastics Society. Unpublished paper, Department of Child Health, Charing Cross and Westminster Medical School, London.

# 12 Social skills and physical handicap[1]

ANDREW P. THOMAS
*Charing Cross and Westminster Medical School, London*

> It is obviously important that pupils with special educational needs, whether they are in ordinary or special schools, should acquire the basic educational skills. It is equally important that they should develop social competence as well as vocational interests, which will give them a realistic awareness of employment opportunities and help them to achieve personal satisfaction in their future life. In the case of pupils with disabilities so severe that they may never be able to work, basic education and instruction in the skills of daily living such as shopping or using public transport should go hand in hand. Moreover, a special effort should be made to enable pupils who have spent their entire school career in special schools to overcome any feelings of isolation and to cope with adult life, in particular to share as closely as possible in the everyday activities of other people without disabilities. (Warnock Report, DES, 1978: para. 10.18)

Adolescence is generally considered to be a time of increased social activity and rapid expansion of a teenager's social circle, yet many young people with physical handicaps grow up in a socially impoverished environment. Due to restricted access and mobility, and in some cases, the lowered expectations of others, physically handicapped teenagers are given little preparation for living an independent adult life (Fox, 1977; Anderson *et al.*, 1982). Independence training in schools generally focuses on practical skills such as washing and dressing. While these are certainly necessary skills, independence needs to address wider issues such as decision-making and the ability to interact with others in society.

However, where independence training is provided in schools, this usually occurs too late in the curriculum and is frequently described as inadequate (Thomas & Bax, 1987). Consequently, many physically handicapped young people have little experience of everyday social events such as shopping in the supermarket, using public transport, choosing and buying fashionable clothes, eating in public, going on holiday, or enjoying an active outdoor social life. While handicapped adolescents may share the same desires as other young people to develop personal independence, experience a rewarding social life and explore their adolescent sexuality, they are often without the opportunity to satisfy these desires. Even in late adolescence, many physically handicapped teenagers are heavily dependent upon parents or other adults for even the most basic of activities of daily living. While a degree of physical dependence may be inevitable, parents can, and often do foster 'independence of spirit' by encouraging young people to make choices and decisions for themselves (Morgan, 1972b). However, problems relating to the way the young people interact with society are still likely to occur. As Younghusband *et al.* (1970) have pointed out, there is a surprising failure to recognise the acute problem of isolation from their peers that confront many of the more seriously handicapped adolescents, with the consequence that many young people with handicaps become socially isolated and experience difficulties in social relationships (Anderson *et al.*, 1982).

It is likely that the social problems associated with physical handicap begin early in the young person's life and indeed Richardson *et al.* (1964) have found that disablement in *children* is associated with lower levels of self-confidence, greater self-deprecation, and for boys in particular, difficulties in interpersonal relations. Clarke *et al.* (1977) found that the social relationships of children with disabilities were frequently impaired. These children were more likely to play alone, less likely to engage in imaginative play, more likely to engage in passive activities by listening or watching others, less likely to communicate with other children and more likely to have one-way rather than two-way speech patterns. In addition, there is growing evidence that both children and adolescents with a physical disability are likely to have difficulties with skilled social behaviour (McMichael, 1971; Anderson, 1973; Tew, 1973; Fulthorpe, 1974; Jowett, 1982).

Social skill may be conceptualised as part of a broader construct known as social competence and defined as those cognitive functions, behaviours or abilities which enable a person to perform competently at particular social tasks and in particular social situations (Foster &

Ritchey, 1979; McFall, 1982). The cognitive functions include such abilities as empathising with or understanding other people's feelings, recognising social behaviours, and predicting and evaluating the consequences of these behaviours. The behaviours themselves may be verbal or non-verbal and include eye contact, facial expression, body movement and posture, and tone of voice (Argyle & Kendon, 1967). To be socially skilled involves the use of a variety of cognitive functions and social behaviours that lead to positive consequences for the interactants. Social competence, therefore, is dependent on a composite of skills such as determining which verbal and non-verbal behaviours are appropriate for a given situation, the fluent performance of those behaviours in appropriate combinations, the accurate perception of other people's behaviours and the constant modification of one's behaviours in the light of feedback from others. Skilled social behaviour includes a number of macro-skills such as going shopping and going to parties, as well as a large number of interactional micro-skills such as starting and ending a conversation, skills in observation, listening and speaking, as well as the expression and recognition of attitudes and emotions.

To what extent do adults with disabilities have difficulties with skilled social behaviour? Paradoxically, while there is a growing literature concerning children and young teenagers (Conger & Keane, 1981; Schinke, 1981; Foster, 1983), there is very little published research concerned with physically handicapped adults. However, a recent study by Jowett (1982) does provide some useful information and suggests that the deficits in social skill can be substantial. In her study, 177 former students of St Loyes College for Training the Disabled for Commerce and Industry were asked to complete a postal questionnaire, one aspect of which dealt with potential difficulties in a number of social situations. Twelve situations had been identified by the authors, the young person being asked to rate whether each of the situations presented any difficulties. The rating scale consisted of five points: no difficulty, slight, moderate or great difficulty, and avoidance of the situation if possible. Of the 177 asked, 150 returned the questionnaires (84% response rate) of whom 54% were physically disabled. Overall, 93% of the young people rated themselves as having at least some difficulty in the 12 social situations. Seventy-three per cent rated themselves as having moderate or great difficulty, and for 56% the difficulty was severe enough to make them avoid social situations altogether. Common characteristics were a lack of social confidence, and difficulties with keeping a conversation going (38%), starting a friendship (38%), and going out with someone to whom they were attracted (32%).

From the existing literature (e.g. Goldberg, 1974; Anderson *et al.*, 1982) one might expect differences in social skill deficits to occur between the sexes and according to the type of disability. While Jowett's sample comprised young people of both sexes and with a range of handicaps, no detailed breakdown of results by physical handicap or sex of respondent is presented. A second difficulty in interpreting her results lies with the method of collecting the social skills information. Postal questionnaires were used and in such cases there is the attendant problem that responses may have been influenced by parents or guardians. Thirdly, the absence of an age-matched non-handicapped comparison group makes interpretation of Jowett's results difficult. Nevertheless, the study does provide some useful information about social skill deficits and provides a backdrop for a more recent study concerned with adolescents and young adults with physical handicaps.

One hundred and eleven physically and multiply handicapped adults living in the areas defined by the Paddington and North Kensington, and the Wycombe South Buckinghamshire District Health Authorities took part in a study designed to provide a detailed picture of a physically handicapped person's health and social problems. (The background to this study and preliminary results are reported in Thomas *et al.*, 1985, 1987; and Bax *et al.*, 1985). In addition to their involvement in a comprehensive health and social interview, 57 young people with physical handicaps rated as mild (17%), moderate (66%), or severe (17%) using the Pultibec system (Lindon, 1963), and with IQs greater than 80 were also asked to take part in a self-report social skills pilot study. Where there were reading and/or writing difficulties the questions were read to the young person and their answers recorded by the interviewer. Of the 57 young people taking part in the study, 31 (54%) were boys and 26 (46%) were girls; 34% were recorded as having cerebral palsy, 25% as having spina bifida, with the remaining 41% representing a variety of other physical handicaps and syndromes. All were aged between 18 and 25 years (the boys' mean age was 21.2 years; the girls' mean age, 20.7 years).

For comparative purposes 194 non-handicapped young people (66 boys, 128 girls) were asked to complete the same social skills questionnaire. At the time of the study, the young people were Youth Training Scheme (YTS) day-release students attending Milton Keynes College ($N = 86$) or were students attending St John's College, York ($N = 51$) or Birmingham Polytechnic ($N = 57$). All were aged between 18 and 25 years (the boys' mean age being 19.8 years; the girls' 19.9 years).

Fourteen social situations were selected from the work of Trower *et al.* (1978) representing 'life skills' (e.g. going into a shop) and 'social skills' (e.g. asking questions). All the young adults in the study were asked to rate themselves according to the degree of difficulty they experienced (if any) in the 14 social situations using a four-point rating scale: no difficulty, some difficulty, great difficulty, and avoid if possible. The handicapped and non-handicapped groups' responses to the social situations are presented in summary form in Table 12.1 together with the results of a series of chi-squared analyses.

Overall, the analyses indicated that similar proportions of the handicapped (49.4%) and non-handicapped (48.4%) groups experienced difficulties in social situations. However, while the non-handicapped experienced difficulties that were of a mild nature (some difficulty: non-handicapped group = 41.4%, handicapped group = 33.4%), the adults in the study with physical handicaps experienced proportionally more difficulties of a severe nature (great difficulty/avoidance: non-handicapped group = 5.9%, handicapped group = 15.5%). Indeed, 96% (92% of the females and 100% of the males) of the handicapped sample rated themselves as having difficulties in social situations and 71% of the males and 69% of the females said that they experienced difficulties in as many as five or more social situations. Differences between the sexes were also particularly marked, with 12.9% of the handicapped males compared to only 0.6% of the non-handicapped males reporting difficulties of a severe nature. Of the handicapped females, 19.5% reported severe difficulties in social situations compared to 9.1% of the non-handicapped females. In comparison with the non-handicapped group, both males and females with physical handicaps experienced significantly greater difficulties with life-skills situations such as going shopping and going to parties, over and above the problems of access and mobility. However, while females experienced greater difficulties with self-disclosure in the form of talking about themselves and their feelings, males had greater difficulties with conversational micro-skills such as disagreeing with others and taking the conversational initiative.

As the study was carried out through the use of interviews, an opportunity was provided to gain an impression of the reliability of the social skill self-ratings. Scores obtained from the self-report questionnaires generally appeared to be accurate though it was felt that many of the young handicapped people understated or underestimated their difficulties. Anecdotally, many of the young people in the study appeared markedly socially unskilled. Difficulties with beginning conversations, instigating

Table 12.1 *Difficulties experienced by handicapped and non-handicapped young people in 14 social situations(%)*

| | Degree of difficulty (males) | | | | | | | |
|---|---|---|---|---|---|---|---|---|
| | None | | Some | | Great | | | |
| | *NH* | *H* | *NH* | *H* | *NH* | *H* | $\chi^2$ | *p* |
| 1. Going into a shop to buy something* | 97.0 | 51.6 | 3.0 | 38.7 | 0 | 9.7 | 30.1 | <0.001 |
| 2. Going to parties* | 80.3 | 58.1 | 18.2 | 25.8 | 1.5 | 16.1 | 9.4 | <0.01 |
| 3. Going to a pub/cafe* | 93.9 | 51.6 | 6.1 | 35.5 | 0 | 12.9 | 24.8 | <0.001 |
| 4. Mixing with people at the Day Centre/ College/work | 84.8 | 64.5 | 15.2 | 29.0 | 0 | 6.5 | 6.8 | <0.05 |
| 5. Making friends of your own age | 54.5 | 64.5 | 43.9 | 22.6 | 1.5 | 12.9 | 6.2 | <0.05 |
| 6. Going out with someone you are attracted to | 36.4 | 29.0 | 57.6 | 41.9 | 6.1 | 29.1 | 12.6 | <0.01 |
| 7. Going into a room full of people | 47.0 | 54.8 | 51.5 | 41.9 | 1.5 | 3.3 | 0.99 | NS |
| 8. Meeting strangers | 31.8 | 51.6 | 65.2 | 45.2 | 3.0 | 3.2 | 6.1 | <0.05 |
| 9. Approaching others — making the first move in starting up a friendship | 34.8 | 25.8 | 62.1 | 48.4 | 3.0 | 25.8 | 11.8 | <0.01 |
| 10. Making ordinary decisions affecting others (e.g. what to do together in the evening) | 90.9 | 51.6 | 9.1 | 38.7 | 0 | 9.7 | 15.1 | <0.001 |
| 11. Taking the initiative in keeping a conversation going | 74.2 | 35.5 | 24.2 | 48.4 | 1.6 | 16.1 | 14.3 | <0.001 |
| 12. Disagreeing with what other people are saying | 80.3 | 51.6 | 18.2 | 35.5 | 1.5 | 12.9 | 10.3 | <0.01 |
| 13. People looking at you | 71.2 | 70.9 | 25.8 | 25.8 | 3.0 | 3.3 | 0.003 | NS |
| 14. Talking about yourself and your feelings | 54.4 | 54.8 | 40.9 | 32.3 | 4.5 | 12.9 | 2.6 | NS |

| | Degree of difficulty (females) | | | | | | | |
|---|---|---|---|---|---|---|---|---|
| | None | | Some | | Great | | | |
| | *NH* | *H* | *NH* | *H* | *NH* | *H* | $\chi^2$ | *p* |
| 1. Going into a shop to buy something* | 92.2 | 50.0 | 7.8 | 38.5 | 0 | 11.5 | 34.6 | <0.001 |
| 2. Going to parties* | 43.8 | 53.8 | 53.9 | 19.2 | 2.4 | 27.0 | 25.8 | <0.001 |
| 3. Going to a pub/cafe* | 75.8 | 61.5 | 23.4 | 11.5 | 0.8 | 27.0 | 42.8 | <0.001 |
| 4. Mixing with people at the Day Centre/College/work | 68.0 | 65.4 | 30.5 | 19.2 | 1.6 | 15.4 | 11.7 | <0.005 |
| 5. Making friends of your own age | 51.6 | 61.5 | 47.7 | 15.4 | 0.8 | 23.1 | 28.9 | <0.001 |
| 6. Going out with someone you are attracted to | 15.6 | 38.5 | 62.5 | 26.9 | 21.9 | 34.6 | 12.2 | <0.005 |
| 7. Going into a room full of people | 18.8 | 50.0 | 73.4 | 38.5 | 7.8 | 11.5 | 13.3 | <0.005 |
| 8. Meeting strangers | 19.5 | 42.3 | 68.0 | 34.6 | 12.5 | 23.1 | 10.3 | <0.01 |
| 9. Approaching others — making the first move in starting up a friendship | 25.8 | 42.3 | 58.6 | 42.3 | 15.6 | 15.4 | 3.1 | NS |
| 10. Making ordinary decisions affecting others (e.g. what to do together in the evening) | 66.4 | 61.5 | 32.0 | 34.6 | 1.6 | 3.9 | 0.74 | NS |
| 11. Taking the initiative in keeping a conversation going | 48.0 | 50.0 | 44.9 | 34.6 | 7.1 | 15.4 | 2.3 | NS |
| 12. Disagreeing with what other people are saying | 44.1 | 57.7 | 47.2 | 34.6 | 8.7 | 7.7 | 1.7 | NS |
| 13. People looking at you | 26.8 | 34.6 | 53.5 | 38.5 | 19.7 | 26.9 | 1.9 | NS |
| 14. Talking about yourself and your feelings | 44.9 | 38.5 | 44.1 | 30.7 | 11.1 | 30.8 | 7.1 | <0.05 |

*Excludes problems of mobility and access
Males: Handicapped (H), $N$=31; non-handicapped (NH), $N$=66
Females: Handicapped (H), $N$=26; non-handicapped (NH), $N$=128
All $\chi^2$ calculations performed using raw frequency data

socially unskilled. Difficulties with beginning conversations, instigating discussion, poor meshing skills in the form of over-long silences and the inability to keep a conversation going were common characteristics, particularly for the males in the study.

The social problems that a handicapped person experiences are frequently related to other people's reactions to physical disability, the young person's own feelings about his/her disability and the degree to which he/she is able to integrate into society and lead a normal social life. In her study of children with cystic fibrosis, Burton (1975) makes the point well: 'when one considers the development of any chronically sick child one is assessing behaviour which results not only from the disease but more especially from the whole amalgam of social experiences'. The experiences that may contribute to the social isolation of a physically handicapped teenager, and consequently an impairment in social skill, are numerous, and include undemanding and restricted school experiences, a lack of social experience, stress, stigma, and problems of self-image and self-esteem.

While few young people with physical handicaps will have reached their full potential both educationally and socially by the age of 16 (Brand *et al.*, 1969; DES, 1978), only a minority of physically handicapped young people continue to receive formal education after this age (NUT, 1982; Bookis, 1983). At a time when further education may be particularly important in helping a young person to 'catch up', many handicapped teenagers are cut off from an environment in which their educational and social skills may be encouraged to develop further. In addition, a general finding of recent research studies is the over–protective nature of the education system for the handicapped. While the Court Report (DHSS, 1976) recommended that much wider recognition should be given to handicapped adolescents' need for counselling to prepare them for adulthood, the Warnock Report (DES, 1978) found that information and advice about relationships, sex education and counselling tended to be handled very poorly in schools. This is particularly unfortunate, for as Anderson & Spain (1977) have pointed out, the restricted social contact that handicapped teenagers have due to restricted mobility and communication problems means that they have even less opportunity to 'pick up' such information and skills from alternative sources than do many of their non-handicapped peers. The consequence of this is that a large proportion of physically handicapped school-leavers have little preparation for adult life. They generally leave school earlier than their peers and with poorer educational attainments, little educational and social maturity, minimal social experience, and often find difficulties in establishing and maintaining social relationships (Anderson & Spain, 1977; DES, 1978).

Having left school, the three major indicators of adult status today are being in work, having an active social life, and enjoying a relationship with a partner. For young people with limited mobility and/or impaired speech these major aspects of adult life may seem difficult or impossible to attain. While work experience and full-time employment are important for self-esteem (e.g. Banks & Jackson, 1982; Warr, 1978, 1982; Warr & Jackson, 1983) the 1976 survey of 393 handicapped 18-year-old school-leavers for the Warnock Committee (Walker, 1980, 1982a,b) concluded that handicapped young people were very seriously disadvantaged in the labour market. Realising their lower educational attainments (Prior & Linford, 1981; Lonton *et al.*, 1983; Smith, 1983), poor job prospects, lack of social life, and limited opportunities to socialise, many teenagers in Anderson *et al.*'s (1982) study mentioned that much of the time they felt depressed and isolated from their peers, both socially and in terms of the work opportunities open to them.

Becoming socially isolated may also become a problem for many physically handicapped teenagers (Dorner, 1973; Lorber & Schloss, 1973). Studies by both Dorner (1975, 1976, 1977) and Rowe (1973) have indicated very high levels of social isolation. For example, in Dorner's (1975) study of 13–19-year-olds with spina bifida, 31 of the 59 (53%) young people had had no social contact with a friend of their own age for at least a month prior to the interview. An indication of just how restricted a disabled young person's social life can be is provided by Anderson *et al.* (1982). Based on the frequency of social contacts obtained from self-reports and reports of their parents, the authors rated the young persons' social lives as satisfactory, limited or very restricted. While 94% of the non-handicapped group were considered to be leading satisfactory social lives, this was true for only 21% of those with disabilities. Just 6% of the non-handicapped young people were said to lead limited or restricted social lives compared to 29% of the young people with disabilities.

Close friendships, living together and marriage are also less likely for a person with a physical handicap (Evans *et al.*, 1975; Laurence & Beresford, 1975). Of the handicapped group in Anderson *et al.*'s (1982) study 46% said that they did not have a special friend, yet this was true for only 21%of the non-handicapped group. Similarly, just 2.2%($N$ = 186) of the 16–25-year-olds with cerebral palsy were married in Ingram *et al.*'s (1964) classic Scottish study. As a comparison, figures given by the Registrar General for Scotland suggest that approximately 18.4% of the male and 33.4%of the female general population would have expected to have married by the time of the survey. The very low marriage rates of youths with handicaps such as cerebral palsy is little different today. One-fifth of the seventy-six 16–27-year-olds in Castree & Walker's (1981) study of spina bifida and cerebral palsy had a boyfriend or girlfriend and only three of the 57 (5.3%) people with mild or moderate disabilities in Thomas *et al.*'s (1987) study were married. When parents in Anderson *et al.*'s (1982) study were asked to describe the kinds of difficulty in forming personal relationships that their teenage children had, they usually mentioned shyness, lack of self-confidence, and self-consciousness. While these are problems that many young people have at this age, with increased awareness of appearance and physical characteristics, someone with a physical disability is particularly prone to shyness and timidity in peer relationships. Significantly, Anderson *et al.* commented that the infrequent contact with friends tended to keep relationships at a rather superficial level, compared with non-handicapped teenagers who had the opportunity to see their friends more often and thereby develop a deeper understanding of each other.

There is a general consensus that visible handicaps and disabilities evoke negative attitudes in those without them — disabled and handicapped people are often seen as different from others (Yuker *et al.*, 1960; Richardson, 1976; Altman, 1981; Furnham & Pendred, 1983; Furnham & Gibbs, 1984). These publicly held stereotypes in turn lead to more restrictions on behaviours and opportunities for disabled people (Schroedel, 1978). As Bloom (1976:22) has pointed out, 'the real trouble lies not so much in the disability but in the extraordinary stigma that is an inherent part of our culture'. A poignant example of this is recorded by Henrich & Kriegel (1961) and is to be found in Goffman (1968:47): 'A group of us in our early teens had gone to the beach for the day. I was lying on the sand and I guess the fellows said "I like Domenca very much but I would never go out with a blind girl". I cannot think of any prejudice which so completely rejects you'. Attitudes such as these, Altman (1981) argues, are important because they have an effect on a handicapped person's interaction with the general public; a person's reaction to disability, both in public and private, plays an important contribution in the development of a handicapped person's self-esteem and self-confidence, and in turn the way they interact with society.

Self-image and self-identity are particularly important aspects of social development during adolescence as this is a time when both handicapped and non-handicapped young people are particularly sensitive about their appearance and how others think of them. Based on work carried out with children with facial burns, Goldberg (1974) has concluded that the self-image of a person is most likely to be affected when the impairment is visible to others. While able-bodied young people are able to explore their self-image and define their role in society, by for example, dating, belonging to a group, engaging in 'deviant behaviour', or participating in activities such as going to the pub or a rock concert, it is much more difficult for people who have visible handicaps and disabilities which in some way restrict their mobility. Furthermore, the non-handicapped do not expect disabled people to engage in the usual adolescent behaviours such as swearing, smoking, being a member of a group and sexual experimentation (Morgan, 1972a). As Philip & Duckworth (1982) point out, handicapped teenagers are therefore faced with a 'double-blind' — they may wish to appear normal, but they are in fact expected to be somehow better than normal, and at the same time, because of restrictions due to poor access and mobility, they face situations in which it is difficult for them to act like an able-bodied teenager.

It is clear that adolescents with physical and/or communication difficulties are liable to face social handicaps. Rutter *et al.* (1970a,b) have suggested that restrictions of this kind can lead to feelings of little worth, and there is also evidence of elevated rates of emotional disturbance. Dorner's (1975) study of 63 teenagers with myelomeningocele indicates a high incidence of depression (68%), particularly for girls (81%) and those with severe mobility problems (75%). Clinical evidence of emotional distress and disturbance has also been reported by Freeman (1970) and a study of the social adjustment of 62 young adults, aged 16–35, with cerebral palsy by Rowe (1973) suggests elevated rates of low self-esteem. Using the Social Adjustment scale of the California Test of Personality, Rowe found that 85% of his cerebral palsy client group had below average social adjustment scores. Anderson *et al.* (1982) also sought information about physically handicapped young persons' ability to cope with new situations. Collecting information from both the parents and the young people themselves the authors found that 44% were rated by their parents as being definitely or somewhat fearful of new situations, compared to only 22% of the non-handicapped comparison group. Using self-reports this fell to 30%, but reported fearfulness by those with physical handicaps was still in excess of the comparison group (20%).

The literature indicates that by the time many physically handicapped young people have reached their teenage years, they have very restricted educational, social and emotional experience when compared with their able-bodied peers. As a consequence, they are disadvantaged in terms of work aspirations, enjoying a social life and developing friendships and relationships. Associated with this socially isolated background may be signs of depression, fearfulness and anxiety when coping with difficulties, low self-esteem, lack of self confidence, and an impairment of social skill (e.g. Anderson, 1973; Fulthorpe, 1974). For the disabled young adult, Anderson *et al.* (1982:135) felt that 'the majority definitely needed advice about how to cope with strangers, and . . . seem a group for whom social skills training, including role-playing, might be valuable'.

Richardson (1976) has suggested that handicapped young people need a high level of social competence to overcome the initial worries associated with handicap, yet the research literature indicates that many are deprived of the social experiences necessary for the development of social competence and social skill. Gresham (1981) has conceptualised social skill problems as occurring in three distinct categories: first, 'skill deficits', which are due to an individual not having learned the cognitive and overt social behaviours needed to succeed in social interaction; second, 'performance deficits', whereby the skills are present in an individual's repertoire, but are not performed; and third, 'self-control deficits', which includes the emission of high rates of aversive behaviour. Social competence and social skill may therefore be seen to imply the use of social rules, even though these rules may be used automatically, and without the knowledge of the user (Argyle, 1979). As a common characteristic of socially unskilled interaction, social rules appear to be continually broken or go unheeded (Trower *et al.*, 1978). The interaction therefore becomes unpredictable and is viewed unfavourably by others (Bryan *et al.*, 1976; Kiesler *et al.*, 1967), which only serves to impair the interaction still further. A corollary to this is the need to train handicapped people to avoid behaviours which lead to negative evaluation by peers and to develop social skills which are positively evaluated by peers.

Social skills training (SST) rests on the assumption that social interaction can be construed as a type of motor skill, involving the same processes as, for example, playing a game of cricket or riding a bicycle. Argyle & Kendon (1967) argue that the advantage of this approach is that, as we have considerable information about motor-skill processes, the concepts and ideas developed in the study of motor skills can be applied to social interaction.

Six processes that are considered to be common to both motor skills and social behaviour have been identified by Argyle and Kendon. These are the setting of distinctive goals; selective perception of verbal and non-verbal cues; central translation processes; motor responses; feedback and corrective action; and the timing of behavioural responses. A performance in a social situation can be seen as having a distinct goal made up of a number of sub-goals. The main goal, for example, of an interviewer would be to obtain particular types of information, the sub-goals including putting the interviewee at ease and establishing rapport. The selective perception of cues refers to the process whereby attention is paid to particular types of information which are relevant to achieving the objectives of the interactants. One might, for example, be particularly keen to place an interviewee at ease in a situation and consequently would selectively perceive cues considered to indicate stress or nervousness. What is attended to will depend not only on the person's plan and motives but also on how well the other person is known, social stereotypes, and beliefs about the other person. Having obtained information through the selective perception of cues the central translation process, which represents the decision-making machinery, prescribes a course of action based on the information coming into the system. Over time, one learns behavioural strategies in response to particular types of perceptual information. The central translation process, having made a decision in the light of previous experience, implements this in the form of a motor response which corresponds to an actual social behaviour. Feedback and corrective action refer to the ways in which individuals may change or modify their behaviour in the light of feedback from others. Finally, the timing of responses is of importance, for example, in choosing the most appropriate moment to disagree with someone, or the right time to interrupt a conversation.

Argyle (1967) has argued that if social behaviour is seen as a skill then SST makes it possible to raise the quality of normal social behaviour so that it becomes more efficient, more enjoyable and more acceptable to others. Any improvement in social interaction skills may have implications not only for the personal and social aspects of a young person's life but also extends his/her ability to obtain and retain some form of daytime occupation or employment (Irvine *et al.*, 1978).

Trower *et al.* (1978) provide a detailed account of the procedures involved in SST. Initially, a list is constructed of the particular social difficulties that a person experiences in particular social situations, using self-report checklists, questionnaires and rating scales, or by filmed interview. Having identified the specific skill deficits, these can then be taught by a variety of methods such as through demonstrations, modelling, role-play, and by using immediate feedback from a video-tape-recording. (Examples of these methods and commentaries may be found in Trower *et al.*, 1978; Gresham, 1981; Wilkinson & Canter, 1982; Spence & Shepherd, 1983). Trower *et al.* (1978) subdivide social skills training into a number of different skills including skills in observation, listening, speaking and meshing. Recognising emotions from non-verbal cues is an example of an observation skill (e.g. Ekman & Friesen, 1975). Typically, clients are taught to recognise different emotions from photographs of others, and are asked to role-play the various emotions, using video tape as a way of providing immediate feedback. An example of a listening skill requires the use of appropriate head nods and verbal listener responses (e.g. 'uh huh') as a way of indicating interest and attention to the conversation (e.g. Yngve, 1970). Speaking and meshing skills refer to the regulation of the social interaction. Changing the topic of the conversation requires some forewarning in the form of 'by the way', or 'that's right, but'. Without these skilled topic changing behaviours the interaction can become unpredictable and thereby viewed unfavourably by others (e.g. Thomas *et al.*, 1983; Thomas, 1985). Meshing skills are used to regulate the conversation enabling, for example, the flow of the conversation to be negotiated using turn-taking, turn-offering and turn-yielding cues (e.g. Duncan, 1972; Duncan & Fiske, 1977; Thomas & Bull, 1981).

The effectiveness of SST is still being debated in the literature (see e.g. Gresham, 1981; LeCroy, 1982), although there are now a number of studies using acceptable follow-up procedures for measuring social skill which have indicated that skills taught to adolescents can be maintained over time (e.g. Sarason & Ganzer, 1973; Oden & Asher, 1977; Spence & Spence, 1980; Avery *et al.*, 1981). The current state of the literature suggests that SST with physically handicapped children does have the potential of facilitating social skill development, and several studies have shown that handicapped children are better accepted by their peers after an SST programme (Ballard *et al.*, 1978; Rucker & Vincenzo, 1970; Strain & Timm, 1974; Strain, 1977).

While there have been a number of studies concerned with the assessment and teaching of social skills to adolescents with learning delay or who have been diagnosed as delinquent (e.g. Pease, 1979; Spence & Marziller, 1979; Kelly *et al.*, 1979; Deshler & Schumaker, 1983), there is a lack of comparable programmes for the physically handicapped. However, it is encouraging that the physically handicapped are beginning to be seen as suitable clients for SST. A recent survey of the provision of speech therapy in the 23 educational establishments run by The Spastics Society indicated that up to 65% of them incorporated the teaching of social interaction skills into their programme. This included the encouragement of movement and gesture while communicating (65%), suppression of inappropriate body movements (57%), and teaching conversational skills (65%), such as listening and turn-taking (Thomas & Coombes, 1986).

However, a follow-up study concerned specifically with social skills training for the physically handicapped found that while social skills were recognised as being a major area for development, the methods and teaching programmes used were frequently unsatisfactory (Thomas & Cornwell, 1986). The development and implementation of SST programmes usually incorporate four main steps: initial formal assessment indicating the main problems and situations to be faced by those to be trained; the selection of the most appropriate teaching techniques for dealing with the problems; the training itself; and final and follow-up assessments designed to assess the degree to which any improvements in skilled social behaviour are maintained. Of the 23 further education establishments for the physically handicapped taking part in the study, none used any formal method for determining the type of social skills needing attention, relying solely on 'general observation'. Observation is perhaps the most face-valid method of assessing social skills and has been extensively used (see Gresham, 1981). However there are disadvantages in terms of assessment bias, lack of predictive validity and low correlations with measures of peer acceptance which limit the usefulness of naturalistic observation as a method of assessing social skills (Kent & Foster, 1977; Gottman, 1977). More reliable techniques of assessment include structured observation using detailed social skills checklists (e.g. Trower *et al.*, 1978; Wilkinson & Canter, 1982) and teacher/instructor ratings (Bolstad & Johnson, 1972). While there are a large number of training programmes currently available only three (13%) establishments employed specific SST programmes in the curriculum. Use of role-play as a means of training appropriate facial expressions, observation and meshing skills was used by only one school. Otherwise, role-play was used as a means of practising social activities such as answering the telephone and shopping. Video-recorders were available in all the schools, although they were used mainly for the benefit of the staff rather than as a means of self-monitoring and immediate feedback in SST. While most of the schools were aware of the need for improvements in social skills, the implementation of training procedures had more to do with basic social competence and life skills than with the more subtle interpersonal sub-skills as described by Trower *et al.* (1978). As Ellis & Whittington (1983) have pointed out, SST remains comparatively rare in schools and is very likely to appear in a debased form as a component in social education or life-skills programmes.

## Conclusion

While both handicapped and non-handicapped young adults experience marked difficulties in social situations, the physically handicapped are significantly more likely to experience social difficulties of a severe nature. While the social difficulties of the non-handicapped are likely to dissipate over time with increasing maturity and a widening social circle, this is less likely for the physically handicapped as problems with mobility and access to outdoor activities tend to restrict their social life and opportunities for social interaction. As Anderson *et al.* (1982) have pointed out, social skills training would seem to be of value for young people with physical handicaps.

There is a general indication in the literature that suggests SST has the potential of facilitating improvement in social skills for the handicapped, and several studies have shown that after SST handicapped children are better accepted by their peers. While this is encouraging, there are several areas for concern that need to be addressed.

Firstly, LeCroy (1982) has pointed out in his review of SST with adolescents that many training programmes are constructed simply on the basis of face validity and do not teach skills which have been empirically derived. Normative data concerning effective social behaviour are still very sparse, particularly for adults and for specialist groups such as those with physical handicaps. While the social skill analyses presented here provide an indication of the type and magnitude of social skill deficits that are associated with physical handicap, a prerequisite for the design of an SST programme is the systematic identification of the type of social skills problems experienced by young people with physical handicaps. While self-report questionnaires provide a wealth of valuable information, they are prone to the problems of under-reporting and represent only one side of the social interaction. Of equal importance is how the handicapped young person is viewed by others in social interaction, for, as Kiesler *et al.* (1967) have pointed out, if the interaction becomes halting and unpredictable it is viewed unfavourably by others. Consequently, combining behaviour ratings of video-taped interactions (e.g. Trower *et al.*, 1978) with self-reports would provide both 'subjective' and 'objective' measures of the social skills problems that a physically handicapped young person experiences in social interaction.

Second, the survey of Spastics Society Further Education establishments (Thomas & Cornwell, 1986) indicated a considerable need for SST packages tailored specifically for physically handicapped clients. The content of these training packages, Gresham (1981) argues, should be selected empirically on the basis of skills which discriminate the handicapped from the non-handicapped. Historically, collecting such information has been limited by the analytical methods available. As Ellis & Whittington (1981, 1983), Thomas *et al.* (1983, 1985) and Thomas (in press) have pointed out, social routines in SST programmes are rarely specified in any detail, primarily due to a lack of methods for classifying and analysing the structure of conversation. In recent years however, a number of methods for content analysis (reviewed by Thomas *et al.*, 1982) have become available and a number of sophisticated sequential and structural methods including chain analysis and Markov processes (e.g. Clark, 1983; Thomas *et al.*, 1983, 1985; Thomas, in press) and conjoint analysis (Collett & Lamb, 1982) have been used successfully in the identification of individual conversation and interaction skills. In addition, discriminant analysis techniques such as those used by Gottman (1977) with socially isolated children may also help in establishing an empirical basis for the selection of skilled behaviours for inclusion in an SST programme.

Third, there is also a need to investigate more fully the most appropriate techniques for teaching social skills to young people with different types of handicap. For example, the cognitively based techniques such as modelling and coaching have been most successful with either non-handicapped or mildly handicapped young people, while techniques such as primary reinforcement and token reinforcement have been most successful in the teaching of specific behaviours to more severely handicapped young people. Research is now needed to investigate the most appropriate techniques for use with different types and combinations of handicap. For example, the adolescent who is both physically and mentally handicapped or the adolescent disabled by spina bifida and hydrocephalus with problems of self-image as well as the need for SST would require different social skills packages, and may require different training techniques.

Finally, the evidence regarding the generalisation and maintenance of social behaviours after SST is still rather deficient as only a handful of studies have demonstrated any generalisation of trained social behaviour to other settings. In addition, there is also a paucity of evidence for the maintenance over time of trained social behaviours. While Oden & Asher (1977) did demonstrate a maintained increase in peer acceptance for up to a year after SST this study is an exception as most demonstrations of maintenance of social skills are of the order of two to three weeks. It is important, therefore, that any SST package for the physically handicapped incorporates a series of long-term follow-up assessments so that the maintenance of skilled social behaviour can be monitored.

In conclusion, an increasing number of research studies have indicated that many physically handicapped young people are likely to be isolated from their peers, and experience problems of self-esteem and self-image, the consequence being that many report considerable difficulties in social situations and social relationships. While the extent of these problems is of sufficient magnitude to warrant intervention, SST programmes tailored to the needs of physically handicapped adults are not generally available. A need has therefore been identified for the compilation of SST packages for the physically handicapped. The contents of these training programmes should be selected empirically on the basis of social skills which discriminate between the handicapped and the non-handicapped, incorporate both 'subjective' and 'objective' methods of assessment, and employ follow-up assessments designed to monitor the maintenance and generalisation of trained social behaviours.

## Note to Chapter 12

1. I would like to thank Martin Bax for his constructive comments, Rachel David (Birmingham Polytechnic), Richard Mallows (College of Ripon and York, St John) and Bill Parkinson (Milton Keynes College) for the comparison questionnaires, Lorraine Wilder and Joy Allsop for their assistance with the preparation of the manuscript, all those who generously completed the questionnaires and the Spastics Society and the Association for Spina Bifida and Hydrocephalus for financial support.

## References

ALTMANN, B. 1981, Studies of attitudes towards the handicapped: The need for a new direction, *Social Problems*,28, 21–37.

ANDERSON, E. M. 1973, *The Disabled Schoolchild: A Study of Integration in Primary Schools*. London: Methuen.

ANDERSON, E. M. & SPAIN, B. 1977, *The Child with Spina Bifida*. London: Methuen.

ANDERSON, E. M., CLARKE, L. & SPAIN, B. 1982, *Disability in Adolescence*. London & New York: Methuen.

ARGYLE, M. 1967, *The Psychology of Interpersonal Behaviour*. London: Allen Lane.

— 1979, Sequences in social behaviour as a function of the situation. In G. P. GINSBURG (ed.), *Emerging Strategies in Social Psychological Research*. Chichester: Wiley.

ARGYLE, M. & KENDON, A. 1967, The experimental analysis of social performance. In L. BERKOWITZ (ed.), *Advances in Experimental Social Psychology*, Vol 3. New York: Academic Press.

AVERY, A. W., RIDER, K. & HAYNES-CLEMENTS, L. A. 1981, Communication skills training for adolescents: A five month follow-up, *Adolescence*, 16, 289–98.

BALLARD, M., CORMAN, L., GOTTLIEB, J. & KAUFMAN, M. J. 1978, Improving the social status of mainstreamed retarded children, *Journal of Educational Psychology*, 69, 605–11.

BANKS, M. H. & JACKSON, P. R. 1982, Unemployment and the risk of minor psychiatric disorder in young people, *Psychological Medicine*, 12, 789–98.

BAX, M., SMYTH, D. & THOMAS, A. P. 1985, The health and social needs of physically handicapped young adults. End-of-grant report to the Spastics Society and ASBAH, Charing Cross and Westminster Medical School.

BLOOM, F. 1976, An aspect of social services for the handicapped child in the community, *Talk*, 79, 22–25.

BOLSTAD, O. D. & JOHNSON, S. M. 1972, Self-regulation in the modification of disruptive classroom behaviour, *Journal of Applied Behaviour Analysis*, 5, 443–54.

BOOKIS, J. 1983, *Beyond the School Gate. A Study of Disabled Young People aged 13–19*. London: Royal Association for Disability and Rehabilitation (RADAR).

BRAND, J., SHAKESPEARE, R. & WOODS, G. E. 1969, Psychological development of the severely subnormal after 16 years of age, *Developmental Medicine and Child Neurology*, 11, 783–85.

BRYAN, T. S., WHEELER, R., FELCAN, J. & HENEK, T. 1976, 'Come on dummy': An observational study of children's communications, *Journal of Learning Disabilities*, 9, 53–61.

BURTON, L. 1975, *The Family Life of Sick Children*. London: Routledge and Kegan Paul.

CASTREE, B. J. & WALKER, J. H. 1981, The young adult with spina bifida, *British Medical Journal*, 283, 1040–42.

CLARK, D. D. 1983, *Language and Action: A Structural Model of Behaviour*. Oxford: Pergamon Press.

CLARKE, M. M., RIACH, J. & CHEYNE, W. M. 1977, Handicapped children and pre-school education. Report to the Warnock Committee on Special Education, University of Strathclyde.

COLLETT, P. & LAMB, R. 1982, Describing sequences of social action. In M. VON CRANACH & R. HARRE (eds), *The Organization of Human Action*. Cambridge: Cambridge University Press.

CONGER, J. & KEANE, S. 1981, Social skills intervention for the treatment of isolated or withdrawn children, *Psychological Bulletin*, 90, 478–95.

DEPARTMENT OF EDUCATION AND SCIENCE 1978, *Special Education Needs*. Cmnd 7212. London: HMSO (Warnock Report).

DEPARTMENT OF HEALTH AND SOCIAL SECURITY 1976, *Fit for the Future*. Cmnd 6684. London: HMSO (Court Report).

DESHLER, D. D. & SCHUMAKER, J.B. 1983, Social skills of learning disabled adolescents: characteristics and intervention, *Topics in Learning and Learning Disabilities*, July, 15–23.

DORNER, S. 1973, Psychological and social problems of families of adolescent spina bifida patients: a preliminary report, *Developmental Medicine and Child Neurology*, 15, Supplement 29, 24–26.

— 1975, The relationship of physical handicap to stress in families with an adolescent with spina bifida, *Developmental Medicine and Child Neurology*, 17, 765–76.

— 1976, Adolescents with spina bifida — how they see their situation, *Archives of Disease in Childhood*, 51, 439–44.

— 1977, Sexual interest and activity in adolescents with spina bifida, *Journal of Child Psychology and Psychiatry*, 18, 229–37.

DUNCAN, S. 1972, Some signals and rules for taking speaking turns in conversations, *Journal of Personality and Social Psychology*, 23, 283–92.

DUNCAN, S. & FISKE, D. W. 1977, *Face-to-face Interaction: Research, Methods and Theory*. Hillsdale, NJ.: Lawrence Erlbaum.

EKMAN, P. & FRIESEN, W. V. 1975, *Unmasking the Face: A Guide to Recognising Emotions from Facial Clues*. Englewood Cliffs, NJ.: Prentice-Hall.

ELLIS, R. & WHITTINGTON, D. 1981, *A Guide to Social Skill Training*. London: Croom Helm.

— 1983, *New Directions in Social Skill Training*. London: Croom Helm.

EVANS, K., HICKMAN, V. & CARTER, C. O. 1975, Handicap and social status of adults with spina bifida cystica, *British Journal of Preventive and Social Medicine*, 28, 85–92.

FOSTER, S. 1983, Critical elements in the development of children's social skills. In R. ELLIS & D. WHITTINGTON (eds.), *New Directions in Social Skill Training*. London: Croom Helm.

FOSTER, S. L. & RITCHEY, W. L. 1979, Issues in the assessment of social competence in children, *Journal of Applied Behaviour Analysis*, 12, 625–38.

FOX, A. M. 1977, Psychological problems of physically handicapped children, *British Journal of Hospital Medicine*, May, 479–90.

FREEMAN, R. D. 1970, Psychiatric problems in adolescents with cerebral palsy, *Developmental Medicine and Child Neurology*, 12, 64–70.

FULTHORPE, D. 1974, Spina bifida: some psychological aspects, *Special Education and Further Trends*, 1, 17–20.

FURNHAM, A. & GIBBS, M. 1984, School children's attitudes towards the handicapped, *Journal of Adolescence*, 7, 99–117.

FURNHAM, A. & PENDRED, J. 1983, Attitudes towards the mentally and physically disabled, *British Journal of Medical Psychology*, 56, 179–87.

GOFFMAN, E. 1968, *Stigma: Notes on the Management of Spoiled Identity*. Harmondsworth: Penguin Books.

GOLDBERG, R. T. 1974, Adjustment of children with invisible and visible handicaps: congenital heart disease and facial burns, *Journal of Counselling Psychology*, 21, 428–32.

GOTTMAN, J. M. 1977, Towards a definition of social isolation in children, *Child Development*, 48, 513–17.

GRESHAM, F. M. 1981, Social skills training with handicapped children: a review, *Review of Educational Research*, 51:1, 139–46.

HENRICH, E. & KRIEGEL, L. 1961, *Experiments in Survival*. New York: Association for the Aid of Crippled Children.

INGRAM, T. T. S., JAMESON, S., ERRINGTON, J. & MITCHELL, R.G. 1964, *Living with Cerebral Palsy*. Clinics in Developmental Medicine, no. 14. London: The Spastics Society Medical Education and Information Unit with Heinemann Medical.

IRVINE, P., GOODMAN, L. & MANN, L. 1978, Occupational and educational needs of the learning disabled. In L. MANN, L. GOODMAN & J. L. WIEDERHOLT (eds), *Teaching the Learning Disabled Adolescent*. Boston: Houghton-Mifflin.

JOWETT, S. 1982, *Young Disabled People: Their Further Education, Training and Employment*. Windsor, Berks: NFER–Nelson.

KELLY, J. A., WILDMAN, B. G., UREY, J. R. & THURMAN, C. 1979, Group skills training to increase conversational repertoire of retarded adolescents, *Child Behaviour Therapy*, 1: 4, 323–36.

KENT, R. N. & FOSTER, S. L. 1977, Direct observational procedures:

methodological issues in naturalistic settings. In A. Cinenero, K. Calhoun & H. Adams (eds), *Handbook of Behavioural Assessment*. New York: Wiley.

Kiesler, C. A., Kiesler, S. G. & Pallack, M. S. 1967, The effect of commitment to future interaction on reactions to norm violations, *Journal of Personality*, 35, 585–99.

Laurence, K. M. & Beresford, A. 1975, Continence, friends, marriage and children in 51 adults with spina bifida, *Developmental Medicine and Child Neurology*, 17, Supplement 35, 123–28.

LeCroy, C. W. 1982, Social skills training with adolescents: a review. In C. W. LeCroy (ed.), *Social Skills Training for Children and Youth*. New York: Haworth Press.

Lindon, R. L. 1963, The Pultibec system for the medical assessment of physically handicapped children, *Developmental Medicine and Child Neurology*, 5, 125–45.

Lonton, A. P., O'Sullivan, A. M. & Loughlin, A. M. 1983, Spina bifida adults, *Zeitschrift für Kinderchirurgie*, 38, Supplement 2, 110–12.

Lorber, J. & Schloss, A. L. 1973, The adolescent with myelomeningocele, *Developmental Medicine and Child Neurology*, 15, Supplement 29, 113 (abstract).

McFall, R. 1982, A review and reformulation of the concept of social skills, *Behavioural Assessment*, 4, 1–33.

McMichael, J. K. 1971, *Handicap: A Study of Physically Handicapped Children and their Families*. London: Staples Press.

Morgan, A. 1972a, Attitudes towards the sexuality of handicapped boys and girls, *Forward Trends*, 16, 62–66.

Morgan, M. 1972b, Like other school leavers? In D. M. Boswell & J. M. Wingrove (eds), *The Handicapped Person in the Community*. London: Tavistock Press.

NUT 1982, *Survey of Educational Provision for 16-19 Year Olds with Special Needs*. London: National Union of Teachers.

Oden, S. & Asher, F. R. 1977, Coaching children in social skills for friendship making, *Child Development*, 48, 495–506.

Pease, J. 1979, A social skills training group for early adolescents, *Journal of Adolescence*, 2, 229–38.

Philip, M. & Duckworth, D. 1982, *Children with Disabilities and their Families: A Review of Research*. Windsor, Berks: NFER-Nelson.

Prior, D. & Linford, M. 1981, The young physically handicapped in Hounslow: a study of adolescents and young adults with severe locomotor handicaps. Research and Planning Section, Social Services Department, London Borough of Hounslow.

Richardson, S.A. 1976, Attitudes and behaviour towards the physically handicapped. In D. Bergsma & A. E. Pulver (eds), *Developmental Disabilities: Psychologic and Social Implications*. New York: Alan R. Liss.

Richardson, S. A., Hastorf, A. H. & Dornbusch, S. M. 1964, Effects of physical disability on the child's description of himself, *Child Development*, 35, 893–907.

Rowe, B. 1973, A study of social adjustment in young adults with cerebral palsy. Unpublished BMSc dissertation, University of Newcastle-upon-Tyne.

Rucker, C. N. & Vincenzo, F. M. 1970, Mainstreaming social acceptance gains made by mentally retarded children, *Exceptional Children*, 36, 679–80.

Rutter, M., Tizard, J. & Whitmore, K. 1970, *Education, Health and Behaviour*. London: Longman.

Rutter, M., Graham, P. & Yule, W. 1970, A neuropsychiatric study in childhood. *Clinics in Developmental Medicine*, 35/36. London: Spastics International Medical Publications and Heinemann Medical.

Sarason, I. G. & Ganzer, V.J. 1973, Modelling and group discussion in the rehabilitation of delinquents, *Journal of Counselling Psychology*, 20, 442–49.

Schinke, S. 1981, Interpersonal skills training with adolescents. In M. Hersen, R. Eisler & P. Miller (eds), *Progress in Behaviour Modification*, Vol.2. New York: Academic Press.

Schroedel, J. 1978, *Attitudes towards Persons with Disabilities: A Compendium of Related Literature*. New York: HRC.

Smith, A. D. 1983, Adult spina bifida survey in Scotland: educational attainment and employment, *Zeitschrift für Kinderchirurgie*, 38, 107–9.

Spence, A. J. & Spence, S. H. 1980, Cognitive changes associated with social skills training, *Behaviour Research and Therapy*, 18, 265–72.

Spence, S. & Shepherd, G. 1983, *Developments in Social Skills Training*. London: Academic Press.

Spence, S. H. & Marziller, J. S. 1979, Social skills training with adolescent male offenders. I: short term effects, *Behaviour Research and Therapy*, 17, 7–16.

Strain, P. S. 1977, An experimental analysis of peer social initiations on the behaviour of withdrawn preschool children: some training and generalisation effects, *Journal of Abnormal Child Psychology*, 5, 445–55.

Strain, P. S. & Timm, M. A. 1974, An experimental analysis of social interaction between a behaviourally disordered preschool child and her classroom peers, *Journal of Applied Behaviour Analysis*, 7, 583–90.

TEW, B.J. 1973, Spina bifida and hydrocephalus: facts, fallacies and future, *Special Education*, 62:4, 26–31.

THOMAS, A. P. 1985, Conversational routines: a Markov chain analysis, *Language and Communication*, 5: 4, 287–96.

— in press, Describing the structure of conversation using Markov chains, chain analysis and Monte Carlo simulation, *Journal of Literary Semantics*.

THOMAS, A. P., BAX, M. & SMYTH, D. 1987, The provision of support services for the handicapped young adult. Report to the Association for Spina Bifida and Hydrocephalus (Department of Child Health, Charing Cross and Westminster Medical School, London).

THOMAS, A. P., BAX, M., COOMBES, K., GOLDSON, E., SMYTH, D. & WHITMORE, K. 1985, The health and social needs of physically handicapped young adults: are they being met by the statutory services? *Developmental Medicine and Child Neurology*, 27: 4, Supplement no. 50.

THOMAS, A. P. & BULL, P. E. 1981, The role of pre-speech posture change in dyadic interaction, *British Journal of Social Psychology*, 20, 105–11.

THOMAS, A. P., BULL, P. E. & ROGER, D. 1982, Conversational Exchange Analysis, *Journal of Language and Social Psychology*, 1, 141–55.

THOMAS, A. P. & COOMBES, K. 1986, A survey of the provision of speech therapy services in centres administered by, or affiliated to the Spastics Society. End-of-grant report to the Spastics Society. Dept. of Child Health, Charing Cross and Westminster Medical School, London.

THOMAS, A. P. & CORNWELL, A. 1986, Social skills training and physical handicap. Report to the Spastics Society. Department of Child Health, Charing Cross and Westminster Medical School, London.

THOMAS, A. P., ROGER, D. & BULL, P. E. 1983, A sequential analysis of informal dyadic conversation using Markov chains, *British Journal of Social Psychology*, 22, 177–88.

TROWER, P., BRYANT, B. &ARGYLE, M. 1978, *Social Skills and Mental Health*. London: Methuen.

WALKER, A. 1980, The handicapped school-leaver and the transition to work, *British Journal of Guidance and Counselling*, 8, 212–23.

— 1982a, Unqualified and Unemployed, *Concern*, 43, 4–9.

— 1982b, *Unqualified and Unemployed: Handicapped Young People and the Labour Market*. London: National Children's Bureau with Macmillan.

WARR, P. B. 1978, A study of psychological well-being, *British Journal of Psychology*, 69, 111–21.

— 1982, Psychological aspects of employment and unemployment. *Psychological Medicine*, 12, 7–11.

WARR, P. B. & JACKSON, P. 1983, Self-esteem and unemployment among young workers, *Le Travail Humain*, 46, 355–66.

WILKINSON, J. & CANTER, S. 1982, *Social Skills Training Manual: Assessment, Programme Design and Management of Training*. Chichester: Wiley.

YOUNGHUSBAND, E., BIRCHALL, D., DAVIE, R. & KELLMER-PRINGLE, M. 1970, *Living with Handicap: The Report of the Working Party on Children with Special Needs*. London: National Bureau for co-operation in Child Care/National Children's Bureau.

YNGVE, V. H. 1970, On getting a word in edgewise. In *Papers from the Sixth Regional Meeting of the Chicago Linguistic Society*. Chicago: Chicago Linguistic Society.

YUKER, H., BLOCK, J. & CAMPBELL, W. 1960, *A Scale to Measure Attitudes towards Disabled Persons*. New York HRC.

# 13 The role of cuelessness in social interaction: An examination of teaching by telephone[1]

D. R. RUTTER
*University of Kent at Canterbury*

## Introduction

Previous research suggests that non-verbal cues play a significant part in social interaction — especially those transmitted visually (Argyle & Cook, 1976; Short, Williams & Christie, 1976; Harper, Wiens & Matarazzo, 1978). Experimental research on visual signalling began in the 1960s and the first of the literature was concerned with 'looking' and 'eye-contact'. From time to time during social encounters, we look at one another in the region of the eyes, and sometimes our eyes meet to make eye-contact. The most pressing task was to explore the pattern and structure of looking, and a number of regularities soon emerged. People looked more when they listened than when they spoke, for example; eye-contact was generally broken very quickly; and the pattern of looks seemed to follow very closely the pattern of speech. What is more, there were marked and consistent individual differences, and personality, sex, and psychopathology were each important sources of variance.

From structure, the literature moved quickly to function, and one of the earliest suggestions was that looking served principally to express our emotions. Emotion, it was argued, affected both how much we looked ourselves and how we interpreted other people's looks, and soon an enormous literature had grown. But, at the same time, looking also helped people to regulate the flow of conversation and to monitor one another for feedback and, while emotion might sometimes be central, information was important, too.

With the growth of interest in information, a new line of research now began to develop, for what gradually emerged was that looking and eye-contact were much less important than had been traditionally thought. What mattered most about visual contact was not that it allowed us to look at the other's eyes but that it gave access to the whole person — the face, the hands, the posture, and so on, just as much as the eyes. *Seeing* the whole person was the most important part of visual communication — but the problem was to find a way of exploring it experimentally.

The question of seeing was one which particularly concerned myself and my colleagues, and the solution we adopted, along with others (see Short, Williams & Christie, 1976) was to compare face-to-face encounters, where seeing was free to occur naturally, with audio-only encounters, where it was precluded altogether since subjects communicated from separate rooms over a microphone-headphone intercom. The differences, we predicted, would be considerable, and three principal effects were detected. First, the outcomes or conclusions of debates were less moderate and compromising in the audio condition than face-to-face (Morley & Stephenson, 1977). In the absence of visual cues, we suggested, subjects were able to disregard interpersonal considerations and were free to concentrate instead on the 'inter-party' issues, with the result that the objective merits of the arguments prevailed and the stronger case won. Second, there were corresponding effects upon the content of what people said (Stephenson, Ayling & Rutter, 1976). On the one hand, audio conversations were depersonalised in comparison with face-to-face conversations, with less reference to the people involved and a noticeably more antagonistic flavour and, on the other, they were task-orientated and less often strayed from the point. Third, there were differences also in linguistic style and, in particular, audio conversations were markedly less spontaneous than those held face-to-face, with noticeably less interruption (Rutter & Stephenson, 1977). The role of visual communication, we argued at the time, was to allow the participants to converse spontaneously and interrupt freely by enabling them to send and receive the non-verbal signals which maintain the interaction and prevent the breakdown which interruption might otherwise threaten.

By the late 1970s, then, we had reached the conclusion that seeing was a significant part of social interaction, and that its effects extended to content, style and outcome. Other groups too were reaching similar conclusions — but there was still one issue which worried us, and it concerned the methodology of our experiments. Whenever we had tried to examine seeing, we had simply compared face-to-face with audio, but face-to-face and audio differ in two respects — physical as well as visual separation in the audio condition — and to be confident of our conclusions we had to find some way of disentangling the two variables. The solution we adopted was to introduce a variety of intermediate conditions — closed-circuit television, which allowed visual contact but kept the subjects in separate rooms, and curtain and wooden-screen conditions, which did the opposite — and the results were striking. For both content and style (outcome was not examined), the new conditions lay almost always between the other two. In other words, we had discovered a dimension, and the term we adopted was *cuelessness* (Rutter, Stephenson & Dewey, 1981; Kemp & Rutter, 1982). From face-to-face, to closed-circuit television, curtain and wooden screen, to audio, the number of social cues declines — from visual cues and physical presence cues face-to-face to neither in the audio condition — and it was cuelessness which could account for all our previous results. The more cueless the encounter, the greater the feeling of psychological distance, and so the more depersonalised and task-orientated the content and, in turn, the less spontaneous the style and the less moderate and compromising the outcome. The aggregate of social cues was what mattered most, not just the cues from vision, and content, style and outcome were all related together, which had not been appreciated before. From looking and eye-contact, the literature had progressed to seeing, and now it had arrived at cuelessness. It was cuelessness, we believed, which offered the most promising theoretical framework for the future (Figure 13.1).

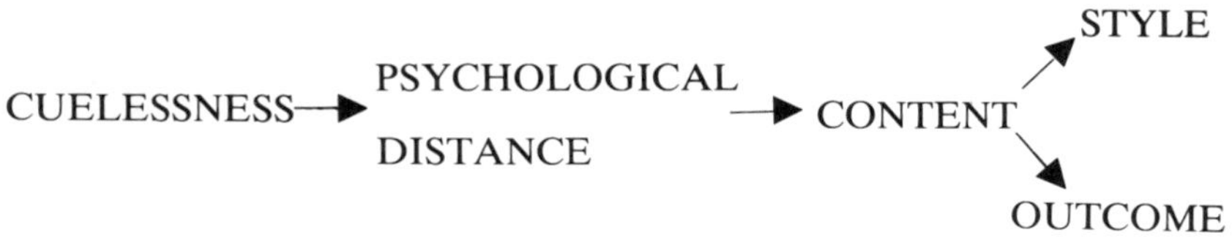


FIGURE 13.1 *Cuelessness*

By now, we had reached the late 1970s, and considerable progress had been made towards integrating the literature both empirically and theoretically. There was, however, one major limitation in our work which concerned us, and that was that almost all the data had come from laboratory research, and we were simply unable to say how well the findings would generalise outside. Applied research allows one to test and extend one's existing findings and theories and to exploit everyday settings as sources of new issues and approaches, and we were anxious as well to try to help solve practical problems. There were two main areas to which we therefore turned — social behaviour in blind people, and teaching and learning by telephone — and it is the latter which provides the focus for the remainder of this chapter.

Teaching by telephone began in Iowa, in the 1930s, and today it has spread throughout the world, particularly the USA and Europe. Many systems have been developed, but the most common in this country is the 'conference call', in which participants use their domestic telephones and are bridged together by an operator. The lines are open, so that everyone can hear and speak directly to everyone else, and up to eight people can normally take part. By exploring telephone tutorials, we believed, and comparing them with face-to-face sessions, we would gain a useful test of our model and findings, as well as some data of practical value to the Open University. We therefore set up a programme of research.

The first of our findings were published in Rutter & Robinson (1981), and the most extensive of our studies — the one to be reported in this chapter — is described in detail in Rutter (1984,1987). Ten tutorial groups were followed for the whole of an academic year, five from Education and five from the Social Sciences, and four sessions from each were recorded, two telephone and two face-to-face. Our objectives were threefold: to provide as detailed an analysis as we could, concentrating in particular on the tutor's strategy and the discourse structure of the two types of meeting, and the ways in which content, style and outcome fitted together; to test whether our findings would generalise from faculty to faculty and from course to course; and to explore whether people might adapt to cuelessness over time as they developed ways of overcoming its constraints.

## Method

Five Education and five Social Science groups took part in the experiment, all of them from full-year post-foundation courses based in the Open University's South-East region. Each was scheduled to hold from four to nine face-to-face tutorials throughout the year and, towards the middle, two telephone meetings were added (at the project's expense) in such a way that at least one face-to-face meeting fell between them. The telephone sessions were held over a conference call, and up to eight students were able to take part. Most of the tutors (like the students) were inexperienced at telephone teaching — though one or two had used it on previous courses — but all had had at least a little training from the Open University. Tape-recordings were made of the two telephone sessions and, in general, four of the face-to-face sessions, and our eventual analyses were based on four recordings altogether from each group — the two telephone sessions, and the face-to-face sessions which immediately preceded and followed them, giving face-to-face, telephone, telephone, face-to-face for each group (Figure 13.2).

| | | | | | | | | | | | | | |
|---|---|---|---|---|---|---|---|---|---|---|---|---|---|
| Education | 1 | F | F | $\underline{F}$ | T* | $\underline{\mathrm{F}}$ | $\underline{T}$ | $\underline{\mathrm{F}}$ | $\underline{T}$ | $\underline{F}$ | F | F | F |
| | 2 | F | $\underline{F}$ | T* | $\underline{\mathrm{F}}$ | $\underline{T}$ | $\underline{\mathrm{F}}$ | $\underline{T}$ | $\underline{F}$ | F | | | |
| | 3 | F | F | $\underline{F}$ | $\underline{T}$ | $\underline{\mathrm{F}}$ | $\underline{\mathrm{F}}$ | $\underline{T}$ | $\underline{F}$ | F | F | | |
| | 4 | F | F | $\underline{F}$ | $\underline{T}$ | $\underline{\mathrm{F}}$ | $\underline{T}$ | $\underline{\mathrm{F}}$ | $\underline{F}$ | F | F | | |
| | 5 | F | $\underline{F}$ | $\underline{T}$ | $\underline{\mathrm{F}}$ | $\underline{\mathrm{F}}$ | $\underline{T}$ | $\underline{F}$ | F | | | | |
| Social science | 1 | F | $\underline{F}$ | $\underline{T}$ | $\underline{\mathrm{F}}$ | $\underline{\mathrm{F}}$ | $\underline{T}$ | $\underline{F}$ | F | | | | |
| | 2 | F | $\underline{F}$ | $\underline{T}$ | $\underline{\mathrm{F}}$ | $\underline{T}$ | F | $\underline{F}$ | | | | | |
| | 3 | F | $\underline{F}$ | $\underline{\mathrm{F}}$ | $\underline{T}$ | $\underline{\mathrm{F}}$ | $\underline{T}$ | $\underline{F}$ | F | | | | |
| | 4 | F | $\underline{F}$ | $\underline{T}$ | $\underline{\mathrm{F}}$ | $\underline{T}$ | $\underline{F}$ | | | | | | |
| | 5 | F | $\underline{F}$ | $\underline{T}$ | $\underline{\mathrm{F}}$ | $\underline{T}$ | F | $\underline{F}$ | F | | | | |

*Recording abandoned because of technical problems.
Underlining means recorded; italics with underlining means recorded and analysed

FIGURE 13.2 *Experimental sessions*

The first stage of our analysis was to prepare verbatim transcripts, and the middle half-hour of each session was selected, and analyses conducted, of content, style and structuring. To examine outcome, we relied on postal questionnaires, and the response rate was 88% for tutors and 74% for students. For all our data, there were wide discrepancies between sessions in the numbers of students present, and we decided to treat the data in the way we had chosen in Rutter & Robinson (1981). For content, the scores for students were totalled for each recording and, for style, structure and outcome, they were averaged, giving one value for the combined students and one for the tutor. The data were then analysed by analysis of variance (Figure 13.3), with faculty (Education/Social Science) a between-subjects factor, and medium (face-to-face/telephone), occasion (first/second), and participant (tutor/student) within-subjects factors (Winer, 1971: 571). Where analysis of variance was inappropriate — in the qualitative items from the outcome questionnaire — non-parametric analyses were used instead, and the totals and means were replaced by frequencies.

| | | Face-to-face | | | | Telephone | | | |
|---|---|---|---|---|---|---|---|---|---|
| | | Occasion 1 | | Occasion 2 | | Occasion 1 | | Occasion 2 | |
| | | Tutor | Student | Tutor | Student | Tutor | Student | Tutor | Student |
| Education | 1 | | | | | | | | |
| | 2 | | | | | | | | |
| | 3 | | | | | | | | |
| | 4 | | | | | | | | |
| | 5 | | | | | | | | |
| Social science | 6 | | | | | | | | |
| | 7 | | | | | | | | |
| | 8 | | | | | | | | |
| | 9 | | | | | | | | |
| | 10 | | | | | | | | |

FIGURE 13.3 *Experimental design*

## Results

The first of our analyses examined content, and our prediction was that, in comparison with face-to-face tutorials, telephone tutorials would be noticeably task-oriented and depersonalised. The scoring was based on Conference Process Analysis (Morley & Stephenson, 1977), refined and extended from the version we had developed in Rutter & Robinson (1981), and each utterance was divided into units of two lines of typescript (or less if the utterance was shorter), and each unit was coded once. In the event, many of the possible codes were used very seldom, and we chose eventually to base our statistical analyses on just 23 categories (Table 13.1). To be included, the category had either to account for a mean of 1% or more of the units or to be an index of personal content — a criterion which was essential for our theoretical purposes since personal contributions were relatively uncommon and would have been almost excluded by the 1-per-cent rule. Together, the 23 categories accounted for 93.8% of the units.

The results are given in Figure 13.4, and what emerged in particular were two principal findings. First, only four of the measures produced a significant main effect of medium and, in every case, the effect was against prediction — more offering of academic information face-to-face ($F(1,8) = 6.4$; $p < 0.05$), less responding with personal examples ($F(1,8) = 7.7$; $p < 0.05$) and personal information about one's study methods ($F(1,8) = 6.1$; $p < 0.05$), and less acknowledgement ($F(1,8) = 5.9$; $p < 0.05$). Second, however, and this was the important result, for eight of the measures there was a significant interaction between medium and participant and, in every single case, the effect of cuelessness was to exaggerate the difference between tutor and students. The effects were for seeking expansion ($F(1,8) = 16.4$; $p < 0.01$), seeking information about personal study methods ($F(1,8) = 10.1$; $p < 0.05$), seeking personal examples ($F(1,8) = 6.6$; $p < 0.05$), seeking academic opinions ($F(1,8) = 7.7$; $p < 0.05$), replying with information about personal study procedures ($F(1,8) = 5.6$; $p < 0.05$), replying with personal examples ($F(1,8) = 7.7$; $p < 0.05$), procedure ($F(1,8) = 9.5$; $p < 0.05$), and acknowledgement ($F(1,8) = 13.3$; $p < 0.01$). The interactions, in fact, accounted for the significant main effects of medium, for supplementary *t*-tests (Winer, 1971:199) revealed that only the tutors were affected by medium for acknowledgements ($t(9) = 3.1$; $p < 0.025$), and only students were affected for replies with personal examples ($t(9) = 2.8$; $p < 0.05$) and replies about study procedures ($t(9) = 2.4$; $p < 0.05$). For offers of academic information, neither tutors nor students showed a significant difference between conditions, despite the significant main effect.

TABLE 13.1 *Principal categories of content*

| *Seek* (S) | *Offer* (O) | *Reply* (R) | *No mode* |
|---|---|---|---|
| Expansion (Exp.) | Information — academic (Inf. ac.) | Information — academic (Inf. ac.) | Agreement (Ag.) |
| Confirmation (Conf.) | Information — personal procedures (Inf. per. proc.) | Information — personal procedures (Inf. per. proc.) | Procedure (Proc.) |
| Information — academic (Inf. ac.) | Information —personal examples (Inf. per. eg.) | Information — personal examples (Inf. per. eg.) | Academic procedure (Ac. proc.) |
| Information — personal procedures (Inf. per. proc.) | Information — OU (Inf. OU) | Opinion — academic (Op. ac.) | Acknowledgement. (Ack.) |
| Information — personal examples (Inf. per. eg.) | Opinion — academic (Op. ac.) | Reply (no resource) (R) | |
| Opinion — academic (Op. ac.) | Opinion — OU (Op. OU)<br>Advice — OU (Adv. OU)<br>Appraisal — academic (App. ac.) | | |

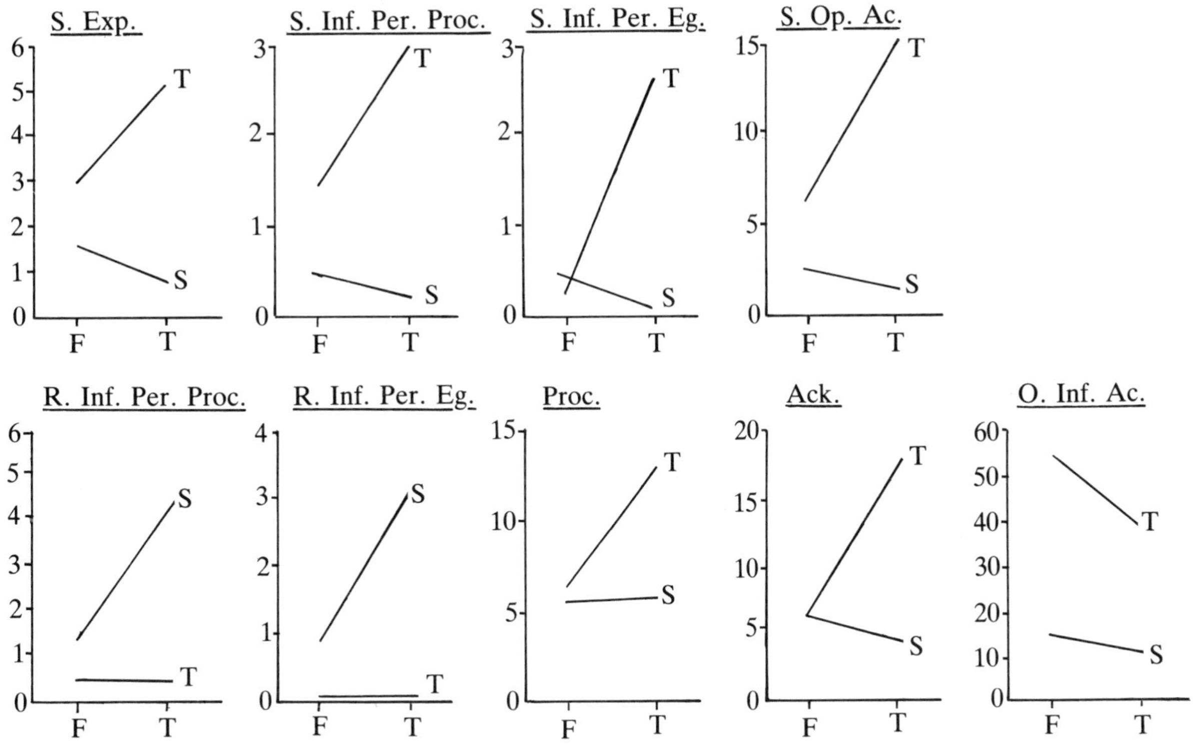


*Note*: F and T are face-to-face and telephone; T and S are tutor and student. Other abbreviations as in Table 13.1

FIGURE 13.4 *Mean values for content*

What had happened, very simply, was that the telephone had led participants into more sharply focused perceptions of their roles, so that tutors became even 'more like' tutors and students even 'more like' students. Thus, tutors spent most of their time over the telephone structuring the proceedings and asking questions — seeking opinions about academic issues, and seeking everyday examples from the students' lives to support their opinions; asking about the students' study habits; and then acknowledging the replies — while students spent their time giving answers. Role perception is central to task-orientation, and similar effects have been found in our previous work (Stephenson, Ayling & Rutter, 1976; Morley & Stephenson, 1977; Rutter & Robinson, 1981). The fewer the social cues, the greater the perceived distance between the participants, and so the more sharply focused the perceptions of role and the more clearly differentiated the behaviour. There were no main effects for faculty, it should be added finally, and there were few effects of occasion and few subsidiary interactions.

The second of our analyses examined style and structuring, and there were two predictions, the first that telephone tutorials would be less spontaneous than face-to-face tutorials, the second that they would be more deliberately structured by the tutor. The results are given in Figure 13.5, and both predictions received good support. Interruptions were more frequent face-to-face, especially for students (interaction $F$ for overlapping interruptions, $F(1,8) = 5.5$; $p < 0.05$), while filled pauses ('ers' and 'ums') were less frequent ($F(1,8) = 68.3$; $p < 0.001$), and laughter and acknowledgement signals were especially common among students face-to-face ($F(1,8) = 12.6$; $p < 0.05$; and $F(1,8) = 16.2$; $p < 0.01$, respectively). Questions by the tutor, the principal means of structuring the proceedings, were more frequent over the telephone than face-to-face, both questions directed to particular individuals ($F(1,8) = 12.8$; $p < 0.01$) and those to the group in general ($F(1,8) = 8.4$; $p < 0.05$), and there was once again a noticeable pattern, as the findings for content had indicated already. Over the telephone, the sequence of utterances was almost always tutor–student–tutor–student, with very little student–student interaction, while face-to-face there were just as many switches from student to student as from tutor to student and student to tutor. The only other important effects concerned the amount said, and tutors, it emerged, spoke more words overall than students ($F(1,8) = 5.9$; $p < 0.05$), in longer ($F(1,8) = 8.9$; $p < 0.05$) but less frequent ($F(1,8) = 9.9$; $p < 0.05$) utterances, and this time the differences were most noticeable face-to-face.

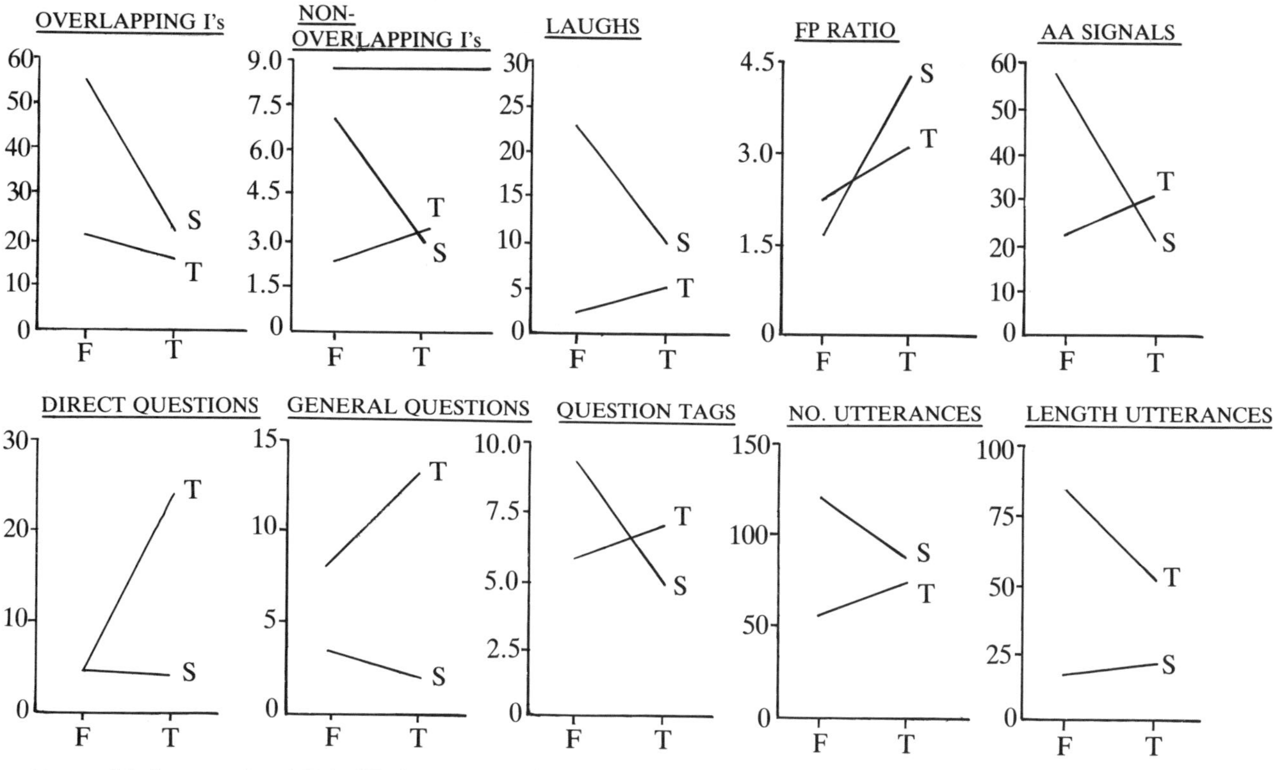


*Note*: I is interruption; FP is filled pause; AA is acknowledgement signal. Other abbreviations as in Figure 13.4

FIGURE 13.5 *Mean values for style*

The third of our analyses examined outcome, and there were two sets of measures, both extracted from the postal questionnaires distributed at the end of each session. The first was based on a variety of open-ended questions about what had happened during the tutorial, and the second came from a checklist of twenty-four adjective scales intended to tap task-orientation, depersonalisation, spontaneity, and the subject's overall evaluation. Only one of the open-ended items was answered by an appreciable number of subjects — the number of topics which had been raised during the session — and neither that nor the majority of the adjective scales revealed any difference between the two conditions. There were just three significant main effects of medium (Figure 13.6) — with telephone tutorials perceived as more 'formal' ($F(1,5) = 10.6$; $p < 0.05$) and 'tiring' ($F(1,5) = 8.6$; $p < 0.05$) than face-to-face, and less 'humorous' ($F(1,5) = 9.5$: $p < 0.05$) — and beyond that there was nothing of importance. In general, both face-to-face and telephone tutorials were evaluated very favourably, by tutors and students alike.

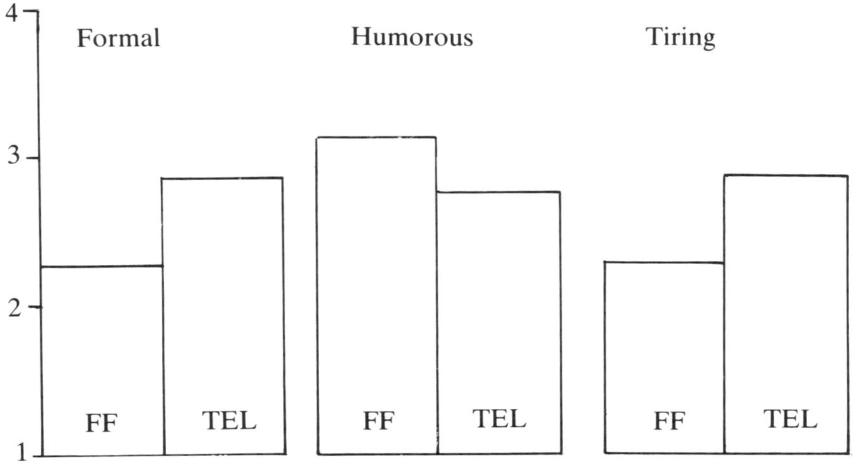


*Note*: FF is face-to-face; TEL is telephone

FIGURE 13.6 *Mean values for outcome*

The fourth and last of our analyses concerned the relationships between the three sets of dependent measures — content, style and outcome — and it was here that we were to find some of the strongest support of all for our predictions. According to our model, the primary effect of cuelessness is upon content, and style and outcome are influenced indirectly, through the mediation of content. The way we had explored the relationships in our previous research was simply to examine the correlations, but now we went on to use multiple regression. If the model was correct, content would predict style and outcome, not merely correlate with them, and it was that which multiple regression allowed us to test.

The first stage of the analysis was to reduce the measures to a manageable number, and for that we used factor analysis. Seven factors emerged for content, three for style, and six for the perceptual measures of outcome. For each of the sixteen factors, the variable which loaded the most strongly was then selected, and both style and outcome were regressed on content, each of the nine measures one at a time. All seven content variables were used as predictors in the equations, and two types of analysis were conducted, simple multiple linear regression to estimate the total variance explained, and stepwise regression to determine the rank-ordering of the predictors.

The first of the analyses examined style (Table 13.2), and all three of the measures were predicted very strongly by content, the variance explained being 69% for the first (spontaneity), 63% for the second (speech quantity), and 56% for the third (questioning). More important still, however, the relationship for the first factor was exactly what our model predicted — the less task-oriented and the more personal the content, the more spontaneous the style. Altogether, the evidence was among the most persuasive we had found.

The second of the analyses examined outcome (Table 13.3), and this time there was rather less support for our predictions. The more task-oriented the tutorial — that is, the more it followed the typical pattern of question and answer — the less favourable the overall evaluation (factor 1) and the greater the reported anxiety (factor 2), but beyond that there were no significant relationships.

The third and last of the analyses again examined outcome, but this time using style rather than content as the predictor. According to our model, style and outcome should be independent — for each is influenced only by content and not by the other — and that is exactly what we found. There was no single significant effect, and the average

TABLE 13.2 *Relationships between content and style*

| | | Cumulative $MR^{2}$ | Standardised |
|---|---|---|---|
| *Factor 1: Spontaneity* | | $MR^2=0.69$ | |
| Step 1 | Agreeing | 0.45 | 0.77*** |
| Step 2 | Seeking & offering academic information & confirmation | 0.57 | –0.34*** |
| Step 3 | Offering & replying with personal information | 0.66 | 0.33*** |
| *Factor 2: Speech quantity* | | $MR^2=0.63$ | |
| Step 1 | Offering & replying with academic information | 0.28 | 0.43*** |
| Step 2 | Offering & replying with personal information | 0.43 | 0.41*** |
| Step 3 | Seeking & offering academic information & confirmation | 0.52 | 0.24** |
| Step 4 | Open University | 0.57 | 0.29*** |
| Step 5 | Tutor seeking & commenting | 0.60 | 0.20* |
| Step 6 | Replying with opinions & personal examples | 0.62 | 0.15 |
| *Factor 3: Questioning* | | $MR^2=0.56$ | |
| Step 1 | Tutor seeking & commenting | 0.54 | 0.79*** |

*$p<0.05$ **$p<0.01$ ***$p<0.001$

TABLE 13.3 *Relationships between content and outcome*

| | | *Cumulative* $MR^2$ | *Standardised* $\beta$ |
|---|---|---|---|
| *Factor 1:* | *Evaluation* | $MR^2$=0.12 | |
| Step 1 | Offering & replying with academic information | 0.07 | –0.27 |
| *Factor 2:* | *Anxiety* | $MR^2$=0.18 | |
| Step 1 | Offering & replying with academic information | 0.13 | 0.35** |
| *Factors 3–6* | | | |
| No steps | | | |

$^{**}p<0.01$

examine the relationships between our dependent measures. Tutor's strategy, discourse structure, and the relationships between content, style and outcome had all been examined successfully, and in general our model had received good support. The second objective was to examine how the findings from our earlier study (Rutter & Robinson, 1981) would generalise, especially across faculties and from course to course within faculties, and what had emerged was a pattern very similar to before, but stronger, with little evidence of differences between either faculties or courses. Much more important than those sources of variance was the medium of communication, and especially its effects upon role performance, for, the more cueless the setting, we found, the more the participants retreated into 'traditional' patterns of behaviour — 'tutor behaviour' for tutors and 'student behaviour' for students. The third and last of our objectives was to explore whether people would adapt to cuelessness as they became accustomed to its constraints, and the short answer, confirming the previous literature, was that they did not. There were few effects of occasion and no interactions at all with medium.

Finally, we come to our conclusions — both practical and theoretical — and the first of the *practical* conclusions is this. Despite the differences between face-to-face and telephone teaching, the telephone is a perfectly acceptable medium for tutorials. Content, style, and outcome all differ, it is true — though how to measure academic aspects of outcome is still not resolved — but tutors and students alike report satisfaction. More attention to training, we hope, may bring the two media closer still, but the most important limitations of the telephone remain technical — the poor quality of the lines, and the inability to accommodate more than a handful of people.

As for our *theoretical* conclusions, the first point to make is the very welcome one that what we had discovered in the laboratory held equally well in the field, and sometimes indeed the effects were even stronger. Content, style and outcome were all affected in ways which were consistent with our model — though they were not always quite the ways we had expected — and the dependent measures were related together, exactly as we had predicted. The most important effects of cuelessness were to influence people's *perceptions* of their task and role and, the fewer the cues, the more 'traditional' or 'stereotyped' they became. The fewer the social cues, the greater the psychological distance, and from psychological distance came the effects upon content, and from content the effects upon style and outcome.

Throughout our project, cuelessness has continued to provide the most useful framework for theoretical integration. Despite the clarity of our findings, however, a variety of problems of interpretation have arisen as the investigation has developed, and the result has been a number of refinements to our model. The first set of problems concerned the definition and measurement of cuelessness, and the second the mechanisms by which cuelessness operates. To end the chapter, I should like to discuss the implications of them both.

The first of the problems arose from an experiment by Rutter *et al.* (1984), in which for the first time we introduced groups of more than two people — and it was an issue which occurred again in the tutorials. The problem was that, although there were now more cues available than in dyads — both face-to-face and in the other conditions — people seemed unable to make use of them. In social interaction, just as in any other task, our capacity to process information is limited, and the addition of extra participants meant that less and less information could be absorbed from each one. The important measure, we therefore concluded, was not *available* cues but *usable* cues, and it is that on which our model is now based.

Other problems of definition and measurement have been less easy to tackle. Should we not be able to quantify cuelessness precisely, or can we only rank-order our experimental conditions? What are the most important of the cues which each medium makes available, how do they combine, and what happens when they are removed? Indeed, is removal itself all that matters, or might degradation be important, too? And, are not certain cues more salient than others, and does not salience change as the encounter develops and as people apply selective attention? All are important questions but, as yet, it is only fair to acknowledge, we have no firm answers.

Our second set of problems concerns the mechanisms by which cuelessness operates. When we first presented our model, in Rutter & Stephenson (1979) and Rutter, Stephenson & Dewey (1981), we assumed that cuelessness had a *direct* effect upon behaviour. Gradually, however, we came to recognise that there is a mediating variable, *psychological distance*, and two important implications followed. The first is simply that psychological distance may also be influenced by a variety of factors quite apart from cuelessness. The purpose of the encounter, for example, may well be one, and so too may the relationship between the subjects and their degree of familiarity with the setting. Each is likely to have its own independent effects upon psychological distance, but there will also be interactions between them, and changes over time.

The second implication takes us back to role perception. Role perception, I have argued here, is central to task-orientation, and a useful demonstration was reported in Morley & Stephenson (1977). Using material of their own from simulated union–management negotiations, and also transcripts from Stephenson, Ayling & Rutter (1976), they were able to show that, whether the speaker of a particular utterance was from the union side or the management side was much more frequently identified correctly when the speakers had met over a sound-only link than when they had met face-to-face. Just as in our present work with the Open University, role differentiation appeared the likely interpretation.

There are, however, two final comments to make. First, in many encounters, participants do not have 'prescribed' roles — everyday conversations between friends, for example — and there we would not expect any particular pattern to emerge, for role differentiation will develop only when the roles are reasonably defined at the outset. Second, as we have seen already, sometimes one's role over the telephone is explicitly to behave in an *intimate*, *personal* way — Samaritans and hotline counsellors, for example. Here, our 'normal' findings of reduced personal content will disappear or even reverse (e.g.

Rutter *et al.*, 1984; Kemp & Rutter, 1982), for the 'traditional' distinction between 'task' and 'person' will break down because to be personal *is* the task. Nevertheless, the key remains psychological distance, for the *anonymity* of the system this time encourages psychological *proximity*, and it is cuelessness which makes that anonymity possible. Of all the variables to pursue in the future, the evidence suggests, role and task are likely to be particularly rewarding.

The third and final implication concerns the relationship of cuelessness to the other main concept in the literature, social presence (Short, Williams & Christie, 1976), for it may appear that there is now very little difference between them. For practical purposes, we concede, that may well be true but conceptually they remain quite distinct in at least four respects. First, while our model explicitly separates social cues from the 'set' of psychological distance, the concept of social presence does not. For us, cuelessness merely *influences* set; for Short, Williams & Christie, social presence *is* that set. Second, while at least in principle we can specify and quantify in advance what produces the experience of psychological distance, Short, Williams and Christie cannot, for the social presence of a medium is measured only at the end of the encounter, and there is no way of knowing how the judgement is reached or what underpins it. Third, social presence says nothing about the relationships between content, style and outcome, and it is concerned exclusively with people's impressions of encounters and media. And, finally, there is a difference above all in the aims with which the models were developed. While social presence was intended for applied problems in telecommunications, cuelessness is concerned with theoretical issues in social psychology — and those, we believe, are the more significant.

## Note to Chapter 13

1. Our research was supported by the Economic and Social Research Council of Great Britain.

## References

Argyle, M. & Cook, M. 1976, *Gaze and Mutual Gaze*. London: Cambridge University Press.

Harper, R. G., Wiens, A. N. & Matarazzo, J. D. 1978, *Nonverbal Communication: The State of the Art*. Chichester: Wiley.

Kemp, N. J. & Rutter, D. R. 1982, Cuelessness and the content and style of conversation, *British Journal of Social Psychology*, 21, 43–49.

Morley, I. E. & Stephenson, G. M. 1977, *The Social Psychology of Bargaining*. London: Allen & Unwin.

Rutter, D. R. 1984, *Looking and Seeing: The Role of Visual Communication in Social Interaction*. Chichester: Wiley.

— 1987, *Communicating by Telephone*. Oxford: Pergamon.

Rutter, D. R., Dewey, M. E., Harding, A. & Stephenson, G. M. 1984, Medium of communication and group size: effects of cuelessness on the content, style, and outcome of discussions. Unpublished. University of Kent at Canterbury.

Rutter, D. R. & Robinson, B. 1981, An experimental analysis of teaching by telephone: theoretical and practical implications for social psychology. In *Progress in Applied Social Psychology*, Vol. 1, Chichester: Wiley, 345–74.

Rutter, D. R. & Stephenson, G. M. 1977, The role of visual communication in synchronising conversation, *European Journal of Social Psychology*, 7, 29–37.

— 1979, The role of visual communication in social interaction, *Current Anthropology*, 20, 124–25.

Rutter, D. R., Stephenson, G. M. & Dewey, M. E. 1981, Visual communication and the content and style of conversation, *British Journal of Social Psychology*, 20, 41–52.

Short, J. A., Williams, E. & Christie, B. 1976, *The Social Psychology of Telecommunications*. Chichester: Wiley.

Stephenson, G. M., Ayling, K. & Rutter, D. R. 1976, The role of visual communication in social exchange, *British Journal of Social and Clinical Psychology*, 15, 113–20.

Winer, B. J. 1971, *Statistical Principles in Experimental Design* (2nd edn). New York: McGraw-Hill.

# 14 'Out of their minds': An analysis of discourse in two South African science classrooms

JOHAN MULLER
*University of the Witwatersrand, Johannesburg*

## Social arrangements and discourse

> Education may well be, as of right, the instrument whereby every individual, in a society like our own, can gain access to any kind of discourse. But we well know that in its distribution, in what it permits and what it prevents, it follows the well trodden battle lines of social conflict. Every education system is a political means of maintaining or of modifying the appropriation of discourse (Michel Foucault, 1972:227).

It is probably fair to say that school science has been more prone than other subjects taught at school to being regarded as a body of information very much like 'truth', existing in some independent pre-social space. For most teachers and students, though certainly not for all of them, communicating about science is communicating about something objective, natural and real. The communicative question is mostly taken as how best to transfer this truth to students. A special sort of classroom practice is the result. My starting assumption for studying this practice is that communicative routines must not be studied apart from other social practices. To take this seriously means engaging in a double analytical task. On the one hand, it means considering social arrangements to understand why they are so ineluctably reproduced in the classroom. On the other, it means showing how actual communicative routines produce those social arrangements in a differentiated and subtle way.

Very few studies attempt to conceive of the link between social arrangements and social interaction. This lacuna is all the more evident when micro-sociological studies of classroom communication and discourse are considered. On the one hand are the conventional sociolinguistic accounts which see discourse as already *pre-structured* and participants as enacters of anterior structures of linguistic order (see, for example, Sinclair & Coulthard, 1975). On the other hand are the ethnomethodologically inclined investigators who object that by emphasising structure, sociolinguists use discourse and communication as an index for something else and risk missing the real nature of communication — the fact that it *accomplishes* structure (Mehan, 1974).

What both positions have in common, however, is that when they consider the social context, they see it as something external to communication, though neither position might want to go as far as Barnes & Todd (1981) in seeing context as a separate level of organisation above that of discourse itself.

I want to retain something of the sociolinguistic sense that there are certain forms of classroom discourse which pre-exist actual classroom encounters, and I also want to retain the notion of accomplishment. But it is important to see that social context is not something external to discourse, or to people.[1] Considering discourse as a social practice means seeing it as the way in which people enact social relations. Life in science classrooms involves participants taking up certain positions within science discourse. Those positions owe their form to a complex interplay of personal predilections and competencies, discourse structure and material limits.

This view of classroom discourse helps to avoid some pitfalls, the major one being that of seeing the teacher simply as an agent of social control or an enforcer of dominant meanings (Edwards, 1980). Indeed, the teacher is positioned in discourse just like any other participant, and though the teacher certainly cues the communication more than anyone else, the form of meaning being cued is at least as much disposed by the form of the discourse as by the teacher. This allows me to account for at least one apparent paradox in my transcripts, which is that the greatest amount of social control is quite evidently exercised through the black classroom by virtue of a teacher–student relationship that is demonstrably more informal and comfortable than the one operating in the white classroom.

By seeing classroom communication as one social or discursive practice amongst other practices, the question of context can be conceived as part of discourse. The question then becomes one of the relation of discursive positions to social positions. Discourse structure and social structure both constrain and enable interaction. The question is how they do this in tandem.

## The communicative contract in information exchanges

Classroom discourse is intuitively supposed by most people to be involved with the *exchange* of information or knowledge, whatever else it also finds itself a forum for. Now, whether the exchange is defined as the 'minimum unit of interaction' (Sinclair, 1980) or as the unit most appropriate for understanding the negotiation of information (Coulthard & Brazil, 1981), there is little doubt that classrooms have become the paradigmatic site for studying exchange structure (Sinclair & Coulthard, 1975). It seems sensible, then, to take the exchange as my basic analytical unit. Referring to it as a structural unit entails that there are more or less binding constraints of a certain kind on discursive sequences in the exchange. Put linguistically, that means that utterances in an exchange can be functionally distinguished on the basis of the degree to which they 'predict forward' (Stubbs, 1983), that is, the degree to which they oblige succeeding utterances. For instance, a question obliges or 'predicts' an answer more than an answer 'predicts' any following discursive move.

Considered communicatively, this means also that discourse structure sets up expectations within and between participants which produce powerful frames for organising communication. The frame of the classroom information exchange has the character of a *contractual relationship*. That is to say, students and teachers are bound into the classroom relationship by a common tacit set of expectations about the way knowledge is to be communicated, and the consequent rights, duties and obligations incumbent upon them. These expectations minimally involve the teacher being the 'one who knows' (the *primary knower*) and thus obliged to do certain things because of this; and the students being the 'ones who do not know' (the *secondary knowers*) and thus also obliged to make certain moves because of this.[2]

The first noteworthy feature of the classroom contract is the requirement that the primary knower be a competent practitioner of the knowledge in question, in this case science. The primary knower must be able to *authorise knowledge* in the classroom; he/she must be authoritative. The most important and obligatory slot in the information exchange is therefore when the primary knower 'confers upon the information a kind of stamp of authority' (Berry, 1981: 126). This function can be called K1.

There is an important distinction to be drawn between authoritativeness, which is a communicative function, and competence, which is a component of the background knowledge of teachers. Teachers may be authoritative without being competent. More rarely, they may be competent without being authoritative, a situation more likely to be a feature of university teaching than of school teaching.

A second noteworthy feature of the classroom contract requires that the process of information transmission must reduce ambiguity. That is to say, it requires that K1s will achieve informational closure by eliminating contending accounts in the process of authorising one (hopefully correct) account. Ideally, this closure is achieved when the teacher displays competence in an authoritative K1. In such cases, competence and authority become indistinguishable. Under certain circumstances, closure of a kind can be achieved by a non-competent but authoritative K1. Indeed many teachers get by with just such a strategy. It could be said that in this case the communicative expectation is satisfied even though the likelihood of real understanding on the part of the secondary knowers is drastically diminished. A superficially similar case occurs when a competent and usually authoritative teacher is unable to communicate her competence. This may well be because an adequate explanation rests upon certain knowledge which the students do not yet possess. It may also occur for at least one other reason. Integral to expectations about the transmission process, in schooling in capitalist countries at any rate, is the assumption that knowledge can be completely specified in language. This is simply not so. There is a point at which explanations stop, as Wittgenstein puts it. Linguistic explanations are more likely to stop short of full explication in science than in other subjects, because scientific explanations are very often exemplified in paradigmatic experiments which display the scientific process in a way that purely linguistic or diagrammatic efforts cannot match. Where experimental demonstrations are unavailable, it is unavoidable that some linguistic authorisations will fall short of requisite clarity, and competent teachers may have no option but to authorise an incomplete explanation.

In neither of these two cases of authoritative but inadequate K1s can the communicative contract be said to be broken, although it certainly is strained. From the point of view of the communicative contract, abrogation only occurs when authorisation itself malfunctions, in other words, in cases where the K1 is either *overauthorised* or *underauthorised*. In the first case, the personal rights of secondary knowers are infringed; in the second case, the obligation to reduce ambiguity is not fulfilled, and the secondary knowers contractually short-changed.

Normally speaking, K1s can occur in one of two formats. The first is simply as a monological declaration. Every teacher lapses into monologue at some stage of the lesson. The information exchange proper occurs when the secondary knowers also participate, under conditions of either rights or obligations. For instance, if the primary knower asks a question, one or more secondary knowers is obliged to offer some kind of response which is in most cases a display of a state of knowledge. On the other hand, since it is contractually determined that secondary knowers are in the communicative situation to increase their knowledge, they are also free to ask questions. This freedom can only be exercised within the limits set by the primary knower who, by virtue of her position, is empowered to direct the traffic of discourse — allocate turns, speaking rights and so forth. However, if secondary knowers are somehow, directly or indirectly, prevented from asking questions, or even if they do not feel free to ask questions, then their rights are infringed and the contract is being broken. These rights and obligations incumbent on secondary knowers are conditioned in the discursive structure in the following way.

It is mostly the primary knower's option whether she declares her K1 immediately, or defers it in order first to find out the state of the secondary knower's knowledge. For example:

(C1) **T:** Brownian motion. What is Brownian motion? If you still remember. Anybody, who can remember? . . .
**S:** Is the haphazard movement of particles.
**T:** Haphazard movement of particles (writes on board) . . . you said this is Brownian motion . . .

K1 here is deferred by an elicitation until the third slot in the exchange. This function of deferral can be called dK1. It obliges some kind of *display of knowledge* (K2) from one or more secondary knowers, which in turn obliges the deferred stamp of K1 from the primary knower.

The secondary knower can initiate an exchange by displaying his knowledge (K2) in the form of a question, thereby obliging a K1 from the primary knower. This pattern of exchange deprives the primary knower of the initiative to decide how and when to declare her K1. The resultant form of K1 in this pattern can be highly revealing.

Berry also distinguishes a fourth function in information exchanges, where a secondary knower confirms a knowledge display already given. For example, if in example C1 above, the student had responded to the teacher's K1 with a 'Right', this would be a *confirmation* (K2f). Berry regards K2f as always non-obligatory. In the following pattern, a common one in classrooms, K2f seems to me to be obligatory.

(C2) **T:** . . . then this equation, we say that it is balanced, right?
**S:** Yes.

In this example the students are not required to display their knowledge (K2), rather they are asked to confirm it. The teacher's K1 is clearly predictive, but it requires a very weak form of response. The whole exchange implicitly refers back to a prior accredited K2 — which might or might not have occurred.

I have briefly and informally characterised four exchange functions in terms of obligatoriness and sequentiality:

K1: elicitation of knowledge display
dK1: knowledge display
K2: conferral of authority
K2f: confirmation

They can be regarded as a layer of structure, and each function can occur only once in an exchange, except when the exchange is recursively embedded.

I have so far discussed the contractual features of the discursive structure of classroom information exchanges. The question now arises as to how the social arrangement and the contractual features it embodies becomes mapped onto and imprinted into information exchanges in the classroom.

## From communicative contract to social contract

The social arrangement of any society can be regarded as a set of legal, political and economic contractual relations. The major contractual features of the current South African arrangement that are of importance for this discussion have to do with political, economic and property rights. *Political rights* in the form of the franchise were granted to white males in 1867, and the history books boast that South Africa was the first 'Western' country to extend those rights to (white) females. It has yet to accord those rights to black people of either sex outside of the state-demarcated 'homelands'. *Economic rights* remain colour- as well as class-marked although the economy is undergoing some reform. What that means is that legal colour bars still exist which exclude black people from certain skilled occupations. Even where relaxations have taken place, the weight of segregatory precedent and colour-marked common sense makes it difficult for black people, even where they have had access to the requisite training, to enter certain occupational domains with ease. Careers in science are one of these domains. *Property rights* are indissolubly linked to political and economic rights in that ownership is a powerful factor in the determination of social relations of production. Propertyless labour is a very rightless and exploitable labour indeed. Whites are free to own property in South Africa: black people are able only to lease it outside of the 'homelands'.

This arrangement of South African society into first- and second-class citizens has direct material parallels in the *financial provisions* made for education (see Table 14.1).

TABLE 14.1 *Capital expenditure on education in South Africa, 1982 (rands)**

| | *Expenditure* | |
|---|---|---|
| | *Total* | *Per capita* |
| Black | 414,320,511 | 176.20 |
| White | 1,688,281,000 | 1,021.00 |

*One rand is roughly equal to 25p.

The inadequate provision for black people places a number of physical limits on black teaching possibilities. There is a shortage of classrooms and trained teachers in black schools. This generally means that most black classrooms are overcrowded: the student–teacher ratio in black schools in 1982 was 39.1:1 compared with 18.2:1 in white schools. Because of the numbers, many black teachers find themselves teaching two sets of students in the same classroom every day. There is also a shortage of textbooks, libraries, teaching aids and, most germane to this discussion, laboratory facilities and scientific materials. This means that science is taught predominantly verbally in black schools. The inadequate provisions made also have specific effects on the training opportunities for teachers and the quality of their competence. During the 1970s, while only 3.36% of white teachers were qualified below matriculation level, 85% of black teachers were thus qualified. It would be no exaggeration to conclude that the majority of black teachers are hopelessly underqualified. Finally, the world knowledge of classroom participants is conditioned by the importance the social arrangement places on education. By 1908 all provinces in South Africa had made white education compulsory and free. Compulsory free education for urban black people began to be 'phased in' in 1979, remaining largely the option of school boards. By 1981, little more than 2% of black schools had been affected.

The implication of all of this for learning science is not hard to imagine. A poorly trained science teacher with inadequate facilities is going to be hard put to act as a scientist and to 'display' science, since she has never had the opportunity to internalise the grammar of science sufficiently to do so. The best she can do is to 'drill' the students along the set curricular formulae. It is a commonplace observation in South Africa that black people are disposed to rote-learning. Contrary to popular opinion it is not a personal preference, and even less is it a cultural one. It is an exigency resorted to by people operating within a very particular communicative contract.

This is of course not to say that all white teachers are competent, or that many white classrooms are not characterised by rote-learning routines. It is to say, however, that the odds dispose the emergence of some white students with a competent grasp of what it means to do science (though by no means all of them), and the emergence of far fewer black students with equivalent competence.

The rest of this chapter is an attempt to examine the way in which knowledge is constructed in the information exchanges of two science classrooms, and the way in which this construction is a joint enactment of the social and discursive contract, through the exercise of classroom rights and obligations by teachers and students.

## An analysis of information exchanges in two classrooms

From the four functions of information exchange outlined above, three common patterns of classroom exchange can be distilled. The transcripts of classroom lessons from one white school, 'Vista', and one black school, 'Caritas', will be considered from the point of view of each exchange pattern. The contractual enactments in each classroom will become evident through the analysis.[3]

### Teacher-initiated elicitation exchanges (dK1–K2–K1)

dK1 moves can occur in the form of either nominated or unnominated elicitations. An example of a nominated elicitation occurs in the following Vista exchange:

(V1) **T:** Is the reaction exo- or endothermic, Theresa?
**S:** Exothermic.
**T:** It's exothermic . . .

It is a direct nomination, obliging the student to answer. Vista elicitation exchanges predominantly take this form. Nominated elicitations in Caritas are more indirect, usually being filtered through a student bid first, though even this form is relatively rare:

(C3) **T:** Where are these spaces in the first place? . . . (*Students bid*) Yes, Fina?
**S:** They are between the particles.
**T:** Yes, they are between the particles.

Most of the elicitations in Caritas are unnominated:

(C4) **T:** What is a sphere? (*Students bid*) Yes?
**S:** A sphere is a round figure.
**T:** Yes, a sphere is a round figure . . .

Indirect and unnominated elicitations place far less obligation on individual participants to display K2. Sacks *et al.* (1974) has noted that nominations exert the greatest possible control over discourse, so an initial observation would be that the Vista teacher exerts far greater control over the discourse than the Caritas teacher does, and this control is channelled through a personal and privatised test of knowledge rather than through a joint class accession to understanding as is often the case in Caritas.

This supposition is strengthened by the following two related forms of elicitation exchange found at Caritas but not found at Vista. The first is initiated by a dK1 move marked by a rising intonation:

(C5) **T:** . . . and these electrons have got energy, they revolve around this nucleus, right, and they are negatively — charged) (*simultaneously*)
**S:** charged)
**T:** Okay . . .

This joint production of the answer serves as a display to the class; it is not for individual assessment, and is only a weak test of individual knowledge.

The second form is a call–response routine common in many primary schools:

(C6) **T:** Ar?
**S:** Argon

Note that the K1 is absent. Joint K2 production, when clearly correct, relaxes the obligation for an authorising K1. In fact, it could be supposed that joint K2 production asserts an authority of its own which could dispose the teacher to allow it through, with or without an authorising K1, even when the answer is obviously wrong.

(C7) **T:** Na?
**S:** Ni— (*one student cueing the class*)
**S:** Nitrogen
**T:** Nitrogen.

The call–response chant moves forward with a communicative logic that is very difficult to interrupt. When the teacher repeats the elicitation five minutes later, the class repeats the error without the need for an authorising K1 this time.

(C8) **T:** Na?
**S:** Ni— (*one student cueing the class*)
**S:** Nitrogen
**T:** Ng?

Joint K2 production, following either a rising intonation or an unmotivated dK1, has been likened to catechism.[4] It is very difficult to interrupt catechism since it operates at an almost ritualistic level.

The notion of knowledge as ritualistic is further emphasised by the predominant use of factual or definitional elicitations in Caritas instead of reasoning elicitations. In Fragment C1 above, a definition is produced in response to the query about Brownian movement, even though words like 'haphazard' are regarded as distinctly odd. Commented one pupil in an interview afterwards: 'I wouldn't use them [words like haphazard] when I was communicating' (*sic*). In fact, most elicitations in Caritas are requests for facts or definitions, rarely for explanations, something predisposed by two-part catechistic exchanges.

Many Vista exchanges are also factual, but there is a greater tendency for the teacher to pursue the explanatory reason behind the fact. This results in long recursively structured exchange chains:

(V2) **T:** Now, what about, uh, temperature? If you change the temperature, if you increase the temperature, what effect would it have?
**S:** (*previously nominated*) Saturation would be reached . . .
**[S2:** *quicker*] No . . . take a long time for saturation to be reached, you can only use solid—
**T:** What effect would it have on the equilibrium?
**S1:** Shift to the right.
**T:** Why?
**S1:** Because . . . more will be able to dissolve
**S2:** [dissolve] ja . . .

I have so far been discussing elicitation exchanges which require affirmative K1s. The style of authorisation is better foregrounded when K2 responses are wrong, or more usually, incomplete or inadequate. When faced with an inadequate K2, the Vista teacher becomes pointed:

(V3) **T:** . . . why's it got the greatest value per mole, the last one says minus 572 . . . ?
**S:** Ja, but that's um . . .
**Ss:** That's for two moles . . . just for two moles
**T:** You haven't really answered it properly, have you?

His pointedness more usually leans not only towards the evaluative, but the personal and at times the sarcastic:

(V4) **T:** What does delta H equals −92 kilojoules mean, Howard Gordon?
**S:** (*indistinct*) endothermic reaction
**T:** OK, so what does that mean? Huh? Don't try and prevaricate! You don't know do you?
**S:** I do.
**T:** So what does it mean? That one, what does that mean?
**S:** 92 kilojoules is . . . (*indistinct*)
**T:** You see you don't know (*Ss laugh*)

The main point to note here is that the Vista teacher is very decided and definite about inadequate answers. K2 mistakes regarded by the teacher as avoidable are frequently allocated punishments:

(V5) **T:** Ah Pincus, you may also write a hundred times 'atomic number is not atomic mass' . . . don't you know how to read a periodic table yet? . . . hey?
**S:** I got confused.
**T:** You got confused? (S: Ja) At this stage of your life you don't *need* to get confused about the periodic table.

In a word, he is very authoritative. The students always know exactly whether their K2s are right or wrong.

By contrast, the Caritas teacher is diffident and seems, to the students at least, to be indecisive:

(C9) **T:** Let's get what is in a molecule (*students bid*) yes?
**S1:** Molecules are small pieces of —, of matter
**T:** Ye-m, you're saying molecu-, I won't, I won't mark you for that, I won't say that you are right or wrong; we say that these are small particles of matter (*writes on board*) . . . what about molecules, what are they? (*students bid*) Yes?
**S2:** Atoms are small particles of molecules
**T:** Atoms are small particles of molecules (*writes on board*) so, in short, why — what we are —, (*students bid*) yes?
**S3:** Molecule . . . is a group of atom (coming) together . . .
**T:** Group of atoms . . . grouped, uh, joined together. Well, at least I've got something, I've got an idea.

In this interesting passage, three K2s are produced. None of them is unambiguously authorised, as this subsequent interview with the pupils indicates. About S1's K2, one student remarked:

(C10) **S:** I can say it's right . . . but what makes me not sure about the answer is that . . . the teacher was not sure . . . and so I didn't know the reason which made her not to be sure about it.

About S2's K2, there is just as much uncertainty. One student said: 'I was not sure of her [the teacher's] answer for that.' S2 herself was quite adamant that her answer was right, and had not been negatively authorised:

(C11) **S2:** For what I can say with this, the, the, the using of the language, that is the only thing which is wrong, the statement is right.

It is clear that the Caritas teacher is having trouble communicating her K1s authoritatively. Indeed, in the following student comment, it is apparent that the students do not see the teacher herself as authoritative:

(C12) **S:** Or it might even happen that . . . eh (S2's) anther —, (S2's) answer satisfied . . . eh, the question, not the teacher, you see?

Because the Caritas teacher is not authoritative and not very competent, the students regard 'real scientific knowledge' as lying somewhere 'out there', not as constituted by dK1s or K1s. Classroom operations by teacher or teacher and students are approximations to knowledge 'out there'; in a sense both teacher and students become collaborators in a joint effort to appropriate knowledge. The result is that science comes to be seen as 'their' science (that is, 'white' science) not 'our' science. Because of this view, the students are able to question the competence of the teacher and to ascribe their lack of understanding to the social arrangement that occasions that lack of competence and their own lack of understanding. As far as they are concerned, the causes for their failure lie outside of them. By the same token, this view also tends to block any sense that failure could be for reasons of personal shortcoming.

The Vista situation is almost the complete converse. The teacher there acts so authoritatively, and himself displays the operations of scientific knowledge so competently, that students never doubt his competence. Indeed, the teacher places himself, and is seen by the students as being, 'head and shoulders' above them. Knowledge is consequently 'up there'. Because of this view, the students can only ascribe their failure to understand to some personal shortcoming of effort or ability. The teacher himself reinforces this construal:

(V6) **T:** Either you don't hear me or you don't understand or you are lazy.

**Teacher-initiated confirmation exchanges (K1–K2f)**

This exchange pattern represents a weaker way of negotiating knowledge in that it obliges a claim to knowledge rather than a display of it. The K1 initiating move can be either nominated or unnominated. A nominated sample occurs in the following Vista exchange:

(V7) **T:** . . . so the smaller you make it, the finer you chop it up, the bigger your resultant surface area is going to be, right, Farrel?
**S:** Yes.

Like elicitations, Vista requests for confirmation are predominantly nominated. The Caritas confirmation pattern also follows the one set in the elicitation exchanges, namely that of obliging a joint K2f production:

(C13) **T:** Yes, by using an indicator, then the indicator will show the colour change, okay?
**Ss:** Yes.

Once again, the Vista pattern tends to privatise knowledge appropriation while the Caritas pattern makes it a public venture of confirmation. Of course, there is no guarantee that the confirmation does in fact represent understanding at all, as pupils indicate in their interviews. In many ways this exchange serves a phatic or 'wavelengthing' purpose so that confirmations may well indicate that the students are following the teacher, but need not necessarily indicate that they are understanding what is going on (Stubbs, 1983). However, for a number of reasons, negating K2fs are rare, not least because a general conversational maxim obliges an affirmation unless there is a real and identifiable breakdown of communication. A negating K2f obliges a student to state what is 'not okay'.

**Student-initiated question exchanges (K2–K1)**

The first thing to note here is that student questions differ from teacher elicitations in that they are usually 'real' questions, not requests for display, though students are known to 'test' teachers they regard as less than competent (Labov & Fanshel, 1977). The second is that this is the only exchange sequence initiated and therefore at least partially controlled by students. The primary knower's option of deferring K1 is suspended; indeed, which K1 is at issue is determined by the K2.

The Vista teacher typically responds in one of two ways. He answers the question with an authoritative K1 if he regards the question as a sensible one:

(V8) **S:** What happens if you stop supplying? Like say you put some—, dissolve some salt in water, surely you've reached an equilibrium even though you haven't . . . ?
**T:** No, if it's uh, if it doesn't reach saturation point it will all dissolve.

As frequently however, he responds with a *personal put-down*, with or without the answer to the question:

(V9) **S:** How do you know which goes on the X-axis?
**T:** The one that is mentioned first, Farrel! I mean for three years I've been telling you this and you're still asking!

The teacher himself is very aware of the way he responds, as is evident in this interview excerpt:

(V10) **T:** uh, you know, sometimes . . . you get the odd sort of very foolish question . . . then I blow my top, you know . . . sometimes they don't even know themselves if that's what they're trying to ask . . .

The unintended consequence is that pupils ask fewer questions, and opportunities for clarifying misunderstandings are lost directly because of over-authoritativeness.

(V11) **I:** Do you feel free to ask questions as things go by?
**S:** No . . . No (*a chorus of No's*)
**I:** Why not?

**S:** No, I suppose you're a bit scared in a way . . .
**S:** If you ask like a stupid question like he thinks it is obvious, he'll jump on you . . .

Slower students who do not understand tend to ascribe their lack to their own personal shortcoming, and refrain from asking questions at all:

(V12) **S1:** You're very hesitant to ask questions
**S2:** . . . you're scared to ask that question in case he shouts at you . . . you're not concentrating 100% all of the time, you know you might just doze for a minute, look out of the window, he said something, you didn't (*tape indistinct*) 'ja, but I just said that' and (*tape indistinct*) screams at you
. . .
**I:** Even if you're pretty sure that it is a solid question?
**S2:** You're still a bit doubtful because he might have just said that in a different way which you didn't quite understand . . .

The result is a clear case of Meno's paradox, neatly captured in the following excerpt:

(V13) **S1:** . . . a lot of times like you'll say . . . 'I don't understand what's going on', he'll say 'what don't you understand'.
**I1:** You don't know what you don't understand.
**S2:** Ja, if you knew what you didn't understand, then you'd know it . . .

What seems to be happening in the Vista classroom is that the stronger students are authoritatively inducted into the grammar of science, while the weaker ones lapse into silence and lack of understanding. An *individual sorting mechanism* is effectively implemented by this pattern of classroom discourse.

The pattern in the Caritas classroom is entirely different. Factual K2 questions are given routine definitional authorisations. However, there are a fair number of basic conceptual K2 questions which fall outside the teacher's own realm of competence simply because she is not sufficiently trained. Her typical response is to naturalise the answer by appealing to self evidencies. In the following example, the students have asked how it is possible to form water from hydrogen and oxygen (the tape is indistinct):

(C14) **T:** So we are told, as much as we believe that the earth is round . . . do you believe that an earth is round?
**Ss:** No.
**T:** Huh?
**Ss:** No.
**T:** Do you believe that you see because of your eyes?
**Ss:** Yes (*discussion*)
. . .
**T:** I'm asking you people
**Ss:** Yes
**T:** Do you? Why do you believe it?
**S:** . . . because one its—
**T:** what . . . what is difficult there if you believe that one is really one, what is difficult to believe that two atoms of hydrogen will combine with one atom oxygen? (*Ss mutter*)

What is remarkable in this excerpt is that the students do not automatically accept the naturalising authorisation which the teacher hopes will close out the embarrassing question. This is no doubt because they generally doubt the teacher's authority in a way not possible in the Vista classroom. As a consequence the students ask more questions, pursue the matter with a greater determination, and generally use the teacher as a mediating resource between themselves and the real knowledge 'out there'. Because of the unnominated dK1 moves and the joint student productions, the internal sorting mechanism apparent in the Vista classroom does not operate at Caritas. The overriding feeling here is that the students (and the teacher, too, for that matter) are *sorted as a group* from attaining 'real knowledge', although there is general non-competitive recognition that some students understand more than others. The sorting mechanism is perceived as affecting all the students. And so indeed it does.

## Conclusion

The social contract inflects the exercise of classroom rights and obligations in determinate ways. In the Caritas classroom, this can be seen most clearly in the way that the poorly trained teacher, with inadequate laboratory facilities, *underauthorises* knowledge and hence contravenes the contract (obligation to authorise). The result is that students assert their rights by usurping some allocative functions of the teacher, by questioning accounts, and by developing with the teacher joint strategies for trying to appropriate the external and distant ideal.

In the Vista classroom, the teacher conversely *overauthorises* knowledge by putting individual students on the spot and overreacting to their errors, thereby contravening the contract (the right of secondary knowers to be wrong) in another way entirely. The result is that the students there do not assert their rights, they take the teacher and the knowledge he displays for granted, and they develop strategies for avoiding the discomfort of overauthorisations.

The way these contractual accents are experienced by the students, and what these experiences lead to, comes out clearly in conversation with the students.

## Consequences of the contract

### Charity and hope

The general lack of authorisation in the Caritas classroom means at least two things. The first is that the students frequently do not know whether their K2 knowledge is really right or not, as we have already seen in Fragment C9. The second is that, even when they know that their K2 is wrong, they frequently know neither why not what the right answer really is:

(C15) **S:** In some cases, eh, you may be asking a question, then after answering, you may be told that you are wrong but you are not told the right answer.

It is evident that the teacher is unable to supply adequate discursive explanations. Furthermore, facilities are such that experimental demonstration is almost non-existent.

(C16) **S:** Most of the things in biology, we see them.
**I:** Ja?
**S:** But in physical science, we don't see them.
**I:** Tell me what sort of thing.
**S:** In experiments [I: Ja] . . . in biology, some of the experiments, you can do them yourself, but in physical science . . . you can't.

With the teacher and experimental demonstrations not providing understandable explanations, it is almost to be expected that the textbooks will on their own not fill the breach.

(C17) **I:** What don't you like about your textbooks?
**S:** Experiments.
**I:** Too many experiments ( . . . )
**S:** It has got too many experiments and less explanation.
**I:** Not enough explanation?
**S:** No.
**I:** And when it's got an explanation in the textbook, do you understand, are you happy with the explanation?
**S:** No.

*Ad hoc* assistance is sought where it may be found:

(C18) **S1:** Yes, most of the time if you don't understand, you go to eh, people such as David [I: Ja] he helps us more . . . much, he helps us much . . .

. . .

**S2:** (*whispered*) Ask my sister.
**S3:** Ask my neighbours.

. . .

**S4:** I sometimes . . . ask my father, sometimes he knows the answer and he tells me, but when he doesn't I just ask my brothers and sisters (I: mm) they sometimes help me, but if they don't know, they just tell me that they, they can't help.

Having to do something without understanding what you are doing gives rise to frustration:

(C19) **S1:** But we sometimes get frustrated with the teacher . . . so we don't understand, we find it difficult for us to . . . to just to . . . learn questions without understanding.
**S2:** We are not happy with copying [from the book]. She gives us a lot of [copying] work *(laughter and admonishment from other students*) but we don't understand.

There are three possible paths to follow to cope with this impossible situation. The first is a short-term strategy, designed to get the student through the exam:

(C20) **I:** How . . . are you going to learn to get it right?
**S**: . . . Myself, I thought myself that I'm going to cram.

The second is a medium-term strategy to get out of an ongoing frustrating situation:

(C21) **S1:** Ha . . . I thought myself I'm not going to do science anymore.
**S2:** Next year! (*both laugh*)

The students don't blame the teacher. They like science even though they do not understand it. The blame for the situation is externalised, laid at the door of the system. Although the students never spoke to the white interviewer about it, the sequence of classroom recordings was interrupted by the school being closed due to student unrest. The constant reminder of and resistance to the system consolidates this view. The third path then, an ever-present possibility since the major school disturbances in Soweto in 1976, is reaction against the system of unequal education in particular, and social inequality in general.

**The view from above**

The major problem in the Caritas classroom — the unavailability of explanatory authority — is not an issue in the Vista classroom. This does not mean that everything is understood in the Vista classroom, however. It could almost be said that the Vista teacher presides over an exchange structure that results in good understanding for some but also self-recriminatory lack of understanding for others. It is clear from the interview with this teacher that he intends his nominated dK1s to illustrate general problems, and for the dK1–K2–K1 exchange to provide a joint display to the class as a whole:

(V14) **T:** . . . if I want to illustrate a point, a typical incorrect answer, then I'll ask somebody who I know has a 90% chance of getting it incorrect.

The students, unsurprisingly, do not appreciate his pedagogic tactic and take his interrogations more personally:

(V15) **I:** Does anyone else get this feeling that you get asked questions because you don't know the answer? (*laughs*) (*hands go up*)
A lot of you . . . Jackie . . . yes

**S:** I don't know if a teacher can see you're not concentrating, but sometimes when he goes so fast, then you can't concentrate, and when he asks you a question you don't know the answer and he goes 'but I've just said it' . . . (I: Yes)

Combined with an unfortunately sharp way of dealing with inadequate K2s, this teacher's nominated dK1s generate a personalised and privatised ambience for the appropriation of knowledge. This results in some students being seen as 'picked on' and others being seen as 'safe' from interrogation:

(V16) **I:** Do you think you're safe from questions, though?
**S:** Ja.
**I:** Why?
**S:** Because if he had to ask me, I'd try like . . . answer like sort of any question he tried . . . I dunno . . . he thinks maybe that I know what's going on (I: You know what's plotting)

The class is, interestingly enough, protective of those being 'picked on', and there is a tendency for the class to resist privatisation by defending students that are being pressed by the insistent teacher:

(V17) **T:** . . . the catalyst has no effect on the equilibrium concentration, David. [S: Yes sir] You're the only one that didn't get that right [*S sniggers*]. But you were arguing with him about it, weren't you, they insisted that you were right, I mean you were wrong.
**S1:** I wasn't arguing about this one.
**T:** Oh, but you're always right.
**S2:** Shame, leave him alone.
**T:** Why? Would you rather I picked on you again?
**S2:** Well pick on somebody else ( . . . )

The teacher undoubtedly sees this sort of exchange as light-hearted banter:

(V18) **T:** I prefer a sort of informal atmosphere in the class . . .

The students see it differently:

(V19) **I:** Do you feel comfortable in the science classroom?
**Ss:** No.
**S1:** . . . because he asks you questions and if you don't know them . . .
**I:** Then you get into trouble?
**S1:** Well, you don't get into trouble, but he gets upset.
**S2:** You *do* get into trouble (*laughter*)

This is in marked contrast to the low-key informality experienced in the Caritas classroom, an informality created at least in part by the different style of the Caritas teacher. In the Vista classroom, on the other hand, the riposte and counter-riposte can get quite heated and the battle lines are at times quite explicitly drawn:

(V20) **T:** You're guessing Howard . . .
**S1:** But Howard didn't say a word.
**T:** Who asked you, hey? Who asked you?
**S1:** He's my friend, I take his side.
**T:** Okay, that implies that I'm your enemy, doesn't it?
**S2:** She never said that.

This cohort resistance to excessive privatisation is, by the time these students get to the fifth form, not much more than an expressive gesture though it does signify temporary withdrawal of canonical support from the contract with its structural entailments.[5] Students by this time have already been sorted into the bright or the stupid category — otherwise the teacher would not know whom to ask for his pedagogic displays! The students themselves also know by this time whether science is going to feature in their future work careers or not:

(V21) **I:** Is anybody going to be doing anything that requires matric science?
**Ss:** Dentistry . . . the army ( . . . )
**I:** So I mean how important do you rate your science?
**S1:** Mine's very important . . .
**S2:** If you don't have science, you can't really do much . . .
**S3:** You don't need science for many things.

It may be surmised that S3 has been selected out while S1 and S2 have been selected in to the domain of 'science knowledge'. It can also be noted in passing that the two professions actually mentioned — the army and dentistry — offer practically no access to the few black students that actually come to master school science.

## Concluding comments

It would be unwise to overestimate the generalisability of this analysis. Two points can, however, be made with relative confidence. The first is that the transactions of knowledge observed in these classrooms are not simply a matter of mental operations, but the result of the exercise of certain communicative practices. What that knowledge is and how it is appropriated depends a great deal on the participant's position in the discourse.

The second is that an adequate understanding of what is happening in these two science classrooms could not be achieved without an understanding of the social contract impinging from the society at large. An analysis in terms of pragmatic presuppositions, or positional power, or even discourse structure alone would not help show what makes these two classrooms so singularly different, in both their routines and their effects, or why.

### Notes to Chapter 14

1. This Foucauldian notion of context intrinsic to discourse is brought out nicely in Walkerdine (1982).
2. The terms 'primary knower' and 'secondary knower' are used in Berry (1981). Berry's distinction is related to the one made by Labov and Fanshel between A- and B-events. A-events refer to events to which the speaker has privileged access, B-events to which the hearer has privileged access. The entailments are similar to those pertaining to primary and secondary knowers. For instance, if students make knowledge statements (i.e. statements about B-events), there is implicit in them a 'request for confirmation'.
3. In this and the other discourse extracts that follow, 'C' will refer to the black classroom 'Caritas' and 'V' will refer to the white classroom 'Vista'. These extracts come from a corpus of lesson and interview transcripts collected by Karl Muller. It should be pointed out that the transcripts are not entirely typical. The white teacher possesses a degree in science and a postgraduate teaching certificate. The black teacher possesses a matriculation-level (school-leaving) qualification in science and a non-graduate teaching certificate. This makes the black teacher better qualified than most of her peers. In addition, the class she

teaches is a streamed one, so her pupils are also above average. Finally, the white class is a form five, the black class is a form two. The classes are thus not strictly comparable. I have tried not to compare the classrooms; rather I have tried to characterise the way in which the contract is enacted in each.

4. Valerie Walkerdine calls this style 'pantomime style'. She shows that small children read 'pantomime', not as a 'knowledge game', but as some other kind of participatory game altogether. In both her case and ours, the social requirements of the different game tend to eclipse the cognitive requirements of the 'knowledge game' (see Walkerdine, 1982:162).
5. Expectations about what should happen in classroom discourse are supported most of the time. Utterances which therefore do not question the suppositions or felicity conditions of preceding utterances are said to lend them 'canonical support'. If this support is not forthcoming, the preceding utterances are either queried, or more rarely, rejected (Stubbs, 1983).

**References**

BARNES, D. & TODD, F. 1981, Talk in small learning groups. In C. ADELMAN (ed.), *Uttering, Muttering*. London: Grant McIntyre.

BERRY, M. 1981, Systematic linguistics and discourse analysis. In M. COULTHARD & M. MONTGOMERY (eds), *Studies in Discourse Analysis*. London: Routledge and Kegan Paul.

COULTHARD, M. & BRAZIL, D. 1981, Exchange structure. In M. COULTHARD & M. MONTGOMERY (eds), *Studies in Discourse Analysis*. London: Routledge and Kegan Paul.

EDWARDS, A. D. 1980, Patterns of power and authority in classroom talk. In P. WOODS (ed.), *Teacher Strategies*. London: Croom Helm.

FOUCAULT, M. 1972, *The Archeology of Knowledge* (Trans. A.M. Sheridan Smith). New York: Harper & Row.

LABOV, W. & FANSHEL, D. 1977, *Therapeutic Discourse: Psychotherapy as Conversation*. New York: Academic Press.

MEHAN, H. 1974, Accomplishing classroom lessons. In A. CICOUREL (ed.), *Language Use and School Performance*. New York: Academic Press.

SACKS, H., SCHEGLOFF, E. A. & JEFFERSON, G. A. 1974, A simplest systematics for the organisation of turn-taking in conversation, *Language*, 50, 697–735.

SINCLAIR, J. McH. 1980, Discourse in relation to language structure and semiotics. In S. GREENBAUM (ed.), *Studies in English Linguistics for Randolph Quirk*. London: Longman.

SINCLAIR, J. McH. & COULTHARD, M. 1975, *Towards an Analysis of Discourse: The English Used by Teacher and Pupils*. London: Oxford University Press.

STUBBS, M. 1983, *Discourse Analysis: The Sociolinguistic Analysis of Natural Language*. Oxford: Basil Blackwell.

WALKERDINE, V. 1982, From context to text: a psychosemiotic approach to abstract thought. In M. BEVERIDGE (ed.), *Children Thinking through Language*. London: Edward Arnold.

# Epilogue

In April 1984, the editors organised a two-day conference at the University of York entitled 'Interdisciplinary approaches to interpersonal communication'. The aim of the conference was to bring together researchers in the disciplines of psychology, sociology and linguistics to explore any common ground that might exist between them in the way that they approach the study of conversation. This in itself was a novel enterprise; typically, researchers in different disciplines have worked independently of one another with little communication across disciplinary boundaries.

A number of the chapters in this book were based on papers presented at the conference, together with some invited contributions. The chapters have been organised around five principal themes, namely, Concepts of Interpersonal Communication, Methods of Observation, Transcription Procedures, Data Analysis, and Research Applications. These themes represent particular issues commonly addressed by researchers working on conversation, and have been prefaced by linking sections written by the editors, which highlight the topic of each section and evaluate the different approaches represented by the individual chapters.

The first section, Concepts of Interpersonal Communication, contrasts the differing theoretical perspectives on communication research adopted by exponents of conversation analysis and experimental social psychology. Chapter 1 was written by the editors and presents a social psychological perspective on the study of interpersonal communication. The most important feature of this approach is a belief in the value of the experimental method, which has a number of distinctive characteristics. One of these is that psychological research on communication tends to be conducted in a laboratory setting. This has the advantage of allowing the researcher to exercise control over variables such as the personality of the participants or the topic of the conversation. Experimental research also emphasises the use of statistical tests in the analysis of the data, and the significance of any observed behaviour typically rests on whether or not it occurs at a level above what would be expected by chance. Associated with statistical analysis is the need for categorisation, and another characteristic feature of the experimental approach is a preoccupation with the development of classification systems which are used to categorise the observed behaviour.

The use of the experimental method has important implications for the procedures used by psychologists when carrying out research. For example, the laboratories in which the data are collected may be equipped with zoom lens video recorders, which significantly enhance the accuracy with which interpersonal behaviour can be recorded. In Chapter 1, the editors discuss the results of a study by Rime & McCusker (1976), who showed that the duration of eye-contact was overestimated at greater conversational distances by both one-way mirror and direct sight observers; only the observers using close-up video-recordings of the subjects could provide an accurate assessment of gaze duration. In the same way, tie-microphones may be used to provide independent audio-recordings for each participant. The improvement in transcription accuracy using tie-microphones is substantial; indeed, in the case of simultaneous speech they may provide the only means for distinguishing between speakers' utterances.

Experimental research has been characterised by Duncan (1969) as the 'external variable' approach, where the researcher typically relates behaviour to something which is external to that behaviour — the number of visual cues available to the participants, for example, or their personality predispositions. Duncan distinguishes between this method and what he calls the 'structural' approach, where the researcher attempts instead to discover regularities in the sequential structure of the interaction itself. In contrast to the experimental approach, conversation analysis may be described as a structural approach, and tends to be more descriptive and qualitative than experimental social psychology.

Conversation analysts have criticised laboratory research for being contrived, and they regard many of the category systems used by social psychologists as oversimplified and unrepresentative. This point is clearly illustrated in the second chapter of Section 1, in which John Heritage reviews recent research on conversation analysis and discusses some of the major concepts upon which the approach is based. In this chapter, Heritage takes issue with the conventional classification of brief utterances such as 'mm hm', 'yes', 'oh', or 'really'. Social psychologists have tended to regard these utterances as signals of continued attention to the speaker, and classify them as a single class of events (usually described as back-channels, listener responses or accompaniment signals). Heritage maintains that these brief utterances serve a whole variety of communicative functions, and he argues that their role in conversation is obscured by lumping them together in a single category.

The contrast between the two major theoretical approaches to the study of interpersonal communication discussed in Section 1 is reflected in other sections of the book as well. Section 2, for example, is concerned with the context in which data are collected, whether through carefully controlled laboratory experimentation or through observation in more naturalistic settings. The studies described by Derek Roger in Chapter 4 were based on experimental methods: subjects were pre-selected for participation on the basis of their scores on a personality dominance questionnaire, and they were invited into a social psychology laboratory to discuss topics on which they were known to disagree with one another. Video-recorders were positioned on the wall, and no attempt was made to disguise the fact that the conversations were being monitored. A single microphone was positioned on the table, and in the second experiment reported in the chapter the subjects also wore tie-microphones to provide an independent vocal signal for each participant.

In contrast to the carefully controlled conversational setting used in these studies, Paul Drew (Chapter 5) analyses exchanges between people in a naturally occurring situation. His chapter is based primarily on a detailed analysis of a video-recording of one conversation. The participants in this conversation were the members of a family, two of whom, Betty and Uncle Victor, had not seen one another for some years. Although the presence of the video-recording equipment was known to at least some of the participants (Betty and her mother), there was no attempt in this study to pre-select the participants for observation. Conversation analysts typically assume that the phenomena which are of real interest occur independently of factors such as gender, personality or acquaintanceship, and they are interested in these factors only to the extent that interactants can be shown to orient to such categories in their dealings with each other. Thus, Betty knows who Uncle Victor is, but her response to his question whether she knows him or not is constrained by what conversation analysts refer to as the 'preference organisation' which characterises particular social situations, in this case an occasion where people are reunited after a prolonged separation. Drew's analysis reveals how this preferred social organisation is orientated to by interactants through the minutiae of their conduct.

The third and last contribution in Section 2, entitled 'Family interaction from an interactional sociolinguistic perspective' (Chapter 6) is by Erica Huls. This study is particularly interesting in the context of this book, since Huls used features of both experimental and naturalistic approaches: the participants were pre-selected on the basis of differences in social class, as they might have been in a social psychology experiment, but the data were collected by the more naturalistic technique of participant observation.

Most studies of interpersonal communication are based on a transcription made from either an audio-tape or video-tape record. Making a valid transcription which will adequately reflect the complexity of human communication presents a major problem, and Section 3 illustrates the ways in which the problem has been tackled by researchers from different disciplines. Chapter 7 by Peter Bull, entitled 'Psychological approaches to transcription', outlines three systems which the author and his colleagues have devised for transcribing both speech and non-verbal behaviour. In describing these systems, Bull points out a number of features which they have in common; for example, they were all derived from earlier coding procedures, and hence possess a number of advantages over the earlier systems. The systems are also all hierarchical: they can be used at a general level for categorising broad features of behaviour, but can be used at a more fine-grained level of analysis to provide highly detailed descriptions of events if this is more appropriate. This distinction between levels of analysis may be illustrated by the Body Movement Scoring System (Bull, 1987) which Bull describes in Chapter 7: if the researcher is interested in hand movements he might simply wish to classify them into contact or non-contact movements, but he may wish to classify hand movements further according to the point of articulation involved (elbow, wrist, fingers) or according to the type of activity employed, (e.g., touch, grasp, rub).

The two remaining chapters in this section are concerned not with classifying conversation into pre-existing category systems, but with the ways in which the precise details of conversation can be represented as faithfully as possible in transcription. Conversation analysts have accordingly developed extremely detailed conventions for making transcriptions, which are clearly illustrated by Gail Jefferson in Chapter 8 ( a glossary of the symbols used appears at the end of her chapter). Perhaps the most striking feature of their system is that standard spelling is ignored in order to reproduce on paper as accurately as possible the way the conversation sounds; an example given in the editors' preface to this section is the phrase 'back in a minute', which may be represented in conversation analysis transcription as 'back inna minnit'. Conversation analysts have even been concerned to devise conventions for representing different kinds of laughter: for example, Jefferson (1984) in one excerpt transcribes laughter as 'ihh hh heh heh huh', while in another excerpt a different kind of laughter is transcribed as 'hhhhHA HA HA HA HA'. The final contribution in section 3 (Chapter 9) was written from a linguistic perspective by John Kelly and John Local. These authors are also concerned to achieve as accurate a representation of speech as possible, but take a much wider range of features into account than social psychologists or conversation analysts. Thus Kelly and Local maintain that transcription should allow the analyst to register 'all the discriminable matter in the spoken medium of language', including physical characteristics such as muscular contractions of the cheeks or larynx movements, together with dynamic features of amplitude, rhythm and so forth in speech itself. As the excerpts in their chapter show, the notation system for transcribing speech described by Kelly and Local is far more complex than those used by psychologists or conversation analysts, although the increasing complexity evident in their work must inevitably make it less accessible outside the confines of specialised linguistic analysis.

Once the transcription has been made from the recording, the problem arises as to how to interpret the data so obtained, and a fundamental issue is whether the corpus of data should be analysed quantitatively or qualitatively. Psychologists typically prefer a quantitative approach, relying on the statistical analysis of data derived from the implementation of various classification systems. By adopting this 'external variable' approach, however, Duncan (1969) has argued that the sequential and hierarchical organisation of interpersonal communication may be lost, and the problem is illustrated by the way in which experimental psychologists attempt to deal with time: although sequential information is sometimes obtained through time-sampling procedures, these do little more than carve the conversation up into successive segments that are entered into the analysis as levels of a within-subjects variable. The limitations of this approach to sequential analysis are discussed by Peter Collett in the first contribution in Section 4 entitled 'Time and Action' (Chapter 10). Collett describes a number of procedures, referred to collectively as stochastic methods, where the occurrence of an event depends to a variable extent upon the events which precede it: instead of describing events simply in terms of their frequency in particular segments of the conversation, or attempting to predict precisely what behaviour will follow from a particular event, stochastic procedures provide a distribution of possible outcomes, each with an associated probability of occurrence. The analysis thus establishes probabilities for certain sequences of events over the course of a conversation, and Collett places particular emphasis on his own method of conjoint analysis (Collett & Lamb, 1982), a technique which he claims will provide a visual representation of exchanges between two or more individuals along several different modalities, or will depict the interplay between different modalities in the same individual.

Much of the work in conversation analysis also focuses on sequential structure, but the approach taken differs markedly from the statistical techniques described by Collett. Stochastic procedures attempt to measure the likelihood of occurrence of an event by constructing probability estimates; by contrast, Wootton (Chapter 11) argues that conversation analysts are concerned to identify the nature of constraints existing between utterance pairs such as, for example, requests and grantings/rejections or questions and answers. What is common to both approaches is the assumption that utterance pairs are linked, but whereas in stochastic methods the link is purely a statement about a statistical probability, in conversation analysis the link constitutes an expectation that the first part of a pair will be followed by the second. Wootton argues that the expectation can be traced in a number of ways: for example, if the second part of the pair is not produced, then there may be a follow-up to the first part of a pair which demonstrates that the recipient has not performed an expected action or response. The behaviour of the participants in a conversation is thus constrained by the social organisation referred to by Drew in Chapter 5, where Betty is placed in a dilemma by Uncle Victor's question; when she doesn't respond, he repeats the question.

An important feature of research on interpersonal communication is its potential application in a wide variety of everyday social situations. In the final section, Research Applications, three chapters are presented which focus explicitly on applied issues. The first of these is by Andrew Thomas (Chapter 12) and deals with social skills deficits amongst disabled patients. Social skills training represents one of the major practical applications of research on interpersonal communication, and is based on the view that social skill can be seen as a kind of motor skill, involving the same kinds of processes as, say, driving a car or playing tennis. Thomas points out that social skills problems are particularly acute amongst the physically handicapped, as the results of his own survey show: 96% of the handicapped adolescents who participated in the study reported experiencing difficulty in at least one of the 14 social situations that were described, and more than two-thirds reported difficulty in as many as five or more of the situations. Despite the widespread incidence of these problems, Thomas reveals a general lack of programmes for social skills training amongst the handicapped, although a recent survey that Thomas reports does show a growing awareness of the problem: 15 of 23 educational establishments run by the Spastics Society include training programmes in skills ranging from the control of inappropriate body movements to conversational management and turn-taking.

Derek Rutter (Chapter 13) focuses on the effects of what he calls 'cuelessness' on speech style, content and outcome in telephone tutorials used by the British Open University. Cuelessness refers to the number of cues available to the participants in conversation, ranging from face-to-face interaction, where both visual and auditory cues are presented, to telephone conversations, where only auditory cues are available. Rutter's study employed experimental procedures, comparing subjects who participated in face-to-face or telephone tutorials on a variety of measures derived from the classification of their transcribed verbal exchanges. Rutter concludes from his analyses that the face-to-face and telephone conditions differ on content, style and outcome, but that the telephone still constitutes an acceptable medium for tutorials because both students and tutors alike reported satisfaction with the method.

Section 5 ends with Chapter 14, by Johan Muller, who contrasts the distinctive communicative styles occurring in two South African science classrooms, one from a white school and one from a black school. He argues that these different communicative styles presuppose a social organisation or contract which differs markedly in the two teaching contexts, and that the communication strategies themselves are an essential mediating factor in perpetuating educational inequality in South Africa.

The methodological differences between researchers from different academic disciplines are clearly shown in the contrasting chapters which appear in the various sections of this book. Whereas conversation analysis is based on a number of assumptions about communication, psychologists typically proceed from a belief in the value of a particular method. This in turn determines the way in which psychologists study communication, with a heavy reliance on laboratory-based experimentation, quantification and categorisation. By contrast, conversation analysts typically prefer to study naturally occurring situations, using qualitative methods of analysis.

It may be tempting to conclude, as Robert Hopper does in Section 1, Chapter 3, that the researcher must 'take sides' between the two approaches. However, it is the editors' view that exponents of both traditions have much to learn from one another. Thus, conversation analysis could benefit from the rigours of quantification and inferential statistics to avoid the risks of generalising too much from single examples, while psychologists could benefit from the rigours of close textual analysis in refining the sensitivity of their classification systems. It is the editors' contention that these different approaches are not necessarily incompatible; open-mindedness could be to the advantage of all!

**References**

BULL, P. E. 1987, *Posture and Gesture*. Oxford: Pergamon.

COLLETT, P. & LAMB, R. 1982, Describing sequences in social interaction. In M. VON CRANACH & R. HARRE (eds), *The Organisation of Human Action*. Cambridge: Cambridge University Press.

DUNCAN, S. 1969, Nonverbal communication, *Psychological Bulletin* 72, 118–37.

JEFFERSON, G. 1984, On the organisation of laughter in talk about troubles. In J. M. ATKINSON & J. C. HERITAGE (eds), *Structures of Social Action: Studies in Conversation Analysis*. Cambridge: Cambridge University Press.

RIME, B. & MCCUSKER, L. 1976, Visual behaviour in social interaction: The validity of eye-contact assessments under different conditions of observation, *British Journal of Psychology*, 67, 507–14.

# Index